A
LITERARY
HISTORY
OF
FRANCE

A LITERARY HISTORY OF FRANCE

General Editor: P. E. CHARVET
Fellow of Corpus Christi College, Cambridge

Volume I
THE MIDDLE AGES AND THE RENAISSANCE
by J. P. COLLAS
Professor of French at Queen Mary College, University of London

Volume II
THE SEVENTEENTH CENTURY 1600–1715
by P. J. YARROW
Professor of French at the University of Newcastle upon Tyne

Volume III
THE EIGHTEENTH CENTURY 1715–1789
by ROBERT NIKLAUS
Professor of French at the University of Exeter

Volume IV
THE NINETEENTH CENTURY 1789–1870
by P. E. CHARVET

Volume V
THE NINETEENTH AND TWENTIETH CENTURIES 1870–1940
by P. E. CHARVET

A LITERARY HISTORY OF FRANCE

Volume V

THE NINETEENTH AND TWENTIETH CENTURIES

1870–1940

A LITERARY
HISTORY OF FRANCE

VOLUME V

The Nineteenth
and Twentieth Centuries
1870–1940

P. E. CHARVET

Fellow of Corpus Christi College, Cambridge

LONDON · ERNEST BENN LIMITED

NEW YORK · BARNES & NOBLE INC

First published 1967 by Ernest Benn Limited
Bouverie House · Fleet Street · London · EC4
and Barnes & Noble Inc. · 105 Fifth Avenue · New York 10003

Distributed in Canada by
The General Publishing Company Limited · Toronto

Printed in Great Britain

FOREWORD BY THE GENERAL EDITOR

IN HIS QUEST for the past, the historian proper deals with a variety of evidence, documentary and other, which is of value to him only for the light it sheds on events and on the men who played a part in them. The historian of literature has before him documents in manuscript or print that exist in their own right, books and ever more books, as the centuries unfold. Within the space allotted to him, his first task must be to give the maximum amount of relevant information about them, but, if he is to avoid producing a mere compilation of unrelated and therefore meaningless facts, he is bound to organize his matter into some sort of pattern.

Time itself does this for him to some extent by keeping alive the memory of those writers and books that retain their relevance, and, often enough, setting one school of writers against another, as successive generations seek to establish their own originality by revolt against their immediate predecessors.

At whatever point in time the historian of literature may stand, he is bound to adopt as a basis of his work the patterns time gives him, although he knows well enough that, just as the tide and the waves may alter the patterns they themselves are for ever imprinting on the sands of the sea shore, time, bringing with it changing tastes and values, will alter these patterns, at least in detail or emphasis.

Within these broad natural patterns come problems of arrangement. Here inevitably a degree of arbitrariness creeps in. Some writers are dubbed precursors, as though they themselves had consciously played the role of prophet in a wilderness, others are marked down as 'epigoni' – poor fellows! Had they but known! – others again are lumped together because they are seen to have in common the characteristics of an age, though

79089

they may have had no relations with each other; chronology must often be sacrificed to the need of tidiness. Thus does the historian of literature try to create from the vigorous and confused growth he is faced with, at least on the surface, an ordered garden, where the reader may wander and get an impression to store away in his memory, of neatness and controlled change, an impression helpful, indeed indispensable, as a preliminary to the study of the subject, but not to be confused with the reality.

Nor is this all. Should the historian of literature, need he, smother his personal responses? And if he should (which we doubt and indeed have not tried to do), is this really possible? Within the kindly Doctor Jekyll, recording in detached tones his literary history, seeking to give an objective picture of an age, explaining, elucidating, lurks Mr Hyde, the critic, ready to leap out at the reader on the slightest provocation and wreak his mischief. As in all of us, the levels of his personality that may respond to stimuli are numerous: intellectual, emotional, moral, spiritual; more numerous still the sources of interest whence the stimuli may come: historical and social, psychological, linguistic and stylistic, aesthetic. Literature is a vast catchment area all these streams flow into; a book, a great book is like a burning glass that concentrates the rays of human experience into one bright point; it burns itself into our memories and may even sear the soul.

If he be wise, Mr Hyde the critic will use as his criterion of judgment only the degree to which he feels his own experience has been enriched, his own perceptiveness extended. Thus will he avoid being too rigid or narrow in his attitudes and avoid the temptation of for ever seeking some underlying principle that controls the whole mechanism. Since the corpus of a writer's work is the expression of his experience, since the writer belongs to a given age, a given people, the works may easily become the pretext for an exercise in individual or national psychology. Conversely, the idea of race, the age, the accumulated legacy of history — its momentum, in a word — may be invoked as cause and explanation of the works. Or again, since the works have their place in one or more given art-forms, they may be seen as no more than moments in the evolution of these.

Such ideas and unifying theories have their value no doubt; the people, the society, the age, the art-forms all bear on the question, but who is to assess their impact? They leave the mystery of individual genius and of artistic creation intact; to emphasize them at the expense of the latter is really using the history of literature for other ends. Admittedly books do not spring from nothing, but whether we consider them historically or critically, in the last resort they stand, as we observed at the outset of this foreword, in their own right, and their value depends upon their impact on the individual; every book has three aspects: what the author meant to express, what the book contains, and the image the reader carries away with him; this latter changes with every reader of the book and depends as much upon himself as upon the book and the author.

From its early beginnings in the ninth century down to the present day, French literature can claim a continued existence of 1100 years. What country, beside our own, can boast such literary wealth, such resource, such powers of renewal? The authors of this history, the first of its kind in English, have been only too well aware of the difficulties attendant upon so vast an enterprise. Their hope is that it may give to all readers of French literature a coherent background against which particular periods or writers may be studied and enjoyed in greater depth.

P. E. C.

PREFACE

MUCH OF WHAT appears in my preface to volume IV is relevant here. Since, as I explained there, the abundant growth has meant dividing the plant, 1870 seemed a convenient starting point for volume V. On the other hand, where to end what has no end was more difficult, and opinions will no doubt differ on my inevitably arbitrary decision.

Various factors influenced me, in deciding where I was finally to take leave of the reader: students' programmes, the hesitancy to tackle the contemporary scene, which gives the onlooker of today a sense of rich and disordered profusion, just as previous periods must have appeared to contemporaries.

As it stands, volume V of this History has, in its latter sections, some aspects of a catalogue rather than a coherent structure, which, however arbitrary such structures may be, where life, past or present, is concerned, are a valuable foundation for knowledge and understanding.

Then again, my previous remarks about the dates in the Table of Contents of volume IV apply with equal force to those in the Table of Contents of this volume. Whatever their impact upon men and society, wars cannot put an abrupt end to given periods of literature. Thus, the war of 1914, despite the destructions it wrought, material and social, appears in some ways as an interruption of intellectual and literary movements rather than as a seeding time of new departures, and my last chapter is a very open-ended one; writers who began writing before the last war and are still active, are followed, however inadequately, down to the present day, whilst those who appear after 1940 may receive no mention.

Finally, my debt of gratitude to all those mentioned in the preface to volume IV remains; to Ernest Benn, to Professors

Baxter and Yarrow, to Doctors Fairlie and Combe, to Mrs
J. P. T. Bury, to Mr Henry Boutflower and Mr John Lucas, I
desire once more to express my profound thanks.

P. E. C.

CONTENTS

CONTENTS

PART II

NINETEENTH-CENTURY TWILIGHT AND NEW TRENDS (1890–1940)

§ I THE REVOLT AGAINST SCIENCE (1890–1914)

§ II RESTLESSNESS AND RECONSTRUCTION

Part I

The Authority of Science

§ I NATURALISM (1870–90)

Chapter 1

POLITICAL PESSIMISM
AND SCIENTIFIC OPTIMISM

THE defeat of 1870 and the Commune (1871) not unnaturally inspired much political pessimism. The prestige of France as one of the great powers had suffered; moreover, some eighty years after the French Revolution, the country seemed more politically divided than ever before. 'Monsieur' Thiers was doubtless right when he declared: 'C'est la république qui nous divise le moins', but this lukewarm negative approval of the republic born in the ruins of the Empire was scarcely calculated to win the support of the majority of Frenchmen in whose minds the republican idea, more than any other political form, was still identified with revolution; the leading republican politicians, too, Gambetta notably, had been partisans of 'la guerre à outrance', whereas the country wanted peace. No wonder the parties of the Right, which supported the conclusion of peace with Germany, had a strong majority in the National Assembly; they – Legitimists, Orleanists and, after a momentary eclipse, Bonapartists – were agreed at least on one thing: to stifle the republic in the cradle.

The pessimism of what may be termed the 'Orleanist years (1870–9) of the Third Republic' is clearly reflected in the work and attitudes of the two prominent intellectual figures of the day, Renan and Taine. A month before the outbreak of war Taine had published *De l'Intelligence*. For fifteen years he had been applying his experimental method in literary and art criticism; here in a treatise on psychology he places the keystone to his arch; from books and paintings, as evidence of the mentalities behind them, he comes, with the same method, to examining the mind itself: 'De tous petits faits bien choisis, importants, significatifs, simplement circonstanciés et minutieusement notés, voilà aujourd'hui la matière de toute science.'[1]

Taine had been a fervent admirer of Germany in his earlier days, later he became more drawn to English empirical thinking; thus, he was better prepared than Renan for the disillusionment with Germany created by the war, patriotic feelings apart. Both

[1] Preface, *De l'Intelligence*.

3

shared feelings of horror at the calamity of the 'Commune' (March–May 1871). Under the shock of defeat and civil war Taine turned his attention to French history with the idea of trying to discover an answer to why France had gone down so suddenly in defeat. What had sapped her apparent strength? A satisfactory answer to this question might help to avoid future catastrophes such as 1870 and the Commune. *Les Origines de la France contemporaine* (1875–94),[2] unfinished at his death, is a powerful contribution to the great debate on the Revolution, alluded to in the previous volume, that divided French historians from the outset and to our own day. In condemning Taine as a historian, his opponents[3] accuse him of having made up his mind beforehand; there is indeed little doubt of Taine's attitude to the Revolution. His work is not so much a history as a diagnosis of the ills he believed responsible for France's plight; their origin? – the Revolution.

Our concern, however, is not with Taine's value as a historian but with the conflicting tendencies revealed in Taine himself. Predictably, he applies to the historical field the method he had used with such success elsewhere, the accumulation of 'petits faits ... significatifs ...' in order to isolate 'la faculté maîtresse' that accounts for the man, the movement, the intellectual climate of an age. Thus, underlying the *ancien régime* in the eighteenth century he discerns the growth of what he calls 'l'esprit classique'. In this context the word has only a distant contact with its use in reference to French seventeenth-century literature, none with its Staëlian sense (i.e. Mediterranean); Taine has in mind an attitude he so evidently dislikes and condemns when he suspects its existence, the rigid rationalist ideological spirit he associates with the Jacobins[4] and that inhuman pedagogue ('le pion') Robespierre; in Napoleon, he saw Corsican heredity at work. Taine's hostile attitude to the Revolution is interesting in two ways: first, it reflects the spirit of the early years of the Third Republic, that Indian summer of the Orleanists, hostile to the Revolution, opposed to rigid centralization, pragmatic, spiritually at home in England. 'Un Français', writes Taine,[5] 'rapportera toujours d'Angleterre cette persuasion profitable que la politique n'est pas une théorie de cabinet applicable ... tout d'une pièce, mais une affaire de tact ... (de) transactions, (de) compromis.'

Taine, who by his critical method had been so representative of the intellectual climate of the Second Empire, is now thoroughly

---

[2] Three parts: *l'Ancien Régime, La Révolution, Le Régime moderne* (unfinished).
[3] e.g. Aulard, Seignobos.
[4] The Staëlian meaning could also apply in a certain degree since the Revolutionaries liked to see themselves as 'heirs' of Republican Rome.
[5] *Notes sur l'Angleterre*, preface. See also *Les Origines...*, preface.

representative, but for different reasons, of the French Orleanist 'Whigs' – who gave France the best written constitution the country has had so far.

Secondly, his attitude is a strong pointer to his own moral development. We have seen Taine the critic writing as Stendhal did[6] or Neitzsche might have done, revelling in violent passions and all manifestations of power, at any rate when expressed on canvas; amoralism and anarchy seem at the end of that road.[7] But then comes the Commune. To exalt the Italian Renaissance as a time of violence favourable to the emergence of vigorous personalities and creative geniuses is one thing; to experience a time of violence is another. When that happens, society must be told that the breakdown of social disciplines means the certain and brutal re-emergence of 'le gorille féroce et lubrique . . . qui subsiste, indéfiniment dans l'homme . . .'[8]

As soon as Taine turns from art to politics, the free development of the 'ego' is condemned and gives place to belief in order, social hierarchies, as of the essence of human groups. In *Les Origines* Taine speaks as a stern political and social moralist; he has become a traditionalist; Barrès will later follow him along the path from individualism to tradition.

Nor is this quite the end of the story for Taine. His change of attitude affects his beliefs. The convinced Hegelian he had been believed in the underlying forces contained within and controlling the Universe, measurable, predictable, containing therefore within their dynamic a system of ethics; he could write: 'Le vice et la vertu sont des produits comme le vitriol et le sucre';[9] if so, it follows they can be controlled. Later, for whatever reasons, his optimism gives way to pessimism; we have noted it in *Voyage en Italie*; the chapter on ethics in *Vie et Opinions de M. Frédéric-Thomas Graindorge* (1867) ends on a note of despair, which the emergence of 'le gorille féroce et lubrique' in the Commune did nothing to dispel; his earlier mechanistic beliefs merge into pantheistic belief in Nature as he turns with relief from the human scene: 'Comme en pareil lieu [Fontainebleau] on se détache vite des choses humaines! Comme l'âme rentre aisément dans sa patrie primitive, dans l'assemblée silencieuse des grandes formes, dans le peuple paisible des êtres qui ne pensent pas.' Taine seems on the way to a spiritual belief; he died a Protestant.

Renan's attitudes after 1870 have similarities with Taine's, and differences. There is the same horror at the spectacle of the

---

[6] cf. *Histoire de la Peinture en Italie.*
[7] P. H. Simon, *Domaine héroïque des lettres françaises* (1963), pp. 374–5.
[8] *Origines, La Révolution.*   [9] *Hist. de la Litt. anglaise*, Introduction.

Commune – 'cette syncope morale',[10] as he called it, the same pessimism, which in Renan's case had the added reason that the
fervent admirer of German thought he had remained suffered the
shock of seeing German intellectuals and spiritual leaders justifying and supporting Bismarckian power politics.

Like Taine, Renan's first impulse is to try to understand France's
defeat, diagnose her ills, as a first step to reconstruction; the result
is *La Réforme intellectuelle et morale* (1871), a stimulating work,
but for a country suffering from defeat perhaps an unacceptably
chastening one; his dislike of democracy is evident: 'Un pays n'est
pas la simple addition des individus qui le composent...'; 'La
France s'est trompée sur la forme que peut prendre la conscience
d'un peuple. Son suffrage universel est comme un tas de sable...'[11]
Renan shows himself to be an intellectual aristocrat, aloof from the
crowd.

Aloof is the key word. Whereas Taine is the committed moralist
in *Les Origines* Renan already in *La Réforme intellectuelle* betrays
an attitude of disengagement that will become his more and more
thereafter. His pessimism assumed the form of disenchanted sc
sceptic-
ism; he became an artist in ideas, a dilettante, never expressing
conviction, always ready to set up one opinion against the opposite
and derive satisfaction from the antithesis. '... On peut dire que
pour l'homme cultivé il n'y a pas de mauvaise doctrine; car pour
lui toute doctrine est un effort vers le vrai, un exercise utile à la
santé de l'esprit.'[12] Everywhere the note of disenchantment is the
same: in *Marc-Aurèle*, in *Histoire d'Israël*, in *Discours et Conférences* (1883), in the preface (1890) to *l'Avenir de la Science*.

As a nineteenth-century Montaigne, Renan's success in the cultivated social world, less concerned with a consistent system of philosophy than a stimulating intellectual feast, was great. His influence
was never greater than in the 1880s and early 1890s; a disinte-
grating influence, the key-note of which is given in the remark
Renan is recorded as having made to Paul Déroulède: 'Jeune
homme, la France se meurt, ne troublez pas son agonie.'[13] Irony,
epicueanism, dilettante attitudes, these Renanist traits reappear in
Anatole France, Jules Lemaitre, the early Barrès; stimulants for
the intellect, poor nourishment for the soul.

Soon after Renan's death, France was to enter the great crisis
of the Dreyfus Affair. In such storms men need to discover what

---

[10] *Réforme*. The first essay gives its name to the book. See also first essay,
end: 'Le 18 Mars 1871 ... jour où la conscience française a été le plus bas.'
[11] *Ibid.*, I.   [12] *Ibid.*, I.
[13] See D. Halévy, *Histoire d'une Histoire*, p. 46. Déroulède (1846–1914),
president of 'La Ligue des Patriotes', author of *Les Chants du soldat*; the
remark was probably made during the Boulangiste crisis, Déroulède being
a convinced supporter of General Boulanger.

moral values their lives are anchored to; they could not find them in the graceful intellectual pirouettes or the frigid idealism of Renan and this no doubt is why, after Renan's death, his influence as a spiritual force quickly declined. But he remains as a man of brilliant intellectual and artistic gifts.

Against this background of political pessimism and hostility to the Republic, Naturalism, in its earlier years and in the person of its champion Emile Zola, represents a different attitude. Its seeds had been sown before 1870, in the 'Positivist' age. Within the Positivist scientific structure the biological sciences had come to the fore; thanks to Darwin's *Origin of Species* (1859) the theory of evolution was in the air with its themes of struggle for life, survival of the fittest, permanence of hereditary characteristics, of original types;[14] Taine had greatly fostered the idea of heredity and environment as vital factors in the development of mentalities, Claude Bernard, the physiologist, had shown[15] that by following a rigorous scientific method, the hitherto empirical art of medicine could itself become a science.

Defeat had done nothing to diminish the belief in science as the magic that would transform society; if anything it had been an encouragement in two ways: scientific optimism was a psychological compensation for the political misfortunes of the day, and the belief, which Renan had encouraged, that Germany's victory was due to her scientific superiority, was a further spur.

Marcelin Berthelot (1827–1907), scientist turned politician after 1870, was an apostle of this scientific creed associated by him with republicanism, which in his mind meant freedom from religious ideas and the obscurantism of the Church; thus science and republicanism together were the hope of the future.

Zola had early imbibed the scientific ideas of his generation, his ideas on heredity in particular had been fixed by his reading (1868–9) a book of dubious scientific value, *Traité philosophique et physiologique de l'hérédité*, from the pen of Dr Prosper Lucas, later to figure in the Rougon-Macquart series as Dr Pascal. A republican, like many of the Realist writers, during the Empire, he fully shared the scientifico-republican gospel of Berthelot; 'La République sera conservatrice ou elle ne sera pas', Thiers had declared in an effort to reassure conservative opinion; 'La République sera Naturaliste ou elle ne sera pas', Zola echoed.[16] The novelist must also become a species of scientist, the novel was to become ... 'experimental'.

14 See Martino, *Le Naturalisme Français.*
15 *Introduction à la médecine expérimentale* (1865).
16 *La République et la littérature* (1879).

Chapter 2

NATURALISM IN NOVEL AND DRAMA

I. THE GONCOURT BROTHERS

'IL y a des hommes n'ayant pour mission parmi les autres que de servir d'intermédiaires; on les franchit comme des ponts et l'on va plus loin.' Thus does Flaubert animadvert on human ingratitude and egotism when Frédéric and Deslauriers succeed in shaking off the worthy but importunate Dussardier.[1] The Goncourt Brothers might prompt the same reflection, sandwiched as they are between Flaubert on one side, Zola on the other. With a distant bow of recognition and a flicker of interest towards the celebrated *Journal* readers hurry over the Goncourt bridge only to find themselves ankle-deep in the mud of Naturalism.

Painting had been the brothers' first choice when in 1848 a comfortable inheritance had left them free to decide what direction their interest in the arts should take. Two years of travel followed, with paints and brushes; France, Italy, Belgium, Algeria. But the urge was not strong enough or the talent was wanting. Their interest in painting was, indeed, to remain; they were later to give ample proof of their artistic awareness, their understanding of the painter's mentality,[2] but their creative activity was thereafter to be with the pen. A first novel[3] had the misfortune to coincide with the *coup d'état* (December 1851) and sold sixty copies, but the authors did at least have the bitter-sweet satisfaction of drawing the critics' fire which they decided was preferable to passing unnoticed: 'un feuilleton où Janin nous fouettait avec de l'ironie, nous pardonnait avec de l'estime et de la critique sérieuse.'[4] History and art criticism next absorbed their attention: *Histoire de la Société française pendant la Révolution* (1854); *Le Directoire* (1855); *Portraits intimes du 18e siècle* (1857–8); *Histoire de Marie-Antoinette* (1858); *L'Art du 18e siècle* (three editions 1859–82); *Les Maîtresses de Louis XV* (1860). In 1860 the two brothers returned to the novel with *Charles Demailly*, and in the next nine years published a

---

[1] *Education Sentimentale*, II, 4.
[2] *Manette Salomon.*
[3] *En 18 . . .*   [4] *Journal*, entry for 15 December 1851.

series of novels: *Soeur Philomène* (1861), *Renée Mauperin* (1864), *Germinie Lacerteux* (1865), *Manette Salomon* (1867), *Madame Gervaisais* (1869). Two plays must be added to the list: *Henriette Maréchal* (1865) and *La Patrie en danger* (1868); further, as a background to their literary activity – the diary, tirelessly compiled, day by day, year in, year out.

History and fiction do not at first sight go well together; a controlled investigation and analysis of facts as against creative imagination fettered only by the discipline of probability. But the Goncourt Brothers, as convinced, nay, dedicated disciples of Realism, found the two activities quite compatible; the novel, they maintained, was no more than history in the present tense: 'Les historiens sont des raconteurs du passé, les romanciers des raconteurs du présent', they opine in their diary.[5] In another place they express much the same idea: 'L'histoire est un roman qui a été, le roman est de l'histoire qui aurait pu être.'[6] Thus both to history and the novel they bring the same attitude of mind. History on the level of potentates and powers is not their concern. Their quest is for anecdotes, intimate or curious details, domestic trifles, the cult of 'le bibelot', anything in fact that may in its own way be used as a document to illumine the daily scene and bring the past to life. The study of the present must be undertaken in a similar spirit of enquiry, observant, detailed, systematic. The six novels written in collaboration between 1860 and 1869 bear this out. With the help of a central character whose name the work bears, each is essentially the study of a chosen 'milieu': in *Charles Demailly* the world of journalism and the theatre; in *Soeur Philomène* the hospitals, in *Renée Mauperin* bourgeois circles. *Germinie Lacerteux* takes the reader from high to low life, to streets and bars; with *Manette Salomon* he moves in the world of art, sees the life in the studios crowded with art students, and from them, in *Madame Gervaisais*, he moves to ecclesiastical circles. Each novel presents a 'slice of life', a 'documentary' on the sector of life chosen. This is underlined by the original titles of three of the novels: *Les Hommes de lettres* (*Charles Demailly*), *La Jeune Bourgeoise* (*Renée Mauperin*), *L'Atelier Langiboult* (*Manette Salomon*).

The Goncourt Brothers can claim to have realized to the full the ideals of the Realists, Champfleury and Co.: social studies, documentary novels, established on direct observation, '...sur le vrai, sur le vif, sur le saignant'. Thanks to their position in life, their range of personal experience was broader than that of the earlier Realists and where it did not extend to the sector chosen they took steps to make it so. Thus for *Soeur Philomène* they obtained an introduction to a member of the staff of 'La Charité' hospital; the

<hr />

[5] Vol. II, p. 229. [6] *Idées et Sensations* (1866), p. 96.

Journal contains an account[7] of what they saw, and this with no modifications was incorporated in the novel; to find a landscape for *Germinie Lacerteux* they go to Clignancourt and faithfully record the scene in the *Journal*.[8]

But the novels aim to be more than social studies; as the titles indicate, they are studies of particular characters woven into the texture of the appropriate social background. Without this human element, usually drawn from a true incident either told to the authors (e.g. the story at the source of *Soeur Philomène*[9]) or from their direct experience (e.g. *Germinie Lacerteux*[10]), the works would not be novels at all but remain mere documents destined, when the present they investigate and report on fades into the past, to fall into the net of the social historian. These individual character portraits are unevenly successful. The portrait of the almost pathologically sensitive Charles Demailly[11] – 'Nature délicate et maladive, sorti d'une famille où s'étaient croisées les délicatesses, maladives de deux races dont il était le dernier rejeton...' – seems much like a conflated portrait of the two brothers themselves and has that much significance; interesting too, because evidently reflecting the Realist ideals of the authors is the analysis of Charles' aims in the social novel he plans but fails to write on the bourgeoisie in the nineteenth century.[12] But as a man Charles lacks interest and his final descent into madness is not compelling; the interest seems deliberately focussed on the circumstances that precipitate the crisis, produce given symptoms which require given treatment. In short, the reader's sympathy for a man under mental stress is scarcely touched; neither is he bidden to observe a clinical case.

The study of Soeur Philomène is delicate but her relations with the young surgeon, Barnier, lack definition and are left for the reader to build up as he chooses; the plot of the novel is tenuous in consequence and overweighted with what is evidently a programmatic study of hospital life. Similar criticisms may be levelled at *Renée Mauperin* and *Madame Gervaisais*; indeed, in the preface Edmond appended to the second edition (1875) of the former novel he admits that the plot is secondary and the authors' main concern is a social study: 'peindre, avec le moins d'imagination possible, la jeune fille moderne telle que l'éducation moderne et garçonnière [*sic*!] des trente dernières années l'a faite.'

No doubt the degree of direct personal experience or personal sympathy involved explains why the two best of the brothers' novels are *Manette Salomon* and *Germinie Lacerteux*. In each case

---

[7] Entry for 18 December 1860, *et seq.*   [8] Entry for 8 May 1864.
[9] Entry for 5 February 1860.   [10] Entry for 21 August 1862.
[11] Chap. 16.   [12] Chap. 20.

character and social study are successfully fused. The former gives
a perceptive portrayal of the mental attitudes of models and artists,
in particular that of Coriolis, the most gifted of the artists evoked,
whose artistic ambitions and will to work are gradually sapped and
destroyed by Manette, his mistress, eventually his wife. The latter,
a detailed study of the physical and moral decay of a nympho-
maniac, touched the authors closely, as their *Journal* testifies. Of all
the Goncourt Brothers' novels, *Germinie Lacerteux* can be seen to
mark most clearly the transition from Realism to Naturalism. In
their other novels the emphasis is on the social study; the characters
are little more than pretexts for the study of the 'milieu' they have
their being in; on the other hand, to the extent that the characters
have any existence, they have traces of personal volitions, have a
moral existence in short, a minimum of free will; this it is that
gives particular definition to Coriolis and even to Manette Salomon
herself. Germinie Lacerteux, on the other hand, is a tragic creature
whose physical and moral condition, whose every action are portrayed as a function of a physiological mechanism. Glandular secretions are the controlling factor. The clinical attitude already
discernible in *Charles Demailly* is fully developed; the Naturalists
will have nothing to equal it, nothing to add to the idea of biological determinism in human behaviour except the notion of
heredity.

The powerful light focussed on Mademoiselle de Varandeuil's
unfortunate servant has had the further effect of altering favour-
ably the balance between character and social study so heavily
weighted towards the latter in the other novels. Herself a member
of a class which had hitherto been no more than a cipher in nineteenth-century French literature, a part of the background, and
which was to achieve full literary status only in the pages of
Proust,[13] *Germinie Lacerteux* marks the novelist's right (claimed
in the preface of the first edition) to choose his models in the lowest
orders of society. On this point too the Naturalists had but to
follow the Goncourts' example; they were to do so ardently.

Yet, although *Germinie Lacerteux* is a turning point, Edmond
and Jules are not full-blooded Naturalists. In a sense this novel is
a happy accident, a providential find in their constant quest for the
true-life story or incident suitable for transplanting into fiction,

[13] Is it not paradoxical that in the seventeenth and eighteenth centuries,
those wicked aristocratic not to say feudal times, the valet from Scapin to
Figaro is as good as his master or at least plays as important a part? After
the French Revolution, that dawn of equality and democracy, the 'lower
orders', so-called, are lost sight of until the time of the Naturalists. Find an
interesting servant in Balzac or Stendhal. Flaubert's *Un Coeur Simple* comes
years after *Germinie Lacerteux*. No doubt both facts reflect the relationships
existing between masters and servants before and after the Revolution: close
and easy in the former; formal and aloof in the latter.

illumined by their personal sympathy for a devoted maid.[14] But
what really reveals the distinction between them and the Naturalists is their style. For the Goncourt Brothers' style has a value of
its own; subject-matter is one thing, the presentation another;
form has a value independent of content. This is an affirmation of
the artist's right to forge a style of his own that shall bear the
stamp of his own personality, be at once recognizable as coming
from his pen, apart from what the work it clothes may be about.
This preoccupation with style gives Edmond and Jules a stake in
the land of 'L'Art pour l'Art', and brings them close to Flaubert.
There is, however, a distinction to be made between Flaubert's
quest for perfection in rhythm and sound, in fusion of word and
image, in composition whereby the full potential of a given scene
shall be communicated or suggested to the reader, a difference between that and the ornate, bejewelled self-conscious style of the
brothers Goncourt. This is at its best in the *Journal*; and, sometimes, at its crudest. The abridged edition of nine volumes Edmond
prepared for publication (1887–96) contained only what he called
'la vérité agréable'; he reserved 'la vérité absolue' for a posthumous edition, now available,[15] and, on this point at least, Edmond was wise.

In the *Journal* the authors are speaking in their own name and
can be as impressionistic as they choose: 'dans ce travail qui voulait
avant tout faire vivant d'après un ressouvenir encore chaud, ...
jeté à la hâte sur le papier et qui n'a pas été toujours relu – vaillent
que vaillent la syntaxe au petit bonheur, et le mot qui n'a pas de
passeport – nous avons toujours préféré la phrase et l'expression qui
émoussaient et *académisaient* [Edmond's italics] le moins le vif de
nos sensations, la fierté de nos idées.'[16]

The brothers embarked in 1850 on their project of being the
intimate chroniclers of literary life in their time. The result is an
unselective recital, filled out with much tittle-tattle. The matters
recorded, the scenes depicted, are often trivial, sometimes scabrous,
even scatological: anecdotes about the courtesans of the day from
'la Païva' downwards, table talk – not always high-powered or fit
for any company – of writers, artists and journalists, fellow diners
at the 'Magny' dinners, or habitués of Edmond's 'grenier' at
Auteuil. Striking is the vitriolic attitude of the brothers to all and
sundry, denigrating, always on the alert for the anecdote that will
show a man, be he friend or merely acquaintance, in an unfavour-
able or ridiculous light. Neither of the diarists appears to have had

[14] Rose Malingre, whose secret life they knew nothing of, until after her
death.
[15] *Journal, Mémoires de la vie littéraire (1851–1896), texte intégral,*
établi et annoté par R. Ricatte, Monaco (1956–   ).
[16] Edmond's preface (1872).

any feeling of true friendship for anyone; the only sign of emotion is when Edmond mourns the brother he has just lost, evidently the only being he ever had any affection for.

After Jules' death, Edmond continued solo this literary scavengers' record, lonely, embittered against Daudet and his quondam disciple Zola when he saw himself outdistanced by both.

But when all is said and done the *Journal*, with all its trivia, pettiness, uncritical acceptance of gossip, gives a crowded, vivid impression of the literary life the brothers knew under the Second Empire and Edmond knew after 1870.

The *Journal* is an important source-book, for the authors' friends and acquaintances;[17] for the light it throws on their own complementary mentalities, on their literary work and ideal. Petty they may seem at times in their views or impressions of others, but their judgments on matters literary or artistic can be shrewd, and they have a clear realization of what they themselves as novelists aim to achieve.

'Maintenant il n'y a plus dans notre vie qu'un grand intérêt: *l'émotion de l'étude sur le vrai.* Sans cela l'ennui et le vide. Certes, nous avons galvanisé autant qu'il est possible, et galvanisé avec du vrai, plus vrai que celui des autres, et dans une réalité retrouvée ... maintenant, le vrai qui est mort ne nous dit plus rien ...'[18]

In his preface Edmond presents his brother and himself as '... ambitieux ... de représenter l'ondoyante humanité dans sa vérité momentanée.' The phrase significantly reflects the social historians on a 'boudoir' level that they had originally been, in quest of the vivid impressions of a vanished society. Furthermore, with their acute sense (Edmond's at any rate) of the instability, the fluency, the relativity of human things – 'l'ondoyante humanité ... sa vérité momentanée' – they seem to look back across the centuries to Montaigne and forward to Proust, but without the intelligence of either: the human personality is itself subject to the constant flow of time; who is to say whether the changes we see in others are not in us? 'Quelquefois même, je l'avoue, le changement indiqué chez les personnes qui nous furent familières ou chères ne vient-il pas du changement qui s'était fait en nous? ...' The concession, for Edmond (and Jules, if he had been party to it), is handsome and, thanks to this flicker of generosity, Edmond has caught sight, no more, of a Proustian idea.

The close collaboration between the two brothers lasted close on twenty years. After Jules' death only force of habit brought Edmond back to literature after seven years' interruption: *La Fille Elisa* (1877), an investigation into the life of prostitutes and brothels, is in the line of the social novels the brothers had written

---

[17] Here it should be treated with suspicion.   [18] Entry for 22 May 1865.

in the previous decade. *Les Frères Zemganno* (1879), with its portrayal of circus life, also has a connection with the earlier manner, but the main focus of interest in the book is the study of the intimate spiritual and psychological relationship between the two clowns which affects the very 'turns' they perform. In his last two novels Edmond turns away from Naturalism; as though, outclassed by Zola and his Médan Group, the ageing Edmond[19] refused to compete further in the race. *La Faustin* (1882) and *Chérie* (1884) are studies of women, the former an actress who appears to owe something to the famous tragic actress Rachel, the latter a girl brought up in the high society of the Second Empire. The works are not without merit as studies of the mentalities chosen but, devoid as they are of much plot – deliberately so[20] – they make little impact on the reader. Without even the pretext of the social study, which the Goncourts' earlier works have, they lack a justifying reason for surviving, and indeed have not.

The truth is that, apart from the *Journal*, Edmond's spirit had, as it were, died with his brother in 1870 and that after that date the Goncourts' influence was a spent force.

But it had not been an inconsiderable influence, and a broader influence than may be suspected. In the preface to *Chérie* – the most interesting part of the work today – Edmond recalls the oft-quoted claim made to him by his brother shortly before the latter died: 'On nous niera tant qu'on voudra ... il faudra bien reconnaître un jour que nous avons fait *Germinie Lacerteux* ... le livre-type qui a servi de modèle à tout ce qui a été fabriqué depuis nous, sous le nom de réalisme, naturalisme, etc. ...' The two words jostle each other as though they were synonyms; too close to both, Jules does not appear to distinguish between the schools, but we have already seen that *Germinie Lacerteux* does indeed mark a transition and that Jules' claim is justified.

Edmond records Jules in the same preface as making another claim for themselves: their impact on the taste of their generation, indeed a two-fold impact: a renewed interest in the eighteenth century and the discovery of the arts of Japan. Again the claim is justified. After the Romantic period with its energies and passions, solidified as it were into the weight and clumsiness of Louis-Philippian style furniture – 'la génération aux commodes d'acajou', in Jules' words, as recorded – something of the eighteenth-century grace, falling often into excessive elaboration and fragility, is apparent in the furniture and decorative styles of the Second Empire; 'Japonisme', on the other hand, was a distinct element in French taste after 1870 and lasted well on into the twentieth century. The

---

[19] cf. *Journal*, entry for 18 May 1879 and 26 April 1884.
[20] Preface to *Chérie*.

results may not all have been happy; we may hazard a guess that Swann's Odette and other successful 'cocottes', always in the van-guard of fashion, overcrowded their salons with lacquer tables, bamboo curtains and bronzes of doubtful provenance; none the less, to have extended French awareness to the Far East, as Méri-mée in an earlier generation had extended it to Russia, was in itself no mean performance, and in at least one respect the influ-ence was enriching: the impact of the Japanese coloured print on French lithography.[21]

Furniture styles, coloured prints may lie outside the scope of lit-erature but they lend emphasis to the broad range of Edmond and Jules de Goncourt's interests: painting, social history, art criticism, biography, fiction, drama, art collecting and 'bibelotmania'.

Industry, diversity of talent, perceptiveness in a small way, the brothers had all these, but their very many-sidedness suggests the lack of a compelling urge to go in any one direction. Dedicated though their cult of literature became, we may wonder whether their initial decision to devote themselves to writing was not an intellectual choice prompted by vanity – the determination to make a niche for themselves somehow, somewhere in the hall of fame. Their novels are interesting, both for the social and literary hist-orian, but, with the possible exception of *Germinie Lacerteux*, they are not compelling; they are too cerebral; the fire is not in them. 'Il y a des hommes n'ayant pour mission . . . que de servir d'inter-médiaires. . . .'

II. ZOLA

The works of Emile Zola (1840–1902) fall conveniently into three groups: the early works,[22] the *Rougon-Macquart* series (1871–93) and the third manner, with its strong vein of symbolism.

Nor must we forget that, like so many other writers in the nine-teenth century, Zola was a journalist almost from the beginning of his literary career to his dramatic intervention in the Dreyfus Case; from *Mes Haines* (1866), *Mon Salon* (1866) and *Edouard Manet* (1867) through the articles of his middle years, notably those collected in *Le Roman Expérimental* and *Le Naturalisme au Théâtre* (1880), to *J'Accuse* (1898), Zola was a voluminous, some-times a powerful journalist[23] and a doughty polemist, battling for Manet – much attacked at the outset of his career, for Naturalism, for Dreyfus. Zola's journalism is like a thunderous accompaniment

---

[21] e.g. in the work of Vuillard.

[22] *Inter alia: Contes à Ninon* (1864), *La Confession de Claude* (1865), *Le Voeu d'une Morte* (1866), *Les Mystères de Marseille* (1867), *Thérèse Raquin* (1867), *Madeleine Férat* (1868).

[23] See *Zola Journaliste* by H. Millerand (1962).

to his creative writing; 'De Zola journaliste à Zola romancier, il n'y a aucune solution de continuité.'[24]

We may safely neglect the first group of Zola's work, except to say that at the outset Zola appears to have no interest in the scientific and literary ideas of Naturalism mounting like a wave and presently to submerge the literary scene in France, in Europe. *Germinie Lacerteux*[25] appears to have been a beacon light to Zola: 'Il y a sans doute, une relation intime entre l'homme moderne ... et ce roman du ruisseau ... Cette littérature est un des produits de notre société ... Nous sommes malades de progrès, d'industrie, de science; nous vivons dans la fièvre, et nous nous plaisons à fouiller les plaies ... avides de connaître le cadavre du coeur humain.'[26] Thereafter there was no looking back.

Thérèse Raquin and *Madeleine Férat*, although included in the first group of Zola's work, belong in spirit to the second group. Instead of the romantic inventions of the *Contes à Ninon* or *La Confession de Claude, Thérèse Raquin* aims to be a study in sordid realism. Thérèse and Laurent, wife and lover, murder Camille, the husband, only to live thereafter haunted by the spectre of their victim and in the shadow of mutual distrust until, intending to do away with each other and discovering their common intention, they commit a double suicide at the feet of the aged relative, Madame Raquin, whom a stroke has deprived of movement and speech to denounce the murderers of her son. In *Madeleine Férat* the situation again resolves itself by suicide but the motivation is different: Madeleine marries Guillaume de Viargues, but the husband's jealousy of her former lover, Jacques, destroys their happiness. Madeleine returns to Jacques, after the death of her daughter Lucie; then poisons herself in a fit of remorse. Jealousy, adultery, grief, remorse, suicide – the chain of motivation here appears more acceptable than in *Thérèse Raquin*.

Less acceptable are the physio-psychological notions alleged as explanation of Guillaume's jealousies. Had they been attributed to Guillaume himself the reader could have accepted them as inherent in his mentality; Zola, however, propounds them as objective fact; their interest to the modern reader is merely as a pointer to Zola's awakening awareness of biological and related sciences. His receptiveness, ardent though it quickly became, remained naïve, as his ideas on heredity[27] were to show.

An entry in the Goncourt *Journal* of these years testifies to Zola's 'conversion' and to the neophyte's ardour in planning his contri-

[24] H. Millerand, op. cit.   [25] See above, pp. 10, 11.
[26] *Mes Haines*, essay on *Germinie Lacerteux*.
[27] Absorbed from Dr Prosper Lucas: *Traité philosophique et physiologique de l'Hérédité* ... (1847–50). Zola read this work in the years 1868–9.

bution to the cause: 'Nous avons eu aujourd'hui à déjeuner, notre admirateur Zola... Il nous parle... du besoin qu'il aurait d'un éditeur l'achetant pour six ans 30,000 francs... et par là lui donnerait la faculté de faire "l'histoire d'une famille", un roman en huit volumes. Car il voudrait faire de *grandes machines*...'[28] Thus, before the outbreak of the Franco-Prussian War, the plan of the Rougon-Macquart series was in being, and in fact the first volume already written. From the publication of *La Fortune des Rougon* (1871) until 1893, date of the last volume, with vast industry and often under great pressure,[29] the project, in which Zola aimed to do for the Second Empire what Balzac had done for the Restoration and the July Monarchy, was achieved.[30]

Balzac naturally springs to mind as a standard of comparison. Zola's intentions seem if anything more deliberate and much more systematic. 'Ils racontent... le Second Empire à l'aide de leurs drames individuels', writes Zola[31] of his characters. Is the claim justified? Some of the novels assuredly seem rooted in the period, notably *La Fortune des Rougon* – a study in political opportunism. The Rougon family which for years has lived at Plassans,[32] in narrow petit-bourgeois circumstances, owes its social and financial promotion to the adventurous skill and political flair of Eugène, eldest son of Pierre Rougon and Félicité his wife, née Puech. Setting out for Paris shortly before the Revolution of February 1848, with 500 francs in his pocket, he attaches himself to the fortunes of Louis Bonaparte. Kept informed by Eugène how events are shaping in Paris, Pierre and Félicité skilfully trim their sails to the Bonapartist winds, succeed in making Plassans into a southern Bonapartist stronghold and are duly rewarded after the *coup d'état* of 1851. From the historical standpoint *La Fortune des Rougon* has the merit of showing that the *coup d'état* was not the 'walk-over' it is commonly supposed to be.[33]

In this novel, Zola gives a vivid impression of the events: the early success of the republican rabble, the anxiety of the Bonapartist clique in Plassans, concentrated in their headquarters, Pierre and Félicité's *Salon jaune*, the army's arrival, the brutal

---

[28] Entry for 14 December 1868.
[29] The novels were usually serialised before publication, sometimes before a novel was completed. *Nana* is a case in point.
[30] Preface to *La Fortune des Rougon* (1871).
[31] Preface.   [32] Aix-en-Provence.
[33] In comparison with the ferocity of the 'June Days' in 1848 Paris was indeed passive in December 1851 and the Opposition members of the Legislative Assembly were the Prince-President's easy victims. In the provinces, however, with the President's military forces concentrated on the capital, the position was different; in the centre and the south, particularly, unforeseen resistance was encountered, which Louis-Napoleon, posing as the defender of social order against the red menace, was able to repress harshly. More than 26,000 people were arrested, many deported to Algeria.

repression of which Silvère Mouret[34] is one victim, Pierre's skilful manoeuvres whereby, at the cost of little personal risk, this poltroon succeeds in cutting an heroic figure as the defender of law and order in Plassans.

The attitude of the conservative elements in the town reflects that of the conservative elements throughout the country: a part of the nobility, bourgeosie and peasantry, the Church, all rallied to Louis-Napoleon and to authoritarian rule established by the Constitution of 1852.

La Curée is largely concerned with the activities of Aristide Rougon, alias Siccardot, alias Saccard. Under the wing of his eldest brother Eugène, Aristide launches into Parisian property speculation and development, on a scale Baron Haussmann[35] would have respected. In *La Conquête de Plassans* the reader returns to the provincial scene and the cradle of the family. As a political novel, *La Conquête de Plassans* compares poorly perhaps with the opening scenes of Balzac's *Député d'Arcis* and bears no comparison with Stendhal's *Lucien Leuwen*. None the less, Abbé Faujas, discredited in his own diocese of Besançon, is a priest whom Abbé Troubert would not have disowned, and his intrigues, as agent of the Ministry of the Interior, to bring the town, which in the seven years since Pierre Rougon's activities[36] has slipped into the hands of the Royalists, back to the Bonapartist allegiance, have an aura of truth about them. Anatole France's worldly prelate, Monseigneur Guitrel,[37] schooled by the adversities of a latter-day anti-clericalism, would doubtless have been glad to enjoy the same political support as Faujas had and might even have reflected ruefully that if the Gallican Church in his day was suffering some persecution, Abbé Faujas and his sort were in part to blame.

With *Son Excellence Eugène Rougon* the reader enters the Imperial Court circles in Paris and at Compiègne. The quasi-penniless adventurer from Plassans, true founder of his family's fortunes, becomes President of the *Conseil d'Etat* and Minister of the Interior – shades of Rouher, perhaps? Associated with the authoritarian rule of Napoleon III before 1860, Eugène has no difficulty, to save his position, in adjusting his attitudes when more liberal policies are introduced. Eugène is an adventurer, well-fitted to carve out a career under the Bonapartist colours, which, since the days of Brumaire, under Egyptian suns, in the snows of Russia, or the plains of Waterloo, at Boulogne, at Strasbourg, had been the symbol of

---

34 Son of Ursule, *née* Macquart.
35 Prefect of the Seine department (1809–91).
36 *La Fortune des Rougon*.
37 *Histoire Contemporaine*, see below, pp. 131–2.

adventure, sometimes on the heroic, sometimes on the conspiratorial scale.

The *coup d'état*, measured though it must be on the latter, conferred respectability by its success on the conspirators, who had supplanted the Orleanists, but in their wake came other adventurers, financial and commercial speculators[38] eager to seize the opportunities that seemed at that moment to be opening up. As in the years of the *Directoire*, so now, France seemed a land of opportunity; the French Industrial Revolution was at hand; expansion of the road and railway systems, the creation of shipping companies, the expansion in industrial production, behind all this lay the necessary development of the financial structure, the mobilization of capital, the control and strategy of credit. Zola captures the spirit of all this with success in the second instalment of Saccard's adventures[39] when he turns from property to finance.

Balzac, too, had had his men of money, from Gobseck to Grandet, from Du Tillet to Keller and Nucingen; the first was a mere usurer, the second a man of substance indeed but after all only a miser, counting his gold, piece by piece; the others project an image of lone wolf bankers, operating by – to speak in Balzacian terms – 'de fructueuses liquidations', whatever that meant – did Balzac himself understand? Saccard is a financier on the grand scale, floating joint-stock companies, dazzling the public by the audacity of his schemes, manipulating millions, in the end himself losing touch with reality and bringing down the whole house of cards, in a catastrophe that foreshadows the end of the régime itself.

In the interval, 'la fête impériale', with the gay naughtiness of Offenbach, the mellifluous melodies of Gounod, the brilliant colour confectionery of Winterhalter, the whole scene scented by Parma violets, was no empty expression. Zola endeavours to record both this heyday of the great courtesan and the disasters that brought the whole thing to an end. Neither *Nana* nor *La Débâcle* rank amongst the most successful of the *Rougon-Macquart* series. Nana is an inflated 'outsize' figure. For this aspect of life, Zola's experience was lacking; his magnifying imagination has produced a symbol of the profession rather than a creature of flesh and blood like Balzac's Esther (always Balzac!).

Neither had Zola any direct experience of war, but here his powerful imagination supported by documentation is not so much to be quarrelled with; rather is it his attitude; for him the disasters of 1870 are the expiation for the vicious luxury bred by the Imperial régime, Nana its symbol. The chronicler of a period – in so far as Zola may be called that – has given place to a moralizer with a magnifying eye, recalling Hugo.

---

[38] The word has nothing inherently derogatory.   [39] *L'Argent.*

Even if we set aside *Nana* and *La Débâcle*, the image Zola projects of the Second Empire in the four novels so far discussed, in spite of their merits, is distorted by hatred. Zola, ardent republican that he was, frankly reveals his attitude in the preface: 'ils racontent... le Second Empire à l'aide de leurs drames individuels, du guet-apens du Coup d'Etat à la trahison de Sedan ... une étrange époque de folie et de honte.' With such value-judgments does Zola condemn at the outset the period he chooses to evoke.

Why then, it may be asked, choose it? The example of Balzac, the temptation to outdo him, the fact that the Second Empire had begun (as it was to end) in violence, his very hatred of it must have been strong incentives; in addition, no doubt, the wish, in conformity with the literary ideas he had espoused, to write only from direct experience; where he had none, from contemporaneous sources. But the choice and his scientific cum literary faith involved him in a dilemma. The Realists and the Goncourt Brothers had proclaimed that literature should be social study; most of the remaining novels in the Rougon-Macquart series can claim to be that: *Le Ventre de Paris* – life in the Parisian food markets; *L'Assommoir* – life, poverty and drink in the working class quarters of the capital; *Pot-Bouille* – a study of bourgeois life; *Au Bonheur des Dames* – the multiple shops; *Germinal* – the miners in the north; *La Terre* – the peasantry; *La Bête Humaine* – the railwaymen.

Social study must be the product of careful documentation, direct experience and observation. Zola was conscientious in these respects;[40] but even if the documentation might in part belong to the previous period, the direct evidence from observation could but belong to the time of writing and must perforce relate to the first twenty years of the Third Republic. No wonder then that the allusions in these novels to the Second Empire are discreet and vague. Prisoner of his preface, Zola had no choice; prisoner of his preface and his literary beliefs, inspired by current scientific or pseudo-scientific ideas. The idea of heredity, which Zola had found in the pages of Prosper Lucas, is particularly relevant here. To exploit the idea systematically, as Zola was the first in French literature to do, entails a family structure and the idea of the family imposed a time framework which fitted the Second Empire.

The ramifications of a large family can evidently enable the novelist mainly interested in social portrayal to provide himself

[40] e.g. the documentation and notes for *Germinal* were drawn from at least seven works: *Sans Famille* (Hector Malot), *La Vie Souterraine* (L. L. Simonin), *Le Grisou* (Maurice Talmeyre), *La Science économique et L'Enfer Social* (Yves Guyot), *Le Bassin houiller de Valenciennes* (E. Dormoy), *Maladies, accidents et difformités des Mineurs* (H. Boens-Boissau). See I.-M. Fraudon, *Autour de Germinal, la Mine et les Mineurs*, Droz.

with a broad canvas; the individual members of the family, with their contrasts of character and fortune, may provide ample material in themselves and the pretext for studying different strata of society, different social or economic groups. The lack of that human dramatic interest is what deprives the Goncourt novels – with the possible exception of *Germinie Lacerteux* – of a reason for existing at all. Zola was evidently aware of these advantages, as the preface shows, but he wanted more. His novels were to be more than merely documentary, they were to be . . . scientific, a series of experiments constructed by a new type of scientist working with pen and ink, instead of test tubes and Bunsen burner. Once the initial characteristics – data, in a word – of a family had been isolated in the first generation, the laws of heredity would operate; the novelist had but to record the results. 'L'hérédité a ses lois, comme la pesanteur'.[41] To make the experiment complete another force must be taken into account – environment; Taine and Darwin to the fore! On the basis of these twin forces, heredity and environment, Zola proceeds to build his family through four generations: the legitimate Rougon branch; the illegitimate Macquarts; between and uniting them, the Mourets. The ancestress Adélaïde Fouque, 'Tante Dide', has a streak of lunacy and as a centenarian ends her days in an asylum;[42] her spouse, a gardener by trade, is recorded as having been gross and inert; her lover Macquart a drunkard with criminal leanings. With these initial traits, Zola claims that the temperaments he ascribes to Tante Dide's descendants on the right and wrong sides of the blanket are the inevitable . . . 'determined' consequence of heredity and environment.

Zola is silent on the complex equations that must have been required to find the precise balance between the forces, and well he might be, but with what enthusiasm he must have seized on the confirmation he thought he had found for his conception of the 'modern' novelist's role, in Claude Bernard's *Introduction à l'étude de la médecine expérimentale* (1865), a classic nineteenth-century discourse on method. Here the great physiologist had laid down the distinction between the sciences built on observed facts and those based on experiment; it was time medicine, by following a rigorous method, should pass from being a mere empirical art to the level of experimental science.

Zola's *Roman Expérimental* (1880) is largely a laudatory exposition of Claude Bernard's theses and a claim that the novelist no less than the physiologist can provoke a controlled reaction – an experiment, in a word. Thus and thus would the novelist become the associate of the scientist, add to the sum of human knowledge, contribute to human happiness.

[41] Preface, *La Fortune des Rougon*.   [42] *Dr Pascal.*

In his enthusiasm, Zola forgets that in the novelist's 'experiment', initial data and results are his invention. Truly Zola absorbed scientific ideas like blotting paper, and, like blotting paper, he blurred the edges. The same note of triumph sounds in Dr Pascal's declaration of faith,[43] as he reveals to Clotilde, his niece and devoted disciple, the notes compiled by him for years about those gloomy Atrides,[44] himself their 'sport', their hereditary exception that proves the rule. Not amongst the best novels of the series, *Le Docteur Pascal* is valuable, because its hero, who like Zola has read Prosper Lucas, *is* Prosper Lucas, provides us with the family tree and a kind of 'chanson de geste' of its members from the days of his father, Pierre Rougon's action at Plassans (December 1851) onwards.[45] 'Oui', declares Pascal, 'notre famille pourrait, aujourd'hui, suffire d'exemple à la science, dont l'espoir est de fixer un jour mathématiquement, les lois des accidents nerveux et sanguins qui se déclarent dans une race à la suite d'une première lésion organique...' Pascal must have read the preface to *La Fortune des Rougon*, as he quotes it almost word for word, but he is more prudent; what was certain there is a hope in his mind, and the great day is adjourned to the Greek Kalends.

'Bien sûr, c'est à la science que doivent s'adresser les romanciers et les poètes...', exclaims Pierre Sandoz,[46] speaking for Zola. That Zola, in the wake of the Goncourts, should seize on a corpus of ideas, which by casting new light on the human situation might bring fresh grist to the mills of fiction, is understandable, but the important question in the last analysis is the effect on his art as a novelist. Zola's characters are conceived essentially as physiological mechanisms, temperaments resulting from glandular secretions; they obey impulses, satisfy appetites, they are driven by lusts, sexual instincts and hereditary compulsions: 'La famille n'était guère d'aplomb, beaucoup avaient une fêlure. Lui, à certaines heures, la sentait bien, cette fêlure héréditaire... c'étaient dans son être, de subites pertes d'équilibre... Il ne s'appartenait plus, il obéissait à ses muscles, à la bête enragée.'[47] Occasionally we get a glimpse of sentiments or psychological analysis: Pierre Rougon's struggle between his natural poltroonery and the conviction that to occupy the town hall by force of arms for the Bonapartist cause is a golden chance,[48] Gervaise's dogged but unavailing struggle against adversity,[49] the stolid resignation in poverty of Maheu and his wife,[50]

[43] *Dr Pascal*, chap. 5.
[44] Fittingly, the element of incest is not lacking; Clotilde becomes Pascal's mistress and mother of his posthumous child, b. 1874.
[45] Pascal dies 1873.
[46] *L'Oeuvre* (1886), p. 45. *Oeuvres Complètes*, Fasquelle, n.d.
[47] *La Bête Humaine*, chap. 2.
[48] *La Fortune des Rougon*.   [49] *L'Assommoir*.   [50] *Germinal*.

the greed and mutual suspicion of Old Fouan's sons as in Me.
Baillehache's office[51] they parcel out between them the old man's
few acres, so as to ensure neither has the advantage; all these are
rare cases that have at least a suggestion of humanity, and bring
the characters to life.

Even if it be true, as any reader of Zola might be persuaded,
that man is nothing but an undersized gorilla,[52] yet what gives him
individuality are the thoughts he has, whencesoever these derive,
the problems provided by his environment as they seem to him, the
decisions he makes and why, his relationships with other men. But
such things point to a mind; Zola's characters do not have minds,
only nerve centres, or if they do have minds Zola regards these as
unfathomable: 'c'est l'insondable, l'obscure éclosion de la chair et
du coeur, où personne ne descend.'[53] Inevitably therefore the
centre of interest in Zola's work shifts from the individual. *La
Fortune des Rougon* is a notable exception. The strategy of 'Le
salon jaune', the military antics of Pierre Rougon, his 'capture' of
the town hall, form a very human adventure and are depicted with
a mixture of irony reminiscent of Gogol and of colour from the
palette of Daumier or Goya, that does not subordinate the main
character, at least, to the scene. But usually the interest is focussed
on some object or entity bigger or more powerful than the individual, and that he is seen in relation to. The process has two
stages in Zola. Often his magnifying imagination is content with a
temporary visual effect: 'Et le Voreux, au fond de son trou, avec
son tassement de bête méchante, s'écrasait davantage, respirait
d'une haleine plus grosse et plus longue, l'air gêné par sa digestion
pénible de chair humaine.'[54]

This process is constant in Zola; two notable examples are to be
found in *L'Assommoir*: the laundry, and the street after Gervaise's
wedding feast. But these cases are a kind of momentary hallucination in which, under the contemplative eye of the beholder, an
object or a scene is invested with a mysterious life of its own.

The second and more significant stage occurs when Zola endeavours to invest the object or entity in question with some symbolic significance: the food market,[55] the working class suburbs,[56]
the apartment block,[57] the department store,[58] art,[59] the mine,[60]
the land,[61] the locomotive,[62] money,[63] the army.[64] Many of the

---

[51] *La Terre.*
[52] cf. Taine's '... gorille féroce et lubrique...'
[53] *L'Oeuvre*, p. 27. *Oeuvres Complètes.*
[54] *Germinal*, chap. 1. The image of Le Voreux as some primeval monster
recurs several times in the book.

[55] *Le Ventre de Paris.*   [56] *L'Assommoir.*   [57] *Pot-Bouille.*
[58] *Au Bonheur des Dames.*   [59] *L'Oeuvre.*   [60] *Germinal.*
[61] *La Terre.*   [62] *La Bête Humaine.*   [63] *L'Argent.*   [64] *La Débâcle.*

titles Zola gives to his novels are indications of this tendency. He
is not uniformly successful. To be effective, the symbol must have
relevance for the reader. In *Le Ventre de Paris* Zola has endeav-
oured to create a vast epicurean symbol – joy from the stomach, a
temple of materialistic delights, as a kind of companion piece to
Hugo's cathedral,[65] a symbol of Romantic beauty. The idea that
men are very close to their stomachs may be true, too true perhaps
to be comfortable; but, lacking the leaven of some uplifting idea, it
does not grow into a symbol. With his pyramids of food, basins of
lard, unending strings of sausages, Zola has created no more than
a gigantic still-life, with something of the vigour and joyful sensuality of Rubens. On the other hand, the working-class quarter as a
crucible of suffering, drink, physical decay and death, or the mine
as the seeding ground of social revolution, are powerful symbols
because informed by a breath of charity or a sense of menace any
reader may feel; *L'Assommoir* and *Germinal*, with *La Fortune
des Rougon*, but for different reasons, may probably be regarded
as Zola's most memorable works. What the first two lose in individual life they regain in symbolic power.

The violence and coarseness that are in all Zola's characters are
as surely the hall-mark of his style; that a violent and coarse
personage should speak in character is proper, but Zola seems
incapable of making the distinction between the speech appropriate to a character and the style he as author uses to depict him.

No characters in Zola ever laugh, they explode with laughter;
they never get hot, they sweat like pigs; directly they open their
mouths they bawl or bellow; they do not get angry, they suffocate
with rage; when envious, they burst (like tyres); when hungry, they
devour. *Eclater, suer, hurler, gueuler, suffoquer, crever, dévorer*,
etc., recur constantly; words lose their descriptive value and become mere counters, debased currency.[66] Zola is like an organist
who pulls out the loudest stop, or a painter who puts on his colours
with a palette knife – always.

Nor does he distinguish between the language of a character who
may be presumed to have at least a veneer of education and someone who has none. 'Hein...Quel crétin...', exclaims Madame
Josserand,[67] an unpleasant creature no doubt, but unlikely, with
her sense of bourgeois respectability, to express herself life a fish-
wife. Even Balzac's duchesses, not renowned for their linguistic
sensitiveness, could not fall so low.

[65] *Notre-Dame de Paris.*
[66] By the same token, when Zola wants a colour adjective it is remarkable how often it is yellow: 'salon jaune', 'cheveux jaunes', 'regard jaune',
etc.
[67] *Pot-Bouille.* cf. 'Hell! Said the duchess...' (*The Young Visiters* [sic],
1919). But at the age of nine, Daisy Ashford had more excuse than Zola.

Stylistic excess, no less than any other, spoils the effect. Zola aims at violence, brutality, strength and in the end falls into the ridiculous by his lack of judgment, or slipshod haste. 'Un piano endiablé venait d'éclater en notes sonores', he writes at the beginning of *La Bête Humaine*; a few pages later the same detail slightly developed: 'Et, dans l'effrayant silence, on entendit monter les chants et les rires des demoiselles Dauvergne, dont le piano faisait rage ... C'était Claire qui chantait des rondes de petites filles, tandis que Sophie l'accompagnait, à tour de bras ...'! The frenzied piano ... bursting with sound ... shuddering under the hammer blows of the ham-fisted (we may suppose) Sophie, and all that to give musical support to Claire's nursery ditties. Claire must have been bellowing (*gueulant*) through a megaphone. In writing this passage Zola has not pictured the scene in his mind; he wished to convey an impression of noisy music and that is all that mattered; the result is a parody. Another good example of Zola's slipshod haste is provided by an animated scene in *L'Argent*; of Gundermann's queue of visitors he writes: 'En suite, ce furent deux dames ... Il vint encore un bijoutier ... deux inventeurs, des Anglais, des Allemands, des Italiens, toutes les langues, tous les sexes ... [*sic*!].'[68]

This habit of slipping from a given scene to a generalized impression makes it easy for Zola to see objects not as they really are but as something else – Le Voreux as a primeval beast swallowing men, for instance. Perhaps we hold here the secret affinity that gave him such surprising insight into the art of Manet. Speaking of a picture by Manet, he writes, 'Il a vu ce sujet par larges taches, par oppositions vigoureuses.'[69] Claude, the artist in *L'Oeuvre*, is evidently inspired by Manet, his style is described as 'cette peinture brutale ... des tons violents, des grands traits de pastel sabrant les ombres ...'

The painter, Zola thinks, is concerned not to copy reality but to convey simplified impressions of it, with forms defined by vigorous oppositions of colour, of light and shade. Similarly the writer need not describe reality, he must convey an impression drawn from it: 'Une oeuvre d'art est un coin de la création, vu à travers un tempérament'.[70]

Where the scene or subject Zola describes appeals to his temperament the impression conveyed is effective, often powerful – the still life impression in *Le Ventre de Paris*, the sombre scenes, reminiscent of the tones of Vlaminck, in the mining area of Flanders (*Germinal*), the crude gas-light effects of the theatrical world (*Nana*). But unlike the impressionist painter who is content to

[68] *L'Argent*, p. 97, Fasquelle edn.   [69] *Mes Haines*; article on Manet.
[70] *Mes Haines*; article on 'Les Réalistes du salon'.

record the impression he receives from the chosen 'coin de la création', Zola, being a writer, not a painter (and in a sense, a Romantic writer unaware of himself), must go further and breathe a new life into the visual impression by giving it a symbolic meaning.

As the series of his *Rougon-Macquart* proceeds, a change occurs in the type of symbol Zola endeavours to create. The stomach as man's God, Nature's exuberance in the conservatory of Aristide Saccard's house[71] or in Le Paradou[72], are well in the Naturalist line, in *L'Assommoir* a note of charity not as yet deliberately humanitarian, but more insistent than for example in the Silvère-Miette theme,[73] is heard; *Pot-Bouille* strikes an aggressive social chord;[74] the apartment house is a symbol of bourgeois hypocrisy; in its 'abîmes d'honnêteté' the house conceals a corruption that will in due course bring the rotten class down in ruins; Doctor Juillerat speaks for Zola as he arraigns a whole social class: 'dans son emportement de vieux jacobin sonnait le glas entêté d'une classe, la décomposition et l'écroulement de la bourgeoisie, dont les étais pourris craquaient d'eux-mêmes.'[75]

In *Germinal* the social interest has become more positive: 'Ce fut l'époque où Etienne entendit les idées qui bourdonnaient dans son crâne... pourquoi la misère des uns? pourquoi la richesse des autres? pourquoi ceux-ci sous le talon de ceux-là...?'[76] In *La Terre*, interfering with the Lear-theme[77] and the melodrama, the social interest comes down to the economic problem of small peasant ownership. In *La Bête Humaine*, the locomotive without its crew, plunging blindly ahead dragging its load of drunken soldiery to the war, is presumably a symbol of the Second Empire, that rotten structure of political tyranny and social exploitation, rushing to destruction.[78]

From being a Naturalist Zola seems to be turning humanitarian. Could it be that the pessimism engendered by the Naturalist conception of man – a physiological mechanism, no more – demanded, in Zola at least, some sort of psychological compensation? Or perhaps it would be truer to ask whether the Romantic in him, so akin in imaginative power and method to Hugo, the Romantic largely kept in check hitherto by Naturalist principles, was not asserting himself – and, like Hugo too, but with a more social emphasis, was not adopting the messianic tone?

---

[71] *La Curée.*   [72] *La Faute de l'Abbé Mouret.*
[73] *La Fortune des Rougon.*
[74] There is already an echo of this in *Le Ventre de Paris*: Claude Lantier exclaims: 'Quels gredins que les honnêtes gens'.
[75] *Pot-Bouille*, p. 400; *Oeuvres Complètes*, Fasquelle.
[76] Part III, chap. 3.
[77] Old Fouan driven out by his children.
[78] See conclusion of the book.

Admittedly, in the last novel of the series, Doctor Pascal returns once more to the scientific vein; that we should be at least reminded of ... heredity was essential, after all, with the social preoccupations gaining ground as the gloomy epic of the family unfolded. But even Pascal, in spite of his claim to scientific objectivity, seems infected by his creator's vicarious optimism. Doctor Pascal looks into the future and sees there the gates of human happiness opening at the turn of organized science's golden key. He is therefore the link between the *Rougon-Macquart* and the novels of Zola's last period when Zola gives full reign to his symbolism.

Lourdes (1894), in which we are spared no details of the lamentable army of pilgrims, is animated with pity for their sufferings, indignation at the exploitation, as Zola sees it, by the business interests of piety, both of their pathetic faith and of the innocent Bernadette; *Rome* (1896) carried the attack into the heart of the enemy's camp. L'Abbé Pierre Froment, with crusading zeal, sets out for Rome, in the hope of persuading the Pope to espouse the cause of social progress. From frustration to frustration which recall those of Lamennais, Pierre Froment loses heart and faith, or rather changes his faith from God to science.

Paris (1897), the third volume of the city trilogy, is evoked at the time of the anarchist bombs and the financial scandal of Panama. Zola sees the latter as the outward sign of the inward corruption of a society represented by the hedonist financial shark, Duvillard, the former as the protest of the poor and starving. 'Que tous aient mon courage', cries the anarchist Salvat, under sentence of death, 'et demain votre société pourrie sera balayée, le bonheur enfin naîtra.'[79]

Three cities, the city of suffering, the city of obscurantism, the city of hope – but hope needs nourishment; Zola intended to provide it in four courses: *Fécondité* (1899), *Travail* (1901) were the first two, the third, *Vérité* (1903), was served, posthumously, the fourth, to be named 'Justice', remained unprepared, and we may safely leave the feast untouched as indigestible propaganda.

Not as lay evangelist ratiocinating on his socialist gospel will Zola be remembered in his closing years, but as the author of *J'accuse* (1898) which moved French society, as the anarchists' bombs of a few years before could never have done. 'J'accuse ... J'accuse ... J'accuse ...' The accusing finger points for all time[80] at Generals Mercier, Billot, de Boisdeffre, Gonse and company, leading figures in the Dreyfus case. Throbbing with generous emotion, the Open Letter to France (to give *J'accuse* its real name) is

---

[79] *Paris*, p. 709, Fasquelle edn.
[80] And perhaps unfairly, but that is another story.

splendid pamphleteering, a testimony to Zola's courage and to the power of his pen, at its best (and worst) in violence.

III. THE MÉDAN GROUP AND MAUPASSANT

As a matter of literary history, Naturalism may be said to begin with *Germinie Lacerteux* (1865), but public taste, obstinately wedded to romance in the Romantic style, was slow to accept the new mode; could fiction exist without a commanding central figure for the reader to take to his heart, identify himself with, follow breathlessly from adventure to adventure? The heroes and heroines of Stendhal and Balzac, of Hugo, Dumas *père* and George Sand, arose to say no; Emma Bovary herself could join that exalted company,[81] and quite latterly Jean Valjean. What characters of such commanding stature could the Rougon-Macquart family put forward? Zola had years of an uphill struggle before he could persuade the public to accept a different literary formula, to accept that there were aspects of life other than individual situations, worthy of the novelist's attention. Thanks to Zola, poverty, disease, economic forces, industrial complexes, social groups, a host of phenomena hitherto no more than a distant background, a backcloth, for the hero playing out his part, come into the foreground, are imbued with a life of their own. The author conjures up in the reader's imagination a series of frescoes in which individual characters, seen in relation to the group they belong to or as a cog in a vast mechanism, inevitably shrink in size and incandescent power. Not until 1877 had public taste shifted far enough for Zola to register his first success with *L'Assommoir*. In 1880, the sales of *Nana* both in France and abroad broke all records. Naturalism was at full tide. In 1880, the writers who had gathered under Zola's banner during the previous years published *Les Soirées de Médan*,[82] a collection of short stories, each by one member of the group, and one from the pen of the master. In the Preface the authors claim that the stories stem from a common philosophy, that they are a testimony to the authors' common literary tendencies.

Zola's own contribution to the book scarcely bears out that contention. 'L'Attaque du Moulin' shares with the other stories the background of the war of 1870, but apart from this detail it has little to do with the philosophy of Naturalism; it is a romantic story, not without merit, of love tragically cut short by the ebb and flow of war – the capture of the mill by the Prussians, its recapture by the French; in contrast to the exultant French officer, Françoise mourns over the bodies of her father and her betrothed. The sym-

---

[81] 'Aujourd'hui même dans tous les villages de France . . .'
[82] Zola had bought a house at Médan in 1877.

pathy and sentimentality the characters are bathed in are more akin to the war stories of Alphonse Daudet than to Naturalism's interpretation of human actions in terms of glandular secretions and its portrayal of the meaningless lunacy of war.

The remaining stories pull out both stops. The characters in 'Boule de Suif' obey their animal appetites; the tragi-comic drama is played out against scenes of the French army in a state of dis-integration, the National Guard taking cover prudently in its funk-holes and the arrogance of the Prussian officers, not all that different, incidentally, from that of the French officers, before the catastrophe: 'les officiers de hussards bleus, qui traînaient avec arrogance leurs grands outils de mort sur le pavé, ne semblaient pas avoir pour les simples citoyens... plus de mépris que les offi-ciers de chasseurs qui l'année d'avant buvaient aux mèmes cafés.'

Apart from effective and characteristic notations of colour, Huysmans's vision of war in 'Sac au Dos' is one of confusion, un-preparedness, dirt and dysentery, the latter limiting the hero's ex-perience of war to field ambulances, the insensitive care of army doctors ('montre ta jambe... ta sale jambe... bonne tisane de réglisse'), and to latrines ('où tout le monde opère, sans pudeur, ensemble); 'Sac au Dos' is the flimsiest of stories, but as a series of scenes of sordid realism under the stress of war it has great merit. The same can scarcely be said of the remaining three stories; 'La Saignée' by Henri Céard, aggressively anti-militarist, ascribes the historic Buzenval 'sortie' from the beleaguered capital to the whims of the general's mistress, Madame de Pahauën – Nana on a small scale, and no less of a caricature – and the sexual desires of the general, presumably an unflattering portrait of the military governor of Paris, General Trochu. Léon Hennique's contribution, 'L'Affaire du Grand 7', relates the story of a wartime massacre, but the victims are the inmates of a garrison brothel. In 'Après la bataille', finally, Paul Alexis, good Naturalist that he is, shows how the sexual instinct, strongest of all human motives, overcomes all bar-riers: social prejudices, human grief, even physical suffering. The aristocratic young war-widow falls into the arms of the common soldier beside the coffin of the dead husband, whilst the cart they're riding in trundles along in the darkness at the whim of the old horse.[83]

The collective impact of *Les Soirées de Médan* is considerable; yet without Maupassant's outstanding contribution, the collection would scarcely have survived as more than a title, an aggressive gesture in favour of Naturalism. The names of Henri Céard (1851–1924) and Léon Hennique (1851–1935) have faded; J. K. Huys-mans (1848–1907) did not long remain in the Naturalist camp; his

[83] A modern version of Petronius's Widow of Ephesus.

work survives indeed but in a different context; Paul Alexis (1847–1901) is chiefly remembered as Zola's hagiographer; the brightest star of the Médan constellation was and remains Maupassant.

Guy de Maupassant (1850–93) had served a severe literary apprenticeship at the hands of his friend, god-father and fellow-Norman, Flaubert. Strong echoes of the elder man's vital and lasting influence on his disciple are to be found in the stimulating rather than profound essay on the novel as an art form that Maupassant wrote as a preface to *Pierre et Jean*[84] (1888). 'Pendant sept ans je fis des vers, je fis des contes, je fis des nouvelles. Il n'en est rien resté.[85] Le maître lisait tout, puis le dimanche suivant, en déjeunant, développait ses critiques et enfonçait en moi peu à peu deux ou trois principes qui sont le résumé de ses longs et patients enseignements...'

Could any teacher have had an apter pupil? 'Boule de Suif' is a masterpiece of construction and acute observation. From the general description of occupied Rouen and the attitude of its inhabitants to the Prussians, the story, much as a film might do, quickly focusses on the stage-coach and its inmates. From this point the story moves like a mechanism, with a neatness of design that is intellectually satisfying. To this is added the constant sensuous pleasure of a series of visual images; from Rouen to the stage-coach and its occupants, from the coach to the inn, from the inn back to the coach, the reader sees the succession of events and their protagonists as though he were present himself; this vision, for instance, of Cornudet, that vulgarian democrat, drinking his beer: 'Il avait une façon particulière de déboucher la bouteille, de faire mousser le liquide, de le considérer en penchant le verre, qu'il élevait ensuite entre la lampe et son oeil pour bien apprécier la couleur. Quand il buvait, sa grande barbe, qui avait gardé la nuance de son breuvage aimé, semblait tressaillir de tendresse; ses yeux louchaient pour ne point perdre de vue sa chope, et il avait l'air de remplir l'unique fonction pour laquelle il était né.' The evocative detail clothed in appropriate words: the appraising eye, the shaggy beer-stained beard, quivering with tenderness, the squint developing as the drinker addresses his lips to the froth-capped mug; all these compel the attention even of the most un-

---

[84] Maupassant wrote six novels: *Une Vie* (1883); *Bel Ami* (1885); *Mont Oriol* (1887); *Pierre et Jean* (1888); *Fort comme la mort* (1889); *Notre Coeur* (1890). Often enough they are scarcely more than long, dramatically developing short stories (*Une Vie, Pierre et Jean*). The most satisfactory of them is probably *Bel Ami* which, both as the chronicle of a cad (Georges Duroy) with the ups and downs of his progress via journalism from penury to plenty, and as a picture of Parisian life in the 'eighties, has much to commend it.

[85] Some at least of the verse survives (*Des vers*, 1880) and could be dispensed with.

co-operative reader, force the inertest imagination to evoke the scene. Just as 'Boule de Suif' spreads out her little feast before the hungry eyes of the other travellers, so the story itself is a perpetual feast to the reader's eyes. 'Il s'agit de regarder tout ce qu'on veut exprimer assez longtemps et avec assez d'attention pour en découvrir un aspect qui n'ait été vu et dit par personne. Il y a, dans tout, de l'inexploré...' Such was Flaubert's recorded lesson.[86] Again we may ask: did ever master have apter pupil? Indeed the pupil outstripped the master. Flaubert's descriptive power sometimes overweights his text;[87] the effort to paint pictures with words becomes evident. Never could such a criticism be levelled at Maupassant where description and action are in perfect balance.

'Il avait l'air de remplir l'unique fonction pour laquelle il était né...' This final trait in the description of Cornudet, where, under the eye of the reader, he changes from a human being into a suction pump, is not only comic in itself; it has value for the whole story. Are not all the main characters in their several ways, similarly shown, beneath the thin superficial layer of their humanity, to be either mechanisms driven by physiological urges or soulless creatures obeying sordid material interests? When the spasms of the stomachic muscles with no food to work on have a chance of being allayed, attitudes change from reserve to friendly bonhomie. Later, when the material interests of the travellers are put in jeopardy by Boule de Suif's resistance to the German officer, her new-found friends soon show that moral, religious or patriotic values have only a subordinate place in their minds; finally, when the journey is resumed, mere humanity is forgotten, as the travellers (all but one) satisfy their hunger.

Maupassant's portrayal of human behaviour has a sociological aspect wider perhaps than he thought. The travellers, as they gather before sunrise in the cold of a winter's dawn, are a haphazard assemblage of individuals; imprisoned in their coats and furs, they have no relation to each other. With the dawn comes recognition, the coachload of individuals becomes a microcosm of Rouen society; the social structure with its barriers and conventions takes immediate shape; under the stress of hunger the barriers break; a corporate body is formed, much like lumps of ice melting in a basin. The moral unity of this body corporate is strengthened by momentary patriotic feeling; they form square to protect their defenceless compatriot against the Prussian officer, but the square in its turn breaks up under the attack of material interests, to produce a new grouping that leaves Boule de Suif in isolation, until she has yielded to the social pressures, only to see herself quickly

---

[86] *Pierre et Jean*, preface.
[87] Notably in *Salammbô* and *La Tentation de Saint-Antoine*.

extruded once more from the body social as its other members fit
into their allotted slots and the pattern of society, inhuman, soulless, reasserts itself. Even if we protest that in the end Maupassant
has stretched the bounds of credibility too far, that, in his passion
for formal neatness, he has counterbalanced the earlier coach scene
with a 'pay-off' scene of searing harshness where human egotism
reaches an improbable point, none the less the little coach community before and after the central incident of the story is too
close to human behaviourism to be comfortable.

The pessimism that pervades the story needs no emphasizing,
relieved only by the tenderness the author betrays for Boule de
Suif herself. The prostitute is a creature of instinct; as such she enjoys Maupassant's ready sympathy; she is an outcast, a victim; as
such she excites his pity.

With its rich mixture of comedy and pathos, its artistic perfection, formal excellence, and sociological relevance, its pessimism
finally, 'Boule de Suif' is a masterpiece that reflects better than
any other work the various aspects of Maupassant's art.

In the next ten years and more, Maupassant produced short
stories in an unending flow; and with unparalleled inventiveness;
they seemed to burgeon at the end of his pen like apples on an
apple-tree.[88] They appeared mostly in the *Gaulois* or *Gil Blas*, later
in volume form with one of the stories giving its title to each
volume.[89]

The high rate of production produced some uneven quality.
There are stories that sacrifice probability for the sake of a tense
situation with a dramatic climax (e.g. 'Denis', 'L'Ordonnance',
'Le Testament', 'Un Lâche', 'La Bûche', 'Un Duel'), but even
when ample allowance is made for inferior stories where inspiration may have suffered under the pressures of journalism, a rich
harvest remains; tragic tales (e.g. 'Miss Harriet', 'La Femme de
Paul', 'Mon Oncle Jules', 'Le Petit'), pathetic tales ('A cheval',
'La Parure', 'Hautot Père et Fils', 'L'Histoire d'une fille de ferme',
'Le Baptême', 'Regret', 'Mlle Perle', 'Le Lit 29', 'L'Odyssée
d'une fille', 'Le Papa de Simon'), and a host of comic tales, not
always scabrous, from the practical jokes and lewd farces of
Norman peasants (e.g. 'La Ficelle', 'Le Lapin', 'Farce Nor-
mande', 'Un Normand', 'Une Vente') to the innumerable chron-
icles of harlotry (e.g. 'La Maison Tellier', 'Une Soirée', 'Nuit de
Noël', 'Les Soeurs Rondoli') and 'slices of life' (e.g. 'En Famille',

[88] Jules Lemaitre's comparison.
[89] 'La Maison Tellier' (1881); 'Mlle Fifi', 'Contes de la Bécasse' (1883),
'Clair de Lune', 'Les Soeurs Rondoli', 'Yvette', 'Miss Harriet', 'M. Parent'
(1884); 'Contes du Jour et de la Nuit' (1885); 'La Petite Roque', 'Toine'
(1886); 'Le Horla' (1887); 'Le Rosier de Mme Husson' (1888); 'La Main
Gauche' (1889); 'L'Inutile Beauté' (1890).

'L'Héritage', 'Duchoux', 'Une Partie de Campagne', 'Le Rosier de Mme Husson', 'Le Trou', 'L'Ami Patience' and the whole cycle of *Les Dimanches d'un Bourgeois de Paris*); tales of the war of 1870 both in comic and tragic vein ('L'Aventure de Walter Schnaffs', 'Deux Amis', 'La Folle', 'Mlle Fifi', 'La Mère sauvage'), tales of obsessive fear or the macabre ('Sur l'Eau', 'La Peur', 'Lui?', 'La Petite Roque', 'Le Horla', 'La Main', 'Auprès d'un Mort', 'Une Vendetta').

As a short story writer Maupassant is concerned mainly with creating a sharp impact on our emotions; in some of the longer stories (e.g. 'Boule de Suif', 'La Maison Tellier', 'Histoire d'une fille de ferme', 'En Famille', 'L'Héritage') outlines of individual characters begin to emerge, but this is rare. In general the most that can be said is that the host of silhouettes that appear in his vast canvas belong to certain distinct social groups: aristocratic Parisian society, in town or in their country châteaux for the summer or the shooting season, minor civil servants, Norman peasantry, prostitutes. Not unexpectedly, the mirror Maupassant holds up to society reflects the most vivid image where his experience has been closest; the Norman peasants and the whole framework of their lives from the countryside and farmyard to their speech, *moeurs* and mentality, are portrayed as only an acute observer could, who had spent his boyhood and youth amongst them; not less successful are the minor civil servants, the drabness of their clockwork lives and their petty ambitions. Although two of his greatest tales ('Boule de Suif' and 'La Maison Tellier') have prostitutes as or amongst their main characters, prostitutes as a class, in spite of Maupassant's experience, do not emerge from his pages with the same vigour as the peasantry and the civil servants; they are pretexts for a story and do not evoke that rich 'faisandé' atmosphere conveyed by the paintings of Toulouse-Lautrec. Least successful of all are Maupassant's young men about town, and society women, so reminiscent of the puppets to be met with in the pages of Bourget. Maupassant had enlisted and fought in the war of 1870; yet his very real experience of war seems a little remote from the stories that have that war as a theme. If we set aside the genuinely comic humanity of Walter Schnaffs, most of the stories give either a conventional picture of the Jack-booted hectoring Prussian officer, rather in the patriotic vein to be met with in Alphonse Daudet,[90] or emphasize the senseless cruelty of war, pity for suffering. The comedies of the barrack-room, the mentality of the 'Sous-Off.' type, must be sought in the pages of Courteline or the drawings of Caran d'Ache.

Doubtless, in this wide-ranging social tour, Maupassant, even in

[90] e.g. 'La Dernière Classe', 'Le Siège de Berlin'.

his best vein, does not explore deeply the human situation or analyze exhaustively individual relationships – the framework of the short story is too narrow even if the wish were present – but certain aspects of life and human nature are brought into sharp relief: the perpetual battle between the sexes: 'Ce fut une lutte courte, sans paroles, violente, entre les prunelles seules, l'éternelle lutte entre les deux brutes humaines, le mâle et la femelle, où le mâle est toujours vaincu';[91] the slavery of marriage: 'il ne se sentait pas le courage de se condamner à la mélancolie, à la servitude conjugale, à cette odieuse existence de deux êtres...';[92] men's egotism in the pursuit of love: 'tous les calculs égoïstes des hommes en matière d'amour lui travaillaient l'esprit';[93] bourgeois hypocrisy and egotism – the theme is constant from 'Boule de Suif' onwards; bourgeois pretentiousness,[94] and stupidity – that theme, already present in *Des Vers*,[95] reappears with all Maupassant's 'burgophobia' in one of his fascinating travel diaries:[96] sitting on the deck of his yacht watching the lights of Cannes, his meditations lack all charity: 'je pensais que dans toutes ces villas, dans tous ces hôtels, des gens, ce soir se sont réunis... et qu'ils causent... Est-il rien de plus sinistre qu'une conversation de table d'hôte? J'ai vécu dans les hôtels, j'ai subi l'âme humaine qui se montre dans toute sa platitude... Faut-il être aveugle et saoul de fierté stupide pour se croire autre chose qu'une bête à peine supérieur aux autres! Ecoutez-les... ces misérables! Ils causent... avec ingénuité, avec confiance, avec douceur, et ils appellent cela échanger des idées. Quelles idées?... Il me semble que je vois en eux l'horreur de leur âme comme on voit un foetus monstreux dans l'esprit de vin d'un bocal. J'assiste à la lente éclosion des lieux communs qu'ils redisent toujours, je sens les mots tomber de ce grenier à sottises dans leurs bouches d'imbéciles...' The passage needs to be read *in extenso* to feel the full impact of Maupassant's hatred and powerful invective, seldom surpassed except in the pages of Léon Bloy.[97]

Nor is this all; cruelty, violence, sordid rapacity, cunning, heartlessness, the whole gloomy catalogue of human egotisms is present everywhere in Maupassant's pages, and to crown them all the big universal lie that covers all men's actions: in a vision reminiscent of the elder Brueghel, Maupassant describes his dream beside the open tombs in a cemetery, with the dead writing the truth about themselves in place of what was on the tombstones: 'Et je voyais que tous avaient été les bourreaux de leurs proches, haîneux, déshon-

<hr/>

[91] 'Allouma'.
[92] 'Duchoux'.
[93] 'Le Père'.
[94] 'L'Ami Patience'.
[95] 'Propos des Rues'.
[96] *Sur L'Eau* (1888); the other two are *Au Soleil* (1884) and *La Vie errante* (1890).
[97] See below, chap. 7.

nêtes, hypocrites, menteurs ... qu'ils avaient volé, trompé, ... ces
bons pères, ces épouses fidèles, ces fils dévoués, ces jeunes filles
chastes ... Ils écrivaient tous ... la cruelle, terrible et sainte vérité
que tout le monde ignore ou feint d'ignorer sur la terre.'[98] Even
though the gloom of it all is occasionally relieved by a shaft of
light – some gesture of love or pity, some trait of honesty,[99] the
all-pervading impression is of the deepest pessimism, a pessimism,
like Flaubert's, that seemed inherent in his nature and appears
early,[100] then adopts the determinism of the Naturalist school.[101]
Though Naturalism appears to be Maupassant's favourable climate, his pessimism takes other forms not in line with the attitude
of a thorough-going determinist; in his first novel, *Une Vie*
(1883), the uncompromising naturalistic negation of the soul gives
place to metaphysical questionings;[102] these, it is true, are ascribed
to a character[103] in the novel, and do not therefore necessarily reflect the opinions of the author. But there are many cases where
Maupassant intervenes in his stories and reveals his own attitude as
author, others where the 'je' of the narrator seems indistinguishable from Maupassant himself. The most striking theme is a sense
of solitude: 'on s'aperçoit soudain qu'on est vraiment et toujours
et partout seul au monde ...'[104] This acute sense of the personality
is, to say the least of it, peculiar in a determinist for whom the
personality can be no more than the sum of the impulses registered
at the nerve-centres. The sense of solitude in Maupassant takes a
tragic form, a hallucinatory fear of being shadowed and ultimately
'possessed'; it is already present in *Des Vers*,[105] becomes stronger in
'Lui?' and achieves its fullest expression in 'Le Horla'. Is that
consciousness of the ego not also connected with the claustrophobic
sense of being imprisoned in this 'dull, flat and unprofitable world',
imprisoned in ourselves, that receives its most anguished form in
the introspective meditations of *Sur L'Eau?*[106] Anguish is indeed
the word that characterizes the later form of Maupassant's pessimism, an anguish full of fear, a spiritual anguish, that finds no hope,
no refuge, not even in art as Flaubert did, a spiritual nihilism
greatly influenced by Schopenhauer,[107] 'le plus grand saccageur

---

[98] 'La Morte'.   [99] 'La Parure'.   [100] 'Le Docteur Heraclius Glos'.
[101] 'Boule de Suif'.   [102] Chap. 9.   [103] 'Jeanne'.
[104] 'Les Soeurs Rondoli'. Another striking example where Maupassant
seems to be expressing his own metaphysical anguish through the mouths or
thoughts of his characters is provided by *Bel Ami*, Part I, chap. 6. Norbert
de Varenne on death; and Part I, chap. 8. Duroy on the same subject while
watching over his dead friend Forestier – a situation parallel to that depicted in *Une Vie*.
[105] cf. 'Terreur'.
[106] The travel reminiscences; not the story with the same title, itself a
powerful story of claustrophobic fear.
[107] Zola, be it noted, rejected 'la poésie noire de Schopenhauer' – see *La
Joie de vivre* (1884)

de rêves qui ait passé sur la terre';[108] like the unidentifiable haunt-
ing presence in 'Le Horla', it pursued Maupassant into madness.[109]

IV. DAUDET

'Dichtung und Wahrheit' – the title might fittingly apply to the
chronicle Alphonse Daudet (1840–97) gives of his early years in
Le Petit Chose (1868): childhood at Nîmes, sundrenched happiness
in the old family house flanked by the printed-calico factory; the
move to Lyon (1848), economic paralysis having finally throttled
the business in that year of revolutions, the father's struggle against
adversity, unrewarded in the end; the break-up of the home, Monsieur Eyssette becoming a business traveller, Madame Eyssette a
patient poor relation boarding with unsympathetic cousins, the
narrator's elder brother Jacques alone remaining at Lyon, struggling along as best his mediocre talents allowed ('Jacques, c'est un
âme'[110]) against life and the cockroaches.

After the family diaspora the interest concentrates on 'Le Petit
Chose's' own experiences (1855–7) as that lowest form of life
within the French school system, 'le répétiteur', commonly known
as 'le pion';[111] gloomy years of poverty and isolation, with flashes
of kindness here (the old servant's welcome; the sympathetic understanding of L'Abbé Germane, reminiscent of L'Abbé Pirenne's
attitude to Julien Sorel[112]), callous indifference there ('La classe
moyenne', 'L'Ami Roger'). On discovering 'L'Ami Roger's' false-
ness, the author writes: 'C'est là dans cette tonnelle noire et froide
que j'ai appris combien les hommes peuvent être méchants et
lâches; c'est là que j'ai appris à douter, à mépriser, à haïr...'
Perhaps; yet the story reflects no such attitudes. The bitterness 'Le
Petit Chose' claims to have learned is absent. Suffering, both moral
and physical, he had in plenty from Lyon to Sarlande, thence to
the Parisian attic which he shared with his brother until the latter's
death, but it is recorded with no self-pitying sentimentality; the
overall impressions are of whimsical humour, pathos, human sympathy and tenderness.

In reality, Daudet does not appear to have shared 'Le Petit
Chose's' misfortunes, not at least in Paris, where success smiled on
him at once;[113] he soon became a secretary to the Duc de Morny
(1860–5).[114] Daudet in the household of Morny suggests a com-

---

[108] 'Auprès d'un mort'.
[109] Syphilis also contributed. He died of general paralysis of the insane
in Dr Emile Blanche's Mental Nursing Home.
[110] Petit Chose. M. Eyssette's usual indulgent description of his elder
son.   [111] At Sarlande in the book; at Alais in reality.   [112] Rouge et Noir.
[113] See article by L. Babesco, Revue d'histoire littéraire de la France,
January 1964.   [114] Half-brother of Napoleon III.

parison with the wayward La Fontaine in that of Nicolas Foucquet. The light verse and comedies Daudet purveyed for the society of his wealthy patron have melted away much as 'Le Songe de Vaux', but the experience Daudet gained of Parisian high society in the last decade of the Second Empire was to be of value to him later. Meanwhile occasional visits to his native Provence enriched the storehouse of the born story-teller who was to reveal himself in *Lettres de mon Moulin* (1869). The very qualities that ensured the success of *Le Petit Chose* shine through abundantly in the *Lettres*; nor must we omit the occasional note of astringent tragedy. Daudet also visited Algeria which was to provide him with inspiration and colour for Tartarin, that engaging pantaloon, that mighty hunter, with little fire in the pot-belly, who, weary of shooting at his cap, sets out for Africa in the hope of meeting game more worthy of his steady eye and iron nerve.

Les Aventures prodigieuses de Tartarin de Tarascon (1872), though published after the Franco-Prussian War (1870–1), belong in spirit to the same group as *Le Petit Chose* and the *Lettres de mon Moulin*. Daudet the story-teller is again in evidence, full of a vaguely Rabelaisian verve and non-corrosive humour; the adventures are in effect a series of stories built around a central figure, the other characters are episodic, almost lifeless. Tartarin himself is scarcely seen in the round; much as in a caricature, his creator, drawing upon his knowledge of his southern compatriots, has been content to capture certain characteristic attitudes and to create an image in which all of us (who are not 'Provençaux') will recognize the quintessential meridional, as unlikely to be met with in the flesh as the fabled Aberdonian or Taffy the Welshman of countless tales, but with a permanence assured so long as Provence exists, that favoured region plagued only by the biting Mistral and the unpredictable Durance, as rich in human comedy as its earth and sky are in contrasts of colour, of light and shadow. Provence has a language and a literature of its own; it flourished in the days of Good King René (1409–80); in Daudet's own day it enjoyed a brief renaissance through the poet Frédéric Mistral (1830–1914), author of *Mireille* (1859) and founder of the 'Félibrige' (1854),[115] but Daudet brought Provence with its regional flavour into French literature as no one had before; Tartarin is the first of a gallery of figures who have a family resemblance: *Jean des Figues* (1873) and Pitalugue,[116] *Marius*,[117] *Tabusse*.[118] Tartarin himself was to

[115] A literary group comprising, besides Mistral, Aubanel, Roumanille, Brunet, Mathieu, Tavan, Giéra.
[116] In *Contes de Paris et de Provence* (1887). Both *J. des F.* and the *Contes* are by Paul Arène (1843–96).
[117] By Marcel Pagnol (b. 1895).
[118] By André Chamson (b. 1900).

reappear; so rich a vein of regionalist comedy once uncovered provided Tartarin's creator with a strong temptation to exploit it to the full, but sequels are seldom as good as the original; *Tartarin sur les Alpes* (1885) and *Port Tarascon* (1890) are no exception. If the capers of Tartarin as mountaineer and colonizer are as prodigious as ever, the reader's interest is on the wane; the adventures may be different, the attitudes are the same.

Daudet had fought in the war; like Maupassant he found in his experience another source of inspiration where pathos and a subdued patriotism are often happily blended (e.g. 'Le Siège de Berlin', 'La Dernière Classe'[119]). The war had the further effect of bringing Daudet face to face with the question of what image of himself he wished to leave to posterity. Was he to be no more than the light-weight story-teller, now grave, now gay? The answer is provided by the series of novels that brought him success and prosperity from 1874 onwards, *inter alia*: *Fromont jeune et Risler aîné* (1874), *Jack* (1876), *Le Nabab* (1877), *Les Rois en Exil* (1879), *Numa Roumestan* (1881), *L'Evangéliste* (1883), *Sapho* (1884), *L'Immortel* (1888). Nor must it be forgotten that Daudet wrote for the stage; apart from dramatized versions of many of his novels, his most successful work in this field remains *L'Arlésienne* (1872), which in fact owes more to the dramatic music of Georges Bizet (1838–75) than to the mediocre story of the tragic love and suicide of Frédéric.

The years that saw Daudet's success as a novelist were those of the rise and fall of Naturalism. Zola, always zealous to gather in recruits and disciples, made every effort to dub his friend a Knight of the Médan Order. The task was not easy; Daudet, an exact contemporary of Zola's, had matured as a writer in his own right, had indeed achieved success some years before Zola. But it would have been strange if a movement of such power, European in breadth, had made no impact on a writer closely in touch with its leader in France. The intellectual and artistic relationship may be tenuous but it exists.

Some of the novels may, for example, claim to portray (if not to study in a documentary fashion) different Parisian social strata; *Fromont jeune et Risler aîné* is a story that unfolds in the world of commerce, of the old business houses in the 'Marais';[120] *Jack*, who gives his name to the novel, is an innocent victim of society, and is dragged through a number of different worlds in the course of his pathetic odyssey: a Parisian private school (reminiscent of

---

[119] *Contes du Lundi, passim.*
[120] The fashionable quarter in seventeenth-century Paris, now centre of wholesale trading houses, occupying many of the old 'hôtels'. In recent years much renovation work has been done. The Marais is also largely a Jewish quarter.

'Dotheboys Hall', Mr Squeers and all), the world of pretentious literary hacks and *ratés*, the steel-workers; *Le Nabab* takes us into high society and its hangers-on under the Second Empire, *Numa Roumestan* into the world of politics, with a Provençal flavour, *Sapho* into that of the *demi-mondaines*, *L'Immortel*, as the name suggests, into the world of the Académie Française and of the 'politics' of literature.

Occasionally, in the course of his perambulations through these different worlds, the reader gets a sense of 'milieu' in a truly Naturalist manner. Thus, seen through the meditative eyes of Guillaume Risler, the pay-day scene at the Fromont factory could well figure in a novel by Zola; no one better than the author of *Le Nabab* – and in delicate touches that have nothing of the heavy documentary manner of Zola but are none the worse for that – suggests the new cosmopolitanism, Judæo-Germanic and Levantine, that invaded Parisian society during the Second Empire;[121] or again we find occasional concessions to Naturalist ideas: 'du sang vicié . . . le plus épuisé le plus pauvre'[122] is a description that could well have come from Zola's pen.

Daudet justifiably claimed[123] that his novels were rooted in his day; notes on incidents, personalities observed were stored up in his 'cahier vert' to be used sooner or later as material for a novel. Nowhere is this truer than of *Le Nabab*; the duc de Mora is evidently modelled on Morny. Daudet gives a half-hearted denial in the preface: 'L'auteur a beau se défendre, jurer ses grands dieux que son roman n'a pas de clef . . .' and proceeds in the next paragraph but one to give himself the lie: 'J'ai connu le "vrai Nabab" en 1864 . . .' Thus Daudet's novels may often be 'a slice of life', to use a slogan so popular amongst Naturalist dramatists.

Sometimes a deeper sense of reality is achieved where the main interest shifts from the social group to the characters themselves. *Les Rois en Exil* offers the study of a situation untouched until then. Ruritania was to become popular in England as a land of Balkan adventure – could Anthony Hope have borrowed the idea from Daudet, through Stevenson?[124] There is more than a whiff of Ruritanian politics in the story of King Christian II and his Queen, driven from their Illyrian kingdom and taking refuge in Paris, but the merit of the story lies in the effect of exile on the characters: confidence in quick restoration changing slowly into the desire for action by unrealistic means and final disillusion,

---

[121] *Le Nabab*, chap. 2: 'Un déjeuner Place Vendôme'.
[122] *Les Rois en Exil*, chap. 18: 'La fin d'une race'.
[123] *Souvenirs d'un homme de lettres*, pp. 43–4.
[124] *Prince Otto* (1885), *Prisoner of Zenda* (1894).

false grandeurs and sordid financial expedients to maintain them, the acceptance and exploitation, even to death, of pathetic loyalties.

Numa Roumestan is the study of a meridional politician, *L'Evangéliste* that of a puritanical religious fervour implanted by a dominating personality in an impressionable mind and progressively driving out from the latter all human feeling. Of all Daudet's novels, *Sapho* is probably the best known. Is she merely one more name to add to the exalted company of courtesans, adventuresses, *demi-mondaines* of nineteenth-century French literature? Certain distinctions are necessary here because these appellations imply different attitudes towards the phenomenon.

The courtesan is a truly romantic figure, 'enthroned' in beauty, sometimes 'redeemed' – as though such a detail of supererogation were necessary – by a pure love: Marion Delorme, Marguerite Gautier;[125] the courtesan is an object of envy, admiration, almost of worship. In comparison, adventuress is an ugly word clearly implying condemnation. From within the embattled fortress of bourgeois morality, Augier warns his generation against that dangerous bird of prey – Fathers! Lock up your . . . sons! – alternatively, she becomes merely a figure of melodrama in the pages of Dumas *père* or in the skilful hands of Sardou. The *demi-mondaine* has a suggestion of objective sociological analysis; the lady must be 'positioned' in relation to the established degrees of the social scale, so that her efforts to achieve material security and a foothold in society may be seen for the fraudulent things they are. 'Look well', cautions Dumas *fils*, 'look well at your basket of peaches before you buy them'![126]

Courtesans, adventuresses, *demi-mondaines*, all are the vehicle for facile sentiment, or didactic moralizing, or pretentious social analysis. Prostitutes proper, honestly portrayed practitioners of the ancient profession, appear with the Naturalists, Maupassant in particular. Daudet's Sapho provides another nuance; she is not a prostitute, she is a kept woman.

The three previously mentioned novels have the merit of achieving, within a limited compass, some general validity; from specific psychological portraits they may claim to attain the level of studies of certain mentalities: monarchs in exile, meridional politicians, 'Major Barbaras'. Perhaps the mentality of the 'kept woman' has so little potential that it defies close study; in any case, in *Sapho* the interest is not in the study of a mentality but in the relationship of two characters; the story's the thing, whether Jean Gaussin will succeed in shaking himself free of his passion for Sapho, whether Sapho will succeed in retaining him; the sort of plot that was to

---

[125] *La Dame aux Camélias.*
[126] See *Le Demi-Monde*, II, 8; Vol. IV, chap. 20.

become commonplace in the nineteenth-century and early twentieth-century theatre.[127]

Skilful plot construction is in fact one of the most characteristic
traits of Daudet as a novelist. This in itself distinguishes him from
the thoroughgoing Naturalist, for plots are concerned with people
and what happens to them; they show in the author some sympathy or at least an interest in men as individuals; the Naturalists
regard them as products of social pressures or as determined by
their glandular secretions, in short, as sociological or biological
phenomena. Daudet has great human sympathy, particularly for
the failures of this world – filial piety perhaps?; his pages are
peopled with *ratés* whether they recognize themselves as such or
not: M. Eyssette and Jacques Fromont Jeune, Guillaume Risler,
Delobelle,[128] Jack, Jansoulet,[129] ex-King Christian II and Elysée
Méraut,[130] Numa, Bompard,[131] Jean Gaussin, Astier-Réhu the
Academician.[132] Nor is the prodigious Tartarin an exception, since
never to be taken seriously in life is a form of failure.

Daudet rejects Naturalism in another way too: the constant
emergence in his novels of his own personality in unexpected and
inappropriate places. As a result he often destroys the illusion of
reality he has been at pains to create. Thus after the successfully
realistic pay-day scene in *Fromont jeune*, Daudet intervenes
directly: 'Oh ... les enfants nu-pieds, les tout petits enveloppés de
vieux châles...'[133]

Again, in *Numa Roumestan*, the opening of Book IV is a gratuitous piece of whimsicality out of keeping with a realistic novel. 'Ah!
Natures aimantes', the author exclaims, in reference to Numa,
'comme vous vous donnez...' – the author stands back from his
own creation and addresses him in a lyrical apostrophe that might
have come from the pen of Chateaubriand.

Associated with the Naturalists by ties of friendship Daudet may
have been, and we have seen that he makes occasional concessions
to their ideas. Fundamentally however he remains an independent.
Unlike his friend Zola, he had no new interpretation of reality or
of the human situation to offer; his novels are essentially derivative; the reader is often reminded of earlier novelists: Guillaume
Risler, the disinterested inventor, is a character who could have
stepped out of the *Comédie Humaine*, the scheming Sidonie Risler
has something of Becky Sharp: 'Tout était bien arrangé dans cette
petite tête qui raisonnait froidement le vice...'[134] and of Emma

[127] Scribe's *Une chaîne*; Maurice Donnay's *Amants*; the passionate or
heartless heroines of Bernstein.
[128] *Fromont jeune et Risler aîné.*
[129] *Le Nabab.*
[130] *Les Rois en Exil.*
[131] *Numa Roumestan.*
[132] *L'Immortel.*
[133] *Fromont jeune*, III, i.
[134] Bk. III, chap. 2.

Bovary: 'Elle aurait voulu avoir des histoires...'[135] Jack is a kind of David Copperfield and Oliver Twist rolled into one – Daudet the poetic realist has evident affinities with Dickens; Numa Roumestan recalls no one so much as Tartarin – Daudet the novelist deriving from Daudet the story-teller! That seems the truth. For all his narrative skill, Daudet's novels hover on the brink of oblivion; he remains the author of the *Lettres de mon Moulin*, the creator of 'Le Petit Chose' and of Tartarin.

V. HUYSMANS

'Il comprit l'inutilité des changements de routes, la stérilité des élans et des efforts;...Schopenhauer a raison, se dit-il, la vie de l'homme oscille comme un pendule entre la douleur et l'ennui... le mieux n'existe pas pour les gens sans le sou; seul le pire arrive.' The discomfited Folantin (*A Vau-l'eau*) takes leave of the reader with these sour reflections, which provide the tonality of the earlier works of Joris-Karl Huysmans (1848–1907): *Le Drageoir aux Épices* (1874), *Marthe* (1876), *Les Soeurs Vatard* (1879), *En Ménage* (1881), *A Vau-l'eau* (1882).[136]

If we set aside the first, which is a series of prose poems in the Baudelairian tradition, the remainder correspond broadly in time with the high water mark of Naturalism; they are novels that evidently obey Naturalist formulae: sordid realism, urban working-class quarters, characters that live their daily lives in the treadmill of habit or of economic forces.

But if Zola be the Naturalist norm, Huysmans's adherence to the school does not go deep. In contrast to the gigantic fresco effects that Zola's most characteristic novels provide, Huysmans works on a small canvas; Zola's characters tend to lose their individuality either through their being lost in the mass movement or because they are shown as mechanisms determined by some force bigger than themselves; Huysmans's characters are more clearly delineated; Marthe, old Vatard and his daughters Céline and Désirée, Cyprien Tibaille and his friend André Jaillant,[137] Folantin. No doubt their lives are constricted, their horizons limited as those of Naturalist characters should be, but within this small compass they are shown not as packets of flesh and bone propelled hither and thither by blind forces but as human beings with some degree of choice, or reflection: Céline and Désirée, Cyprien and André, Folantin have their own views on how best to order their lives and

---

[135] Bk. III, chap. 2.
[136] 'Sac au Dos', Huysmans's contribution to *Les Soirées de Médan*, also belongs to this group.
[137] In *En Ménage*.

try to make decisions accordingly. To that extent they come alive in the reader's mind. Even Folantin's pessimism, already alluded to, is different from the damp cloud of pessimism that hangs around some of Zola's characters, for Folantin's is shown to be the result of his own experience, it is his own conclusion about things and the reader is free to pity him or condemn the spineless lack of initiative alone responsible, the reader may think, for his plight; Zola's characters allow the reader no such freedom; he must accept or reject the whole mechanism of which the characters are merely cogs, and if he accepts the pessimistic view, that pervades the whole. The effect may, sometimes, be more powerful; it is certainly less human. In his choice of subject, social strata and background, Huysmans may be faithful to Naturalist formulae but his treatment is different. The idea of documentation with either quasi-scientific or some social purpose is not apparent; instead the author's pre-occupation to exploit his material for artistic effect is manifest; scenes may be sordid but what opportunities for effects of light and shade: 'de grands carrés à lumière éclataient dans les façades sombres...'[138] Or again: 'des éclats de soleils qui perçaient les carreaux de la devanture, allumant le dessous rouge des lettres en cuivre collées sur les vitres...'[139] What opportunities for creating colour patterns: 'Un lapin, ouvert sur un plat...étalait le violet visqueux de son foie sur sa carcasse lavée de vermillon très pâle.'[140] Or again: 'Quelques parapluies encore ouverts mettaient des ronds de couleur sombre, emperlés de gouttes claires aux bords,...'.[141] There are unsuspected beauties, only for those with eyes to see: 'Vue ainsi la rue est toujours splendide et toujours neuve. Elle regorge, si fanée qu'elle puisse être, d'innombrables délices que bien peu comprennent...'[142]

Huysmans's artistic attitude is further revealed by his sense of form. Jejune in substance these early novels may be, revealing little that is original, nothing that is enriching about human nature; they none the less give the reader an impression of design, a neatness of construction not met with in Zola's heavier masonry. Nor must we forget Huysmans's originality as a stylist; the wealth of suggestion he draws from a wide variety of sensuous experience often gives his style the character of a highly flavoured sauce; the artist in Huysmans is aiming to make an impact on the reader by means that lie outside the substance of the work itself; a reminiscence of the Goncourt Brothers' self-conscious 'style artiste' and even of the ideas of 'l'Art pour l'Art'.

Thus, one way and another, Huysmans's allegiance to Naturalism will be seen to lack vigour. In another way, too, he shows himself

---

[138] *En Ménage*, p. 190; *Oeuvres Complètes*, Crès edn.
[139] *Ibid.*, p. 195. [140] *Ibid.*, p. 36. [141] *Ibid.*, p. 361. [142] *Ibid.*, p. 128.

ready to part company with Zola – the personal element that creeps in. When Cyprien and his friends show their attitude of superiority to Céline's crude notions on art and literature: 'dans un roman elle voulait des crimes, dans un tableau des choses douces...', we hear the voice of Huysmans gently mocking the cheap romanticism of the people; and sometimes the attack against romanticism is a more direct author's intervention: 'Ah! si tous tant que nous sommes n'étions pas gangrenés par le romantisme... nous verrions...bien d'autres beautés qui nous échappent!'[143]

From the outset Huysmans tends to identify himself with one or other of his characters: Old Vatard, pillar of the cafés; both André and Cyprien have occasional reminders of him, and the physical description of the latter is clearly modelled on himself: 'Grand et blond, maigre et blême, Cyprien avait une barbe pâle, de longs doigts effilés et pointus.'[144] Monsieur Folantin's bachelor habits and his lonely pessimism surely echo Huysmans's own.

These elements of personal attitudes are as yet discreet; two years later they assert themselves vigorously.

A Rebours (1884) reflects all the intellectual and spiritual turmoil that had been working in Huysmans in the interval and that Naturalism could not dispel. Zola was quick to read the signs. Huysmans recalls[145] Zola's appeal to the erstwhile disciple to fall back into line. A vain hope; whilst paying tribute to Naturalism's contribution to the evolution of the novel: 'l'inoubliable service de situer des personnages réels dans des milieux exacts...',[146] he declares it to have been a blind alley and to have cast all its characters in the one mould of average mediocre humanity. The hero of A Rebours is anything but average or mediocre; Jean des Esseintes[147] is full of aesthetic sensitiveness and awareness in matters artistic and literary, dislikes the civilization he is committed to living in, and tries to contract out of it by organizing a wholly artificial mode of life. The identification with Huysmans himself comes only in the next work Là-Bas (1891). Des Esseintes was no more than a pale image, an intellectual fantasy, Durtal, who holds the centre of the stage, not only in Là-Bas but also in the last group of works, the trilogy, En Route (1895), La Cathédrale (1898), L'Oblat (1903), is the historical reality. In his explorations, both historical and contemporaneous, into occultism (Là-Bas), in the various aspects of his religious experience (the trilogy), Durtal gives us chapters from Huysmans's own experience, moments of the con-

---

[143] Ibid., p. 129.   [144] Ibid., p. 131.   [145] See Preface (1903).
[146] With some of Zola's novels in mind the reader may well demur, but Huysmans goes on to show that in making this claim he is thinking of Flaubert, not of Zola, of L'Education Sentimentale, not of L'Assommoir.
[147] Modelled on Comte Robert de Montesquiou (1855–1921), poet, aesthete, arbiter of taste and fashion, friend of Proust.

flicts and pilgrimage, that led him – and others of his generation[148] – from spiritual darkness into the light of Christian faith.

The break with Naturalism is clear. From *A Rebours* onwards Huysmans, abandoning the harsh deterministic world of Naturalism, returns to what are in effect personal novels. The most inward-looking and enclosed is *A Rebours*. Finding the world about him dull, flat and unprofitable, Jean des Esseintes, last and etiolated scion of a ducal house, determines henceforth to cultivate his own ego by the pursuit of sensuous experience in an artificial world of his own creation.

Of the whims and fantasies of this latter-day dandy, who naturally worships at the shrine of Baudelaire, the gilded and jewel-encrusted tortoise, which soon succumbs to such treatment, and the liqueur cabinet or 'orgue à bouche', providing him with a symphony of tastes, are all that are usually recalled. But in fact des Esseintes' exploration of the sensuous world, his analysis of his own responses, his awareness of 'correspondances' in the Baudelairian sense are immensely stimulating; des Esseintes may be unreal, his experience is not. Furthermore, inward-looking though he is, he provides us unwittingly with what is perhaps the best record of the so-called 'decadent' attitude that became such a marked feature in the literature of the 'eighties. Gilbert's 'greenery-yallery...[149] foot-in-the-grave young man', who could not have failed to recognize des Esseintes as a brother nourished on Schopenhauer, is explored in depth. Thus des Esseintes, like René generations before, but on a deeper, more analytical level, has a significance that extends beyond Huysmans himself.

A Rebours, so Huysmans claims,[150] contains his subsequent works in embryo; des Esseintes does indeed at one moment feel himself drawn to a diabolical perversity[151] such as opens the door to Satanism, at another the pull of religion[152] and the beauties of plainsong, but Schopenhauer dominates.

Des Esseintes' experiment in aesthetic narcissism fails; that way madness lies; to avoid it he must burst out from his claustrophobic world and return to normal life. We can appreciate that, as Huysmans's own sense of spiritual dissatisfaction grew, he should feel the need to make a clean break with the neuropathic des Esseintes and project his mood into a less shadowy character. It may seem paradoxical that as Huysmans's personal experience comes closer

[148] e.g. Bloy, Claudel, Jammes, Maritain, Psichari, Péguy.

[149] To this expression of Gilbert's, there is a parallel in Huysmans, the colour substantive and its adjective he uses frequently – chlorose, chlorotique.

[150] Preface, 1903.

[151] 'le terrible chapitre vi ... et ... certaines parties du ixe ...' (op. cit., p. xvi).

[152] *A Rebours*, chaps. vii and xv.

to his work, identifying itself indeed with the fiction of Durtal, so do the works become less of personal novels; already in *Là-Bas* there are other characters that have some consistence.[153] The process is more marked in the final trilogy;[154] these works are a direct transposition of Huysmans's experience; thus the fictional characters conceal real people – a fact that provides no guarantee that living characters will result, yet here they do live and give a measure of Huysmans's skill as a novelist; with all his concentration on his own, Durtal's, spiritual conflict, he does not lose his power of observing the men and women Durtal comes in contact with.

The core of that conflict is in *En Route*. Recoiling with horror from the orgiastic experience of the black mass Docre officiates at and which Madame Chantelouve had introduced him to, Durtal turns for spiritual comfort to Rome. His doubts and hesitations are not finally dispelled until, on the advice of his friend, the abbé Gévresin, he undertakes a retreat in a Trappist monastery. Here the physically exhausting resistance of the old Adam is finally defeated by the overwhelming impact on Durtal of the monks' saintliness, their charity towards a soul in torment, their life, harsh to the limit of endurance and yet conferring upon those who practise it a serenity flowing from their mystical sense of getting ever nearer to God as all ties with this world are broken.

For Durtal confession and communion follow. Thereafter his problem changes; back once more, but with convinced awareness, in the Catholic fold of his childhood, the question is how shall he order his life so as to maintain it on a high devotional level. Living in the shadow of Chartres (*La Cathédrale*) with all its beauty, direct and symbolic, and even though he enjoys the saintly and stimulating company of Genévrier and Plomb, turns out not to be the answer; only a formal link with a monastic order – of it, yet not in it – can provide the tonifying effect of spiritual concentration (*L'Oblat*). This decision denotes a bias in favour of the regular rather than the secular clergy. Durtal's attitude both to the latter and to the Catholic laity lacks sympathy;[155] the spirit of the great

---

[153] Madame Chantelouve des Hermies, Carhaix. The satanic Chanoine Docre, modern counterpart of Gilles de Retz or Rais, that fifteenth-century blue-beard, whom Durtal is researching on, remains little more than a sinister force in the background.

[154] L'Abbé Gévresin, M. Brunot, Le Père Siméon, L'Abbé Plomb, Madame Bavoil, M. Lampre, Mademoiselle de Garambois, the Abbot and Prior of the Benedictine abbey of Le Val-des-Saints, Ligugé in reality.

[155] In company with other writers of the Catholic revival, notably Léon Bloy (who, however, was anything but friendly to Huysmans [see *La Femme Pauvre*, chaps. 30 and 31, *passim*]). Huysmans was apt to take the view that the soft attitude of compromise with the spirit of the age, a view attributed to many Catholics, both priests and laymen, was more dangerous to the pure fount of Catholicism than the frank hostility of its enemies.

mystics of the Middle Ages was what moved him; and only amongst the regular clergy did he find it. Equally important was his choice of order – the Benedictines of Val-des-Saints.[156] The impact of the Trappists had been decisive in the initial stage of his conversion, but with all their saintliness their mode of existence was unlovely, and not the least powerful element in Catholicism's hold on Durtal was the beauty of its liturgy and its music. Only with the Benedictines could he receive this nourishment, for theirs was the tradition of beauty in ritual and religious music – 'cette idée de luxe pour Dieu';[157] Dom Guéranger (1806–75) at Solesmes had revived the primitive Roman liturgy; Dom Pothier (1835–1923), his brother abbot at Ligugé, had revived plainsong. The artist in Huysmans is as active as ever; the aesthetic chord in his nature vibrates again, this time under the touch of religion. Following here in the tradition of Chateaubriand, Huysmans explores, with artistic penetration and a learning beyond the scope of Chateaubriand, the immense contribution of Catholicism to the arts, notably architecture, using and strengthening their impact by the Christian symbolism it has imparted to them.[158] Thus, like A Rebours, the trilogy has a significance that extends beyond the destiny of its hero; its message has permanent human validity.

Nor, in conclusion, must we forget that taken as a whole Huysman's work reflects more fully than that of any other contemporary writer the different intellectual and spiritual movements of the day. Naturalism, 'decadence', of which A Rebours is the breviary[159] and Schopenhauer the intellectual light. Satanism and divers forms of occultism which were the reaction of a generation in flight from the materialism and determinism that had held the previous generation in its iron grip, finally the Catholic revival of the last decade of the nineteenth century, another sign of a generation sick of Positivism and all its works. As a literary force this latter was important; not so in politics, where the tragedy of the Dreyfus affair was directly responsible for the victory of the militant radical-socialists (1902) and their aggressive anti-clericalism – L'Oblat is full of echoes of the struggle and when at last the blow falls, the religious orders, unwilling or unable to get the necessary authorization to remain in France,[160] took the road into exile, the Benedictines from Solesmes to the Isle of Wight,[161] those from Ligugé to Belgium.

Huysmans did not follow them there; impenitent Parisian, he preferred after his provincial exile to return to the capital,

---

[156] Huysmans was at Ligugé for nearly two years – 1899–1901.
[157] L'Oblat, VI.   [158] Especially La Cathédrale.
[159] See R. Baldick, Life of J. K. Huysmans (Oxford, 1955).
[160] Under 'loi sur les Associations', 1902.   [161] Quarr Abbey.

profoundly marked, however, by his experience of Trappists and Benedictines alike; their lives were a permanent offering to God, in service, in penitence, if need be in suffering for the sins of others; Huysmans too was to take the opportunity dying gave him of stoically accepting to suffer as his vicarious offering for the salvation of souls.[162]

VI. MINOR NATURALISTS
VALLÈS, VILLIERS DE L'ISLE-ADAM

The prestige of Zola, the success of the Rougon-Macquart novels, attracted a number of writers under the banner of Naturalism.

Camille Lemonnier (1845–1913), Belgian by birth, was already an established writer (e.g. *Nos Flamands*, 1869) before Naturalism claimed him, notably with *Les Charniers* (1881) about the defeat of Sedan, and *Happe-Chair* (1886), reminiscent of the author of *Germinal* but with factory as its scene instead of coalmines.

The brothers Joseph-Henri (1856–1940) and Justin (1859–1948) Boex, also Belgian by birth, sank their identities in the fecund literary personality known as J. H. Rosny, whose literary début was the Naturalist novel *Nell Horn* (1886). A year later, under their pseudonym, they were amongst the signatories of the *Manifeste des Cinq*[163] attacking Zola. This gesture of independence did not sever them from Naturalist ideas – the pessimism, the baseness and cruelty of human instincts – but they did not restrict their choice of subject to aspects of contemporaneous society, e.g. *Vamireh* (1894), an evocation of the human struggle in prehistoric times. The collaboration between the brothers ceased in 1907. Thereafter J. H. Rosny the elder's evolution is not dissimilar from Zola's own, imagination and even social idealism progressively dominating observation. The preoccupation with society as an organic whole, whilst it is not unconnected with Naturalist formulae, makes J. H. Rosny a forerunner of 'Unanimism'.[164]

Octave Mirbeau (1848–1917), bureaucrat turned journalist and writer, originally a conservative and supporter of 'Le 16 mai', moved towards extreme republicanism and in step with his political views became a Naturalist writer both as a novelist, e.g. *Le Calvaire* (1886), *L'Abbé Jules* (1888), *Sebastien Roch* (1890), and as a playwright.[165]

The Swiss writer Edouard Rod (1857–1910) began as an enthusiastic supporter of Zola (*A propos de l'Assommoir*, 1879), and a conscientious Naturalist novelist (*Palmyre Veulard*, 1881; *La Femme*

---

[162] When dying of cancer of the mouth, he refused all pain-killing drugs.
[163] The other signatories were P. Margueritte, P. Bonnetain, L. Descaves. The occasion was Zola's *La Terre*. [164] See below, pp. 106–7.
[165] See below, p. 143.

de Henri Vanneau, 1884), but thereafter he broke away from the school and became a moralist and student of human passions in an older tradition (e.g. *Le Sacrifice,* 1892; *Les Roches Blanches,* 1895). Lucien Descaves (1861–1949), another signatory of the *Manifeste des Cinq,* is remembered for his early anti-militarism which earned him the publicity of a prosecution and acquittal for insults to the army (1890). *La Caserne, Misères du Sabre* (1887), *Sous-offs.* (1889), with all the bitter satire and none of the comedy of Courteline's scenes of army life,[166] are derived from his own experience as a conscript.

Abel Hermant (1862–1950), in his Naturalist period, shares Descaves' satirical vein (e.g. *Le Cavalier Miserey,* 1887).

Jules Renard (1864–1910) is perhaps better remembered than any of the foregoing. One of the co-founders of the *Mercure de France* (1890), he has also to his credit one literary character, the hero of *Poil de Carotte* (1894), who, as the type of the deprived and ill-treated child, commonly but wrongly[167] supposed to be drawn from the author's own experience, may outlive his creator. Of his numerous playlets which bear the stamp of the Naturalist 'slice of life' formula, at least one, *Le Plaisir de rompre* (1897), has had a revival.

More prominent than any of the foregoing are two writers who in truth belong to an earlier generation but who, different though they are from each other, have some contacts with Naturalism: Jules Vallès (1832–85) and Auguste Villiers de l'Isle-Adam (1840–89).

Revolt is the keynote of Jules Vallès. After the fall of the Second Empire, he joined the Socialist International, founded a newspaper, *Le Peuple,* became a member of the Commune (1871) and fled to London after its fall. The same attitude of revolt and protest is manifest in his literary work; in so far as Naturalism itself has an element of social protest which becomes more insistent as the movement develops from observation of the submerged social classes to its humanitarian implications, there is a link with Vallès's earlier works: *Les Réfractaires* (1866) and *La Rue* (1866), which are collected newspaper studies, acutely observed, on social conditions of low Parisian 'milieux'. The link is maintained when, during his political exile, the bitterness that was in Vallès, inflamed by his personal suffering, flared up vigorously in his high-tension autobiographical trilogy, *Jacques Vingtras* (*L'Enfant,* 1879, *Le Bachelier,* 1881, *L'Insurgé,* 1886).

---

[166] See below, pp. 56–7.
[167] cf. the testimony of Jules Renard's niece Mme Lappoui (*Le Monde,* 13–14 June 1954) and a letter dated 2 November 1890 from Renard to her parents: 'Mettez-vous bien, dans vos chères boules, une fois pour toutes, que je ne fais jamais de personnalités dans ce que je pense écrire…'

Villiers de l'Isle-Adam (1840–89), last scion of an ancient Breton noble house, also has a note of protest in some of his work but of a very different kind. For ever faithful, despite the ill-fortune, financial and literary, that dogged him throughout his life, to his high Catholic and traditionalist background, his protest, just as that of Chateaubriand, his compatriot and spiritual ancestor, would have been had he lived in a Positivist age, is against the scientific materialism of his generation. In this he recalls also the attitude of Barbey d'Aurevilly, although Villiers's position is more complex.

A volume of poems, *Premières Poésies*, which owe something to the author of 'Rolla' and 'Namouna', had been his début; thereafter his chosen forms of expression were the drama (*Elën*, 1865; *Morgane*, 1866; *La Révolte*, 1870; *Le Nouveau Monde*, 1883; *L'Evasion*, 1887; *Axël*, first version 1872, posth. 1890) and short stories, the best known collections of which are *Contes Cruels* (1883) and *Nouveaux Contes Cruels* (1889). Important too for the insight they give into Villiers's complex personality are the longer story *L'Eve future* (1886) and the collection of stories built round the character of Tribulat Bonhomet (1887).

Villiers's friendship with Baudelaire, the admiration for Poe, whom Baudelaire revealed to him, and for Wagner, to whom Baudelaire introduced him, is an important pointer to one, perhaps the fundamental element of his art – its Romanticism. *Elën* and *Morgane* have all the air of Romantic plays; the cruelty and macabre horror of many of his short stories (e.g. 'Isis', 'Claire Lenoir', 'La Torture par l'espérance') belong to the same climate which, in others, takes the form of irony at the expense of different aspects of the society around him: the power of money ('A s'y méprendre'), self-satisfied mediocrity ('Deux Augures'), the stupidity of the crowd ('Vox populi'), the inept scientific enthusiasms of the age, symbolized by that worthy successor of Flaubert's Homais, Tribulat Bonhomet (1887), whose mind, obscured by the mists of commonsense so-called, is impervious to 'la lumière du Rêve', or the materialist paradise that scientific progress holds out to the vulgarian, thanks to the creative skills of inventors such as Edison. In *L'Eve future* Villiers displays an almost Wellsian skill in exploiting scientific data with prophetic fantasy.

Villiers's dislike of the vulgarian joys of the age did not mean his turning away from it. His art, notably the short stories, is often firmly implanted in reality; two of his plays, indeed – *La Révolte* and *L'Evasion* – are in the Naturalist idiom and were performed at the 'Théâtre Libre', a sure sign of their Naturalist orthodoxy.

Romanticist, ironist, realist, Villiers was all of these but the conflict was resolved by his idealism; it shows itself as early as *Morgane*, where, within the framework of a romantic historical action set in the Kingdom of Naples, the heroine and her lover Sergius, in their conspiratorial activities, which are real enough, are symbols of human strivings after ideals unattainable in this world; thus the failure of their conspiracy itself becomes symbolical.

Still concealed in *Morgane*, the idealism is much more evident in *Axël*, Villiers's real spiritual testament, where the hero finally rejects the temptations offered by the powers of the world – wealth, love – and in a Wagnerian apotheosis finds ecstatic spiritual fulfilment in death.

Published posthumously, *Axël* was first performed in 1894. Symbolism was then in the ascendant; minds had become attuned to Villiers's art which was seen to be akin with ideas then current. When Sergius exclaims,[168] 'Apprends, Sorcière,... que, fort du sentiment de mon éternité, je ne permets pas à ce que tu es convenue d'appeler le Réel d'être jamais autre chose pour moi que ce qui se passe sous mon front!', he was saying something which Symbolists, under the influence of Schopenhauer, were to adopt as an article of faith – true reality lies beyond appearances; the dreamer alone may apprehend it.

The idealism of Villiers de l'Isle-Adam, foreshadowing that of the Symbolists, is of a very different order from that of Georges Ohnet (1848–1918), who deserves mention here merely as the purveyor of idealism fed on unimpeachable moral sentiments and woven into well-constructed tales, as commonplace in substance as in form, which appeal to the romantic reader of every generation. With novels such as *Serge Panine* (1881), *Le Maître de Forges* (1882), *La Grande Marinière* (1885), Ohnet is the successor in the Naturalist period of Octave Feuillet and his 'Juleps'.

VII. BECQUE

The Romantics had had to contend with opponents in entrenched positions in the theatre and schooled by a rigid tradition, which had also formed public taste. To overcome these forces, to crystallize a diffused dissatisfaction, to propose new dramatic ideals and to achieve these, took several years.

The Naturalists had had difficulty enough to establish their ideas in the novel; the Goncourt Brothers, as the forerunners, had never enjoyed much favour; not until the success of *L'Assommoir* (1877) did Zola force public attention; even then the critics were by no means disarmed.

When the Naturalists turned their eyes towards the stage they, like the Romantics, had great odds to contend with: men of great talent and established reputation, critics like Sarcey whose press

[168] *Morgane*, III, 8.

articles were oracular pronouncements making or marring the fortunes of new men, theatre-managers, attentive to the critics and
obedient to a conservative opinion disliking, as always, to be dis-
turbed in its habits, and unable or unwilling to see what is obvious
now, that the Naturalists, like the Romantics before them, had an
excellent case.

For all their claims to realism – contemporary society and its
manners mirrored on the stage, its problems set forth, its vices
attacked – the dramatic conceptions of Dumas and Augier had
hardened into a rigid formula: characters invariably drawn from
high society; a plot designed to focus attention on a given problem;
a situation depending on previous events so that much explanation
between characters for the benefit of the audience has to be got
through before the plot can move; plays moving along well-oiled
and established grooves; dramatic tension, using the rigid social
conventions of the day and artificial aids (letters and the like),
building up to the inevitable climax of the duel, fought out of ear-
shot between the fourth and fifth acts, and leading, after the right
man has been put out of action, to a dénouement that answers the
problem or smoothes out the difficulty or in some way is a solution
to the initial data of the play. Thus, like the Romantic theatre in
its day, the social theatre had become artificial; artificial in plot,
artificial more fundamentally in that the plays were arbitrary
constructions to illustrate or prove some point.

The Naturalists had good grounds for dissatisfaction; their
spokesman, Zola, voices it in the articles he wrote as dramatic
critic,[169] subsequently collected (1881) in *Le Naturalisme au
Théâtre* and *Nos Auteurs dramatiques*: 'Notre Théâtre aurait tant
besoin d'un homme nouveau ... un tempérament (the word is
characteristic) puissant dont le cerveau novateur vînt révolutionner
les conventions admises et planter enfin le véritable drame humain
à la place des mensonges ridicules qui s'étalent aujourd'hui ...'[170]
The problem, as Zola sees it, is how to get rid of the artificiality of
the drama of the day; how to give life to these puppet men and
women who in the end are all so similar, who walk in and out of
drawing rooms as though pulled by invisible wires and whose words
and actions seem so unrelated to their everyday lives. The so-called
realism of the social theatre had not amounted to more than giving
labels to characters – banker, financier, author, doctor, etc.; in the
plays they were never engaged in their professional activities but
always in some problem of the author's choosing.

The question invites attack on the plot as the core of the artificial

[169] For four years from 1876 first with *Le Bien Public* then with the
Voltaire, see: *Naturalisme au Théâtre*, preface.
[170] Op. cit., I: 'Le Naturalisme'.

structure. Without it a play falls apart into a series of 'tableaux' loosely knit together. With this idea in mind the dramist may hope to achieve his aim of throwing 'a slice of life' on the stage; characters will not be involved in some well-riveted chain of cause and effect contrived by the dramatist; they will be 'discovered' by the rise of the curtain, going about their daily lives, a fact that gives more importance to the realism of décor; at the end, as the curtain falls, they will not have achieved a solution to some problem; they will shuffle on with their 'unsolved' lives, impelled as always by their own natures, their glandular secretions.

It may be added that, in line with the spirit of Naturalism, the characters and the scenes are more likely to be drawn from the lower than the upper strata of society.

To proclaim a doctrine is one thing; to put it into practice is another. The Goncourt Brothers had given an early model of the new ideas in *Henriette Maréchal* (1865); mother and daughter love the same man; outraged father shoots at retreating figure in the house; daughter throws herself in the way and is killed. The three acts loosely tied by a plot reduced to its simplest form; the first act in particular is a pointer to the Naturalist ideas of tableaux destined to convey impressions of the characters' lives rather than subordinated to a plot; admittedly Madame Maréchal and Paul de Bréville meet at the opera ball, but, if the plot itself had been more complex and therefore demanded economy of time, that meeting would probably have been treated as the starting point of the plot before the action of the play began.

The play in retrospect can be seen as an interesting experiment some fifteen years ahead of public taste which at the first performance took immediate exception to the crudities expressed by the masked revellers.

Not till after the impact of *L'Assommoir* had launched Naturalism on its successful way in the novel, could such plays hope for a hearing. Thereafter, and strengthened by Zola's campaign as dramatic critic, Naturalism achieved a foothold on the stage. It became the fashion to draw plays from Naturalist novels; *L'Assommoir*, dramatized in 1879, was the first of a series over the next ten years drawn from the novels of Zola, the Goncourt Brothers, Maupassant and Daudet. The fashion is in line with Naturalist ideas: Naturalism claims to get away from romantic fiction, which focusses interest on the individual; it endeavours in the novel to bring a given social group within its scope; some individuals may be in the foreground, others in the distance, but all are part of one social organism, all are subject to the same social pressures and physiological urges; their actions are determined; the novelists' task is to paint the individual as part of the group; thus, only thus, can the novelist dedicated to scientific truth as he, as all, must be, hope to give a true picture of life.

The dramatist will be equally dedicated to a true representation of life and what easier way to achieve that, to get away from the artificiality of Dumas and Co., than to plunder the rich store of Naturalist novels? Thus would they realize their ideal of 'a slice of life' on the stage. They tended to overlook the fact that whereas the novelist can nourish the reader's interest by description and analysis as well as action, the dramatist has only the latter – conflict of some kind, either in a chain of well-connected events, plot, in a word, or psychological, and reflected in the dialogue.

To the Naturalist, plot-interest spelt artificiality, whilst psychological interest was equally denied them since it was absent from novels, portraying men as bundles of physiological urges.

The only successful dramatist in the chronicles of Naturalism is Henri Becque (1837–1899). His play *Les Corbeaux* (performed 1882) is a milestone in the story of Naturalism's conquest of the stage. When Becque became (1876) dramatic critic of *Le Peuple*, he had little to his credit as a dramatist: the libretto of an opera by Joncières; *Sardanapale* (1867), a farce; *L'Enfant Prodigue* (1869), a drama; *Michel Pauper* (1870), a thesis play in favour of divorce; *L'Enterrement* (1871), which might have come from the pen of Dumas. Of these, only *Michel Pauper*, the story of a workman-inventor who marries above him, takes to drink and dies in a fit of *delirium tremens* when on the verge of a discovery worth a fortune, gives promise of what *Les Corbeaux* was to achieve. Pauper vaguely foreshadows Coupeau in *L'Assommoir*; a workman as hero was something new on the stage, so new in fact that the critics,[171] enslaved to the Dumas-Augier dramatic formula with its ingenious variants on love and adultery in high life, ironically referred to Becque as a member of 'L'Ecole brutale'.

Zola, as we have seen, began his campaign for a dramatic revolution in the year that saw Becque's appointment to *Le Peuple*, and, though he could not claim Becque as a disciple, his influence is evident in *Les Corbeaux*. The five years between the writing and performing of *Les Corbeaux* are a measure of the 'sales resistance' to the new ideas of public, critics and theatre managers to whose pleas for changes in the play Becque remained deaf. In the interval Becque had written two one-act plays, *La Navette* (1878) and *Les Honnêtes Femmes* (1880). A comedy, *La Parisienne* (1885), a few minor playlets (e.g. *Le Départ*, 1897; *Une Exécution*, 1897), an unfinished play, *Les Polichinelles*,[172] complete Becque's not very abundant production.

Les Corbeaux ensures Becque's place in the history of the

---

[171] e.g. Sarcey and Barbey d'Aurevilly.   [172] About financiers.

drama; *La Parisienne*, his masterpiece, survives in its own right. *Les Corbeaux* portrays the Vigneron family – widow and three daughters – vainly trying in their ignorance of the law to defend their inheritance, after the sudden death of M. Vigneron (end Act I), against Vigneron's business associate, Teissier, Bourdon the lawyer and others; a cruel drama where simplicity of structure and faithful observation of reality are the keynotes. No bravura passages or tirades for effect, no 'raisonneur' to uphold honest morality with a wit so obviously the author's; a dialogue style attuned to the characters, a plot that does not seek to prove anything but portrays three different stages in the decline and fall of a defenceless family, in short a brilliant application of the Naturalist formula, and yet, if anything, less brilliant than *La Parisienne*. If the plot of *Les Corbeaux* is reduced to its simplest form, in *La Parisienne* it can scarcely be said to exist at all. Becque gives here the finished picture he had sketched in *La Navette*: husband, wife, lover; the lover's (not the husband's) jealousy of a rival disturbs the three-cornered *ménage*; when the rival cools, the situation reverts to 'normal'. Nothing could be more banal. The interest resides exclusively in the characters and the relations between them: the husband, vulgar materialist concerned with his own career and obtusely trusting; the jealous lover; between them the attractive scheming Clotilde. The dialogue does not strain after effect, it relies on its naturalness. The illusion of a moment in the lives of real people being lived, a moment of human experience that neither begins nor ends at any significant point, that proves nothing, that simply is, that illusion is brilliantly achieved.

But the play does more than reflect the Naturalist dramaturgy and its 'slices of life' ideal; it has classic simplicity – 'toute l'invention consiste à faire quelque chose de rien . . .'; stripped of the elegance, pathos and social significance of Molière, Clotilde's salon is a pale reflection of Célimène's with two very bourgeois types, the cynical Dumesnil and the jealous Lafont, in place of Philinte and Alceste. *La Parisienne* has not dated, because in its simplicity there is nothing to become the prey of time except perhaps its brittle cynicism which reflects Naturalist attitudes and the harsh experience of life that was Becque's lot, and which the success of *La Parisienne* after the struggle for recognition of his earlier years may have done something to soften.

That success he owed in part to André Antoine (1858–1943), founder and director of the 'Théâtre Libre' (1887–96). The story of this minor employee of the Paris Gas Co., who had a passion for the theatre and who, with neither backers nor money, created a small troupe of amateur zealots and a 'pocket' theatre, shows what faith can do. Debts forced Antoine out of business (1894),

but during his management the 'Théâtre Libre' had become a
forcing house for new dramatic ideas, had given Naturalist plays
the chance of a sympathetic hearing, had welcomed the work of
foreign dramatists and had created a new style of acting in keeping with the illusion of reality that the new drama was aiming to
create.[173] Antoine also inspired a number of younger actor-
managers,[174] who ensured permanency to the acting traditions of
the 'Théâtre Libre'.

Outstanding amongst the comic writers of the period is Georges
Courteline (1861–1929),[175] outstanding because he rises beyond
the comedy of plot or situation to genuine observation of manners
and character. With the exception of Jarry,[176] he is the only writer
of comedies in this period to have created comic characters with
a life of their own. They may not compare in stature with those of
Molière because they are not full-length studies – Courteline's
plays, though mostly dating from after the Naturalist period, are
usually short 'slices of life' in the Naturalist mode – but they make
a little gallery: e.g. Boubouroche, the good-natured petit-bourgeois,
who gives his name to the play (1893), forever deceived by friends
and mistress, and whose ire, quickly aroused and quickly allayed,
falls on the wrong victim, Me. Barbemolle,[177] the eloquent advo-
cate ready to switch from defence to prosecution in the same case,
Capitaine Hurluret, the gruff but good-hearted officer, and Flick,
the N.C.O.[178] in excelsis, the police commissioner,[179] the police
constable.[180] Often there is an element of caricature; most are
seen against the background of the life that has fashioned them:
the law courts, the barrack-room, the police, bureaucracy.[181]
In all these institutions Courteline has seen above all a source of
laughter. One comic effect in Courteline is worth recalling because we believe him to have been the first to exploit it: a scene
of excitement or indignation (e.g. Un Client sérieux) where several
characters talk at once. The audience may lose the effect of what
is being said, but the loss is more than compensated for by the
comedy of the situation, which derives from genuine observation
of life: a scene between angry people, so long as it remains on the
level of words and gestures, is funny to the detached onlooker;
the participants, intent upon expressing their own feelings and

[173] No more declamation and rhetoric; the stage is a room with one wall
removed; actors must turn their back on the audience if naturalness demands it, etc. . . .
[174] e.g. Copeau, Lugné-Poë.
[175] Georges Moinaux.
[176] See below, pp. 145–6.
[177] Un Client sérieux (1897).
[178] Les Gaietés de l'Escadron (1886).
[179] Le Commissaire est bon enfant (1899).
[180] Le Gendarme est sans pitié (1909).
[181] Messieurs les Ronds-de-Cuir (1893).

opinions, taking no notice of what the other parties to the dispute have to say, have lost something of their humanity and taken on the absurdity of gesticulating puppets.

Another comic effect exploited skilfully by Courteline (e.g. in *Les Gaietés de l'Escadron*) is that of pursuit – one character looking for another and never meeting him. Effective though this is, it is evidently more artificial than the other; both effects are farcical but are none the worse for that. In Courteline, what heightens their value is that they are mingled with comedy derived from character and often informed with savage irony at the harsh injustices of life.

Betrayed by his friend, Philinte, Courteline's Alceste[182] speaks for his creator:

> Las de l'humain commerce et de sa turpitude
> Il m'est permis d'aller...
> Traîner au fond d'un bois la tristesse de vivre,
> En tâchant de savoir, dans leur rivalité
> Qui, de l'homme ou du loup, l'emporte en cruauté.

[182] *La Conversion d'Alceste* (1905).

Part I

§ II   SYMBOLISM (1880–1900)

Chapter 3

POLITICAL OPTIMISM
AND PHILOSOPHICAL PESSIMISM

CONTRARY to all expectations and despite the efforts[1] of its enemies, the Republic survived. By 1880 the political climate had changed, the republican idea had taken root in public opinion. When Marshal MacMahon resigned (1879), the first generation of true republican politicians – the 'Opportunists' – came into power; the new men – Grévy, Ferry, Gambetta, Freycinet – were determined to build a republic in spirit as well as in name. The attack on the positions of the Church began and, at the same time, the reorganization of State primary education on the triple basis of 'gratuité, obligation, laïcité'; with moments of quiescence this double *Kulturkampf* was not to end until the expulsion of the religious orders (1903) and the separation of Church and State (1905).

The success of the Republic's taking root is shown by its ability to weather the storms that were to beat on it.[2] The new men, Ferry in particular, were even prepared to look overseas and build a new colonial empire for France. Clearly the political pessimism of the early 'seventies had disappeared for a time.

By 1880 the success of Naturalism was at its height, and yet, in contrast to the growing political confidence, the rationalist fervour and scientific optimism that had marked the years of struggle began then to dry up under a chill wind of philosophical pessimism blowing from beyond the Rhine.

Schopenhauer's ideas as expressed in *Die Welt als Wille und Vorstellung* (1818) had attracted Leconte de Lisle in the 'fifties, owing to their similarity to Buddhism; after 1870 their influence gathered momentum, particularly in the 'eighties when Schopenhauer's works were being translated (1886–90). Schopenhauer's teaching rests on the idea that the world, as man apprehends it on the phenomenal level, is no more than a representation in the human

---

[1] The defeat of Thiers (1873), the election of MacMahon to the presidency (1873), the attempted Restoration (1873–5), the Constitution (1875), the '16 mai' (1877).

[2] Boulangisme (1886–9), Panama Scandal (1892), Dreyfus Affair (1898).

61

mind. On the noumenal level, underlying all the representations we have of reality, is the will, in effect the force of Nature, the life force. Active in all phenomena, it is yet blind, unconscious of itself in the mineral world, in plant and animal life; only men, slaves though they are of the instinct to resist the forces of destruction, to survive in a word, are conscious of their enslavement; but, thanks to that very consciousness, which intelligence confirms, men may come to see how the will to exist exploits its victims, and find the way to liberation from evil and suffering, inseparable from life, by, as it were, contracting out of it; the practice of chastity will eliminate the species, that of asceticism the passions; thus and thus will the ruthless will to exist be cheated of its inheritance.

Beside this path of escape that the 'saints' – in Schopenhauer parlance – alone will tread, he indicates another, which was much more eagerly followed, that of the escape to art. Art is composed of the images man gives of his 'representations' of reality, the images of images in fact, but whereas the latter images die with the minds they exist in, the former, being projections of the latter on to the physical plane, exist independently and are not subject to man's transience. Thus by art man may transcend his suffering and defy the will.

Schopenhauer put music above all other arts; organized sound penetrates to the core of our being, induces that reverie, that *Innerlichkeit* which is the highest form of prescience. Reverie or *Innerlichkeit* enables us to break through the representational world that envelops us, and that the other arts are confined in, stimulating in us by the power of musical suggestion, Symbolism in a word, our immediate apprehension of the truth the composer desires to convey.

These ideas, naturally enough, confirmed Wagner in his own ambition of creating, around the old Teutonic myths and their ultimate destruction by the power of Christian love,[3] a dramatic poem, an artistic synthesis in which his music, weaving its themes about the whole structure, with the intricacy of an abundant virginia creeper, would suggest, by the power of its symbolism, the inner realities of Teutonism. Wagner is a Symbolist in music, a painter in music, the arch-priest of *Gesammtkunst*. Without discovering Schopenhauer, Baudelaire's philosophy (using the term in the broadest sense) had moved in the same direction; his satanic pleasure in flaying sin, which he both enjoys and recoils from, seems akin to Schopenhauer's satisfaction in denouncing the evil of the will; the affinities he felt in Wagner's music with his own belief in the poetic potential of symbols aroused his enthusiasm.[4] Baude-

---

[3] *The Ring.*
[4] cf. his essay on 'Richard Wagner et Tannhäuser à Paris'.

laire – Wagner – Schopenhauer preside like the three members of an artistic Trinity over the triumph of Symbolism. Baudelaire by his intuitive understanding that the springs of true poetry did not lie in Parnassian territory, Wagner with his conception of music as an inspiration for the poets, and behind or above them, Schopenhauer, who provided the devotees of the temple with precisely the philosophy they needed: metaphysical anguish for the decadents (Laforgue and Company), a gospel of beauty for the aesthetes (Huysmans, Montesquiou and others), a poetic doctrine for the Symbolists, and for all and sundry a sense, a disturbing, sometimes even an exciting sense, of the all-pervading mystery. 'Une vérité nouvelle ... est entrée ... dans la littérature et dans l'art ... vérité toute métaphysique ... Cette vérité ... libératrice et rénovatrice, c'est le principe de l'idéalité du monde. Par rapport à l'homme, sujet pensant, le monde, tout ce qui est extérieur au moi, n'existe que selon l'idée qu'il s'en fait. Nous ne connaissons que des phénomènes, nous ne raisonnons que sur des apparences; toute vérité en soi nous échappe; l'essence est inattaquable. C'est ce que Schopenhauer a vulgarisé sous cette formule simple et claire: le monde est une représentation. Je ne vois pas ce qui est; ce qui est, c'est ce que je vois.'[5] This esotericism became fashionable and took different forms;[6] theosophy,[7] occultism, mysticism, exercised a powerful attraction on writers and artists; religious conversions amongst them were not infrequent,[8] whilst to those who could not willingly abandon rationalist attitudes, freemasonry appeared to offer a refuge where rationalist idealism merged conveniently with mysticism; hence, no doubt, its popularity and expansion at the time.[9]

No better example of the prevailing climate can be found than Joséphin Péladan (1858–1918), fecund if now forgotten author of novels, plays and essays,[10] founder of a *Rosicrucian* salon (1892–8) and self-proclaimed 'Sâr'.[11]

---

[5] See R. de Gourmont, *Premier Livre des Masques*, preface.

[6] C. Chassé, *Les Clés de Mallarmé*, chap. 2, and R. Griffiths, op. cit., Part II.

[7] Madame Blavatsky (1831–91) had founded the Theosophic Society in 1875 and was by now enjoying great success.

[8] e.g. Huysmans, Bloy, Claudel, Maritain, Péguy.

[9] Politicians of the moderate Left, later radical-socialists, were supposedly very prone to it.

[10] e.g. *Comment on devient mage* (1892); *Comment on devient fée* (1893); *La science, la religion et la conscience* (1895).

[11] 'Sâr, ce monosyllabe, intrigua d'abord les bons reporters ... C'était le synonyme de roi chez les vieux Mésopotamiens; c'est des Sârs et non des Césars, que viendraient les Tsars russes.' (H. Mazel, *Aux Beaux Temps du Symbolisme, 1890–5*, 1943, p. 190.)

Chapter 4

PRE-SYMBOLISTS

I. MALLARMÉ

L A vie de professeur dans un lycée est simple, modeste, calme. Nous y serons tranquilles. J'y vise', wrote Stéphane Mallarmé (1842–98) to his friend Henri Cazalis (June 1863). He achieved this simple, modest ambition but experience scarcely confirmed his belief in its peacefulness. From occasional discreet references in his letters we may judge Mallarmé, the teacher of English he became in 1863, to have been neither successful nor happy: 'je suis peu respecté, et même, parfois, accablé de papier mâché et de huées...' (to H. Cazalis, July 1865). Yet the profession to which he gave thirty years (1863–93), at Tournon, Besançon, Avignon, and finally, from 1871, Paris, goal of his ambitions, enabled him to divide his life into two separate compartments: the exterior social one, where he spent the minimum time, and the inner sanctuary where, with the shutters closed on the outside world, he escaped to the dream-world – 'rêver', 'le rêve', are favourite words with him – of poetry. Mallarmé's production is light: a thin volume of poetry – *Poésies* (first published 1887, first complete edition 1913) containing sixty-four poems in all, including the two longest poems, 'Hérodiade' and 'L'Après-Midi d'un Faune' (1876),[1] an unfinished prose piece 'Igitur' (1869), 'Un coup de dés jamais n'abolira le hasard' (1897), a translation of Poe's poems (1888), a number of essays and other fugitive pieces.

Broadly speaking the poems fall into two groups: the early poems leading up to 'L'Après-Midi d'un Faune' and the remainder. No rigorous cleavage divides the two, but the differences between them make it possible to speak of Mallarmé's first and second manner.

The poems in the first group do not for the most part raise any problems of interpretation; some convey personal emotion ('Apparition', 'Renouveau', 'Brise Marine'); a distinctly Baudelairian note is occasionally sounded, Baudelaire in his Romantic attitudes:

[1] An earlier version (1865) was entitled 'Improvisation d'un Faune', and then 'Monologue d'un Faune'. In its final form, the poem may have been completed as early as 1866.

the poet's suffering and isolation ('Le Guignon'), his disgust with the crude realities of this world and the follies of men ('Les Fenêtres': 'Mais, hélas! ici-bas est maître', etc.), prostitutes as creatures of sorrow rather than joy, vice, remorse ('Angoisse'). Beside the poems that are the direct communication of personal mood ('Apparition', 'Soupir', 'Les Fenêtres', 'Renouveau', 'Angoisse', 'Brise Marine'), some, by their greater complexity of syntax, and indirect communication by means of symbols, already point to a different conception of poetry in mode or function or both ('Las de l'amer repos où ma paresse offense', 'Azur', 'Aumône', 'Don du Poème', 'Hérodiade'). Then, after what may well be regarded as Mallarmé's supreme achievement – the final version of 'L'Après-Midi d'un Faune' – come the short poems, mostly sonnets, of the second group, where the reader needs a key to open the mysterious treasure-house.

Clearly Mallarmé's ideas had undergone some transformation. During his formative years, Parnassian poetry was in the ascendant. He had many contacts with the group; his closest friend Henri Cazalis (1840–1909; in poetry, Jean Lahor) was one of them; he professed admiration, one wonders with how much sincerity, for the work of François Coppée,[2] later, and with greater sincerity no doubt, for Heredia's Les Trophées;[3] he contributed to the Parnasse Contemporain (1866) and to the second number (1871), which is proof enough that the hallmark of Parnassianism was on his work.

On the other hand many of Mallarmé's ideas on the nature of poetry carry him well away from those of the Parnassian era. The intellectual climate[4] of the 'Parnasse' was Positivism and the faith in science to achieve objective truth, with, as a corollary, rejection of religious faith. Only on this latter point is Mallarmé in accord; to Cazalis he writes of his religious struggle and rejection of 'ce vieux et méchant plumage, terrassé, heureusement, Dieu'.[5] But though he rejects God, poetry provides him with a spiritual experience that Positivism cannot admit; in an earlier letter to Cazalis he writes: 'Malheureusement, en creusant le vers à ce point, j'ai rencontré deux abîmes, qui me désespèrent. L'un est le Néant, auquel je suis arrivé sans connaître le Bouddhisme...'[6]

---

[2] Propos sur la Poésie, edited by H. Mondor, p. 97; letter, April 1868: 'votre volume m'a été droit au coeur'.

[3] Op. cit., p. 196; letter, October 1895: 'un petit bouquin éternel'.

[4] Mallarmé, incidentally, uses the word in this sense; cf. op. cit., p. 104; letter to Cazalis, April 1870: 'mes climats intérieurs'. Could he have been the first to do so? It suggests the change soon to become evident from the clear rationalist outlines of Positivism to the blurred 'atmosphere' of Symbolism.

[5] Op. cit., p. 87, May 1867.

[6] The other abyss is his bad physical health.

How different this is from the attitude of Parnassian poets; at the highest intellectual level (e.g. in Leconte de Lisle and Heredia) poetry will be scholarly and antiquarian, at other levels it will content itself with evoking the external forms of things. Moreover, Leconte de Lisle saw the poet's role as that of teacher, above the crowd, yes, aloof perhaps, but, as teacher, necessarily in contact with it. Mallarmé's idea of poetry is more aristocratic. Evidently his meditations on poetry, his efforts to extract from the dross of life the pure essence of things, like a milligram of radium from a ton of pitch-blende, were so intense that they amounted to a kind of poetic mysticism, as esoteric as any other mystical experience, which the coherent language of prose cannot adequately describe. In the letter of May 1867 to Cazalis, Mallarmé speaks of it thus: 'ma Pensée s'est pensée et est arrivée à une conception pure. Tout ce que... mon être a souffert, pendant cette longue agonie, est inénarrable, mais heureusement, je suis parfaitement mort, et la région la plus impure où mon Esprit puisse s'aventurer est l'Eternité... j'avoue du reste... que j'ai encore besoin, tant ont été grandes les avanies de mon triomphe, de me regarder dans cette glace pour penser, et que si elle n'était pas devant la table où je t'écris cette lettre, je redeviendrais le Néant. C'est t'apprendre que je suis maintenant impersonnel, et non plus Stéphane que tu as connu – mais une aptitude qu'a l'Univers Spirituel à se voir et à se développer, à travers ce qui fut moi.' Physical exhaustion, an intense refinement of thought, a fading of the individual personality into the universal spirit or nothingness; echoes of Leconte de Lisle's philosophy on the latter point? Perhaps, but with all the difference between an inert intellectual concept and intense spiritual experience.

In another letter[7] Mallarmé returns to the loss of awareness of his body that accompanies this spiritual experience: 'je sens mon coeur... et le reste de mon corps oublié, sauf la main qui écrit et ce coeur qui vit... Je suis véritablement décomposé...' But the price must be paid to achieve the sense of oneness with the Universe: 'et dire qu'il faut cela pour avoir une vue très une de l'Univers.'

That a spiritual experience such as this should inform the whole of a poet's attitude towards his art is understandable; he believes he has had a vision of the mystery of the Universe; his duty as a poet is to proclaim its ineffable beauty; to Cazalis he writes:[8] 'je te dirai que je suis depuis un mois dans les plus purs glaciers de l'Esthétique – qu'après avoir trouvé le Néant, j'ai trouvé le Beau – et que tu ne peux t'imaginer dans quelles altitudes lucides je

---

[7] See op. cit., p. 93, May 1867, to E. Lefébure.
[8] Op. cit., p. 77, July 1866.

m'aventure...'. What vehicle is worthy and capable of such a trust but poetry? Again to Cazalis:[9] 'j'ai fait une assez longue descente au Néant pour pouvoir parler avec certitude. Il n'y a que la Beauté – et elle n'a qu'une expression parfaite – la Poésie.'

The magnitude of the task gives an edge to his enthusiasm: 'J'ai voulu te dire simplement', he writes to Aubanel,[10] 'que je venais de jeter le plan de mon Oeuvre entier, après avoir trouvé la clef de moi-même... Que je prévois qu'il me faudra vingt ans pour ces cinq livres dont se composera l'Oeuvre...'

The years 1866 and 1867 were evidently crucial in Mallarmé's life as a poet. They left an indelible mark on him; some twenty years later we find him faithful to his young convictions; in answer to a request from Léo d'Orfer for a definition of poetry he writes: 'La Poésie est l'expression, par le langage humain, ramené à son rhythme essentiel, du sens mystérieux des aspects de l'existence; elle doue ainsi d'authenticité notre séjour et constitue la seule tâche spirituelle';[11] just over a year later he writes to Verlaine: 'à part les morceaux de prose et les vers de ma jeunesse et la suite ... j'ai toujours rêvé et tenté autrechose,... Quoi? C'est difficile à dire: un livre,... en maints tomes, un livre qui soit un livre, architectural et prémédité, et non un recueil des inspirations de hasard fussent-elles merveilleuses... j'irai plus loin, je dirai: le livre, persuadé qu'... il n'y en a qu'un... l'explication orphique de la Terre, qui est le seul devoir du poète et le jeu littéraire par excellence...'[12] Underlying all its manifestations the Universe is one, and poetry is its song; to capture and transcribe it in words is the poet's task; like the alchemist of old, the poet has his 'grand oeuvre' to pursue; its realization gives genuine value to the poet's life ('doue d'authenticité notre séjour').

These idealist views would in themselves have sufficed to change the nature of his poetry – 'Hérodiade' symbolizes the ethereal, almost inaccessible, idealism he flees to from the horror of reality; the poem seems to correspond with the 'purs glaciers de l'Esthétique' and the 'altitudes lucides' of the letter already quoted. After thinking of 'Le Néant' as an abyss, he evidently looks upwards to the ideal heights of beauty he wants to scale. Poems such as 'L'Azur', 'Aumône', 'Don du Poème' and 'Hérodiade' seem to reflect the high endeavour that animated him in the years 1866 and 1867.

But side by side with his idealism another force is at work. His letters, particularly those of the 'sixties, frequently refer to his fear of the drying up of his creative power, of sterility. Is this obscurely

---

[9] Op. cit., pp. 88–9, May 1867. [10] Op. cit., p. 79, July 1866.
[11] Op. cit., p. 134, June 1884.
[12] Op. cit., pp. 142, 143, November 1885.

connected, on a metaphysical level, with his experience of 'Le Néant'? However exalting the spiritual experience, the notion if conceived as an abyss is by definition empty, and if as heights, frigid. Or is it to be related with the physiological ailments to which an occasional reference occurs in the earlier letters? Be that as it may, the fear of sterility, accompanied by bouts of pessimism, alternates with periods of optimism; 'Igitur' was undertaken in an effort to destroy the 'monster', as Mallarmé called it,[13] but remained unfinished and unpublished,[14] a rough sketch, whence thirty years later will be drawn 'Un coup de dés jamais n'abolira le hasard'.

Sterility is, moreover, transformed into an ideal (e.g. 'Hérodiade'), and Mallarmé returns again and again to ideas and images allied to it – purity, chastity, virginity, winter as the sterile season, the whiteness of snow, ice, mirrors, diamonds, gems, flowing hair as the essential attribute of woman's beauty; all these suggest a frigid type of beauty; they are symbols that could derive either from Mallarmé's idealism, or from the fear of his own sterility; the endeavour to scale esoteric peaks and the discouragement born of a conviction that the wells of inspiration are drying up may both have contributed to the characteristics of the second manner: concentration, abstruseness, a suspicion of meagreness.

Mallarmé's ideas on the technique of poetry, which show him to have been a highly deliberate artist, are also a vital factor. An early pointer to them is provided by his article entitled 'Hérésies artistiques, L'Art pour tous'.[15] In it Mallarmé stresses the sacred nature of poetry and in consequence the need for it as for all things sacred (e.g. religious) to be wrapped in mystery. Poetry without mystery becomes the prey of the vulgar, the subject of lessons in school, as though it were just another science, the victim of pedagogues' commentaries. Other arts have techniques that deny access to them by the uninitiated (notably music); only poetry, the greatest of them all, lacks this vital defence: 'la musique étant pour tous un art, la peinture un art, la statuaire un art – et la poésie n'en étant plus un ... on abandonne musique, peinture et statuaire aux *gens de métiers* [his italics] et comme on tient à sembler instruit on apprend la poésie.'

He rejected Taine's theories on art because: 'Taine ne voit que l'impression comme source des oeuvres d'art, et pas assez la réflexion. Devant le papier, l'artiste *se fait*. Il ne croit pas par

---

[13] Letter to Cazalis, November 1869, cited by Chassé, *Les Clefs de Mallarmé* (1954), chap. 6.
[14] *Oeuvres Complètes*, Pléiade, pp. 429 *et seq.*
[15] Published in *L'Artiste*, 15 September 1862. See Noulet, *Dix poèmes de Stéphane Mallarmé*, avant-propos, p. 11. Part of the article is reproduced by Noulet as an appendix.

exemple qu'un écrivain puisse entièrement changer sa manière, ce qui est faux, je l'ai observé sur moi...'[16]

Mallarmé's poetic practice amounted to a revolution in the use of words or phrases, in syntax, in style; words have special meanings that are either peculiar to Mallarmé (e.g. agonie, vierge, aboli) or a return, with the help of Littré,[17] to archaic usage; phrases, like those of the *Précieuses*, are often a disguise for an ordinary object or idea (e.g. 'espoir du corridor' for death as way to eternal life, ['Toast Funèbre']); the involved syntax arises from Mallarme's banishing all words he regards as not rigorously essential to his purpose; conjunctions, relative pronouns, even prepositions, all those slaves of ordinary language lacking resonance or colour, are pitilessly expunged, thereby not only increasing the poet's own metrical difficulties but producing a contortion of sentence arrangement with unattached appositions and absolute clauses; a first task in penetrating the meaning of a Mallarmé poem may be to re-establish the logical order; in style Mallarmé's principle was indeed sound: to Jean Moréas he writes: 'Tout ce que vous faites en ce moment illustre cette donnée exacte qu'il faut, si l'on fait de la littérature, parler autrement que les journaux[18] ...' He applied this principle not only to verse but also to prose.[19]

Mallarmé's attack upon the norms of linguistic communication produces a vigorous effect of compression. Effect is the important word, and with that purpose in mind he expresses other views on the structure and conception of a poem that are original and point to his understanding of how to rivet the reader's attention, in short the art of communication, with the emphasis on the word art, and on a subtle level. 'Il faut toujours couper le commencement et la fin de ce qu'on écrit. Pas d'introduction, pas de finale', he writes to Cazalis;[20] the opening of 'L'Après-Midi d'un Faune' is a good example of the precept: 'Ces nymphes, je les veux perpétuer...'; and again to Cazalis: 'Peindre, non la chose, mais l'effet qu'elle produit';[21] like an intaglio, whose design becomes apparent only when impressed on sealing wax. This idea is related to his equally original exploitation of the psychological truth that if the reader can be persuaded or forced to create his own image of what the poet has in mind the effect will be all the more powerful.[22]

---

[16] *Propos*, pp. 52–3. Letter to Lefébure, February 1865.
[17] Chassé, op. cit., chap. 3.   [18] *Propos*, p. 147, October 1886.
[19] e.g. 'Divagations' and 'La Musique et les Lettres'. The latter is a lecture delivered at Oxford and at Cambridge in March 1895. One wonders what his audiences could have made of this piece, frankly boring and jejune!   [20] *Propos*, p. 42, April 1864.   [21] *Ibid.*, p. 46, October 1864.
[22] For a good example, see in *Vers et Prose Morceaux Choisis* (1893), 'Le Nénuphar Blanc', the passage beginning 'Résumer d'un regard la vierge absence... mon idéale fleur', and, of course, the well-known passage: 'Je dis: une fleur! et hors de l'oubli...' in 'Divagation Première'.

Together these precepts also fit in with the general theory that inspires Mallarmé's second manner: a poem is a mystery for the reader to unravel: 'Nommer un objet, c'est supprimer les trois quarts de la jouissance du poème qui est fait du bonheur de deviner peu à peu; la suggérer, voilà le rêve...'.[23] He did all he could to suppress notes, earlier versions, etc., that might help the readers in the task.

Thus under the impulse of his idealism and the ideas on poetic technique it fostered, Mallarmé gradually shifts from his first to his second manner, from direct statement to esotericism, from discursiveness (very relative) to intense compression, from definition of things to suggestions,

> Le sens trop précis rature
> Ta vague littérature.

Discouragement at his failure through lack of creative power (as he believed) to realize his ambitious ideas of 'poésie pure' and 'le grand oeuvre' may have had a share in the progress towards hermeticism – 'out of weakness cometh forth strength'.

Evidently Mallarmé has moved away from Parnassian ideas to Symbolism. His emphasis in his later years on the affinities between poetry and music is further evidence; Wagner's musical themes suggest the characters in the operas; poetry must strive after a similar evocative power; in the end indeed it must become a kind of musical composition with words ('Un coup de dés'). Yet to label Mallarmé's two manners as Parnassian and Symbolist respectively is an over-simplification, for the tendency towards Symbolism begins early (e.g. 'Hérodiade') and characteristics of Parnassianism persist in his second manner.[24] There is much in common between his divided loyalties and those of the painter Gustave Moreau, who hovered uneasily between Realism and Symbolism.[25] The happiest marriage between 'Parnasse' and Symbolism in Mallarmé's work is afforded perhaps by 'L'Après-Midi d'un Faune'; the concentrated workmanship, the frank paganism inspired by Boucher's painting 'Pan et Syrinx' – a classical legend in terms of eighteenth-century naughtiness, so often echoed in the poetry of Chénier, re-expressed in the jocund sensuality of Banville's 'Diane aux Bois' (1863),[26] what more Parnassian? On the other hand, the subject is transposed into a faun's erotic visions; the scene unfolding in a Sicilian glade under oppressive heat is suggested, not

---

[23] 'Enquête'.
[24] e.g. particularly his cult of form, of 'La difficulté vaincu' and 'rime riche' (influence of Banville). Mallarmé never liked the liberties the Symbolists took with the traditional verse forms: 'Divagation Première', and 'La Musique et les Lettres' – 'On a touché au vers...', etc.
[25] Chassé, op. cit., chap. I.
[26] Martino, *Parnasse et Symbolisme* (1925).

described, and in this form will lend itself perfectly to the dreamy music of Debussy.

To understand the evolution of Mallarmé's poetry, with the underlying factors that account for it and its significance in relation to the contemporary poetic scene, is one thing, to find the key to any given poem of the second manner is another. There are or have been two schools of thought: the earlier clung to the mystery as a virtue in itself. The Symbolists, with their beliefs, derived from Schopenhauer's philosophy, belonged to it: the only valid truth about the exterior world and all its manifestations is what the subject represents them to be for himself. A poem of Mallarmé's, therefore, may have different symbolic values for different people and even different values for the same person at different times.

The other school of more recent date[27] believes there is a key to each poem; it even claims in some of the abstruser poems to find trivial and even scatological subjects.[28]

This school may be right in its interpretations – in the absence of Mallarmé to confirm them, who is to say? In any case, thanks to them, the modern reader can, following Mallarmé's own principle of the value of surprise, enjoy the poems of the second manner (e.g. 'Sainte', 'Toast Funèbre', 'Le vierge, le vivant et le bel aujourd'hui', the group of 'Tombeaux') at more levels than one, and relish in the end, at least on the aesthetic level, the quintessential distillation of his pessimistic appraisal of man's helplessness in the Universe ('Un coup de dés').[29]

As his second manner developed and his poems became more shrouded in mystery, Mallarmé's personal influence on his younger contemporaries grew stronger. His letters bear striking witness to the fact. From 1880 the salon of the Rue de Rome and the sage who presided there were a fountain-head of new poetic magic.

II. VERLAINE

Like Mallarmé, Paul Verlaine (1844–96) contributed to the *Parnasse Contemporain* of 1866. His first volume of collected poems, *Poèmes Saturniens*, appeared in the same year. Many of the poems, written while Verlaine was still at school, drew their inspiration from older or contemporary poets. The narrator of 'Après Trois Ans' must have read 'Tristesse d'Olympio'; 'Cavitri' could have been from the pen of Leconte de Lisle, 'César Borgia'

---

[27] e.g. Thibaudet, *Poésie de Stéphane Mallarmé*; E. Noulet, *Dix poèmes de Stéphane Mallarmé*, Chassé, op. cit.

[28] Chassé, op. cit.

[29] *Un Coup de dés, avec commentaire par C. Soula.*

from that of Heredia. Baudelaire, too, has evidently stood god-
father to some of them:

> Roule, roule ton flot indolent, morne Seine –
> Bien des corps ont passé, morts, horribles, pourris,
> Dont les âmes avaient pour meurtrier Paris.
>
> ('Nocturne Parisien')

There is a general, if assimilated, Baudelairian influence; the dark
colours of Baudelaire have been softened into a grey wistfulness –
Paysages Tristes.

But, however strong Parnassian and other influences, the *Poèmes
Saturniens* contain a number of poems where Verlaine's original
contribution to French nineteenth-century poetry comes out
strongly; they are mostly to be found in the sub-section *Paysages
Tristes*.

> La lune est rouge au brumeux horizon:
> Dans un brouillard qui danse, la prairie
> S'endort fumeuse . . .   ('L'Heure du Berger')

This short poem is a perfect evocation of twilight; word-painting,
perhaps, in the Parnassian manner, but gone are the clear-cut con-
tours and hard light; instead the picture is in a low colour-key;
the descriptive words blur the outlines; the scene evoked is reminiscent of a picture by Corot in his second manner (e.g. *Souvenir de
Mortefontaine*). 'L'Heure du Berger', though giving no hint of
the poet's own mood, is a fitting introduction to the best of the
Poèmes Saturniens, where Verlaine's gentle wistfulness is closely
attuned to the uncertain transient hours of twilight or dawn and,
by the same token, to the melancholy of autumn.

> Une aube affaiblie
>   Verse par les champs
> La mélancolie
>   Des soleils couchants . . .   ('Soleils Couchants')

Here, and in 'Promenade Sentimentale', the direct notations of
nature are like the accompaniment of the poet's mood:

> Le couchant dardait ses rayons suprêmes
> Et le vent berçait les nénuphars blêmes
> Moi, j'errais tout seul, promenant ma plaie
>   ('Promenade Sentimentale').

In 'Le Rossignol' mood and scene are more closely mingled:

> Comme un vol criard d'oiseaux en émoi
> Tous mes souvenirs s'abattent sur moi,
> S'abattent parmi le feuillage jaune,
> De mon coeur mirant son tronc plié d'aune
> Au tain violet de l'eau des Regrets
> Qui mélancoliquement coule auprès . . .

The poet is still using the form of the simile, 'Comme un vol criard . . .', but the image of the birds coming down on the tree in its yellow autumn dress is so clear that it almost has the force of a symbol, though perhaps the phrase 'L'eau des Regrets' which suggests an allegory in the manner of 'La carte du Tendre' weakens it (only momentarily, however, for quickly the tree and bird's song recapture the imagination:

> L'arbre qui frissonne et l'oiseau qui pleure.)

In 'Chanson d'Automne' the fusion between mood and image is complete:

> Les sanglots longs
> Des violons
> De l'Automne . . .

In 'L'Heure du Berger' the skill of the poet is concentrated on evoking a scene, in 'Promenade Sentimentale' and 'Le Rossignol' the reader is not allowed to forget the poet's own personality, in 'Chanson d'Automne', although the poet is present, the balance in the first stanza between image, rhythm and music is so successful that, for a transient moment, the poet's mood becomes our own; identification is complete. Hackneyed the stanza may have become, but that is a measure of its success.

In *Poèmes Saturniens* the poet is already in quest of the effects, and the technical means to achieve them he will later prescribe in his 'Art Poétique'[30] – even if he did not regard them as firm principles: musicality

> De la Musique avant toute chose . . .

and the value for that of irregular lines, blurred outlines

> . . . l'indécis . . .
> . . . rien que la nuance,

away with eloquence.

> Prends l'éloquence et tords-lui son cou ;

beware of rhyme!

> Oh! qui dira les torts de la Rime.

The Parnasse is thrown overboard!

In 1866 Verlaine had not moved that far, but the experimenter in new metres is awake and his ear sensitive to the emotional value of tonal and other effects: the mixed four and three syllable lines of 'Chanson d'Automne'; the five syllable lines of 'Soleils Couchants'; the decasyllabics of 'Promenade Sentimentale', 'L'Heure du Berger' and 'Le Rossignol', mostly divided into two unequal

[30] Written 1874, published 1884 in *Jadis et Naguère*.

hemistiches; the weakening of the caesura, 'enjambement' – both means of giving greater fluidity; the obsessive effect of repetition (e.g. in 'Mon Rêve familier', 'Promenade Sentimentale') and the rhythmical and tonal effects of long adverbs (e.g. *mélancolique-ment, imperturbablement*) – two favourite devices of Verlaine's; the music of certain vowels; variations of rhyme schemes;[31] 'internal' rhymes.

In all these ways which he was to develop and whereby he unshackled French prosody from its Parnassian chains, Verlaine gave his own stamp to the poems in *Poèmes Saturniens* we have discussed; by technical means in fact rather than by any original thought content; 'Chanson d'Automne' is a technical success, no more.

> . . . ceux-là qui sont nés sous le signe SATURNE,
> Ont entre tous . . .
> Bonne part de malheur . . .

Verlaine writes in his dedicatory poem. That he should have chosen Saturn, literary influences apart,[32] must have been due to an appraisal of his own anxious nature, so easily subjugated by external influences rather than from any direct experiences of misfortune; he was twenty-two and, unlike Baudelaire, had no youthful grievances to look back upon; impulsive and irresponsible as he was, sorrow lay in the future.

> Et je m'en vais
> Au vent mauvais
> Qui m'emporte
> Deçà, de là . . .   ('Chanson d'Automne')

The dead leaf blown hither and thither, skilfully suggested by the rhythm, is a prophetic commentary on Verlaine's life.

Les Fêtes Galantes (1869) develops the technical skills already evident in *Poèmes Saturniens*. Mallarmé, no mean judge, long regarded them as his friend's masterpiece in musicality and delicacy.

The title evokes a vision of the eighteenth century Verlaine shared with other poets and writers of his day,[33] a vision with more tenderness and melancholy than was always present in the refined urbane spirit of that period, although there are signs of it in the painter Watteau. The moonlight (e.g. in 'Clair de Lune' and 'En Bateau') is a Romantic addition, the 'correspondances' (e.g. 'A Clymène') come from a nearer source, and in the end the

[31] In connection with the last two points, the first stanza of 'Nevermore' consists of four alexandrines ending in feminine rhymes, which was against all accepted canons: automne, atone, monotone, détone.
[32] Baudelaire calls *Les Fleurs du Mal* 'un livre saturnien . . .'; Poem No. 3 in Hugo's *Les Contemplations*, Bk. III, is entitled 'Saturne'.
[33] Gautier, Hugo, Banville, Nerval, Baudelaire, Glatigny, Ed. and J. de Goncourt.

pastoral fantasy with its pasteboard décor fades on a note of despair (e.g. 'En Sourdine') and even a note of eeriness (e.g. 'Colloque Sentimentale') which is Verlaine's own.

But the grey mists dissolve in the warmth of true love; *La Bonne Chanson* (1870) is a moment of sunshine; away with café life and absinthe; instead:

> Le foyer, la lueur étroite de la lampe;
> La rêverie avec le doigt contre la tempe
> Et les yeux se perdant parmi les yeux aimés . . .

The tender vision of conjugal happiness, which prefigures a picture by the *intimiste* painter Vuillard, which the poet sings with sincerity and his wealth of metrical ingenuity, was realized,[34] only to be shattered by Rimbaud who tore into Verlaine's life like a tornado.

The war of 1870 which had made of Verlaine a 'mobile guard' made no impact on his poetry; it was as though the brutal fact of war lay outside his range, but Rimbaud gave Verlaine's pessimism, instinctive and literary until then, a basis in personal suffering. As though under a spell, Verlaine abandoned wife and child for Rimbaud. The flight with Rimbaud to England, and thence to Belgium, the revolver shot fired in drunken anger, the prison sentence for wounding, were a prelude to the life of drunken debauchery which was mostly Verlaine's thereafter, except for a few years, while the influence of his religious conversion was still active; this brief interlude was spent partly as a teacher of French in England, and partly in a financially disastrous attempt at farming.

Romances sans Paroles (1874), *Sagesse* (1881) are the fruit of his middle years; the sufferings of the man have enriched the poet. After the short interlude of joy (*La Bonne Chanson*), *Romances sans Paroles* bear the signs of harsh experience:

> Il pleure dans mon coeur
> Comme il pleut sur la ville . . .

Like the other poems in the section *Ariettes Oubliées*, the four short stanzas of this poem, which are like a musical variation on a theme in a lost poem of Rimbaud's, 'il pleut doucement sur la ville', carry no title; the imprisoned poet, looking inward on his grief, requires no outward stimulus; the heart is numbed by indefinable sorrow, the soul weighed down by the memory of vanished happiness:

> O Triste, triste était mon âme . . .

The poet's grief forms many of the poems of *Sagesse* too (especially Section III), though religious conversion brings moods of humility, gratitude, hope, serenity.

[34] Verlaine married in 1870.

In addition to 'Art Poétique' already referred to, *Jadis et Naguère* (1884) contains poems of both profane ('Jadis') and sacred ('Naguère') inspiration; thereafter Verlaine veers between these two attitudes; the naïve sincerity of the personal confession continues now in pious mood: *Amour* (1888), *Bonheur* (1891), *Liturgies Intimes* (1892); now in a mood of expansive sensuality: *Parallèlement* (1889) – a title that underlines his 'other' or 'lower' self's coexistence; *Chansons pour elle* (1891), or frank eroticism; *Odes en son honneur* (1893), but though the superlative craftsman remains, the poet has little new to say.

He had attained the summit of his achievement in *Romances sans Paroles* and *Sagesse* because the sincerity of the man and the inspiration of the poet are in balance, because, in spite of drink and debauchery or, for that matter, the fervours of faith and repentance, the artist remains in control, stretching to the limit the rhythmical possibility of French verse within the traditional structures ('vers libéré' was Verlaine's ideal, not the 'vers libre' which comes later), exploiting the musical resources of the language, exploring as never before the poetic aura of words, the symbolic potential of images, expressed with cunning simplicity: the rain (*Ariettes Oubliées*), the faltering snow on the mournful plains (*Ariettes Oubliées*), the solitary tree in the empty sky (*Sagesse*), the notes of the hunting horn dying on the distant hill (*Sagesse*), all symbols of Verlaine's heartbreak, have lost none of their suggestive power. To the Symbolists they were to be a powerful inspiration. As Verlaine was sinking into the mire, they discovered him; his reputation, hitherto limited, rose; the 'pauvre Lélian' of *Les Poètes Maudits* (1884) became the 'Prince of Poets'.

III. RIMBAUD

In contrast to Verlaine's gentle cadences, the poetry of Arthur Rimbaud (1854–91) is like hammer blows on metal. That he started writing poetry at an early age is suggested by the practised skill apparent in the alexandrines of his first extant poem – 'Les Etrennes des Orphelins' (1869). The subject is strongly reminiscent of Hugo in sentimental vein, or François Coppée, but in choosing the subject Rimbaud may have had personal motives.

> ... ces enfants sont sans mère,
> Plus de mère au logis! – et le père est bien loin ...

Rimbaud's father, a regular officer, had in fact deserted his wife and four children after returning from the wars;[35] Madame Rim-

---

[35] He had campaigned in Algeria and the Crimea.

baud was not dead but, bigoted and severe, showed no outward affection. Arthur, the 'deprived child', seems in the poem to be objectivizing his sense of loss; it was as though he had no mother; poetry is a consolation. During the next three years poetry assumes a vital role in Rimbaud's life, but quickly changes in character.

The year 1870 was important in his development; the pious repressed child taking refuge in solitude suddenly becomes a rebellious adolescent, the 'angry young man' in the making. 'Ce jeune homme sera le génie du bien ou du mal' was the prophetic comment of his headmaster.

The age of innocence is over ('Première Soirée'); the passive acceptance of what life brings, so characteristic of a child, gives way to more positive attitudes, to a determination to go in search of the happiness that must exist . . . somewhere:

> Je ne parlerai pas, je ne penserai rien
> Mais l'amour enfin me montera dans l'âme,
> Et j'irai loin, bien loin, comme un bohémien
> Par la Nature. ('Sensation')

In exclamatory tones that have a Parnassian ring, the youthful poet proclaims his new-found faith in the frank sensuality of the ancients:

> Je crois en toi! je crois en toi! Divine Mère,
> Aphrodite marine! . . . ('Soleil et Chair')

But the optimism that illumines these poems is quickly obscured; instead a mood of aggressive cynicism; 'Aphrodite marine' becomes an ugly hag ('Vénus Anadyomène'); the provincial life of his native Charleville, Christianity, both weights of oppression to him, become objects of hatred ('A la Musique', 'Soleil et Chair' – *passim*, 'Le Mal'); republican fervour, both in the spirit and manner of Victor Hugo, provides a psychological compensation for his unhappiness ('Le Forgeron'); the outbreak and the disasters of the war add fuel to his hatreds ('Le Mal', 'Rages de Césars', 'Le Dormeur du Val').

The impact of the war may also have quickened in Rimbaud the latent hope of liberation, the desire to escape from the hideous dream his life at Charleville had become; a series of attempted flights followed, towards Paris (August 1870), towards Belgium (October 1870[36]) and again to Paris (February–March 1871). None succeeded; the first ended in prison for travelling without a ticket;[37] of the second, little is known except that a number of

---

[36] The German armies by then were threatening Paris.

[37] He was rescued from Mazas by the schoolmaster Georges Izambard who, being a poet and a republican, had gained Rimbaud's confidence and was one of his rare friends; Paul Demeny, also a poet, was another.

poems in happy mood – e.g. 'Rêve pour l'hiver', 'Au Cabaret-
Vert', 'La Maline', 'Ma Bohême' – seem to be echoes of this short
odyssey which, like the first, brought him to Douai,[38] and like the
first ended in the hated Charleville. The third time he succeeded
in getting to Paris, only to suffer disappointment; he did not meet
the Parnassian poets in the cafés, as he had dreamed of doing; ten
days of physical privation and sleeping under bridges convinced
him that even Charleville was the lesser evil; he returned thither
on foot just before the Commune broke out in Paris.

The odds were against him, inevitably, in such ill-conceived
efforts to escape, or not so much ill-conceived as unpremeditated;
lacking all experience of what lay beyond his horizons, the youthful Rimbaud obeys the compulsions of his dreams. The mood of
revolt built on their ruins can be measured in 'Les Poètes de sept
ans', his pitiless contempt of human decrepitudes and indignities
in 'Les Assis' and 'Accroupissements', of human naïve stupidity in
'Les Pauvres à l'Eglise'.

The winter months of 1870–1, between the second and third
attempted escape, were sombre. Outward signs of Rimbaud's revolt were not wanting: refusal to return to school, long hair, dirt
and dishevelment, a pipe smoked with symbolically inverted bowl.
With no immediate prospect of escape Rimbaud is driven in on
himself:

> Je vis assis, tel qu'un ange aux mains d'un barbier . . .
> . . . . .
> Tels que les excréments chauds d'un vieux colombier,
> Mille Rêves en moi font de douces brûlures . . .
>
> ('Oraison du Soir')

It was a period of gestation, nourished by disordered reading at
the town library which had remained open despite the war; books
on occultism, spiritualism, Indian philosophies, particularly absorbed him. If physical escape was denied him for a variety of
reasons – war, lack of funds, youthfulness – he could perhaps build
up some spiritual compensation.

Now a new conception of the poet's function and consequently of
poetry appeared to him. Before, poetry had been an escape from
his childhood's distresses, then a cathartic release for pent-up feelings of revolt and hatred; now, with the revelation of the poet as in
truth a magician but of a modern type, poetry is to be the faithful
recording of his visions.

After the failure of his third attempt at physical escape, Rimbaud evidently turned with fervour towards this new avenue of
salvation at a moment of spiritual bankruptcy: 'Mon triste coeur

[38] Izambard, an orphan, had his home there, with Mlles Gindre who
had brought him up.

bave à la poupe . . .' ('Le Coeur du Pître'). In a letter to Izambard (13 May 1871), in another to Demeny (15 May), he gives free rein to his enthusiasms; the ideas pour out in a disordered array but the pattern is clear, though one wonders what his two friends, poets perhaps but grounded on the lower slopes of Parnassus, made of it. To Demeny he explains the first duty of the aspirant poet: 'la première étude de l'homme qui veut être poète est sa propre connaissance, entière; il cherche son âme, il l'inspecte, il la tente, l'apprend. Dès qu'il la sait, il doit la cultiver; cela semble simple . . . Mais il s'agit de faire l'âme monstrueuse . . . Je dis qu'il faut être *voyant*, se faire *voyant*.'

The poet-seer is to be the architect of a revolution which, more significant than social or political convulsions, is to attack all normal conceptions of the human personality, by plunging into its mysterious depths: 'sa propre connaissance, entière'. How? Both letters give the answer in similar terms: 'par un long, immense et raisonné *dérèglement* de *tous les sens*. Toutes les formes d'amour, de souffrance, de folie; il cherche lui-même, il épuise en lui tous les poisons, pour n'en garder que les quintessences . . .'[39] (echoes of Baudelaire!). Poetry will be the notation of all this: 'il (the poet) devra faire sentir, palper, écouter ses inventions; si ce qu'il rapporte de là-bas a forme, il donne forme; si c'est informe, il donne de l'informe . . .'[40] Here lies the explanation of the much greater inaccessibility of Rimbaud's later poems.

The letter to Demeny reveals and indeed expresses its author's admiration for Baudelaire[41] in whom he saw the first 'voyant' of French poetry, but there is an important difference Rimbaud seems unaware of, or at least does not mention, between Baudelaire's 'voyance' and his own – the purpose. Baudelaire moves on an aesthetic plane, in search of beauty, Rimbaud's aim is a psychological and moral renovation; the poet must be 'un multiplicateur de progrès', a leader of men, in a much deeper sense than ever understood by Leconte de Lisle.[42]

Were the letters no more than an ecstatic declaration of purpose? The suffering Rimbaud knew was involved, and accepted, the split personality ('Je est un autre . . .'), the sense of being the plaything of a superior power ('Si le cuivre s'éveille clairon . . .') could derive from his reading in the occult; but the authoritative, dedicated tone points to some experience already acquired – 'je m'encrapule le plus possible . . .'? A passage in *Une Saison en Enfer* supports the view that the process of initiation had begun: 'J'aimais les peintures idiotes . . .etc.';[43] all things, be it noted,

[39] To Demeny.
[40] Ditto.
[41] The Baudelaire of *Correspondances*.
[42] See Vol. IV, chap. 19.
[43] *Délires II*, 'Alchimie du Verbe'.

which being either unrepresentational or not on the level of Rimbaud's personal experience, could have powers of suggestion, partake of otherness.[44] 'La vieillerie poétique', he continues, 'avait une bonne part dans mon alchimie du verbe.

'Je m'habituai à l'hallucination simple: je voyais ... une mosquée à la place d'une usine ... un titre de vaudeville dressait des épouvantes devant moi.

'Puis j'expliquai mes sophismes magiques avec l'hallucination des mots!'

The letters to Izambard and Demeny were written only a few days before the fall of the Commune. In spite of the last sentence of the letter to Demeny, it seems unlikely that Rimbaud was an eye-witness of the fighting that crushed it, but, rebel that he had become, his sympathies lay with the Communards ('L'Orgie Parisienne ou Paris se repeuple') and their defeat was a further blow to his morale. In June and July 1871 he appears to hover between contrary directions; at one moment he harbours thoughts of death ('Les Soeurs de Charité'), at another he is writing the mysterious 'Voyelles', variously interpreted, but which if the author's own subsequent allusion to it[45] is to be accepted (and why not?), was at the time of composition connected with poetry's part in the poet's function as seer; at yet another time his desire to escape wells up and he writes 'Le Bateau Ivre'.

With some exceptions (e.g. 'flottaison blême', 'échouages hideux'), the descriptions ring true and could come from direct observation, but in 1871 the sea, with its power, its storms, its ever-changing colours in polar and torrid zones, had not yet come into Rimbaud's youthful experience; reading or book illustrations seen in childhood could alone have coloured his imagination.[46]

Only in the last three stanzas of the poem does the experience become direct and they are the most moving:

> Mais, vrai, j'ai trop pleuré! ...

The whole poem seems prophetic of Rimbaud's own later years of vagabondage; in his last letters from Ethiopia, where as a trader in gems and ivory (white and black?) he was making money, there is a note of nostalgia for home; similarly here in the last stanzas Rimbaud evokes an image of his own childhood:

> Si je désire une eau d'Europe, c'est la flâche
> Noire et froide où vers le crépuscule embaumé
> Un enfant accroupi plein de tristesses, lâche
> Un bateau frêle comme un papillon de mai ...

---

[44] See Yves Bonnefoy, 'La décision de Rimbaud', *Preuves*, No. 107, January 1960.
[45] See *Une Saison en Enfer*, *Délires II*, 'Alchimie du Verbe'.
[46] The Voyages of Captain Cook, and Jules Verne's *Vingt Mille lieues sous la mer* have been suggested.

the small boy who, as he launched his paper boat on the puddle, had imagined its progress down a vast river of the Americas into the Seven Seas.

Childhood was still near in time and yet remote; his memories of it were vivid because so close and yet he could look at them from beyond the gulf fixed in him by the deep revelation he had had of what poetry ought to be: 'Ah! cette vie de mon enfance ... quelle sottise c'était. – Et je m'en aperçois seulement!'[47] He had become dedicated.

This intensity of purpose drove him to the final successful effort to break away from Charleville. To Verlaine, whom he admired, he wrote enclosing some of his poems and asking for hospitality. 'Venez chère grande âme, on vous attend.' 'On vous désire', was the reply, and to Paris, with his mother's acquiescence, he went.

The 'dérèglement de tous les sens' was about to begin in earnest; it was to last two years (August 1871–July 1873); its victim was the spellbound Verlaine. Only the fanatical sense of mission can explain Rimbaud's callous destruction of his companion's happiness: 'Pitoyable frère! Que d'atroces veillées je lui dus! ... presque chaque nuit, aussitôt endormi, le pauvre frère se levait, la bouche pourrie, les yeux arrachés ... et me tirait dans la salle en hurlant son songe de chagrin idiot.

' J'avais en effet, en toute sincérité d'esprit, pris l'engagement de le rendre à son état primitif de fils du soleil – et nous errions, nourris du vin des cavernes et du biscuit de la route, moi pressé de trouver le lieu et la formule.'[48]

Of the poems written in 1872 some seem directly related to the experience (e.g. 'Bannières de Mai', 'Chanson de la plus Haute Tour', 'L'Eternité', 'Honte', 'O Saisons O Châteaux'), but the most important of its fruits are the *Illuminations* (1875) in which, abandoning verse forms presumably to give the most immediate notation of his visions ('si ce qu'il rapporte de là-bas a forme ...', etc.), he takes to prose poems: 'J'ai tendu des cordes de clocher à clocher; des guirlandes de fenêtre à fenêtre; des chaînes d'or d'étoile à étoile, et je danse.'[49]

But seldom do the *Illuminations* display such a euphoric picture of visionary states. The experience, often gruelling, is recorded in *Une Saison en Enfer* (1873); played out, now in a Paris garret, now in London, now in Brussels, it ended with a pistol shot, prison for Verlaine, spiritual bankruptcy for Rimbaud; the journey into the sub-liminal world leads man either into madness ('Les rages, les débauches, la folie, dont je sais tous les élans et les désastres'[50]) or back to the commonplace world, clutching at a shadow: 'Moi!

---

[47] *Saison en Enfer*, 'L'Impossible'.   [48] *Illuminations*, 'Vagabonds'.
[49] *Ibid.*, 'Phrases'.   [50] *Saison en Enfer*, 'Mauvais Sang'.

moi qui me suis dit mage ou ange, dispensé de toute morale, je suis rendu au sol, avec un devoir à chercher, et la réalité rugueuse à étreindre! Paysan!'[51]

In 1875 Rimbaud walked out of literature to roam the world, convinced, it seems, that the six (known) years of his poetic activity had been wasted. He was twenty-one. His path was to take him to many parts of Europe, as far east as Java, to Cyprus, Aden, Ethiopia, and back finally to Marseilles where he died a Christian, so his sister Isabelle alleged.

But even though for him the great experiment had failed, he was profoundly wrong in thinking his experience was to bear no fruit. The words of his letter to Demeny are prophetic; of the poet he intends to be he writes: 'Qu'il crève dans son bondissement par les choses inouïes et innombrables: viendront d'autres horribles travailleurs; ils commenceront par les horizons où l'autre s'est affaissé!'

For the Symbolists the author of 'Le Bateau Ivre' and 'Voyelles' was one of them; for the Surrealists the author of *Une Saison en Enfer* was one of them; Paul Claudel was to return to the Catholic fold, thanks to the author of the *Illuminations*; Existentialists, Communists, Fascists claim him too; truly Rimbaud more than any other nineteenth-century French poet stands on the threshold of the twentieth.

IV. DECADENTS AND SYMBOLISTS

Mallarmé, Verlaine, Rimbaud, these are the great names in the pre-Symbolist years. In a lower bracket may be mentioned the poets who have in common an attitude which in due course was to be described as 'decadent': Charles Cros, Tristan Corbière, Jules Laforgue. Théophile Gautier, in his preface to the 1869 edition of *Les Fleurs du Mal*, had defended the idea of decadence in art which, he said, 'n'est autre chose que l'art arrivé à ce point de maturité extrême que déterminent à leurs soleils obliques les civilisations qui vieillissent.' Later, Verlaine was to take up the idea: 'Je suis l'Empire à la fin de la décadence',[52] and in 1882 Laforgue was using the term as a label for the young poets of the day. Thereafter the word gains ground; Huysmans gives the idea definition in the character of des Esseintes;[53] the word became a term of derision with newspaper critics who disapproved of the new poetic movement; Vicaire and Beauclair published a book of pastiches entitled *Les Déliquescences d'Adoré Floupette, poèmes décadents* (1885). Anatole Baju thereupon published a poetry

---

[51] *Ibid.*, 'Adieu'.   [52] *Jadis et Naguère* (1881): 'Sonnet de Bérénice'.
[53] *A Rebours* (1884). See above, chap. 2.

journal called *Le Décadent*, as a rallying-point for young poets of the day.

Charles Cros (1842–88), philologist and scientific inventor,[54] was also a humorist ('le Hareng Saur', 'le Bilboquet', 'l'Obsession') and the poet of *Le Coffret de Santal* (1873) and *Le Collier de Griffe*[55] (posth. 1908), of which the dominant note is pessimism disguised under a biting irony. Like Cros, Tristan Corbière (1845–75), the sea-dog from Brittany, has only a minor part; indeed 'part' is perhaps the wrong word since it suggests some influence, however small, on the play in progress; whether Corbière can be said to have had any is doubtful; Parnassian ideas, stale though they were becoming, were still too strong, and Corbière's work, quite foreign to them, made no impact, although he was one of the poets chosen by Verlaine for his gallery of *Poètes Maudits* (1884). Corbière's *Amours Jaunes* (1873) had been published at his own expense and a second edition (posth. 1891) was also ill-timed; by then the Symbolist poets were in full, though, in a sense, discordant song, since there was little agreement on what the melody should be, and Corbière's little voice was drowned in the chorus. A later generation, however, may see that this minor poet, uninfluenced by prevailing orthodoxies, has a note of originality. His love and knowledge of the sea is a genuine if not very deep vein of inspiration,[56] he knew the men of the sea, the joys and skill of their struggle against wind and weather, their contempt for landsmen:

> On ne les connaît pas, ces gens à rudes noeuds.
> Ils ont le mal de mer sur vos planchers à boeufs;
> A terre – oiseaux palmés – ils sont gauches et veules
> On ne les connaît pas – Eux: que leur fait la terre?

Hugo, a landlubber, waxes sentimental, as anyone may who lacks direct experience of his theme, about the sailor's sad fate;[57] how refreshingly astringent is the professional's reply:

> Allons! C'est leur métier; ils sont morts dans leurs bottes![58]

Likewise his knowledge and love of Brittany; Corbière can scarcely be classed as a regionalist poet if by that we mean a poet who has specialized in giving the tales and songs, the folklore of his birthplace, a permanent place in literature,[59] but Corbière knew Brittany as he knew the sea; he had the Breton scene in his eye and heart:

> Bénite est l'infertile plage
> Où comme la mer tout est nud.

[54] Coloured photography; also had the idea of the 'phonograph' before Edison.
[55] *Poèmes et Proses* (1944), Gallimard.
[56] e.g. 'Gens de Mer'. [57] In 'Oceano Nox'.
[58] Op. cit. [59] e.g. Anatole Le Braz for Brittany.

Sainte est la chapelle sauvage
De Sainte-Anne-de-la-Palud.[60]

Corbière could perhaps have become a great poet of the sea or of
Brittany; two things interfered: first, the ironic side of his nature
which blurred observation, avoided the expression of deep emotion or drowned the sob under bitter laughter; secondly, his decision (1872) to forsake Brittany for Paris, in pursuit of 'Marcelle'.[61]
For the remainder of his short life he lived isolated and unknown. Had he then met the poets who like himself were exploring
new territory, perhaps his own genius would have been enriched.
Instead he was thrown back on his own resources: his disordered
reading – Hugo, Musset, Baudelaire, Banville; his love, to be both
nursed and derided, his skill and obvious enjoyment at the un-
orthodox acrobatics of rhyme and language; a dandy, an amateur,
he remains, a 'pagliaccio', hiding the sob under a hollow laugh:

Poète, en dépit de ses vers;
Artiste sans art – à l'envers;
Philosophe – à tort, à travers.
Un drôle sérieux . . .[62]

The elements of 'decadence' apparent in Cros, more visible in
Corbière, are much more pronounced in Jules Laforgue (1860–87).
What in Cros and Corbière had been little more than effort to
escape from the tyranny of Parnassian form and find new rhythms
in which to clothe their native melancholy, becomes a more deliberate search both for poetic originality in the wake of Baudelaire and a philosophic basis to underpin his 'decadent' view of
life. Like the specialists in Shaw's *Doctor's Dilemma* who are interested only in their own specialisms, be it the 'Phagocytes' or the
'Nuciform Sack', Laforgue admired particularly in Baudelaire the
symptoms of his own disease; for him Baudelaire was the epitome
of 'décadence': 'quel nerfs plaintifs! Quelles narines ouvertes à
tout!'[63]
But, setting aside any comparison of poetic quality all to the
advantage of Baudelaire, we may discern a difference in register
between the master and the neophyte. Whether tortured by a
sense of sin, or revolted by his sordid weaknesses, whether taking
refuge in art or escaping to the distant Isles, Baudelaire, in his
anguish, remains within the compass of his and our poor humanity; Laforgue strives to be cosmic:

Le jour qu'elle quittera ce monde,
Je vais jouer un Miserere

[60] Op. cit., *Armor*: 'La Rapsode Foraine et le Pardon de Sainte-Anne'.
[61] Armida-Josefina Cuchiani whom he had met in 1871.
[62] Op. cit., 'Epitaphe'.   [63] *Oeuvres complètes*, Vol. 4, p. 119 (1923).

Si cosmiquement désespéré
Qu'il faudra bien que Dieu me réponde!
('Complainte de l'organiste de Notre-Dame de Nice',
Le Sanglot de la Terre.)

Schopenhauer has profoundly marked him. The early poems in
Le Sanglot de la Terre (posth. 1901) constantly echo the idea that
life is a sinister meaningless joke:

Eternité! pardon. Je le vois, notre terre
N'est, dans l'universel hosannah des splendeurs
Qu'un atome où se joue une farce éphémère
('Farce éphémère, *Le Sanglot*)

and the poet's anguished search for enlightenment:

Oui moi, je veux savoir! Parlez! pourquoi ces choses?
Où chercher le témoin de tout?...
('Curiosités déplacées', *Le Sanglot*)

But the influence of another German philosopher, Hartmann,
came as some corrective to Schopenhauer's. Hartmann's doctrine[64]
about the life force which, unconscious, blind, therefore evil, anim-
ates the universe, which all conscious beings derive from and are
controlled by, seems scarcely less pessimistic than Schopenhauer's,
except that it provides for a certain form of progress, the perpetual
deepening of consciousness in the Universe; man cannot control
the life force but at least he may come to terms with it by understanding his position. Laforgue thereby achieved a certain stability
in fatalistic resignation:

Oui ce monde est bien plat: quant à l'autre, sornettes.
Moi, je vais résigné, sans espoir à mon sort,
Et pour tuer le temps, en attendant la mort
Je fume au nez des dieux de fines cigarettes...[65]
('La Cigarette', *Le Sanglot*)

This mood inspires Laforgue's subsequent work: *Les Complaintes*
(1885), *L'Imitation de Notre-Dame la Lune* (1886), *Derniers Vers*
(posth. 1890); resignation perhaps but with its psychological compensation – an impertinent posturing, a gesture of defiance by the
brave poor thing fighting down his sobs.

Baudelaire, the man, had expressed his suffering with deep sincerity and passion; but Baudelaire the poet communicates that
suffering in terms derived from his experience and observation of
the world around him; the impact on the reader is all the greater
because, although the communication is by no means always indirect, his own experience of life can take the measure of the
poet's, understand, even enter into it; we forget the poet's egotism,

[64] *Philosophie des Unbewuszten* (1865), translated into French 1877.
[65] See also *Les Complaintes*, 'Préludes Autobiographiques'.

because it becomes our own. Laforgue would fain follow Baudelaire's example, nay outstrip him by his inventive originality;
Baudelaire wrung poetry from the day-to-day, even the sordid;
Laforgue will reduce metaphysical ideas to the level of a music-
hall ditty, arrest our attention by his dislocated rhythms, and un-
abashed puns, fling together in unpredictable association the most
disparate objects to achieve effects of contrast and bathos; what
better way, the poet seems to imply, of conveying a sense of the
inanity of life beneath 'la céleste Eternullité'?[66]

But how inferior it all is to the work of the master! Skilful
originality of form sometimes; sincerity – yes, but sincerity is not
enough. The truth is that short of Lucretian calibre, metaphysics
are a glacial level for poetic inspiration; Laforgue's antics do not
enrich our experience of the subject; they seem to be there to
sustain the interest the subject itself cannot provide; they draw
our attention away from it to the poet's own attitude; thus the
very vastness of the theme serves to underline the poet's own
egotism we are unwilling to identify ourselves with, and we quickly
tire of this baying to the moon, this whimpering in the moonlight.
The best of Laforgue is to be found in the *Vers Libres* of *Derniers
Vers* where often the poet is more ready to look outwards and
colour the surrounding scene with his melancholy:

> Noire bise, averse glapissante,
> Et fleuve noir, et maisons closes,
> Et quartiers sinistres comme des Morgues . . .

The climate of 'decadence' persists in such poets as Laurent
Tailhade (1854–1919), the elegiac poet of *Le Jardin des Rêves*
(1879), *Un douzain de Sonnets* (1882) and *Vitraux* (1891)[67] and
the trenchant satirist of *Au pays du Mufle* (1891) and *A travers
les Groins* (1899);[68] in Georges Rodenbach (1855–98), poet[69] and
novelist,[70] for whom the melancholy of the old towns and canals
of his native Belgium reflect his own; in Ephraïm Mikhaël (1866–
90), whose sadness[71] closes round him like the mists in a Verlain-
ian landscape and seems to presage his early death:

> L'ennui descend sur moi comme un brouillard d'automne
> ('Crépuscule Pluvieux')

By 1885, however, the young poets of the day were no longer
satisfied with the word 'decadent' as label for their poetic aspira-

---

[66] *Complaintes*, 'Préludes autobiographiques'.
[67] All collected in *Poèmes Elégiaques* (1907).
[68] Both republished as *Poèmes Aristophanesques* (1904).
[69] *Le Règne du silence* (1891), *Les Vies encloses* (1896).
[70] *Bruges – la Morte* (1892).
[71] *Oeuvres, poésie, poèmes en prose* (posth. 1890).

tions. Jean Moréas (1856–1910), whose early poems – *Les Syrtes* (1884) – had been in the 'decadent' manner, was the first to voice the new discontent, the first, with Baudelaire's famous poem[72] in mind no doubt, to propose another word as a standard the new school could gather round. Paul Bourde, writing in *Le Temps* (6 August 1885) had reviewed with little sympathy the work of the 'Décadents'; Jean Moréas replied in *Le Dix-neuvième Siècle*, suggesting 'Symbolisme' as a better description of the new poetry. A further article by him in *Le Figaro* (18 September 1886) is a veritable manifesto of Symbolism as he then conceived it: 'Ennemie de l'enseignement, de la déclamation, de la fausse sensibilité, de la description objective, la poésie symboliste cherche à vêtir l'idée d'une forme sensible...'

Moréas was not alone in his efforts to define the aims of the new poetry. As in the heroic days of Romanticism, the poetic enthusiasms of the hour produced a plethora of critical articles, reviews and journals, mostly ephemeral, launched by aspirants to influence and the glory of founding a literary school: e.g. *Lutèce, Le Symbolisme, La Vogue, La Revue Indépendante, La Plume, La Pléiade* (to become *Le Mercure de France*), *Entretiens politiques et littéraires, La Revue Blanche, Ecrits pour l'Art*.

The babel of controversy bears witness to the poetic ferment of the Symbolist era. The cult of poetry was at its height, a disinterested and, under the influence of Mallarmé, often a rather esoteric cult which, if it was of vital interest to its devotees, was less attractive to the public at large. Symbolism, like a palace revolution, was of little concern to those outside and, as often happens, the participants, united in their dislikes – in this case Parnassian poetry and the Naturalist philosophy with its roots in Positivism, were disunited in their constructive ideas. True, René Ghil (1862–1925) did not eschew science; his poetry, uniting Baudelaire's idea of synaesthesia – 'Les parfums, les couleurs et les sons se répondent...' – to Rimbaud's belief in the almost magical potential of words – 'Alchimie du verbe' – aimed at using words for their sound value and colour suggestion, and at establishing Symbolism on a methodical scientific study of sound and its psychological effects. 'L'instrumentation verbale' was Ghil's expression,[73] and, following out his theory, all his poems were to be, as it were, orchestrated into a poetic symphony entitled *Oeuvre*.[74] Ghil's poetic notions bear the stamp of the enthusiastic self-mystification prevalent at that time.

[72] *Correspondances*.
[73] See his *Traité du Verbe* (1886).
[74] Of the three 'movements' *Oeuvre* was to comprise: 'Dire du Mieux', 'Dire des Sangs', 'Dire de la Loi' – the first two only were completed, the former 1889–1909, the latter 1898–1920.

Though himself a believer in metrical emancipation, Ghil stands apart from the 'Vers-libristes' group whose real theorist was Gustave Kahn[75] (1859–1936), the materialist and rationalist poet of *Palais Nomades* (1887), *Chansons d'Amant* (1891), *Livre d'images* (1897). How significant from a Symbolist angle are the titles: *Palais Nomades* and *Livre d'images*! Palaces are not fixed structures but nomadic because the poet carries with him wherever he goes his own 'ideal' palaces of ideas and impressions, and the exterior world is the pretext for a succession of subjective images; the whole suffused with a dark pessimism:

> Rien dans le passé, rien dans le présent,
> Encore un lambeau d'heure évanouie! ...
>   ('Voix de l'heure implacable', *Les Palais Nomades*)

Verlaine seems very close in the rhythms and blurred landscapes:

> Chantonne lentement et très bas ... mon coeur pleure ...
> Tristement, doucement ...
> Il fait froid, il pâlit quelque chose dans l'heure – ,
> Un vague très blafard étreint l'âpre sonneur.
>   ('Chantonne Lentement', *Ibid.*)

The new prosody attracted a large number of poets, e.g. Stuart Merrill (1863–1915), Francis Vielé-Griffin (1864–1937), both American born, Max Elskamp (1862–1931), Grégoire Le Roy (1862–1948), André Fontainas (1865–1948), Albert Möckel (1866–1945), Charles van Lerberghe (1861–1907), all Belgians, Rémy de Gourmont (1858–1915), Saint-Pol Roux (1861–1940), Adolphe Retté (1863–1930), Camille Mauclair (1872–1936), Henry Bataille (1872–1922).[76]

Prominent amongst the 'vers-libristes' is Paul Fort (b. 1872), founder of the 'Théâtre d'Art' (1890), later 'l'Oeuvre', where as a counter-blast to the 'Théâtre libre' a wide repertoire of poetic drama, ancient and modern, French and foreign, was performed. The habit of the spoken word may have influenced Paul Fort in his use of the 'vers libres'; in any case the fecund author of *Ballades françaises et chroniques de France* (1897–1937) stretches the form to the point where it becomes rhythmical prose.

But surely the outstanding member of the group by his versatility and range of inspiration is the Belgian, Emile Verhaeren (1865–1916). The lesser Symbolists like other lesser poets before them are derivative; they take refuge in a house already built and dwell there in twilight melancholy. Verhaeren is robust even when

---

[75] See his critical articles in *La Revue Indépendante* (1888) and the preface to *Livre d'images*.
[76] For short studies of these and other Symbolist poets, see R. de Gourmont, *Le Livre des Masques* and *Deuxième Livre des Masques*.

his mood is dark, as it often is. He is both a Realist and mystical.
Les Flamandes (1883) are vigorously realist:

> Ces hommes de labour, que Greuze affadissait
> Les voici noirs, grossiers, bestiaux – ils sont tels
>
> (*Les Paysans*)

Les Moines (1886), *Les Soirs* (1887), *Les Débâcles* (1888), *Les Flam-
beaux Noirs* (1890) are the record of spiritual tribulation and loss
of faith. The poet withdraws into himself but soon emerges from
the inner sanctuary to face society anew with its sadnesses – *Les
Campagnes hallucinées* (1893), *Les Villages illusoires* (1895) – and
its struggles – *Les Villes tentaculaires* (1895). The fervent soul
finds a new faith: the creative spirit of modern man, e.g. *Les
Visages de la vie* (1899), *La Multiple Splendeur* (1906), and an
idyllic peace in the happiness of home and country, e.g. *Les
Heures Claires* (1896), *Les Heures du Soir* (1911), *Les Blés Mouv-
ants* (1912), only to be shattered in the end by war – *Les Ailes
Rouges de la Guerre* (1916).

Verhaeren was as sensitive to the literary influences of his day
as to the life around him. He moved from Parnassianism through
the Symbolism of his middle period to the classicism which, as we
shall see, was to be another offshoot of the Symbolist movement,
but everywhere he sets the stamp of his originality; he has a magnifying eye; his figures have the proportions of those of Rubens;
his domestic series recall lesser Flemish masters. The most lasting
impression of Verhaeren is that of his native Flanders, the dark
plains a prey to the relentless wind like the hound of heaven:

> Les grand'routes tracent des croix
> Dans l'air livide et froid,
> Ou voyagent les vents déchevelés
> A l'infini, par les allées.
>
> ('Novembre', *Les Vignes de ma Muraille*)

The 'vers libristes' may justifiably be regarded as the central core
of the Symbolist movement, for in these poets are to be found its
essential characteristics in form and substance: the tyranny of
prosody in its traditional forms is rejected, particularly the alexandrines, in favour of unfettered rhythms, governed only by the
poet's individual ideas; rejected also is plastic descriptive and
narrative poetry. Poetic inspiration must flow from the soul, in
musical cadences, like song; delicate shades of meaning, pure sensation such as those of Impressionist pictures, reverie, these are the
stuff of poetry, expressing themselves in allusive symbols which
draw the reader's inner eye and give him an intuitive apprehension
of the idea behind them, a flight from the modern world – reality
– to the world of fantasy and medieval bric-à-brac, with corre-
sponding pleasure in verbal and syntactical archaisms.

Madame de Staël would no doubt have detected in all this the very characteristics of 'the literatures of the north'. What satisfaction she would have had in noting the number of Flemish poets amongst the 'vers libristes' group! And further support for this theory was in store, for here was another group of poets who, fleeing the misty north, were returning to the plastic beauty of 'southern literatures', and – oh joy! – its founder was a Greek!

Jean Moréas[77] (1856–1910) had started as a 'Decadent' (*Les Syrtes*, 1884), and had then become the champion of Symbolist theory.[78] His poems of this period – *Les Cantilènes* (1886) – have the free rhythms of the 'vers-libristes', and their inspiration, influenced now by medieval legends, now by Mallarmé-an ideas, shows the direction of Moréas's development. Soon this 'Pèlerin Passionné', as he styled himself, was founding the 'Romance School' which was to explore the ancient treasure-house of medieval French language and poetry – e.g. *Sylves* (1894). Nor was this the end of Moréas's poetic pilgrimage. The very word 'romance', in its linguistic sense, invites the poet to push his quest further into the past – the classical world opens before him. In *Les Stances* (1899) Moréas reaches the final stage of his poetic journey.

This rediscovery of classical beauty marks a breakaway from Symbolism. Many of the poets who had enjoyed some reputation in their own day[79] soon became anthology poets,[80] then merely names as members of the Symbolist movement. Nor has that been the end of the merciless time process; today, in the latter half of the twentieth century, Symbolism remains as a label covering a period of poetic ferment, but the majority of poets who took part in it have faded;[81] their cult of poetry was disinterested, but it quickly became too narrowly aesthetic to retain a permanent resonance; nothing can wither more quickly than poetry.

None the less, in the wake of their great forerunners – Mallarmé, Verlaine and Rimbaud, the Symbolists were an army of liberation from Parnassian and Naturalist domination, from traditional forms of prosody, from unimaginative use of words and narrowly rigorous syntax.

The most important avenue of escape from Naturalism in the drama was provided by the Symbolist movement, reflected on the stage in the work of Maurice Maeterlinck and Paul Claudel. None

[77] Born at Athens; real name Johannes Papadiamantopoulos.
[78] See above, p. 87.
[79] See R. de Gourmont, op. cit.
[80] e.g. A. van Bever et P. Léautaud, *Poètes d'Aujourd'hui, 1888–1900*.
[81] Poetic anthologies are primarily an indication of the anthologist's personal taste; Thierry Maulnier's anthology, *Introduction à La Poésie Française* (Gallimard, 1939), includes no 'Symbolist' poet; of the pre-Symbolists, neither Verlaine (scandalous!) nor Laforgue (understandable!).

better than they reveal the sense of dissatisfaction with the tyranny of Naturalism and its confining influence on the drama as a vehicle for expressing the human situation. Both belong to the generation which in various spheres – scientific, philosophical as well as literary – was calling into question the supremacy of science and reason.[82] 'Longtemps encore, toujours peut-être, nous ne serons que de précaires et fortuites lueurs, abandonnées sans dessein appréciable à tous les souffles d'une nuit indifférente.'[83] Maurice Maeterlinck (1862–1949) was sensitive to the mystery surrounding human life, to the mystery of death and destiny, of mind, of all the imponderables that weigh so heavy; his early plays, which form the bulk of his dramatic work, are largely inspired by them: e.g. La Princesse Maleine (1889), Les Aveugles (1890), L'Intruse (1890), Pelléas et Mélisande (1892), Intérieur (1894), La Mort de Tintagiles (1894).

The gloom and foreboding that these plays convey correspond with the pessimism of Maeterlinck's philosophy at the time; the little Princess Maleine is doomed to unhappiness and death; in all innocence she brings tragedy to those that love her; similarly the beautiful and passive Mélisande; in Les Aveugles death strikes the old priest and leaves the blind with none to guide them except a small child with sight but too young to help. Death is the principal character in L'Intruse, Intérieure and La Mort de Tintagiles, personified in the latter play by the wicked queen, unseen but active in the other two; in their several ways all the plays symbolize man's helplessness in the face of the hostile force surrounding him.

But then comes a shift in Maeterlinck's attitude; the fundamental pessimism remains, but he is ready to look for hope in life with all its insecure basis: 'Essayons ... de varier l'apparence de l'inconnu qui nous entoure et d'y découvrir une raison nouvelle de vivre et de persévérer ...'[84] Who knows but that our belief in the finality of death may be no more than an evidence of our ignorance: 'rien en elle n'est certain que notre ignorance.'[85]

This flicker of hope inspires Maeterlinck's activity in widely different fields. La Vie des Abeilles (1901), La Vie des Termites (1926), La Vie des Fourmis (1930), L'Intelligence des Fleurs (1907) may not be the work of a specialist in lepidoptera or flora, they betray rather the patient observation of the naturalist philosopher, a Teilhard de Chardin of an earlier generation in quest of significant patterns of life as a means of solving or at least interpreting the enigma at levels where life seems closest to the ultimate impulses. By the same token, Maeterlinck's interest in psychic

---

[82] See below, chap. 6.   [83] Maeterlinck, Théâtre, Vol. I, Preface.
[84] Ibid.   [85] Ibid.

research (e.g. *L'Hôte Inconnu*, 1917) suggests a desire to reach out to the fringes of experience where the known and the unknown merge into one another. The common factor is a sense of quest, quite absent from Maeterlinck's early dramatic work.

In the dramatic field Maeterlinck's changed attitude is marked by *Monna Vanna* (1902); the pale inert characters of the earlier plays give way to characters who know what they want and act in consequence. Human will is a reality; it cannot avoid tragedy but it pushes back the forces lying beyond human control, creates an area where it acts independently, in full knowledge and acceptance of the sacrifice required.

With *L'Oiseau bleu* (1909) Maeterlinck returns to the earlier Symbolist type of drama and yet the later sense of quest is here emphatic, the quest for happiness, momentarily within man's grasp but eluding him in the end; the sense of purpose, revealing the underlying earlier pessimism.

The Symbolist idiom was convenient for a sense of mystery in terms of the drama, but the results are uneven. *La Princesse Maleine*, with its gloomy castle, its dark forest, its fountains that suddenly cease playing, etc., creates a dreamy atmosphere, a 'climate', no more, where poetry may flower; the contact with human life and passions, provided by the scheming Queen of Jutland, is so slight that the symbolism of the play seems to have little human value and is reduced to matters of stagecraft. Much the same may be said of *Les Aveugles*, of *Pelléas et Mélisande*, of *L'Oiseau bleu*; in the first the symbol of the human situation is so general that it loses impact; in the second the atmosphere of *La Princesse Maleine* is again evident and though the human content is stronger through the jealousy of Golaud, the play is mainly re-membered as the libretto for Debussy's music; the third is a fantasy that fades away in its own mysteries, barring only the symbol of the blue bird of happiness. In all the plays the characters them-selves are mysterious, ill-defined; they have little or no individu-ality, they are merely means to emphasize the symbolic message. In contrast, where there is no symbol but instead a moral message, the characters are vigorously drawn – e.g. Monna Vanna.

Yet Maeterlinck's philosophy led him to make one original con-tribution to the theatre. The sense of mystery makes a real impact on us when it touches human experience closely, when, for ex-ample, death creeps in on a waiting household. In *L'Intruse* and *Intérieur* Maeterlinck has evoked such moments with skill. There are no stage tricks in *L'Intruse*; indirectly by what the characters say, by their silences – Maeterlinck's sense of mystery led him to discover the dramatic value of silence – the stealthy approach, the entry, the presence of the unwanted guest are successively apprehended. The impact is powerful enough for us not to feel the lack of characterization, deliberate in this case,[86] so as not to distract attention from the main theme, so powerful indeed that we are tempted to create, out of the anxious family, the room they are assembled in and the darkness outside, our own symbol of humanity enclosed by mystery.

From Maeterlinck to Claudel suggests a parallel with Rousseau and Chateaubriand. As Rousseau's religious feeling was rooted by Chateaubriand in the Christian faith, so the awe that Maeterlinck felt and sometimes communicates is transformed by Claudel into robust Christian belief.[87]

The novel as an art form did not provide congenial soil for Symbolism to take root in. Gide's efforts to write a Symbolist novel[88] are unimpressive. Only one name deserves mention in this context. Henri-Alban Fournier (1886–1914), to give him his real name,[89] was killed in September 1914, like his friend Péguy, who had predicted a great future for him: 'Fournier, vous irez loin, et vous vous rappellerez que c'est moi qui vous l'ai dit...' The prediction has turned out true, though doubtless not in the sense Péguy meant; Fournier has his permanent if small memorial in French literature: *Le Grand Meaulnes* (1913). The only other works of his published during his lifetime are a few essays.[90] His posthumous publications are a collection of poems, *Miracles*[91] (1924), and the four volumes of correspondence (1927) with his friend Jacques Rivière, the critic. Fragments of two other novels, *Colombe Blanchet* and *La Maison dans la Forêt*, also exist.

The correspondence is in the first place the touching record of a cloudless friendship that began on the benches of the Lycée Lakanal at Sceaux, when both delighted in the discovery of the Symbolist poets, notably Régnier: 'ni Racine, ni Rousseau, ni Chateaubriand, ni même Flaubert ne s'adressaient à nous, jeunes gens de 1903; ils parlaient à l'humanité universelle; ils n'avaient pas cette voix comme à l'avance dirigée vers notre cœur, que tout à coup Henri de Régnier nous fit entendre... Quelque chose d'inconnu était atteint dans nos âmes; une harpe que nous ne soupçonnions pas en nous s'éveillait.'[92] The letters which cover the years 1905 to July 1914 reveal the interest both writers shared in

[86] They have no names, merely status: L'Aimé, Le Père, L'Oncle, etc.
[87] For Claudel, see below, chap. 9, iii.   [88] See chap. 9, ii.
[89] He adopted the pen name Alain-Fournier, perhaps as a compliment to 'Alain' Chartier.
[90] In *La Grande Revue, L'Occident* and the *N.R.F.*, 1907–11.
[91] One poem, 'A travers les Etés', points towards *Le Grand Meaulnes*.
[92] J. Rivière. Quoted by M. J. Moore-Rinvolucri, *Modern Languages* (May 1947).

literature and on Alain-Fournier's side a man who was at once a keen observer and a sensitive idealist, characteristics that reappear in the author of *Le Grand Meaulnes*.

The keen observer has had but to look into his own past and evoke a host of sharply defined scenes and landscapes of his childhood, the peasants and villages he knew so well, to write what from one angle is a regionalist novel set in his native Sologne,[93] that melancholy country of sand, pinewoods and stretches of water, 'cher pays sauvage et inutile'.[94] François Seurel, the narrator in the novel, is Fournier, recalling his boyhood's memories, and Fournier the artist, deliberately applying his expressed principle on descriptive writing: 'Redonner chaque petit morceau de réel strictement tel qu'il s'est déposé en nous, sans rien de moins, mais peut-être surtout sans rien de plus. Et si l'image retrouvée, reconstituée, est absolument fidèle, elle doit éveiller chez le lecteur exactement les mêmes impressions que la réalité fait naître . . .'[95]

This authentic regionalist life, however, is enriched by the story of 'Le Grand Meaulnes' and at once the novel has a different dimension. Meaulnes's strange adventure, faintly reminiscent of Verlaine's *Fêtes Galantes*, at the mysterious domaine of 'Les Sablonnières', the vision of Yvonne de Galais, his quest in search of her, the ending on the brink of happiness, suddenly turned to tragedy, have a depth of pathos that recalls both Fromentin's *Dominique* with its equally pathetic 'might-have-beens', and the dream-like quality of Nerval's *Sylvie* where the same characteristics of tightly interwoven dream and clear-cut reality are evident. Meaulnes's love for Yvonne de Galais, like François Seurel's own story, is a transposition of Fournier's experience. Yvonne de Galais was not a figment of his imagination but a girl of that name whom he had seen in 1905 at the Petit Palais picture gallery in Paris, followed as though spellbound, had briefly spoken to later, only to see her vanish again into her world of human relationships he had no contacts with. An authentic experience, an intense joy falling to ashes, leaving him numbly unable to recall the girl's face, clutching at a vision at once beautiful and poignant: 'Je voudrais parler de mon amour. A cette heure, j'ai à peu près perdu son visage, il ne me reste que son expression et sa beauté. . . . A moi qui demandais un grand amour impossible et lointain, cet amour est venu. Et maintenant je souffre . . .'[96] Thereafter there are several allusions to the event, in the correspondence. Eight years

[93] He was born at La Chapelle d'Angillon where his father and mother ran the village school.
[94] *Correspondance*, Vol. IV. To J. Rivière, 12 September 1908.
[95] Quoted by M. J. M-R., op. cit.
[96] *Correspondance*, Vol. III. To J.R., 21 January 1907.

later he has not forgotten it: 'Hier était le huitième anniversaire du jour où j'ai rencontré Yvonne de Galais...'[97]

What more natural than for an experience so mysterious, perhaps so miraculous, to take on in retrospect the character of a nostalgic dream? What more natural than the wish to objectify in fiction an experience so charged with emotion, and thus perhaps break its spell? And so Meaulnes, who in many respects is a solidly planted character possibly modelled on some other boy Fournier had known at the primary school, steps out of the real world of the village into the mysterious world of 'Les Sablonnières' and seems thereafter to live and act as though in a waking dream.

Nor is this all, for the whole adventure, both rooted in reality and fairy-like, seems charged with a symbolic significance for Fournier. Just at the moment when Meaulnes's cup of happiness is filled, it is dashed from his lips. Much as Hernani obeys the call to death from the distant horn, so Meaulnes leaves his wife in obedience to Franz's anguished cry for help. That 'Houhou' from the depths of the wood has an authentic air about it – a memory of childhood surely? – but its mysterious compelling force on Meaulnes, though subsequently accounted for, is the weakest part of the story: it seems to reflect Fournier's own conviction that he was not himself destined to find happiness in this life. 'Ce que Jacques dit de mon enfance est très vrai et très beau. Meaulnes, le grand Meaulnes, le héros de mon livre, est un homme dont l'enfance fut trop belle. Pendant toute son adolescence, il la traîne après lui. Par instants, il semble que tout ce paradis imaginaire qui fut le monde de son enfance va surgir au bout de ses aventures, ou se lever sur un de ses gestes. Ainsi le matin d'hiver où, après trois jours d'absence inexplicable, il rentre à son cours comme un jeune dieu mystérieux et insolent. – Mais il sait déjà que ce paradis ne peut plus être. Il a renoncé au bonheur. Il est dans le monde comme quelqu'un qui va s'en aller.'[98]

There are those who enjoy Le Grand Meaulnes for its solid rustic qualities; in those who know Sologne, Fournier's soberly beautiful evocations will surely call forth an immediate response. Others enjoy its idealism, its delicate unreality and poignancy so reminiscent of the Symbolists. The one form of enjoyment does not necessarily exclude the other, but to the extent that the latter may leave an image of an Orpheus weeping inconsolably for his lost Eurydice, that image is not the true one of Fournier: 'Hier était

[97] *Ibid.*, Vol. IV. To J.R., 2 May 1913.
[98] *Ibid.*, Vol. IV. Letter to J.R., 4 April 1910. Though addressed to Jacques, the letter is evidently meant for both him and his wife, Isabelle, Alain-Fournier's sister.

le huitième anniversaire du jour où j'ai rencontré Yvonne de Galais... Il est terrible d'avouer que je ne suis pas complètement désespéré quand même. Je ne puis croire que Dieu m'a tant montré, tant promis et ne me donnera rien – en ce monde, ou dans *l'autre*, il est vrai.'[99] He had found another love.[100]

[99] *Ibid.*, Vol. IV. Letter previously quoted to J.R., 2 May 1913.
[100] See Mme Simone, *Sous de nouveaux Soleils*, last chapter: 'Histoire d'une amitié et d'un amour'.

Part II

Nineteenth-century Twilight and
New Trends (1890–1940)

§ I THE REVOLT AGAINST SCIENCE
(1890–1914)

Chapter 5

POLITICAL
AND INTELLECTUAL BACKGROUND

THE last decade of the nineteenth century, the early years of the twentieth were a brilliant moment – France had taken her place once more amongst the great powers, she had taken a successful part in the colonial race and carved out an Empire second only in extent to the British, she had formed an alliance with Russia and soon, thanks to the vision of Delcassé, ably seconded by an able diplomat,[1] the Franco-Russian alliance was to be immensely strengthened by the Entente Cordiale. The Republic had not only weathered the storms, including the Dreyfus Affair – the last and most dangerous one, but had grown stronger as a result, firmly implanted now in the loyalties of the majority – politicians, civil servants (the real centre of power), the masses. Presently (1902) the Radical-Socialist party was to win the elections[2] – and seal republican unity by the renewed attack on the Church. Thanks to the Concordat (1802), the Catholic Church was 'established', thanks to the Loi Falloux (1850) and the measures taken in the years immediately after 1870, the Church and the Religious Orders in particular had a powerful influence in the educational system; at the end of the nineteenth century the Church and the Religious Orders seemed the only important element still remaining of moral opposition to the Republic; thus, to expel the Orders and denounce the Concordat would at one stroke rid the body politic of its last 'impure' elements.

The 'Loi sur les Associations' (1903) and the separation of Church and State (1905) were seen not so much as an attack upon the liberties of individuals and conscience, as measures designed to ensure the moral unity of the nation. Thus would internal peace be forged, founded on a single and single-minded educational system for the young and a communion of all, in republican philosophy.

[1] Paul Cambon.

[2] And keep power, incidentally, as the core of all those ministerial reconstructions that were so marked a feature of the Third Republic, until 1936, when Léon Blum and the Socialists took the lead, at the head of the 'Front Populaire'.

The only cloud on the political horizon was Germany. Busy with the development of her industrial and military power, she had started late in the colonial race and felt defrauded of her 'place in the sun'. The shadow of the German menace was to grow longer after 1905,[3] but although men were not lacking to foretell war,[4] to feel disquiet at the relative strengths of France and Germany, both in population and industrial power, France could at least feel secure under the umbrella of the Triple Entente.[5]

Socially the scene was no less brilliant. On a lesser scale perhaps than in Edwardian England, the prosperity none the less was great; Paris, one of the great capitals of the world; the Exhibition of 1900 seemed the climax and symbol of the prevailing euphory. Nor do material joys necessarily mean intellectual stagnation; in fact, the period was full of intellectual ferment; there was a sense of quest for something to replace what Zola had called 'la grande poésie noire de Schopenhauer',[6] which had had its day; the 'taedium vitae' of the Decadents and their refuge in aestheticism could no longer satisfy; in euphoric times men are not usually inward-looking.

But Schopenhauer had left his mark none the less; we have alluded to the puerilities of 'Sâr' Péladan; even these show a more positive attitude to the great mysteries than the 'contracting out' of the Decadents – perhaps, who knows, occultism or a black Mass may be the key that unlocks the gates? More important however is the post-Schopenhauer discontent with science; external reality is an illusion, Schopenhauer had pointed out; science deals with matter, analyses, dissects it, breaks it down into its elements, accumulates data about it, but in the end what more does it do than express the great illusion in intellectual terms? Life in the meantime escapes through the meshes of this static net, without yielding up its secret; nor does science provide us with moral values, something to live by or for.

In an article[7] that caused a stir at the time, Brunetière echoed these discontents and proclaimed the bankruptcy of science: 'ce sont des philosophes', he writes, 'qui ont enfin le courage de dire: 'ma science n'empêche point mon ignorance de la réalité d'être absolue ... langage symbolique, admirable système de signes ... plus la science progresse, plus elle s'éloigne de la réalité pour s'enfoncer dans l'abstraction ... La croyance au contraire ne se repaît pas d'abstractions mais de réalités et ... tend à l'action.' Brunetière himself became a Catholic, nor was his an isolated

---

[3] 'Coup de Tanger'.   [4] cf. Péguy. See below, p. 109.
[5] The Entente Cordiale extended to include Russia.
[6] La Joie de Vivre, chap. 3.
[7] See Revue des deux mondes, 15 October 1896: 'Les bases de la Croyance'.

case. The religious revival is a vital feature of the period, a revival, eager as previous revivals were not,[8] to put faith to the test of historical and archaeological research,[9] of philosophic thought.[10]

The new climate is particularly well reflected in the philosophy of Henri Bergson (1859–1941). The essential ideas of his philosophy are to be found in his thesis, *Essai sur les données immédiates de la conscience* (1889), and in *Matière et Mémoire – Essai sur la relation du corps à l'esprit* (1896). These works had established him in philosophical circles; his influence spread to wider intellectual and social spheres when he was appointed to a chair at the Collège de France (1900), and drew crowded audiences to his lectures by the brilliance of his style and eloquence. The seal on his public reputation was set by his *Introduction à la métaphysique* (1903) and especially by *L'Evolution Créatrice* (1906).[11] Bergson appeared to offer a way of escape from the 'impasse' to which reason and the scientific spirit seemed to lead – reason by its modes of thinking offers us only an unending series of concepts; concepts are static and finite, they can do no more than render things intelligible to us, they do not enable us to seize the underlying truths. A critique of the notion of time[12] shows the difference between rational concepts and underlying reality. Time is an arbitrary construction, indispensable certainly to our needs as human beings in a material world and in society, but it does not properly express the true nature of life which is continuous movement; the notion of time is like a series of isolated dots, it is spatial, quantitative; life is like an ever-flowing stream from which every attribute is removed except the essential qualitative notion of movement; time is a static concept; life's essential quality is 'la durée', not only on the biological level where the 'élan vital' exercises a continuous pressure to express itself in living forms, but also on the level of the psyche. 'La durée toute pure est la forme que prend la succession de nos états de conscience quand notre moi se laisse vivre, quand il s'abstient d'établir une séparation entre l'état présent et

---

[8] e.g., Chateaubriand, Lamennais.

[9] e.g. Mgr Louis Duchesne (1843–1922).

[10] e.g. Maurice Blondel (1861–1949), author of *L'Action* (1893), much influenced by the pragmatism of William James; also the Oratorian Father Laberthonnière (1860–1932), editor of *Les Annales de la Philosophie Chrétienne*, and the Dominican Father Sertillanges (1863–1948), who, together with Blondel and Edouard Le Roy (1870–1954), philosopher and mathematician, defended 'fidéisme' (so-called because of its emphasis on the core of faith in religion); the prevailing climate of Bergsonism was favourable to the development of their ideas.

[11] Other works: *Le Rire* (1900), *Les Deux sources de la morale et de la religion* (1932), *La Pensée et le mouvant* (1934). The last named is a collection of essays (1903–23) with an introduction in two parts, which provides a useful guide to his leading ideas.

[12] *Les Données immédiates de la conscience*.

les états antérieurs.'[13] If we are to achieve a satisfactory apprehension of the nature of existence, we must abandon metaphysicians and sensualists or empiricists and rely on intuition. Bergson's distinction between time and duration is the starting point
for his theory of the psyche, a spiritualist theory, freed from all
taint of determinism. In *Matière et Mémoire* he examines the
faculty of memory in relation to the body and again, on the basis
of his theory of the spiritual nature of 'la durée', rejects the idea
that memory is primarily like a series of photographic plates stored
up in the brain cells. From psychology Bergson moves in *L'Evolution Créatrice* to a consideration of all life, all living organisms
propelled by the triumphant upward thrust of the 'élan vital'
against the downward pull of matter. There are moments when
Bergson seems more of a poet than a philosopher: 'Comme le
plus petit grain de poussière est solidaire de notre système solaire
tout entier, entraîné avec lui dans ce mouvement indivisé de
descente qui est la matérialité même, ainsi tous les êtres organisés,
du plus humble au plus élevé, depuis les premières origines de la
vie jusqu'au temps où nous sommes et dans tous les lieux comme
dans tous les temps, ne font que rendre sensible aux yeux une
impulsion unique, inverse du mouvement de la matière et, en
elle-même, indivisible. Tous les vivants se tiennent, et tous cèdent
à la même formidable poussée – l'animal prend son point d'appui
sur la plante, l'homme chevauche sur l'animalité et l'humanité
entière, dans l'espace et dans le temps, est une immense armée qui
galope à côté de chacun de nous, en avant et en arrière de nous,
dans une charge entraînante capable de culbuter toutes les résist-
ances et de franchir bien des obstacles, même peut-être la mort.'[14]

Proclaiming as it does the spiritual nature of experience, providing thereby a channel of escape from materialism, biological
determinism and a chance to re-conquer spiritual freedom, Bergson's philosophy and its triumphantly lyrical description of the
'élan vital', which suggests much the same conception as the
divine creative power, encouraged the religious revival.[15] All
branches of life were affected; in politics there were Bergsonians
of the Right and Bergsonians of the Left. On the Right, Nationalists and Patriots who, ignoring Bergson's origins,[16] hailed him as a
glorious French phenomenon able to counter nefarious German
philosophical influences; military thinkers who held that as the
'élan vital' was the idea of a French philosopher it must be a
peculiarly French characteristic and pinned their faith to the
'élan'[17] of the French soldier as a counterweight to German

---

[13] *Ibid.*, chap. 2.   [14] *Evolution Créatrice*, chap. 3, conclusion.
[15] 'Dédouaner la religion' was the current description.
[16] He was a Polish Jew.   [17] The 'vital' was conveniently dropped.

superiority in numbers.[18] On the Left, Syndicalist thought also seized on the revolutionary 'élan' of the workers' 'élite', inspired by the myth, in the Sorelian[19] sense, of the 'General Strike' and direct action, to compensate for the weakness in organization of French trade unions.

In literature, Proust immediately springs to mind, with his recapture of the past as a continuum of personal experience, but, in a general way, a philosophy that emphasized the inner spiritual nature of reality, liberated the creative instinct from the slavery of rationalist construction and encouraged esotericism; latter-day Symbolists, Alain-Fournier, Proust, Apollinaire, post-impressionists, Fauvistes, Surrealists would have existed, without Bergson, but Bergsonism encouraged their view that art and literature were not to be a reflection of superficial reality, but inner creative exploration and the communication of spiritual experience.

The influence of Friedrich Nietzsche (1844–1900), which began to be felt from 1900,[20] is as important as Bergson's. For those who were dissatisfied with science, at least to the extent of finding there no incentive for living, but who were not on that account willing to accept faith, the ideas of Nietzsche provided the moral stimulus they needed. Nietzsche, with his Lutheran background, had intended to be a pastor, but his loss of faith not only prevented him pursuing that course, but led to his building a philosophy that was both an attack on Christianity and a kind of moral counterpoint to it. The idea of a world without God had appalled him; he had found joy for a time in the philosophy of Schopenhauer[21] and the ideas of Wagner,[22] but in the end Nietzsche came to preach a doctrine of individual self-reliance. For Christian morality, source, as he came to believe, of false moral values, of mediocrity and weakness, he substituted the morality of the Superman, of the strong, creative spirit, of the joy in Nature and the Earth,[23] of the 'Will to Power' which is supreme good, whereas all that is weak is bad; Christianity is not only false but harmful because it teaches pity for the weak and the idea of equal rights, inexistent in Nature.

Since God is non-existent and with him has gone sin and a moral

[18] A factor in the doctrine of the 'Offensive', so costly to the French in the early stages of the 1914 war. See M. Earle, *Modern France* (chapter on 'The concept of *Elan Vital*. A rationalization of weakness' by J. Bowditch).

[19] Georges Sorel (1857–1922), author of *Réflexions sur la Violence* (1908).

[20] See van Tieghem, *Les Influences Etrangères sur la Littérature Française*, p. 236.

[21] See Bonifazi, *Christendom attacked* (1953), chap. 3.

[22] Bonifazi, op. cit., chap. 3.   [23] cf. Gide, *Nourritures Terrestres*.

order, 'nothing remains except that man himself, by a titanic effort and infinite heroism, should make life mean something to which, with his whole being, he can say 'Yes'.[24]

Here was a doctrine to put heart into a man. Since science could not penetrate to the core of life, the only way to get there was by direct experience, by living life to the full and on an heroic level. The impact of this new gospel was probably more powerful than Bergson's idea of 'l'élan vital'. The latter had its value as a new spiritualist interpretation of life, but there is still something static about an interpretation, however refreshing; Nietzsche provided a philosophy of action and his influence was to spread to politics and literature. The monarchism of Charles Maurras and the *Action Française* group admittedly owes more to traditionalist thinkers, notably Bonald, more recently the sociologist Pierre Le Play (1806-82); but the nationalism of Barrès, with its effort to tap the deepest springs of national energy, the heroic anti-intellectualism of Péguy, the 'fervour' of Gide, all bear the Nietzschean stamp. Nor was Nietzsche's influence to be limited to the first decade of the new century; we shall find it active in the years after the First World War and later as a source of Existentialism. Whilst Naturalists, Symbolists and their 'epigoni' were slowly going into liquidation at the end of the nineteenth century, Bergson and Nietzsche stand at the threshold of the twentieth.[25]

[24] Bonifazi, op. cit., chap. 4.
[25] As a commentary on the attitude of the younger generation of the day, see *Jean Barois*, Part III, the discussion between Barois and his young interviewers Tillet and Grenneville.

Chapter 6

NEO-SYMBOLISTS AND OTHERS

THE new intellectual climate was not favourable to Symbolism; away with esotericism and etiolated pessimism! The poetic torrent of Symbolism splits up into a collection of minor rivulets. The host of post-Symbolist poets may not have been ready for the bold explorations that were to mark the post-war years and of which signs were soon to appear in other arts,[1] but, tired of 'inwardness', they were beginning to look outwards once more, tired of aesthetic sophistication, they were to find refreshment in simplicity.

Moréas's 'Romance School' attracted a number of quondam Symbolists: e.g. Ernest Raynaud (1864–1936), Maurice du Plessys (1864–1924), Raymond de la Tailhède (1867–1938), Pierre Quillard (1864–1912), the pagan Charles Maurras (1868–1952), whose innate classicism or 'Mediterraneanism' was revealed to him in a quasi-mystical experience,[2] and most notably Henri de Régnier (1864–1936).

Other poets, as could be expected, found refreshing pastures in a return to Nature; Maurice Le Blond (*Essai sur le Naturisme*, 1895), Saint-Georges de Bouhélier (1867–1947) interpret 'le naturisme' not in a Rousseauist sense of a flight to Nature as consolation for the hostility of man, but as a glorification of Nature and man's place in it: 'Nous chanterons les hautes fêtes de l'homme. Pour la splendeur de ce spectacle, nous convoquerons les étoiles et le vent. Une littérature viendra qui glorifiera les marins, les laboureurs nés des entrailles du sol et les pasteurs qui habitent près des aigles.'[3]

Francis Jammes (1868–1938) finds joy in evoking the beauties of his native Béarn, and presently (1906) his conversion to Catholicism was to provide his deliberately naïve Virgilian poetry with a new inspiration;[4] the same, but in a minor key, applies to Charles

---

[1] e.g. Futurism and cubism in painting; the impact of the Russian ballet; the music of Stravinsky.
[2] See *Antinéa* (1911), *passim.*
[3] St G. de B., quoted by Pierre-Henri Simon, *Hist. de la Litt. Contemp.*, Vol. I, p. 62.
[4] e.g. *Les Géorgiques Chrétiennes* (1911–12).

Guérin (1873–1907); Louis Le Cardonnel (1862–1936) is a purely religious poet.[5]

Another group – 'Les Fantaisistes' – of which P. J. Toulet (1867–1920)[6] was the chief, and Tristan Derême (1889–1941), J. Pellerin (1885–1941), J. M. Bernard (1881–1915) members, mingled humour with their themes, deliberately simple and objective: the joys of friendship, the bitter-sweet joys of love, the passing of time.

Prominent amongst a number of poetesses[7] is Anna de Noailles (1876–1933), in whose fervent and discreetly sensual poetry a pantheistic Romanticism in the vein now of Lamartine, now of Hugo, reappears, but with no religious echo:

> J'affirme, . . .
> Qu'il n'est rien qui survive à la chaleur des veines!
> (*L'Honneur de souffrir*, VI, 1927.)

thus death and total extinction are the spur to poetry:

> J'écris pour que le jour où je ne serai plus
> On sache comme l'air et le plaisir m'ont plu . . .
> (*Le Coeur innombrable*, 1901)

Another aspect of the return, in the pre-war years, to a broad and simple humanism is provided by the group of artists and writers who formed themselves (1906) into a lay monastic community at the Abbaye de Créteil: Raymond Arcos (b. 1881), Charles Vildrac (b. 1883), Georges Duhamel[8] (b. 1884), G. Chennevière (1884–1921), Luc Durtain (b. 1881) and others. In *L'Etape nécessaire* (1906) Durtain wrote the group's manifesto; Jules Romains (b. 1885) was in contact with them later (1909). He had already felt the appeal inherent both in Zola's novels of men's collective struggles, and in Verhaeren's poetry of the mysterious life of human communities; he it was that gave the Abbaye group their 'charter', and their ideas a name, in his poems (*La Vie unanime*, 1908; *Prières*, 1909).

The effort to escape from the traditional framework of bourgeois attitudes and the inevitable individualism of the cultivated man, back to the earthiness of the simple life, the compassion for the poor and the humble, points to the source of the 'Unanimists'' design for living – Tolstoy; their joy in fraternal solidarity, their belief in the divine nature of collective effort as a source of poetry derive from Walt Whitman.

The 'Unanimists' are interesting as a sign of the new-found op-

---

[5] *Poèmes* (1904), *Carmina Sacra* (1912).   [6] *Contrerimes* (1921).
[7] *Inter alia* Renée Vivien (1877–1909), Lucie Delarue-Mardrus (1880–1945), Catherine Pozzi (1882–1934).
[8] Duhamel, Pasquier series, Vol. V, *Le désert de Bièvre*.

timism that was beginning to recapture some poets' allegiance
before the outbreak of war was to smother it.

Equally characteristic and much more important because so
deeply nourished by the new spiritual aspirations of his generation
is Charles Péguy (1873–1914); his *Cahiers de la Quinzaine* are at
the very heart of the intellectual, religious, social and literary questions, of the controversies from the Dreyfus Affair to the outbreak
of the 1914 war. Yet, paradoxically, this robust and noble character, both publicist and poet, is less well-known in England than he
deserves. Even in France his reputation, though secure, is perhaps
more due to events than to his having won, like his contemporary
Claudel, a large audience. The reason is that those wishing to find
Péguy must seek him in a mass of unrelated writings that are a
burning commentary on current events and attitudes; the massive
volumes invite the surgery of abridgment and 'selected passages',
which they have duly received.[9]

Brought up in poverty by a widowed mother, Péguy had won
his way by scholarships to the Ecole Normale Supérieure itself
(1894). In the process he had built for himself that solid foundation
of classical and modern scholarship that enabled him to write with
such penetrative understanding of Greek literature,[10] of Cornelian tragedy,[11] of philosophy;[12] he had discovered Romain
Rolland, and Bergson to whose thought he remained permanently
attached.

That he was able to climb to the top of the intellectual ladder
was due, apart from his natural gifts, to the educational system of
the Third Republic, of which the principal builder was Jules Ferry,
and the chance it offered to clever boys from the poorest homes.
Yet this brilliant product of the system showed no affection for his
alma mater; he had left the Ecole Normale prematurely, to the
Sorbonne he was always hostile, because he suspected in the pun-
dits of that ancient house the faults of the intellectual: the pedantry
that reduces scholarship to a deadening soulless process of documentation (M. Lanson's 'fiches') instead of its being a guide and inspiration for life; the habit of thinking that knowing is as good as
doing, of contracting out of life instead of committing yourself to
it body and soul as Péguy did, and perhaps of a certain intellectual
arrogance, bred of critical ability and knowledge. None better than
Péguy reflects the anti-intellectualism of the day, which is an aspect
of the revolt against science. Thus, at the outset of his career, we

[9] *Morceaux Choisis – Prose*; *Morceaux Choisis – Poésie*. N.R.F.
[10] *Cahiers*, VII, 7, *Les Suppliants parallèles*.
[11] *Oeuvres posth.*, N.R.F. (1923). *Note conjointe sur M. Descartes et la Philosophie Cartésienne.*
[12] *Cahiers*, VIII, 11, 'Bar-Cochebas'.

see Péguy, rightly or wrongly, cutting himself off from the academic world he could have belonged to – a first step along the road
of spiritual isolation he was to tread.

After leaving the Ecole Normale, he had started a socialist book-
shop, which quickly foundered, and he had married (1897); then
his true vocation was revealed to him by the Dreyfus Case, which,
though it had begun in 1894, did not burst into flame until Zola's
intervention with *J'accuse* (1898). Péguy became a Dreyfusiste and
founded a periodical (January 1900) which initially was intended
as a forum for discussion of all the problems raised by 'l'Affaire'.
'Nous demandons simplement', he wrote in a passage characteristic
of his style and attitudes, 'qu'on dise la vérité, rien que la vérité!
Dire la vérité, toute la vérité, rien que la vérité; dire bêtement la
vérité bête, ennuyeusement la vérité ennuyeuse, tristement la vérité
triste . . .' Péguy's socialist friends gave the *Cahiers de la Quinzaine*
six months at most; they reckoned without Péguy's doggedness;
surrender on any front was foreign to Péguy; the six months
stretched to fourteen years, precarious though survival sometimes
was; the *Cahiers* are the central pillar of Péguy's life, his chief
memorial.

Socialism, for Péguy, was an ideal of human solidarity and love;
no one has written more movingly of grinding poverty ('la misère'):
'On confond presque toujours la misère avec la pauvreté; cette
confusion vient de ce que la misère et la pauvreté sont voisines . . .'[13]
Not the economic, but the moral aspect of the problem was Péguy's
concern; the redistribution of wealth was a matter of no importance: 'autant il est passionnant, inquiétant de savoir qu'il y a encore des hommes dans la misère, autant il m'est égal de savoir si
hors de la misère, les hommes ont des morceaux plus ou moins
grands de fortune; je ne puis parvenir à me passionner pour la
question célèbre de savoir à qui reviendront, dans la cité future, les
bouteilles de champagne, les chevaux rares, les châteaux de la
vallée de la Loire; j'espère qu'on s'arrangera toujours; pourvu
qu'il y ait vraiment une cité, c'est-à-dire pourvu qu'il n'y ait aucun
homme qui soit banni de la cité . . .'

He soon discovered his socialist friends to be politicians, concerned
with party discipline, public opinion, parliamentary strategy, power,
all things that may need or at any rate invite compromise with
principle or conscience. Such things were not for Péguy; socialism
as he understood it – yes, the socialists – no! A further reason for
his divorce from them was provided by 'l'Affaire'. In the early
days, few Frenchmen were on Dreyfus's side; those who think that

---

[13] *Cahiers*, IV, 3, 4 November 1902. This essay is a commentary on
Jean Coste by Louis Lavergne, which portrays the poverty of many primary
school teachers of the day.

from the outset the issue was a straight one between the Right (Church, army, high society, the 'Establishment' in a word) and the Left (radicals, radical-socialists, socialists, Jews, free-thinkers, intellectuals) are wrong. The radicals and radical-socialists, as the spiritual descendants of the Jacobins, were patriots who believed Dreyfus to be a spy; the socialists thought of him as a capitalist (splendid syllogism; all Jews are capitalists, Dreyfus is a Jew; *ergo* ...); even the ranks of French Jewry tended to be against this black sheep, as they believed, who was bringing trouble and discredit upon them. Only slowly did the Right-Left pattern emerge; the socialists rallied to Dreyfus. Péguy, however, was far from making up his quarrel with them on that account; in *Notre Jeunesse* (1910), one of the greatest of his pamphlets, he tells us why: two distinct phases succeeded each other in the case: the first, the only pure one, was that of the Dreyfusistes; the second, that of the Dreyfusards, who climbed on to the band-waggon for what they could get out of it – to wit, for the Left, the discomfiture of the Roman Church, the separation of Church and State, the consolidation of 'l'Etat laïque' – the old story: ideals, when they get administratively organized, become sordid interest, 'mystique' fades, 'politics' begin: 'la mystique républicaine, c'était quand on mourait pour la République, la politique républicaine, c'est a' présent qu'on en vit.'[14] Thus Péguy became an outcast or rather cast himself out from amongst the socialists, as well as the intellectuals. By 1905, the Dreyfus case, with its consequences – 'Loi sur les Associations', expulsion of the Religious Orders, separation, was passing slowly into the wings. But another crisis burst, this time on the international scene: Tangier, the Kaiser's histrionics, the German press campaign against Delcassé. Prophetically, Péguy saw that war lay somewhere along this road. The patriotism of the peasant springing to the defence of his soil was at once awake in him.[15]

Since the days of General Boulanger[16] patriotism had been a theme of the Right; was Péguy then to find new friends in that camp? Not at all; the patriotism of the Right was infected with 'Maurrasism'; the idea of France, for Maurras, was an intellectual concept that meant expulsion from the French 'family', of Jews, Protestants and generally 'métèques' of all kinds. Péguy's patriotism excluded no one, was solidly republican, neither nationalistic nor aggressive; merely far-seeing, and personally dedicated.[17]

No wonder that with it should have flowered his cult of Joan of Arc. In 1897 he had finished a verse play called *Jeanne d'Arc*; as the dedicatory verses show, its inspiration was humanistic and

[14] *Notre Jeunesse, Oeuvres Complètes*, N.R.F. Vol. 4, p. 250.
[15] *Notre Patrie* (1905).   [16] 'Boulangisme' (1886–92 approx.).
[17] He was killed near Villeroy, in the battle of the Marne.

vaguely socialist; he now recast the play and renamed it *Le Mystère de la Charité de Jeanne d'Arc* (1910). The figure of the 'Maid of Orleans' had become immensely precious to him. Orleans, his native town, the scene of one of the Maid's achievements, the peasant girl, in whom all the values Péguy held to seemed enshrined: charity, patriotism, a sense of mission, and, in line with the ideas of the Catholic revival, of personal sacrifice for the purchase of others' salvation, spiritual voices that brought her comfort, furthermore a simple faith, and, withal, commonsense, earthy realism. Péguy, without renouncing his former ideals, enriching them on the contrary by a sort of Bergsonian creative evolution, had returned to the Christian faith (1908); his new play reflects this. Yet, here again, for a variety of reasons[18] he did not seek a haven in the Catholic Church: a certain degree of anticlericalism, his refusal to enter a fold whence so many were excluded by the attitudes of Catholics themselves, and condemned to damnation – 'Je marche avec les juifs parce qu'avec les juifs je peux être catholique; avec les catholiques je ne le pourrais pas.'[19] Amongst the number, incidentally, were his wife, faithful to the views they had shared at the time of their marriage, and his children, who were not baptized. His intellectual position was therefore complicated by a personal tragedy. His faith remained individual, non-conforming, a matter of private prayer and Christian charity, of supplication to the Virgin as mediatrix.

Thus, to the end, Péguy remained spiritually isolated: a scholar against the intellectuals, a socialist against the party, a patriot against the nationalists, a Christian outside the Church, always in the very 'eye' of the polemical storms that divided intellectuals from reactionaries, Catholics from anti-clericals, patriots from pacifists; to this fact his *Cahiers de la Quinzaine* bear testimony.

His *Mystère de la Charité de Jeanne d'Arc* enjoyed some success; the war and his death in battle brought increased attention to his work. The publication of the complete works[20] was another step. The Vichy régime tried at one moment to exploit his cult for Joan of Arc, but the man who had written 'Tous les régimes de faiblesse, tous les régimes de capitulation devant l'ennemi sont aussi ceux des plus grands massacres de la population militaire et de la population civile. Rien n'est meurtrier comme la faiblesse et la lâcheté'[21] was difficult to bring into line. The 'Resistance' and the post-war years were his without reservation. Today, at last, he is established as one of the moral forces likely to remain permanent, because what

---

[18] See R. P. Duploye, *La Religion de Péguy* (Paris, Klingcksieck, 1965).
[19] Quoted by R. P. Congar, *Le Monde*, 17 August 1965.
[20] N.R.F. edition, started in 1920.
[21] *Cahiers*, XIV, 9: 'L'Argent (suite)', 1913.

Péguy writes rings true. But his style, which is as distinctive as that of Proust, does not make access to him easy; abundant, deliberately repetitive, it moves as slowly as a deep broad river. Like a cunning peasant, Péguy never comes straight to his point; he likes a circuitous route; his eloquence builds up steadily, circles and eddies round a subject, goes back to the starting point, starts off on the same and yet not quite the same track; he enjoys words, can be funny,[22] or cruelly ironical,[23] powerful or prolix.

His poetry has the same character as his prose; at times movingly eloquent and incantatory:

> Adieu, Meuse endormeuse et douce à mon enfance
> Qui demeures aux prés, où tu coules tout bas . . .[24]

or again:

> Heureux ceux qui sont morts pour la terre charnelle,
> Mais pourvu que ce fût dans une juste guerre.
> Heureux ceux qui sont morts dans les grandes batailles,
> Couchés dessus le sol à la face de Dieu . . .[25]

at others deliberately naïve and homely:

> Je comprends très bien, dit Dieu, qu'on fasse son
> examen de conscience.
> C'est un excellent exercise . . .[26]

at others overweighted with words; it has no relation to the poetry of his contemporaries, except the prosody which varies from rhythmical prose to free verse or regular alexandrines, but everything to do with the values, human and spiritual, he lived and died for: Joan of Arc, France, the Christian virtues of faith, hope and charity, the power of prayer, the intercession of the Saints, of the Virgin Mary, all these are the stuff of his poetic inspiration in, for example, *Jeanne d'Arc* (1896–7), *Le Mystère de la Charité de Jeanne d'Arc* (1910), *Le Porche du Mystère de la deuxième vertu* (1911), *Le Mystère des Saints Innocents* (1912), *La Tapisserie de Sainte Geneviève et de Jeanne d'Arc* (1913), *La Tapisserie de Notre Dame* (1913), *Eve* (1913); human beings – Joan of Arc, Saint Geneviève, material things – the Cathedral of Chartres, the cornfields of Beauce stretching out like a golden sea – all are informed

---

[22] e.g. his portrait of Jaurès, prominent Socialist and brilliant orator (d. 1914): 'Il m'expliquait toujours tout cela. Il expliquait toujours tout. Il savait admirablement tout expliquer . . .'. 'Courrier de Russie' (*Oeuvres Complètes*, N.R.F., Vol. 2, p. 358).

[23] e.g. his attack on Fernand Laudet, 'Un nouveau théologien', or on C. V. Langlois, in 'Langlois tel qu'on le parle' (*Oeuvres*, N.R.F., Vol. 13).

[24] *Jeanne d'Arc*, 1896–7.

[25] *Eve. Prière pour nous autres Charnels. Cahiers*, XV, 4 (1913).

[26] *Mystère des Saints Innocents* (1912).

with God's purpose; the word made flesh, for only so can it be understood:

> Car le surnaturel est lui-même charnel
> Et l'arbre de la grâce est racine profonde
> Et plonge dans le sol et cherche jusqu'au fond
> Et l'arbre de la race est lui-même éternel.[27]

[27] *Eve*, 'La double racination'.

Chapter 7

'COMMITTED' WRITERS AND OTHERS

WHILST Zola's successors continued with diminishing returns to work the seams of Naturalism, other novelists sought to reflect the intellectual currents and fervours of the day and became in effect 'committed' writers for whom the novel was not so much a form of art as a form of action; from here to didacticism is a short step, mostly taken by the writers in question who, like Péguy but in a different field, remain closely integrated with their age.

At first sight Léon Bloy (1846–1917) does not appear to conform to the above description, standing as he does isolated in the landscape, like an erratic block of granite, blackened by fire from heaven, isolated by what he believed with some reason to be a conspiracy of silence on the part of contemporary writers.

Brought up as a free-thinker, Bloy had become a Catholic under the influence of Barbey d'Aurevilly, when as a youth of eighteen he came to Paris for the first time from his native Périgueux. Thereafter chance was a word without meaning for him: 'le mot Hasard était un intolérable blasphème qu'il s'étonnait toujours, malgré l'expérience de son mépris, de rencontrer dans des bouches soi-disant chrétiennes.' Not chance therefore but divine intention had brought him in contact with Barbey, instrument of his conversion, Barbey and the Catholic traditionalists, past and contemporaneous, Barbey had made him read: de Maistre, Bonald, Donoso Cortès,[1] Blanc de Saint-Bonnet.[2] The republican anti-clerical teaching Bloy had imbibed from his father was swept aside; the mystical side of his nature, inherited perhaps from his mother and her Spanish forbears, was aflame and was to burn with a lurid brightness.

After fighting in the war of 1870, Bloy returned to Paris in 1873. Much of the impact he thereafter made upon the journalistic and literary world of the capital, and the fierceness of his spirit may be

---

[1] 1809–53. Spanish exile and Catholic philosopher.
[2] 1815–80. Exalted Catholic writer; with Veuillot and Hello, he greatly influenced the revival of Catholic literature in the last quarter of the nineteenth century. See R. Griffiths, *The Reactionary Revolution ... 1870–1914* (1966), p. 29.

gauged from the pages of his personal journal, published in several volumes: *Le Mendiant Ingrat* (1898), *L'Invendable* (1909), *Le Pèlerin de l'Absolu* (1924), and from the largely autobiographical novels: *Le Désepéré* (1886) and *La Femme Pauvre* (1897); Caïn Marchenoir the hero's tragic life is a reflection of Bloy's own harsh experience.

The fictional crust of the two novels is thin; the volcano that was Bloy erupts, destroying the illusion of fiction, while his hatreds spill over like molten lava in a stream of invective, brutal, corrosively ironical and polemical, vituperative, often scatological. In his critical and polemical writings, e.g. *Propos d'un entrepreneur de démolitions* (1884), *Un Brelan d'excommuniés* (1889), the manner is the same.

Burning with a mystical faith, Bloy was torn in two directions. Like Huysmans he had leanings towards the monastic life, but a difference of emphasis divides them. The scholar and artist in Huysmans was drawn to the Benedictine order, to their scholarship, the grandeur of their liturgy and plainsong. The aesthetic response to religion was not in the forefront of Bloy's preoccupations;[3] the Trappists or the Carthusians, whose silent and austere lives are not only a liberation for the individual[4] but a perpetual propitiation for the sins of men, were his ideal. At a peculiarly distressing moment of Caïn Marchenoir's life, the young man is recorded as wanting to become a monk at La Grande Chartreuse, but the Carthusian Father Athanasius, to whom Bloy's *alter ego* confides his idea, dissuades him – 'Vous êtes un homme de guerre et de perpétuelle inquiétude.'[5] And so Bloy-Marchenoir gives free rein to his other compulsion, which is to write, regarding as a sacred charge the duty of writing the truth as he sees it, be the cost to himself what it may; of his prospective appointment to the staff of a Parisian newspaper Marchenoir exclaims: 'cet arrangement, ... qui va surtout me donner le moyen tant désiré d'accomplir ce que je regarde comme le strict devoir d'un écrivain: dire la vérité quelle qu'elle soit et quels qu'en puissent être les dangers.'[6]

For Bloy, the exalted moralist, the cant, the self-seeking and other forms of egotism, the triumphant mediocrity – all things of which he saw or believed he saw abundant proof in the literary world of Paris – were as a red rag to a bull; writers who could prostitute their gifts for success were an offence that this 'demolition contractor' felt obliged to clear away. What writer of the day,

---

[3] cf. Marchenoir: 'Alors, que voulez-vous que je vous dise? Si l'Art est dans mon bagage, tant pis pour moi!' *La Femme Pauvre*, Part I, chap. 33.
[4] 'Les Chartreux ... sont les seuls hommes libres et joyeux dans notre société de forçats intellectuels ...' (*Le Désespéré*, Part II).
[5] *Le Désespéré*, Part II.   [6] *Ibid.*, Part IV.

if prominent or successful, was safe from his attacks: Paul Bourget,[7] Georges Ohnet, Renan, Daudet,[8] Zola, Veuillot, Catulle Mendès,[9] countless others,[10] sometimes in their own names, sometimes under a scarcely-veiled pseudonym.

But Bloy was not wholly destructive in his intentions. If chance did not exist, it followed that history was the ordered pattern of God's divine purpose, 'a vast liturgical text'.[11] Marchenoir's great ambition is to write a work that would show this vital truth about history: 'Dégager de l'histoire universelle un ensemble symbolique, c'est à dire prouver que *l'histoire signifie quelque chose* [his italics], qu'elle a son architecture et qu'elle se développe avec docilité sur les antérieures données d'un plan infaillible....'[12] This attitude is reflected in Bloy's historical writings; his biographical studies of three great figures in history are in reality variations on the theme of God's chosen instruments: Christopher Columbus, 'The most unique of all the divine senseless people';[13] of Napoleon he comments: 'so what is called genius would simply be that divine will made flesh..., become visible and tangible in a human instrument, brought to its highest degree of power and precision, but incapable, like a compass, of going beyond its ultimate circumference';[14] Joan of Arc was a victim of one of 'these vast injustices... indispensable to the working out of an enormously mysterious plan, which we cannot understand.'[15]

Like Péguy, a few years later, he opposed the virulent anti-semitism of the century's closing years, for what people could provide a clearer testimony of the divine purpose in history than the race whence sprang the saviour of the world? In reply to Edouard Drumont (1844–1917), author of *La France juive* (1886), he wrote *Le Salut par les Juifs* (1892).

His belief in the divine design of history drove him to deny free will; he speaks of 'l'holocauste préalable du Libre Arbitre tel du

---

[7] Alexis Dulaurier, in *Le Désespéré*, Part I.

[8] Gaston Chaudesaigues, *ibid.*, Part IV. The name must be an allusion (scarcely veiled indeed!) to the complaint Bloy believed him to suffer from.

[9] Properce Beauvilliers, editor of *Le Pilate*, *ibid.*, Part IV.

[10] See particularly *ibid.*, Part IV, the journalists' dinner Marchenoir is invited to, by Beauvilliers.

[11] *L'Ame de Napoléon* (1912). Introduction.

[12] *Le Désespéré*, Part II.

[13] *Christophe Colomb devant les Taureaux* (1890). A redraft of his first published work, *Le Révélateur du Globe* (1884), which attacked the *advocati diaboli* who had opposed Columbus's beatification. This was to have been laid before the Vatican Council (1870); the war interrupted the Council's sittings, and the matter was not proceeded with. The revised work's odd title derives from the fact that a descendant of Columbus, the Duke of Veragna, who had sided with the opponents of the beatification, was also a breeder of bulls for bull-fighting.

[14] *L'Ame de Napoléon*. Introduction.

[15] *Jeanne d'Arc et l'Allemagne* (1915).

moins, que la raison moderne peut le concevoir.'[16] In that case, he might have reflected that the victims of his abuse were also part of God's purpose, and tempered his attacks with charity. But there was evidently a manichean element in his attitude. As an instrument of God's justice, his duty was to do what he could to promote the destruction of the evil one in his manifestations of the day. Unjust he may have been, but avenging angels, laying about them with flaming swords, cannot be sure of cutting down only the froward.

Bloy is remembered in the role of avenging angel, rather than as an interpreter of history, for his view of history proves nothing but his own mystical belief; remembered for his unequalled invective power.[17] With this weapon he sought to goad his contemporaries out of their complacency; for the wounds he inflicted he paid the expected price: spiritual isolation and the conspiracy of silence, as the most efficient means of smothering this turbulent firebrand; nor was the suffering confined to the intellectual level; it struck him in his flesh, hunger often, poverty always, and, at least until his marriage with Jeanne Molbech in 1890, a chain of harsh personal sorrows. But Bloy-Marchenoir could not be deterred from his predestined path, 'Car il ne pouvait se dispenser de donner son fruit, ce pommier de tristesse.'[18]

The traditionalist temper of Bloy's Catholicism is at the core of the Catholic renaissance of the 1890's; his bitter denunciations of the materialism on every hand spare no one, least of all the lukewarm Catholics who shied away from the exalted ideal of vicarious suffering, and the liberal Catholics, whose efforts to relieve poverty by social work conflicted with Bloy's conception of the dignity attaching to the poor and of their vital role in the divine order of society. His attitudes are more reminiscent of the Inquisition than of the Bergsonian climate in which the Catholic renaissance of the 'nineties flowered; yet Bloy's bitter denunciations of the materialism of his generation stems from his fervent belief in an authoritarian ordering of the world and human society: 'Jusqu'à la venue de l'Esprit qui renouvellera la face de la terre, les hommes en général doivent être gouvernés avec le bâton, que ce bâton soit une trique de chef de bande ou une crosse épiscopale.'[19] This attitude is in line with that of other authoritarian writers of the day, notably the slightly younger Bourget, and reflects the anxieties and dissatisfac-

---

[16] *Le Désespéré*, Part II.
[17] Which he had cultivated by his study, *inter alia*, of St Jerome's Vulgate, Juvenal, Tertullian, the medieval Latin writers, Rabelais; nor should his master, Barbey d'Aurevilly, be omitted from the list.
[18] *Le Désespéré*, Part II.
[19] *Mon Journal*, quoted by M-J. Lory, *La Pensée religieuse de Léon Bloy*. See R. M. Griffiths, op. cit.

tions felt by the writers of the high Catholic Right in face of the future being prepared for France by democracy.

The poet had died young in Paul Bourget (1852–1935); Parnassian mode, fragility, languid pessimism and all, neither he nor his works (*La Vie Inquiète*, 1872; *Edel*, 1878; *Les Aveux*, 1882) were greatly missed. In his place appeared the penetrating critic of *Les Essais de Psychologie Contemporaine*,[20] and finally the novelist which Bourget was to remain for over fifty years.

Bourget's novels fall broadly into three categories: the early novels (*L'Irréparable*, 1884; *Cruelle Enigme*, 1885; *Un Crime d'Amour*, 1886; *Mensonges*, 1887); the novels of psychological analysis (*André Cornélis*, 1887; *Cosmopolis*, 1893); and the novels with a didactic purpose (*Le Disciple*, 1889; *L'Etape*, 1903; *l'Emigré*, 1907; *Le Démon de Midi*, 1914; *Némésis*, 1918).

The first group are little more than well-built stories in a high-society setting; all Bourget's novels, indeed, share these two characteristics – the neatness in plot construction of a 'well-made play' and characters who are either socially impeccable or, if they are not, are apt to suffer from being in social circles that are not theirs.[21] In this context, Bourget was no more than the fashionable novelist of his day; he has a gallery of characters, men with flowing moustaches in high stiff collars, dress coats, drain-pipe trousers and button boots, women in wasp-waisted 'tailor-mades', large hats and muffs, all of flawless physical and moral elegance, distinguishable as the class that occupied the 'high life' scene in the 'eighties and 'nineties, indistinguishable as individuals.

With no more literary baggage than this, Bourget would no doubt have sunk into the same oblivion as his successful forerunners in the *genre*, Octave Feuillet and Georges Ohnet. But the second group of his novels had more claim to attention; here the stories in themselves, losing nothing in their dramatic nature, are less important than the analysis of the emotions they give rise to in the protagonists. The interest of *André Cornélis* lies not so much in that modern Hamlet's suspicions, justified, of his stepfather, Terremonde, unjustified, of his mother, for having encompassed the death of his father, but in the complex of emotional relations involving the three characters.

Le Disciple marked a new and important departure. From the plot angle the mixture is as before but stronger: seduction, double suicide planned but carried out only by one of the parties, trial of the other, acquittal immediately followed by condign punishment (or murder, according to the point of view) by avenger-brother.

[20] See below, p. 149.
[21] e.g. Robert Greslou (*Le Disciple*), Jean Monneron (*L'Etape*).

Strong meat, but what caused the intellectual stir was not the misfortunes of Robert Greslou, this pale unattractive shadow of Julien Sorel, but the reasons for his corruption and downfall – the determinist views propounded by the gentle old philosopher devoid of malice, Adrien Sixte;[22] these Greslou had imbibed, and had determined to make them the rule of his life.

Here was a vigorous condemnation of the philosophies that had held sway for the past quarter of a century. True, a reader might have objected that Bourget may show them to be dangerous, but that what is dangerous is not on that account untrue; indeed, the consequences that follow with clockwork precision from Greslou's choice seem rather to show how effective, therefore, on a pragmatic assessment at least, how true the philosophy is; not the philosophy, only those that misapply it stand condemned.

Be that as it may, Bourget's didactic intention is clear and the preface addressed to 'Youth', warning them against both the gross materialism of the 'struggle-for-life' and the arid cynicism of the nihilist (Naturalists and Decadents despatched at a blow) underlines it. Henceforth the bulk of Bourget's works move from the plane of analysis of individual sensibility to the plane of moral or metaphysical preoccupations with a social intention: the social barriers and false democratic myths in France resulting from the Revolution and their impact on individuals (*L'Etape*), the relationship between men in different age and social groups (*L'Emigré*), the value of the religious instinct (*Le Démon de Midi*), human destiny (*Le Sens de la Mort, Némésis*); important questions, important books, perhaps, but novels? The answer depends on what the reader looks for. If it be characters whose existence he can believe in, he is unlikely to find them in Bourget; without being false, their attitudes seem unreal, because Bourget is not thinking so much of creating individual characters as of excogitating ideas for them to express; the conversation between M. Ferrand and his daughter[23] is a model of this process; as an exposition of the Revolution's deleterious effects, cogent perhaps, as an exercise in the fictional creation of a girl, disastrous! From *Le Disciple* onwards, the moral clinician of the *Essais* has reappeared in the novelist. The novel must be made to serve Bourget's social and political purpose.

As a youth Bourget had been an eyewitness of the Commune, the last of the revolutionary convulsions that had afflicted France with rhythmical repetition since 1789. Bourget had come to the conclusion that the underlying cause of this misfortune lay in France's betrayal of her traditions, religious and historical; for France Catholicism and Monarchy were the pillars of social order; Joseph de Maistre, Bonald, Comte, Balzac, Taine, Fustel de

[22] Taine, to the life?   [23] *L'Etape*, opening pages.

Coulanges, had said the same or at least upheld authoritarianism, Maurras was to build up the political threat to the Republic; Bourget, a social philosopher rather than a politician, places his pen at the service of the same ideal.

René Bazin (1853–1932), Emile Baumann (1868–1941) and Henri Bordeaux (1870–1963) belong to the same 'spiritual family' as Bourget. They defend traditional values, in rather conventional terms; French life – in rustic provincial settings very often[24] – is shown to be at its best in all classes, peasantry, bourgeoisie, nobility, when rooted in the old loyalties – Church, country, family. Bazin's *Les Oberlé* (1901) is a good example of a conventional representation, taking as its model the sentimental image many Frenchmen had of Alsace after the war of 1870, a province torn from France, as flesh from flesh, with the old, the right loyalties still active – witness the Oberlé family divided against itself; Madame Oberlé abetting the son's escape across the frontier to serve France; the father, sunk in material interests, approving the daughter's love for a Prussian officer.

Baumann's novels[25] are concerned mainly with the idea, so thoroughly rooted in Catholic reactionary circles, of vicarious suffering.

Henri Bordeaux enjoys the distinction of a literary production extending over sixty-six years.[26] Such fecund regularity forces the sort of respect, almost affection we may feel for a clock, with a sympathetic face, telling the time year in year out. Entrenched in *La Revue des deux mondes*, that citadel of tradition and respectability, Bordeaux is almost an institution in himself, highly respectable for the sincerity of his beliefs,[27] and his sound qualities, which are apt to be lost sight of in the unending production flow, as a regionalist painter of his native Savoy, e.g. *Le Barrage* (1927), a simple tale that tells of a mountain hamlet's life sacrificed in the interests of water power for the plains, and that foreshadows the best stories of André Chamson.[28]

What more brilliant conquest for the Roman Church than Ernest Psichari (1883–1914), this son of a free-thinker[29] and grand-

---

[24] e.g. Bazin: *La Terre qui meurt*, 1898; *Le Blé qui lève*; Baumann: *La Fosse aux Lions*, 1911; Bordeaux: *Les Roquevillard*, 1906; *La Robe de laine*, 1910; *La Neige sur les pas*, 1912.

[25] e.g. *L'Immolé* (1908), *La Fosse aux Lions* (1911), *Le Baptême de Pauline Ardel* (1914).

[26] 1894, a group of literary studies, *Ames Modernes*, to 1960, date of the last novel, *Le Flambeau Renversé*.

[27] Which he practised as well as preached; mobilized in 1914 as an infantry captain, he took part in the attack on the Fortress of Vaux, in the battle of Verdun.

[28] See below, p. 233.

[29] Jean Psichari, born at Odessa in 1854, was of Greek origin.

son by his mother of Ernest Renan, this scholar-soldier, converted in 1913, killed in action at St. Vincent-Rossignol in Belgium at the age of thirty-one.

His previous soldiering had been in Africa and the three books that constitute his literary legacy – *Terres de soleil et de sommeil* (1908), *L'Appel des armes* (1912), *Le Voyage du Centurion* (written 1913, posth. 1915) – are a series of African impressions. *L'Appel des armes* is in addition an apology for the profession of arms, in the person of the hero, Captain Nangès, who might have stepped out of the pages of Vigny's *Servitude et Grandeur militaires*. *Le Voyage du Centurion*, Psichari's most permanent memorial, is the story of a journey that is both physical and spiritual. Maxence, at the head of his camel patrol,[30] is depicted on a service mission against rebel tribesmen in the Adrar desert of Mauretania; the life of the colonial soldier, confident in the value of his pacifying and civilizing mission is evoked. But at the same time, like the Centurion of the New Testament, like Psichari, whose *alter ego* he is, Maxence is in search of a God of whom his upbringing has left him ignorant and whom he discovers through his reverence for his own profession and the mysterious hold over him of the desert: 'Le désert ceignait ses reins . . . Et rien, en effet, ne venait troubler cet admirable déroulement de vie intérieure que l'Afrique réserve à ses élus.'[31] Ernest Psichari was not the only French officer to feel the call of the desert. Charles de Foucault (1858–1916) had become a solitary missionary in the Sahara, where he was assassinated; had Ernest Psichari survived the war, his intention was to follow in Foucault's footsteps and become a monk.

Of all the 'committed' writers none is more powerful, none more characteristic of the spirit of the day than Maurice Barrès (1862–1923). Barrès came to Paris in 1883; he was twenty-one. His native Lorraine had had time to make an indelible mark on his mind and spirit, a fact that was to appear in his various activities: politics, journalism, literature.

No less than others of his time, Barrès was sensitive to the winter of discontents that Naturalism's high summer gave way to. Unlike some (e.g. Anatole France) he could not shrug it off by adopting an attitude of Pyrrhonism. Thus in one sense his journey through life was a restless quest for a secure spiritual anchorage. At the same time the urge to provide a guiding light for his generation was at least as strong in him as in his contemporary Paul Bourget. Both provide a diagnosis of the moral ills of the youth of the day: 'c'est de manquer d'énergie et de ne savoir où s'intéresser que

---

[30] Méharistes.   [31] Chap. 3.

souffre le jeune homme moderne.'[32] Bourget in fact lays greater emphasis on analysis than on cure, throughout his abundant works. Barrès is more positive, though the message varies.

Could science really be relied on to create human happiness? The picture of humanity as painted by the Naturalists scarcely encouraged the belief, in spite of Zola's professions of faith; the loss of confidence in that possibility engendered a new mood; if the promises of science were empty husks, the individual must rely on his own moral resources. This attitude is reflected in Barrès's first three works, a trilogy to which he gave the general title of *Le Culte du Moi*. *Sous l'oeil des Barbares* (1888), *Un Homme Libre* (1889), *Le Jardin de Bérénice* (1891) are three parts of an exercise in egotism conducted by the author's 'alter ego', Philippe. First the revolt against the disciplines and pressures of school and society, against the 'Barbarians', in a word, who seek to mould the young man in their own image. But this form of spiritual independence is merely a by-product of thraldom to the Philistines; even though supported by scepticism and irony[33] it is not enough. To be proof against its enemies – acedia, metaphysical anguish, *ennui* and the like – the spirit must organize its own discipline: self-knowledge by analysis, cultivation of euphoric moods, of intense and exquisite experience, co-ordination of the spiritual mechanisms. Such a programme is more fruitful in association, more successfully followed when its devotees are uninterrupted by contacts with the outside world;[34] Philippe finds a kindred spirit in his friend Simon; together they pursue the inward exploration they hope will lead them to genuine spiritual freedom. Such is the theme of *Un Homme Libre* (1889). But these exercises do not fully satisfy Philippe's search for spiritual fulfilment. Had he not written in *Sous l'oeil des Barbares*, 'Prenez d'ailleurs le moi pour un terrain d'attente sur lequel vous devez vous tenir jusqu'à ce qu'une personne énergique vous ait reconstruit une religion'? Thus, with all its inner organization, the 'ego' is in a state of 'disponibilité', seeks to be committed. The young Barrès himself had found what he believed was a good cause to fight for when he rallied to General Boulanger and was elected to the Chamber as a *boulangiste* deputy for Nancy (1889).

Philippe, like his creator, turns to politics. The construction of the inner citadel will be incomplete without its outer bulwark: dedication to the Boulangist cause. Yet this theme is not the main purpose of *Le Jardin de Bérénice* (1891); it lies in the contrast he observes between his own inner restlessness, which remains in spite

[32] *Sous l'oeil des Barbares.*
[33] '... nous ne méprisons pas le scepticisme, nous ne dédaignons pas l'ironie ... forte garantie de liberté.' Shades of Renan! *Ibid.*
[34] Shades of Huysmans's des Esseintes! *A Rebours*, see above, chap. 2, v.

of all, and the effortless serenity of his mistress Bérénice. What is her secret? Philippe believes he discovers it in her acceptance, unquestioning, even unconscious, of the mould heredity has cast her in; she hails from Lorraine and lives contentedly in the traditions Lorraine has woven in and about her. Into Philippe's mind creeps the doubt whether the spiritual self-sufficiency he had aimed at is the proper basis of a code for living, whether indeed it is a possible one. Are not the fibres of a man's being rooted in his heredity and traditional environment?[35] Can he cut away, merely by saying so, from a past of which he is in effect a projection into the present?

The *Déracinés* were presently to reject the pretention, but Barrès was not yet ready to throw his egotism overboard; the pursuit of spiritual independence is still the theme in *L'Ennemi des Lois* (1892), but its hero, André Maltère, has none the less learned from Philippe's reflexions to strive for it no longer by the cultivation of intellectual and aesthetic experience but by attention to the hidden urges of his nature, the elements, in fact, that the past has implanted in him. 'Je m'accuse', he declares, 'de désirer le libre essor de toutes mes facultés et de donner son sens complet au mot exister. Homme et homme libre, puissé-je accomplir mes destinées, respecter et favoriser mon impulsion intérieure, sans prendre conseil de rien du dehors...'[36]

Du Sang, de la Volupté et de la Mort (1894), a sheaf of essays garnered mostly from visits to Spain by the restless traveller Barrès was always to be, also belongs in part to the *Culte du Moi* group. Delrio, in the first essay,[37] is an image of des Esseintes, and indeed all the essays reflect the aestheticism of Huysmans's hero. 'Ordonner intelligemment ses sensations' is the principle man should adopt, if he wishes to extract the most from life. Yet in the last essay Barrès recognizes the ultimate bankruptcy of his egotism as he had sought to construct it hitherto, and is clearly in search of a more solid foundation to build on.[38] Barrès gives us the result of that search in his next three works, *Les Déracinés* (1897), *L'Appel au Soldat* (1900) and *Leurs Figures* (1902), which together form the trilogy with the general title of *Roman de l'Energie Nationale*.

The seven young men whose destinies we are invited to follow from the end of their school days at the Nancy lyceum (*Les Déracinés*) through the stormy Boulangist days (*L'Appel au Soldat*) to the sordid tragi-comedy of Panama (*Leurs Figures*), provide their creator with a double theme to which the title of the first volume

[35] Shades of Taine!   [36] *L'Ennemi des Lois*, Crès edn., n.d., p. 12.
[37] 'Un Amateur d'Ame'.
[38] Barrès provides us with a number of passages which show how he spanned the intellectual gulf between the two trilogies: e.g. *Scènes et Doctrines du Nationalisme*, Vol. I (1902, *passim*); *Amori et Dolori Sacrum* (1903), essay entitled 'Le 2 Novembre en Lorraine' (1902).

and that of the trilogy itself are pointers: the attack on the universalist and rationalist spirit of French education, the defence of regional loyalties. The seven young provincials, weaned from the spiritual nourishment of their native Lorraine, seem transformed into intellectuals, uprooted from their native soil, into ambitious shavelings bent, the little Napoleons,[39] on conquering Paris. The success or disaster that attends them varies in direct proportion to the corrosive effect of their education; at the bottom of the ladder Racadot ends on the scaffold, Mouchefrin in sordid poverty as a police stool-pigeon; some rungs higher, Renaudin as a journalist and Suret-Lefort as a barrister, both as unscrupulous deputies. The remaining three, St Phlin, Roemerspacher and Sturel, come unscathed through the etiolating influences of the capital because in them the provincial voices, momentarily stilled, are not dead. Thus, in his search for spiritual energy to feed his egotism with, Barrès, at this point in his development, sees it in the rich humus of loyalties to family, regional life and traditions – race, environment, momentum, as Taine would say; his influence on Barrès had become paramount.[40] But we must not overlook that the title of the trilogy contains the important word 'national'. Barrès indeed looks beyond the confines of his province to the future of the nation as a whole. 'Qu'est-ce qu'une nation'? (1882); Renan had posed the question and had given as a reply a broad uniformity of modes of thinking produced by the combined factors of geography and history. The question preoccupied Barrès, all the more as he condemned the state educational machine for its failure to produce the desired unity, because in its efforts to stamp a uniform impress upon French youth it ignored the inner psychological differences rooted in regional realities and worthy of preservation as a source of spiritual wealth and strength to the nation.

The unity so essential to France in the face of the growing menace of German power must be founded not on a superficial uniformity but on the recognition that France was built of a rich variety of cultures, such is the message inherent in *Le Roman de l'Energie Nationale* and more explicitly in *Les Amitiés Françaises* (1903). Nor is there any break here with the earlier Barrès but rather a deeper understanding of the psyche and a less egotistical application of it. The hidden potentialities that André Maltère[41] had sought to buttress his own spiritual detachment with, are now to be harnessed to the spiritual needs of the nation. How great these were had only recently been shown by the Dreyfus Affair. Barrès had been an uncompromising anti-Dreyfusard. In company

[39] *Déracinés*, Vol. I, 8, 'Au tombeau de Napoléon'.
[40] *Déracinés*, Vol. I, 7, 'L'arbre de Monsieur Taine'.
[41] *L'Ennemi des Lois*.

with many others, he saw the problem in national terms. The Dreyfusards were internationalist, un-French therefore, and incapable of grasping the unimportance of Dreyfus in comparison with the prestige of the military – vital factors in national defence. How could an Emile Zola understand French realities? 'Qu'est-ce que Monsieur Emile Zola? Je le regarde à ses racines: cet homme n'est pas un Français . . . il pense tout naturellement en Vénitien déraciné';[42] to speak in Barrèsian terms: the inner necessities of Zola's nature determined an un-French attitude. On this issue, Barrès joined hands with the extreme nationalist Charles Maurras, only to part company with him on others. For Maurras the only hope of achieving the desired moral unity was on the basis of monarchy and of Catholicism, unacceptable to him as a religion[43] but vital as a factor in the French tradition. This position entailed the exclusion from the national 'family' of all who did not accept these two tenets: republicans of every shade, Protestants and Jews. Barrès, less logically perhaps, but more realistically, rejected such purism. The French Revolution was just as much a part of the living flesh of France as the great ages of the French monarchy and could not be struck out with a pen.[44]

In his next two works, *Au Service de l'Allemagne* (1902) and *Colette Baudoche* (1909), Barrès returns to the theme, at least as important for him as the need for Frenchmen of his day to accept the total legacies of French history, be they never so conflicting, the theme of regionalism, of the particular role the provinces should play on the French scene. Obedient to his own 'inner necessities' Barrès naturally focussed his and our attention on Lorraine; but next door lay Alsace. If Lorraine had been partially, Alsace had been wholly overwhelmed by the disaster of 1870. Thus the two provinces were linked by a common tragedy, their images evoked personal memories of 1870,[45] created the same emotional tensions, but, with his sensitive belief in provincial diversity and a realistic appreciation of different situations, Barrès saw different answers to the question what attitudes Alsatians and Lorrainers should adopt in the face of this common problem – Germany.

For many Frenchmen of the interior, there was only one course open to Alsatians with the cause of France at heart: to cross the frontier and resettle in France;[46] what could those be that did not,

---

[42] *Scènes et Doctrines du Nationalisme*, I, 2.

[43] Hence the eventual condemnation of Maurras's paper *L'Action Française* in 1926 by the Pope.

[44] *Scènes et Doctrines du Nationalisme*, Vol. I: 'Vous pensez que la Révolution a fait dévier les destinées du peuple français . . .', etc.

[45] As a boy of eight, Barrès had seen the Prussian invaders in his native Charmes.

[46] A number went to Algeria. Bazin's *Les Oberlé* (1901) is typical of this attitude.

but active or passive collaborationists? Barrès's strong belief in the
nourishing spiritual values of native soil and traditions naturally
ran counter to such a facile answer which ignored the real terms
of the problem. Could not an Alsatian justifiably ask why he
should be morally compelled to make such a move, which, apart
from the material sacrifices involved, would represent a severance
from friends, customs, language, perhaps religion, a spiritual up-
rooting in fact of the type Barrès had already condemned?[47] Besides, even assuming an Alsatian to be wholly French at heart,
there was the pertinent question whether the best way for an Alsatian to serve France was to quit, thus leaving a vacancy certain to
be filled, under administrative pressure, by a German; on a large
scale this process would be tantamount to abandoning French territory to German settlement for ever. As M. Ehrman, the hero of
Au Service de l'Allemagne, explains, these were the factors that
had weighed on his decision to remain in Alsace, learn to know
German mentality intimately and pay the price – German military
service.

Frenchmen generally were unable between 1870 and 1914 to
see the problem facing Alsatians with the discernment of Barrès;
after 1918, had the French administration shown something of
Barrès's sympathetic understanding of Alsatian mentality, much
bitterness and the 'Separatist' movement might have been avoided.

For Lorrainers the problem was more clear-cut. The attitude
Barrès thinks right had been foreshadowed in the experience of
St Phlin and Sturel at Metz,[48] a city French in language and
customs, exposed to 'Germanizing' pressures. The two young men
leave the city with heavy hearts, aware of the struggle against an
alien administration, awakened to their own duty as natives of the
province: to resist the stealthy invasion by all means in their power.

A similar message emerges from *Colette Baudoche*. The story is
no more than an episode in the life of the heroine, courted by
Herr Asmus, the German schoolmaster working at Metz. Colette,
flattered at first, is disposed to look upon Asmus with a favourable
eye, but soon she comes to appreciate the lack of a common bond
between the worthy, methodical, erudite, ponderous, humourless
Asmus, and herself, the epitome of grace and refinement. The
marriage will not take place. The two characters have no individual life; symbols, the Germanic and the Gallic, they stand
facing each other across a gulf. Lorraine must be a bulwark of
resistance, not a bridge of understanding. Resistance from without
for Lorraine, from within for Alsace, the message is ultimately the

---

[47] *Les Déracinés*, etc.
[48] *L'Appel au Soldat*. Their tour in Lorraine must be one of the earliest
to be undertaken on push-bicycles.

same and enabled Barrès to group the two stories together with the general title – *Les Bastions de l'Est*.

In 1913, Barrès published what, with the possible exception of *Les Déracinés*, remains his masterpiece: *La Colline Inspirée*. The story, founded on fact, of the three Baillard brothers, priests all of them, who in their search for spiritual revival get entangled with an 'illuminé', Pierre Michel Vintras, found a mixed religious community on the hill of Sion-Vaudémont in Lorraine, and are drawn into heterodox attitudes that bring conflict with Rome and final defeat, that story may be seen as a restatement of the theme already developed in *Le Roman de l'Energie Nationale*. But the restatement is in different terms; there the problem was between the nation and its constituent parts, here the problem is religious; there we are shown how a centralized educational machine inspired by a universalist rationalist philosophy may, if successful, dry up the springs of vital energy hidden deep in provincial soil, and lead to spiritual anaemia; here the answer appears different; as between the three stout sons of Lorraine, peasants in priestly habit, and the church, it is the former, the spiritually adventurous, the forces of renewal, that are defeated by the central authority. But the difference is more apparent than real; once Barrès had interpreted the mystery of the human psyche, in Tainian terms, as the product of combined hereditary and environmental forces, tradition becomes a key word. In the conflict between the Baillard brothers and the Church, the latter is the guardian of tradition against all deviationism, and as such prevails. Tradition implies an established order, and order means security. From the venturesome attitude his earliest work suggests, Barrès had long since turned away, without, however, being able to resolve on a rational systematic basis the inherent conflict between the individual and society, between diverse regional traditions and a central government, between the desire for spiritual renewal and traditional authority.

But 1914 was not a moment for smooth intellectual constructions; it called for an upsurge of all the latent energies however diverse, fused by an emotional bond into a single defensive effort. The spirit of the *Union Sacrée* lasted about two years and during that time the prestige of Barrès, the apostle of heterogeneous nationalism, the indefatigable wartime commentator of *L'Echo de Paris*, was at its peak.

In retrospect the fourteen volumes of his *Chronique de la Grande Guerre* add nothing to Barrès's literary stature. The fourteen volumes of the *Cahiers*,[49] on the other hand, are a mine of valuable information on the man, the politician and publicist; on

49 Vols. I to XI (1929–38); Vol. XII (1948); Vols. XIII and XIV (1957).

his religious attitudes, emotionally akin to those of Chateaubriand
and sometimes of doubtful orthodoxy,[50] on his literary art; often
he appears more generous in spirit than in his other writings.[51]
These are mostly in fictional form,[52] and most important are: *Le
Culte du Moi, L'Ennemi des Lois, Le Roman de l'Energie Nationale, Les Bastions de l'Est, La Colline Inspirée*; yet Barrès cannot
be classed as a great novelist. There are moments, notably in *Les
Déracinés* and *La Colline Inspirée*, when the illusion all novelists
must want to create is complete, passages of the former are Balzacian in intensity;[53] at others, Barrès reveals himself as a skilful and
observant chronicler of his times;[54] nothing could be more dramatic than the evocation of the scenes in parliament at the time of
Panama,[55] more feverish than the description of Reinach, the
financier's last hours,[56] more penetrating than the analysis of the
underlying politics of that scandal.[57] In these cases Barrès has
moved from fiction to history and its interpretation, but history
comes alive. Yet, whether in pure fiction or poised between fiction
and fact, his art is scarcely that of the novelist, particularly in the
creation of characters; the men are poorly individuated, the women
scarcely exist. Historical fact, fiction and characters, all are made
to subserve Barrès's main purpose, the communication of a moral
message. Whether as the egotist of the early works, or the traditionalist and fervent Nietzchean nationalist of later years, the neo-
romantic moralist he was provided a code of values that exactly
fitted a generation. Hence its tremendous if short-lived impact,
greatly enhanced by the magic of a style that recalls the best vein
of Chateaubriand.

The revolt against Naturalism had opened the way to new currents in literature; the writers we have been discussing all in their
several ways subscribe to traditional values associated with the
Right in politics; the emphasis is on faith, loyalty, energy, action,
heroism, sacrifice, order, on forces that have their mainspring in
the secret recesses of the soul.

.   .   .

[50] e.g. the idea of the 'Intercessors' in *Un Homme Libre*, the essay on
the pagan statue in Auxerre Cathedral – 'Le Mystère en pleine lumière';
the idea of the 'local spirits' in *La Colline Inspirée*.
[51] e.g. his revised attitudes (Vol. XIV) towards Clemenceau and Renan,
both of whom he had bitterly attacked, the former at the time of Panama,
the latter for his post-1870 pessimism on France's future, cf. Renan's remark to Paul Déroulède: 'Jeune homme, la France se meurt, ne troublez
pas son agonie' – mentioned in *Sc. et Doc. du Nationalisme*, I, 5: 'Une
phrase de M. Renan'.
[52] The remainder are collections of essays.
[53] e.g. the scenes in Racadot's newspaper office, when he is on the verge
of financial shipwreck.
[54] The days of Boulanger in *L'Appel au Soldat*.
[55] *Leurs Figures.*   [56] *Ibid.*   [57] *Ibid.*

In marked contrast stand Anatole France (1844–1924) and Romain Rolland (1866–1944).

Son of a small Parisian bookseller on the Quai Malaquais, Thibault, alias France, variously schoolmaster, journalist, publisher's reader and junior librarian (1876) in the Senate library, published his first work, a critical study of Alfred de Vigny, in 1868. A collection of poems in the Parnassian mode – Les Noces Corinthiennes – appeared in 1876; three years later his first two stories: Jocaste and Le Chat Maigre. Thereafter his reputation grew, slowly at first, both as literary critic and story-writer. His numerous articles of impressionistic criticism, many of them excellent, were published under the collective titles of La Vie Littéraire (1888–92) and Le Génie Latin (1913). But fiction was his main activity: Le Crime de Sylvestre Bonnard (1881), Les Désirs de Jean Servien (1882).

In 1890 he achieved his first great success with Thaïs, which evokes the early Christian era in Egypt. Flaubert had done the same in La Tentation de Saint-Antoine; France's saint, Paphnuce, also has his temptation, in the person of Thaïs the courtesan whom he converts to Christianity – ill-advisedly, for Venus is on the alert, and Thaïs is her instrument of vengeance.

The flow of short stories continued with L'Etui de Nacre (1892) and Le Puits de Sainte Claire (1895); Le Lys Rouge (1894) may claim to be France's first full-length novel, a psychological study set in contemporary society; at the same time the fruit of the author's worldly wisdom is given to us indirectly in Les Opinions de M. Jérôme Coignard (1893) and directly in Le Jardin d'Epicure (1895). In La Rôtisserie de la Reine Pédauque (1893) the worthy abbé also holds the centre of the stage but is presented to us through the eyes of his patient disciple Jacques Tournebroche.

With the secure foundation of his literary reputation came also, thanks to the help and guidance of Madame Arman de Caillavet, a notable 'salonnière' of the period, Anatole France's great success in Parisian society, a valuable help on the road to the Académie Française which opened its doors to him in 1896. L'Orme du Mail was published in the same year. This work with the three following volumes, Le Mannequin d'Osier (1897), L'Anneau d'Améthyste (1899), M. Bergeret à Paris (1901), together form the Histoire Contemporaine. As their general title indicates, these novels are intended to be a contemporary social study. The Dreyfus Affair, which had been smouldering since 1894, burst into flame in 1898; the country was rent in twain. The Histoire Contemporaine, in its later chapters, echoes its author's own strong pro-Dreyfus convictions. French politics and administration, life in general which had provided a broad field for the exercise of Jérôme Coignard's gentle scepticism, now call forth a note of bitter satire: L'Affaire Crain-

quebille (1902) and *L'Ile des Pingouins* (1908). But already in *La Révolte des Anges* (1914) the tone is less bitter; the irony remains, and a disillusioned epicureanism, which is also at the root of what remains France's best novel, *Les Dieux ont soif* (1912), where, against the background of the French Revolution, the author depicts and condemns the fanaticism of the young Jacobin, Evariste Gamelin,[58] whose own fate is sealed by the fate of Robespierre.

In the historical field the figure of Joan of Arc had also attracted him as it had Michelet many years before, and as it attracted Péguy almost at the same time as France. For Michelet she is the symbol of the French people of her day, a romantic heroine, portrayed with anglophobic joy, and pity for her suffering; Péguy exalts in her the robust good sense of the peasant, her mystic piety, her dedication and self-sacrifice to a patriotic ideal, without Michelet's chauvinism. Anatole France, for his part, approaches the subject with a genuine desire to strip away the hagiographical legends that have sprung up in the course of centuries about the quasi-miraculous part played by the 'Maid' in ridding the country of the foreign foe and to see what historical factors conspired to bring about her victories over the English. In the role of historian he shows himself full of appropriate discernment and suspicion in his handling of the evidence. On the other hand, what drew his interest initially to the figure of Joan was not so much a historian's desire to establish the facts on a firm basis, as the rationalist's interest in alleged supernatural phenomena. These must be investigated. What Renan had done for the figure of Jesus, Anatole France would do for Joan of Arc; thus, France in the end is less concerned with creating a historical image than with providing a rationalist interpretation of the data; the Maid's 'voices', her compelling sense of mission, the faith that sustained her – all boil down to a well-authenticated case of hysteria. This 'solution' is as clear as fog; the mystery remains.

The attitude and even at times the vocabulary of this spiritual son of Renan reflects the master: 'elle eut la part la plus belle', he writes, 'celle du sacrifice; elle donna l'exemple du plus haut courage et montra l'héroïsme sous une forme imprévue et charmante ..'[59] The condescension with which, as he sits safely at his desk, he pats Joan of Arc paternally on the head reflects Renan's towards Jesus; the word 'charmante' in the context is simply intolerable. For once France's stylistic taste, usually impeccable, has abandoned him.

Any review of Anatole France's works would be incomplete without mention of his personal reminiscences.

Early on he had started dipping into this store, and he returned

---

[58] Modelled on the painter David.   [59] Preface.

to them several times: *Le Livre de Mon Ami* (1885); *Pierre Nozière* (1899); *Le Petit Pierre* (1918); *La Vie en Fleurs* (1923) are a loosely constructed collection of anecdotes and reminiscences, a mixture of fact and fiction. Bathed in pink light and nostalgic sentiment they have something of the attraction that pervades an album of old family photographs from the pages of which our forbears greet us.

A writer successful in his own day usually suffers a decline after his death. This law operated particularly harshly on Anatole France. After a slow start he had after 1890 conquered the public, the salons, the Academy; by the turn of the century he had become a beacon light for the humanists; towards the end of his life his reputation was world-wide and he achieved the double distinction of receiving the Nobel Prize and being put on the Index; the two facts may conflict, but together they confirm France's significance as an international literary figure.

But soon after his death the attacks began; Surrealists, nationalists, clericals joined in the hunt; Paul Valéry, his successor in the Academy, pronounced the traditional Encomium on his predecessor without mention of his name; Gide and Maurras denigrated him. Nor has France had a much better press in recent years; on the *Histoire Contemporaine* a distinguished critic writes: 'je peux difficilement imaginer lecture moins nourrissante pour l'âme, et finalement plus appauvrissante et débilitante que celle de ces oeuvres également insignes par une incohérence complaisante de la pensée et une absolue sécheresse spirituelle...'[60] Such conflicting judgments are a warning to critics that they express dogmatic opinions at their peril, for standards of value shift.

But Anatole France had something to please most of his contemporaries, at one time or another, notably his successive philosophic attitudes – at first that of an eighteenth-century materialist. We are entitled to regard René Longuemare,[61] the physiologist, as his mouthpiece since the young man's materialist opinions have little to do with the story and are evidently 'planted' for their own purpose. Moral values have no meaning for Longuemare; they are a consequence of physiological or even pathological causes: 'La vertu est un produit comme le phosphore et le vitriol'; 'L'heroïsme et la sainteté sont l'effet d'une congestion du cerveau'. Longuemare is also informed on leaders of contemporary thought: 'la nature est le théâtre d'un éternel carnage... rien n'y vit que par le meurtre' – 'nature red in tooth and claw', 'the survival of the fittest'.

Longuemare's ideas are in tune with the Positivist tradition of which the university, after being the battleground throughout the nineteenth century between clericals and anti-clericals, was in the

---

[60] Madame C-E. Magny, *Figaro Litt.*, 11 December 1948.   [61] *Jocaste.*

late nineteenth century to become the citadel, with historians such
as Seignobos and Aulard, the literary historian Gustave Lanson, the
sociologist Emile Durkheim, the biologist Felix Le Dantec who,
much in the manner of Longuemare, defined intelligence as 'une
matière molle qui vit à 38°' and conscience as an 'epiphenome-
non'.[62] Humanist philosophies have something firm about them;
their protagonists, even though not provided with a faith that gives
any sense to the life of the individual, may at least inflate themselves with the belief that human behaviour is predictable and that
a policy of social progress may be built up accordingly. Anatole
France did not share this optimism. The tragic death of Jules
Servien, butchered by the communards as a result of a misappre-
hension, reflects a bitter pessimism more akin to that of the Naturalists, but it also points to the scepticism that was quickly to submerge his early materialism. The earlier confidence in the power
of science gives way to a conviction that we can know nothing:
'C'est une grande niaiserie que le "connais-toi toi-même", de la
philosophie grecque. Nous ne connaîtrons jamais ni nous ni autrui
. . . Aussi bien est-ce faire un abus vraiment unique de l'intelligence
que de l'employer à rechercher la vérité...'[63] Intelligence cannot
help us assess with absolute justice either men or their works.

This attitude pervades all Anatole France's work between 1880
and 1900. It explains his attitude to history: 'L'histoire n'est qu'un
art ou tout au plus une fausse science';[64] it provides him with a
system of literary criticism which is to have no system at all, with-
hold dogmatic judgment, content oneself with describing personal
impressions; it reflects the scepticism of Renan in his latter day
and, like his, evidently appealed to the pessimism of a generation
that seemed after the shock of defeat in 1870 to have lost confidence in itself, to find nothing particular to live – or die – for, enjoyed Anatole France's artistic hedonism, the disenchanted wisdom
of Jérôme Coignard, the delicate all-pervading irony, which is a
kind of revenge on life, and the condescending indulgence towards
men that masquerades as charity, but is in reality a form of intellectual arrogance. They were not shocked at the picture France
painted of French society in the *Histoire Contemporaine*, for indeed he provided ammunition for every section of opinion: the
anti-clericals could enjoy the foibles, follies and intrigues of the
clergy as seen in a provincial diocese, from the diocesan himself –
Mgr Charlot – down to the intransigent old campaigner, the
Abbé Lantaigne, and his arch-enemy, the supple, ambitious Abbé

---

[62] J. Chastenet, *La France de M. Fallières*, p. 207.
[63] *Jardin d'Epicure*.
[64] M. Pigeonneau in *Balthazar*; cf. Renan: 'ces pauvres petites sciences
conjecturales.'

Guitrel; the republicans could laugh at the paladins of nationalism – Raoul Marcien, Joseph Lacrisse – and at the 'Ligue des Trublions', recruited from dunderheads, adventurers, crooked financiers and the rest, to bring down the Republic – 'la gueuse' – and restore the Monarchy; the parties of the Right could in their turn feel satisfied at the poor figures cut by the representatives of the 'Establishment': the disillusioned Loyer, the Jewish prefect Worms-Clavelin, the crowd of parliamentarians largely preoccupied with avoiding scandals and parliamentary enquiries; the 'outsiders' could sneer at the bone-headed pantaloons that apparently people high-society. All could enjoy the disenchanted pessimism of M. Bergeret, seedy professor – and cuckold of course – talking to his dog, Riquet.

But suddenly a change comes over the scene; an invigorating wind starts to blow. M. Bergeret in Paris is a very different man from what he was in the provinces; he has found a cause and gone crusading. For him as for his creator and indeed for French society as a whole, the Dreyfus Affair was like a flash of light that revealed to men that deep down, under the scepticism and irony they had enjoyed, their lives were after all anchored to certain values to be defended regardless of cost; the nation, the army, the Church, justice for the individual 'Laïcité', all these great causes were or become involved in the conflict; all, without distinction of party, inspired some sincere attitudes, but were also the pretext for misguided or vile actions, and political exploitation. M. Bergeret, like his creator, believed in justice for the individual; both were Dreyfusards.

The Dreyfus case marks a turning-point in Anatole France's political evolution. In his early days he had, if anything, tended towards conservatism; he had recoiled with horror at the 'syncope morale'[65] of the Commune.[66] In the 'eighties and 'nineties his scepticism naturally extended to politics; 'Jérôme Coignard', having seen politicians close to,[67] and become one of the literary lions of the salons, poured out his irony with liberal impartiality, attacking particularly any manifestations of the persecuting spirit and showing little love for parliamentary democracy. What more shocking example, apparently, of the persecuting spirit than the condemnation of Dreyfus and the resistance to revision. Opponents[68] ascribed France's Dreyfusism to the influence of the Jewish Madame Arman de Caillavet; unjustly, for it was consistent with his liberal attitudes of previous years, and since for reasons that

---

[65] Renan's description.
[66] cf. *Jean Servien.*
[67] In the days when A.F. was employed in the Senate Library.
[68] e.g. Charles Maurras, Clemenceau, Barrès, Albert de Mun,

were not all of them good the parties of the Left were revisionist,
France thenceforward became a man of the Left.

A further cause for this new allegiance was his growing inter-
nationalism. Various factors may account for that: his literary
success which was leaping over frontiers, his pity for the individual
– an inverted form of the sceptic's intellectual arrogance perhaps
but genuine none the less – and for human suffering, which, the
Dreyfus case pushing in the same direction, took more and more
the obvious form of pacifism and hostility to the officer class, the
human butchers. On this point he was in close alliance with Jaurès
and the Socialists whose ranks he joined. Like the Socialists, he
was moved by the wave of patriotism that swept the country in
1914, and, though bitterly attacked by the nationalists for using
the word *amitié* in reference to the attitude the French should have
towards the Germans after victory had been achieved,[69] he did
not, like Romain Rolland, become a militant pacifist during the
war. After the war he remained faithful to his socialist allegiance,
except for a short flirtation with the Communists.[70]

Anatole France's career thus falls broadly into three periods: the
early years and up to 1880, when his materialism was uppermost;
the last twenty years of the century which saw his great literary
successes and the flowering of his pessimistic but amused scepticism; the post-Dreyfus period when despite his scepticism he is prepared to take a more positive attitude, to devote himself to causes:
Dreyfus, pacifism, the defence of the individual against persecution
and fanaticism. He became in consequence a controversial figure,
and if this meant on the one hand a certain loss of public acclaim
in France, that was more than compensated for by the ardour of
those who shared his views and by his international reputation.
Moreover, even though many of his former friends found themselves after 1900 in the opposing camp,[71] their admiration still
went to the writer if not to the man.

Now that the causes Anatole France espoused have lost their
passionate content and become matters of history, he stands or
falls by his literary value alone, and to judge from some withering
comments, this seems meagre. As a novelist his merits have indeed
faded. That they should have enjoyed an immediate success is just
understandable: *Le Lys Rouge* with its glimpses of Parisian salon
life, of Florence, of politicians, of society men and women, the
whole flavoured by irony and a dash of salaciousness; the Bergeret
series, much on the same formula but on a wider canvas and with
some heartening idealism to end on; the satire of *L'Ile des*

---

[69] His open letter to Gustave Hervé, published in *La Guerre Sociale*,
22 September 1914.
[70] 1921–2. [71] e.g. Barrès.

Pingouins at the expense of all the great figures in the French past and present;[72] the entertaining anachronisms of *La Révolte des Anges* with Jehovah and Satan fighting it out in Miltonic manner, to the accompaniment of salon chatter and adultery. But how jejune it has all become; how debilitating. The human texture is as thick and springy as a threadbare carpet; one character only – the disillusioned, yet moralizing, the ironical but kindly sage. Whether in the disguise of highly respectable scholars – Sylvestre Bonnard, Sariette,[73] M. Pigeonneau,[74] M. Schmoll,[75] M. Bergeret – or of the down-at-heel pedagogue, M. Godet-Laterasse,[76] or the fraudulent foreign marquis, Tudesco,[77] or the smiling philosophers, Jérôme Coignard, Brotteaux des Ilettes,[78] we recognize at once the large nose (they all seem to have large noses) and the mental attitudes of Anatole France. 'Artiste, on donne sa propre vie à ses créations ou bien l'on taille des marionettes et l'on habille des poupées.'[79] How true. But the great novelist has such wealth and diversity in his psyche that his gallery of characters is as richly diversified as the psyche that created it; apart from the 'sage', Anatole France's characters, men and women, are indeed marionettes and puppets.

To this general stricture on Anatole France as a novelist there is an exception – *Les Dieux ont soif*. Admittedly the author's characteristic irony, his thinly veiled contempt of men, are present here as elsewhere, but three factors have happily blended to make them less obtrusive: his sincere hatred of fanaticism, his interest in the period of the French Revolution,[80] and his very scepticism in its effect on his conception of a historical novel. As a result we have the vigorously drawn portrait of a young fanatic against a background of a period – evoked with scholarly sureness but where the author, rejecting the conventional approach to the men and events that occupy the centre of the stage, endeavours to see them through the eyes of the common folk, as distrustful of politicians as the author himself and for whom the pleasures and difficulties of daily life are at least as important as the struggle for power in the Convention.

In no other novel has Anatole France succeeded in communicating to the reader such a sense of life and vitality; his literary merits must be sought elsewhere; he is an agreeable 'raconteur'; *Jocaste*, *Le Chat Maigre*, *Le Crime de Sylvestre Bonnard* are excellent short stories. *L'Etui de Nacre*, *Balthazar*, *Le Puits de Sainte*

---

[72] A surprising exception is Louis XIV; but Anatole France was devoted to French classical literature, so Louis XIV escapes.

[73] *Le Chat Maigre.*   [74] *Balthazar.*   [75] *Lys Rouge.*   [76] *Jocaste.*

[77] *Jean Servien.*   [78] *Les Dieux ont soif.*   [79] *Sylvestre Bonnard.*

[80] Already apparent in a number of short stories in *L'Etui de Nacre*, and in *Le Livre de Mon Ami.*

Claire, the autobiographical works are full of entertaining anecdotes. He handles his favourite weapon of irony with immense skill.
The pleasure we derive is sometimes purely formal: 'Ma mère, tout
en gardant au capitaine une indulgence de soeur, l'invitait parfois
à moins *caresser* les flacons d'eau-de-vie';[81] 'mon excellent collègue
avait consenti à mourir grâce à deux ou trois attaques d'apoplexies
des plus persuasives';[82] 'Branchut...le regarda avec des *yeux de
homard*';[83] sometimes the suggestion of a human attitude is involved which gives it more weight: 'il fit fusiller sans méchanceté
quelques-uns de ses concitoyens...';[84] 'Schmoll est sans rancune.
C'est une vertu de sa race. Il n'en veut pas à ceux qu'il persécute.'[85]
This is beating Voltaire and Renan at their own game. But
France's irony is at its best in his critical essays, when his unerring
literary taste is offended. Such studies as those on Zola's *La
Terre*[86] or Georges Ohnet's *Volonté*[87] are masterpieces of literary
execution and send us away with a song in our hearts, rightly (or
wrongly) convinced that justice has been done.

Romain Rolland (1866–1944) was a pedagogue by training and
profession;[88] moralizing, his 'faculté maîtresse', to speak in Tainian
terms. Playwright, biographer and novelist, he remains an important, some may reasonably think, a noble figure, but the importance, if it exists, comes more from his moral attitudes than
from his literary achievements; much of his work, indeed, Nobel
Prize notwithstanding,[89] hovers on the brink of oblivion.

His plays (*Saint-Louis*, 1897, *Aërt*, 1898, *Le Triomphe de la
Raison*, the three republished as *Tragédies de la Foi*, 1913; *Les
Loups*, 1898, *Danton*, 1901, *Le 14 Juillet*, 1902) are unlikely to be
revived.

His early biographies (*Beethoven*, 1903, *Michel-Ange*, 1905)
derive a certain authority, the former from his love and knowledge
of music, the latter from his professional avocation as an art historian, but like his later series of lives of great men (*Tolstoï*, 1911,
Mahatma Gandhi, 1923, *Ramakrishna*, *Vivekananda*, 1929–30),
they are written less in a spirit of disinterested scholarship than as
apologias for their author's own loyalties; to this there is one exception, the memorial volume to Péguy (1944), whose friend and
collaborator in the *Cahiers de la Quinzaine* he had been, but whose
ideas were in certain respects so different.

The success that had eluded him in the theatre crowned his

[81] *Sylvestre Bonnard.*   [82] *Ibid.*   [83] *Chat Maigre.*   [84] *Ibid.*
[85] *Lys Rouge.*   [86] *La Vie Littéraire*, I.
[87] *Ibid.*, II, 'Hors de la littérature'.
[88] Entered Ecole Normale Supérieure 1886. Lecturer on History of Art at
Ecole Normale (1895), later at the Sorbonne.
[89] 1916.

fiction. *Jean-Christophe* (1904–12) was a European success, not re-
peated by his post-war writings, which, besides the biographies
previously mentioned, include *Colas Breugnon* (1919), a story, in
Rabelaisian vein, of a Burgundy peasant with a streak of non-
conformity much like Rolland's, *Clérambault* (1920), inspired by
the pacifism that Rolland had preached during the 1914 war and
which is reflected in *Au-dessus de la mêlée*[90] (1914) and *L'Ame en-
chantée* (1922–7), a heavily weighted pacifist manifesto in fictional
form. Thus, Rolland's post-war writings, including his autobiography (*Le Voyage Intérieur*, 1926, 1942), are, like his earlier works,
gestures in the campaign for the gospel of peace and universal love
he had early espoused, and, in a sense, personal apologias. Of all
his works the one that reflects most fully his ideas and beliefs is
Jean-Christophe. In his plays he had pleaded for personal dedication to a faith (*Les Tragédies de la Foi*) and exalted the universalist mystique of the French Revolution. In his lives of Beethoven,
Michelangelo and Tolstoy, he had expressed a Nietzschean cult of
the hero, but of the type he could hold up as an example to humanity, those who achieve joy through suffering; in *Jean-Christophe* there is something of all this and much else besides.

The attraction of fiction when Rolland was submitting himself
to the discipline of historical biography must have been particularly strong. He would endow his character with the musical genius
of Beethoven, and his power – the family name was to be Krafft.
The suffering, the struggle, the ultimate message of joy would all
be there but Jean-Christophe's experience would be in the present
so that he could reflect the ideas and feelings of Rolland's own
generation.

On the framework of these ideas, Rolland has built what is in
effect an 'Erziehungsroman', except that we do not leave the hero
on the threshold of maturity but at the end of his life, after a
chequered career that leads him from his native Rhineland Grand
Duchy to Paris and ultimately to Switzerland. If, with Rolland's
musical knowledge and sensibility in mind, we had hoped to see
him exploit at least the musical potential of his story, to have
enriched our insight into the development of a great musician,
we should be disappointed; instead, we are merely given Jean-
Christophe's life-chronicle and we soon become aware that he is
only rarely a living character, with a mind and feelings of his own,
growing in artistic and moral stature as he acquires experience.
Neither he nor his surroundings are observed closely enough for
us to get the illusion of life; Rolland is too anxious to communicate
his own views for him to keep his inner eye on the character and
scenes he wants to evoke. The result is that Jean-Christophe is

90 Article in *Journal de Genève*, 22–23 September 1914.

more symbol than character; a symbol of the genius who wins through to joy by suffering; a symbol-character in the manner of Hugo. Moreover, Christophe's joy in life is not shown convincingly to flow from his musical gifts; it comes in part from his Tolstoyan pantheistic cult of natural forces: 'Et Christophe entendit, comme un murmure de source, le chant de la vie qui remontait en lui. Penché sur le bord de sa fenêtre, il vit la forêt, morte hier, qui dans le vent et le soleil bouillonnait, soulevée comme la mer ... Le même paysage, hier dans le tombeau, était ressuscité; la vie venait d'y rentrer en même temps que l'amour dans le coeur de Christophe ... Et Christophe rentra dans la bataille divine ...'[91] The trees come to life because the wind blows on them! In a man who had rejected Christianity because it failed to satisfy his reason,[92] this wholly irrational, unscientific and lyrical attitude comes as a surprise.

Another source of joy for Christophe is his friendship with Olivier and Antoinette Jeannin. In the shallow, ambitious, artistic world of Paris Christophe is introduced into, after his flight from Germany, Olivier and his sister represent – again a symbolic note; it is constant in Jean-Christophe – authentic French values, rooted in provincial France.

In these two themes we see why the work, in spite of its being unsatisfying artistically, made such an impact on Rolland's generation. 'Il m'apparaît parfois', notes Gide,[93] 'que ce livre barbare, mal équarri, sans art ... reste ce qui a été produit en France de plus important, ou du moins de plus typique par notre génération.' Those of Rolland's generation who rejected Catholicism but who were dissatisfied with Positivism, found spiritual nourishment in the lyrical worship of the life force; for those again, who on the political plane rejected the nationalist creeds of a Maurras or a Barrès, here was a symbolic bridge across the Rhine whereby the true, the humanist spirit of France could meet the equally true spirit of Germany. In opposition to the prevailing notion strongly held on both sides of the Rhine of the two hereditary enemies preparing for the next conflict, Rolland gave powerful support to the other rather struggling idea, that of the two Germanies, the Prussian Germany, drunk with military glory, and the humane Germany of Goethe, of Weimar, of disinterested peaceful scholarship.[94]

Jean-Christophe, be it remembered, had been forced to flee because he had roughly handled a German soldier. He is a Rhinelander too, be it noted; how often on the political plane, from

[91] Bk. IX.
[92] See Bk. III. 'Léonhard dut constater que Christophe ... avait la prétention de ne se laisser convaincre qu'au moyen de la raison.'
[93] *Journal*, 30 January 1917.
[94] cf. Marcel Prévost, the same theme in *M. et Madame Moloch*.

Napoleon's Kingdom of Westphalia down to the abortive Separatist Movement in 1919, perhaps even to Dr Adenauer, and on the literary plane from Hugo[95] to Renan[96] and Barrès,[97] has the idea of the Rhineland as a separate culture, formed in the cradle of Rome, more closely akin to France than to Lutheran Germany with its Slav admixture, been exploited by French diplomacy and literature.

Rolland's influence, thanks to his *Jean-Christophe*, on one section of younger intellectuals before the 1914 war, can be measured by his correspondence with Jean-Richard Bloch.[98] Forlorn after the death of Christophe in the last volume (1912), Bloch writes: 'Vous nous avez tué Christophe . . . Je crois que vous seul ne pouvez plus mesurer la grandeur du chagrin que vous nous avez causé! Nous l'avions vu naître. C'avait été notre naissance. Il avait grandi pour nous; chacun de nous avait reparcouru son enfance avec lui, l'avait purifiée, comprise et sanctifiée . . .' Evidently, Bloch, who shared Rolland's ardent belief in the tonic value of moralizing literature, had achieved the sense of identification that all great literature has on a reader; we suspect however that *Jean-Christophe*'s impact on Bloch was due more to the moral climate of the day than to the work's intrinsic merit, and the war was to show that their natures if not their ideals were different. Bloch, the Jew, fervently loyal to the spirit of France as he saw it and fearful, in the pre-war nationalist days, of being thought unintegrated in the French family,[99] was in the trenches; Rolland, wholly French by heredity, clinging to his intellectual pacifist position of respect for life, was in Switzerland, whence, in lofty moral isolation, he condemns both sides for betraying true human values and masking brutish ferocity under a cloak of false nationalist idealism.[100]

Without questioning Rolland's sincerity, we may doubt whether he chose his time well for proclaiming his view of the truth, and prefer the attitude of Bloch who, whilst remaining faithful to Rolland's ideals,[101] yet understood his personal duty differently.[102] In another respect, too, *Jean-Christophe* was to have influence. Rolland endeavours, not successfully in our view, to make the

[95] *Le Rhin.*   [96] *Réforme intellectuelle et morale.*
[97] e.g. *L'Appel du Rhin* (1919).
[98] See *Cahiers Romain Rolland*, No. 15; Albin Michel, 1964. (See P. H. Simon in *Le Monde*, 30 December 1964.)
[99] *Et Cie* (1917) has a similar theme: the struggle of the Simler family (Alsatian industrialists) to 'belong' to French society, on settling in France, after 1870.   [100] *Au-dessus de la mêlée.*
[101] 'Ne doutez pas que mon accord avec votre pensée n'a subi aucune atteinte', he writes to Rolland.
[102] To be fair to Rolland, it should be added that he had been crippled by an accident before the war and that he was over military age; but silence would perhaps have better become him.

Rhine play a symbolic role in the work; the great river exercises a mysterious fascination on the boy, its great power suggests the life force, its unending flow has something of the flow of music, it gives Rolland the idea of his novel as a flowing life story, 'un roman-fleuve'; the expression is Rolland's and *Jean-Christophe* is the first of many, published during the inter-war years.

The period contains other novelists in profusion, not wholly forgotten; each in their several ways rooted in their time, they are less marked by the religious or political preoccupations of the day than the writers just mentioned. Thus, for example, Pierre Loti (1850–1923), Elémir Bourges (1852–1925), Paul Adam (1862–1920), Edouard Estaunié (1862–1942), Marcel Prévost (1862–1941), Pierre Louÿs (1870–1925), Pierre Mille (1854–1941), Louis Bertrand (1866–1941), the brothers Jean (1877–1952) and Jérôme (1874–1953) Tharaud, Claude Farrère (1876–1947), and a strong contingent of women writers, *inter alia* Marcel Tinayre (1872–1948), 'Colette' (1873–1954), Colette Yver (1874–1953), Gérard d'Houville (1875–1937), Myriam Harry (1875–1956) and Lucie Delarue-Mardrus.[103]

Both in and out of naval uniform, Pierre Loti[104] was a traveller,[105] yes, if by that we mean a writer who 'goes places', not if we mean a writer who wants to evoke for his readers the beauties of foreign parts, the life of distant societies. The true Loti is to be found rather in novels such as *Aziyade* (1879), *Rarahu* (1880), *Le Mariage de Loti*[106] (1882), *Madame Chrysanthème* (1887), *Japon-neries d'automne* (1889), *Ramuntcho* (1897), where in settings drawn from his travels – Turkey, Tahiti, Japan, the Basque country – he communicates personal sentimental experience; his eye is turned inward on himself rather than outward on the world; his own moods are what interest him.

A latter-day Romantic, in the wake of Chateaubriand, he freshens the latter's colour palette, lightens his technique; instead of the heavy *impasto* style of the First Empire, we get delicate touches of pastel shades – an impressionistic style; not definition, only suggestion, helped by three dot pauses – exoticism, done to Symbolist taste:

> Car nous voulons la Nuance encor,
> Pas la Couleur, rien que la nuance!
> Oh! la nuance seule fiance
> Le rêve au rêve et la flûte au cor!

---

[103] p. 106 n.7.   [104] Real name Julien Viaud.
[105] e.g. *Au Maroc*, 1890; *L'Inde sans les Anglais*, 1903; *Vers Ispahan*, 1904.
[106] Rarahu, lady-in-waiting to Pomaré, Queen of Tahiti, called Julien Viaud Loti, after a flower.

Fortune smiled early on Loti both as man and writer, but he carried with him round the globe the same sense of life's ephemeral fragility that bore on Chateaubriand: 'Toujours, j'ai eu horrible- ment conscience du néant des néants, de la poussière des poussi- ères.'[107]

Julien Viaud's personal vanity found perhaps some solace in the belief that Pierre Loti's forty volumes would be a solid bulwark against the ever-rolling flood, but no! All have been swept away, with the possible exception of *Le Roman d'un Spahi* (1881), *Mon frère Yves* (1883), and at least *Pêcheur d'Islande* (1886), where his picture of Breton women schooled in adversity and resignation by the 'cruel sea' has truth.

But melancholy hangs about all Loti's work like a damp blanket, intellectually and morally it lacks vigour.

Hovering between history and fiction, the two best remembered novels[108] of Bourges have a solidity of construction, a care for descriptive detail and pictorial effect reminiscent of Flaubert.

With a predilection for the romantic background of small Ger- man principalities, Bourges evokes violent and tragic dramas in high places, for which the contemporaneous chronicles of the Hapsburg and Wittelsbach Royal Houses could have provided parallels. A resigned philosophy of destruction and death emerges, compensated for by the escape to beauty.

The titles of the novels suggest decline and fall, *Götterdämmerung* – Wagner is indeed the presiding deity in Bourges' epics of decay.

The epic intention is also evident in the later novels of Paul Adam, the one-time Naturalist,[109] who had felt the call of revolt and, in his most successful vein, evokes scenes from the Napoleonic saga, e.g. *La Force* (1899), *L'Enfant d'Austerlitz* (1902), as mo- ments of power and energy in the nation's life.

With Estaunié we move from epic levels to intimate moral studies of individuals now in provincial settings: e.g. *La Vie Secrète* (1908), *Les Choses Voient* (1913); now in Paris: *L'Ascension de M. Baslèvre* (1921).

Marcel Prévost aims to be a moralist in *Demi-Vierges* (1894) and sounds a warning against 'le flirt...anglo-Saxon';[110] in *Mon- sieur et Madame Moloch* (1906) he develops the theme, popular at the time, of the two Germanies, the peace-loving Germany of the Social-Democrats, of the scholars, like M. Moloch, and the Ger- many that believes in the gospel of force. But principally Prévost set out to be a moralist and more particularly a father-confessor to

---

[107] *Le Roman d'un Enfant* (1899).
[108] *Le Crépuscule des Dieux* (1884); *Les Oiseaux s'envolent et les fleurs tombent* (1895).
[109] *Chair Molle* (1888).
[110] See Bourget's preface.

women, e.g. the continuing series, before and after her marriage, of the *Lettres à Françoise* (1902, '20, '24), preaching a morality, whose prudence, respectability and latitudinarianism ensured the preacher's popularity. There is something of Bourget in Prévost but on a lower level of passionate intensity; he reflects the attitudes of a secure and prosperous bourgeois society, ready to accept moral lessons provided they are worldly-wise and make no uncomfortable demands.

As becomes a son-in-law of Heredia, the Belgian Pierre Louÿs gives a Parnassian flavour to his evocations of life in ancient Alexandria, e.g. *Aphrodite* (1896), but strongly spiced with eroticism.

In *Les Aventures du roi Pausole* (1901), Alexandria is replaced by a land of fancy, its best justification being that it inspired a light opera by Arthur Honegger (1892–1955); the eroticism remains. Better than either of these works is *La Femme et le Pantin* (1898), a story of the then popular formula of unrequited love and cruelty.

Pierre Mille, Louis Bertrand, the brothers Tharaud, Claude Farrère, like Loti before them, take the novel a-travelling. Mille aimed to be the French Kipling. Kipling also inspired the first work of the Tharaud tandem: *Dingley, l'illustre écrivain* (1906). In the long series of their joint works, which bestrides the 1914 war, fiction is often a thin disguise for well-documented studies, both historical and social, of foreign lands: e.g. *La Fête arabe* (1912), *Rabat, ou les heures marocaines* (1918), *L'An prochain à Jérusalem* (1924). Louis Bertrand is drawn particularly to North Africa as a cradle of Western Christianity, e.g. *Sanguis Martyrum* (1918), Claude Farrère to Turkey and the Far East; melodrama against exotic background is his formula: e.g. *L'homme qui assassina* (1907), *La Bataille* (1908).

Amongst the women writers the outstanding figure is Colette. Neither Colette Willy – though Willy[111] was her first husband and early partner or impresario, in literature – nor Colette Yver, her worthy if pedestrian contemporary, but simply Colette.

The Claudine series, largely autobiographical (*Claudine à l'Ecole*, 1900, *Claudine à Paris*, 1901, *Claudine en Ménage*, 1902, *Claudine s'en va*, 1903), had been written under Willy's guidance – she learned much from him stylistically – and published under his name. The entrancing *Dialogues de Bêtes* (1904) were signed Colette Willy – a first step to liberation, achieved in 1906 by divorce, after publishing two other books in collaboration with Willy: *Minne* (1904) and *Les Egarements de Minne* (1905). But liberation from Willy did not yet mean for Colette the independence of a writer with an assured literary reputation; she did make

[111] Henry Gauthier-Villars.

a reputation for herself, but in another sphere, that of the Café-Concert or 'Miousicholl' world, then enjoying golden days and so often brilliantly depicted by Toulouse-Lautrec (1864–1901). As a dancer at the 'Ba-Ta-Clan', and with her partner Georges Wague,[112] she created mime-shows (e.g. le Désir, l'Amour, la Chimère) of the type that formed a regular feature in the programme of these establishments. These years enriched the fund of experience she continued to draw on for her books: e.g. *La Retraite Sentimentale* (1907), *L'Ingénue Libertine* (1909) – a reedition in one volume of the two volumes of *Minne, La Vagabonde* (1910), *L'Entrave* (1913), sequel to *La Vagabonde*.

During the war years, Madame Henry de Jouvenel, as she had become (1912), was mainly engaged in journalism. The inter-war period was to see her at the height of her powers, notably with *Chéri* (1920) – whence a play was to be made, Colette herself taking the part of Léa; *Le Blé en Herbe* (1923) – later filmed; *La Fin de Chéri* (1926); *La Naissance du Jour* (1928) – the book, possibly her greatest, that dwells so tenderly on her mother; *Sido* (1929); *La Chatte* (1933); *Duo* (1934); and *Mes Apprentissages* (1936), which evokes the literary world she had known at the turn of the century before the Colette-Willy ménage had broken up.

Through the Second World War and after, the flow of her books continued, amongst them *Paris de ma fenêtre* (1944); *Gigi* (1945) – a gift for the nostalgic film evocation of *la belle époque* with Maurice Chevalier in a leading part; *L'Etoile Vesper* (1947); *Le Fanal Bleu* (1949). By this time Colette, Madame Goudeket by her third marriage (1935), President of the Goncourt Academy (elected, 1945), Grand Officer of the Legion of Honour (1953), had become a national figure. Few writers can have registered such a record of continuous success.

Memories of childhood and adolescence (*Claudine I* and *II*), of her pets Tobie-Chien and Kitti-la-Doucette (*Dialogues de Bêtes*), of her early womanhood (*Claudine III* and *IV*; and *L'Ingénue Libertine*), back-stage memories (*La Vagabonde, L'Entrave, L'Envers du Music Hall*), writing apprenticeship memoirs (*Mes Apprentissages*), memories of *Sido*, portrait of herself in the evening glow (*L'Etoile Vesper*), much of Colette's output seems directly or indirectly autobiographical, a record full of vividness and vitality; she loved simple things abundantly – animals, children, flowers, her native Burgundy – but she could also get outside herself. She can excel in the pithy short story (e.g. *La Femme Cachée*, 1924) and, within the limits of her deliberately limited canvas, her longer stories (perhaps too slight to rank as full-scale novels?) have a delicate perfection – e.g. *Le Blé en Herbe, Chéri*, the dawn of love,

112 *La Vagabonde*.

and the pathos of the not-so-young woman in love with a heartless gigolo, what more moving. Love is the great, the only theme; love, frankly sensual, its awakening, its joys and frustrations, its ashes and sordid morrows. Let others moralize on man and his destiny, Colette remains on the level of natural instincts; on that level she looks at life with an unsentimental but compassionate eye, belonging to no school, untouched by fashion, content to be natural and, with her concrete, vivid style, one of the outstanding prose-writers of her time. Who would not willingly go with her 'vers la porte invisible par où ils sont sortis de leur enfance'?[113]

While Naturalism held the stage, Becque had many imitators of whom almost nothing remains; exceptions are an early play by Brieux, *Blanchette* (1892), *L'Argent* (1895) by Fabre, *Plaisir de rompre* (1897) by Jules Renard, where something of the illusion of life is achieved, by the objective attitude of the dramatist, and dramatic interest maintained by the characterization and naturalness of the dialogue.

But *La Parisienne* was a summit, after which the direction lay downhill. Life may provide an inexhaustible number of subjects, but if the attitude that lies behind their portrayal remains the same, the works soon lose originality. The Naturalist theatre in its turn fell into a rigid formula, where formlessness and flatness were the dramatic rule, the sordid, the harsh, the brutal, the cynical, invariably the angle of vision. The escape from this dead end followed broadly three directions: first, the dramatists who whilst retaining the realist framework, allow some personal attitude of their own to show itself; Octave Mirbeau (1848–1917) expresses his hatred of the bourgeoisie in terms that hover between aggressive realism and virulent satire;[114] Porto-Riche (1849–1930) and François de Curel (1854–1928) bring back moral and psychological analysis;[115] on a similar plane, Henri Bernstein (1876–1953), with all the skill of Sardou, brings greater dramatic tension and sense of crisis;[116] Paul Hervieu (1857–1915) endeavours to return to the ancient idea of fate to give tragic weight to his moral[117] or social[118] message; Eugène Brieux (1858–1932), from his early Naturalist loyalties, gravitated to aggressive thesis drama[119] or social didacticism.[120]

The euphoric lyricism of Jean Richepin (1849–1926),[121] in

[113] *Blé en Herbe.*
[114] e.g. *Les Affaires sont les Affaires* (1903); *L'Epidémie* (1908).
[115] P-R., e.g. *Le Vieil Homme* (1911). F. de C., e.g. *L'Envers d'une Sainte* (1892), *Les Fossiles* (1892).
[116] e.g. *La Rafale* (1905), *Le Voleur* (1906), *La Griffe* (1906), *Samson* (1907). [117] e.g. *Le Dédale* (1903).
[118] e.g. *La Course du Flambeau* (1901). [119] *La Robe Rouge* (1900).
[120] *Les Avariés* (1902). [121] *Le Flibustier* (1888), *Le Chemineau* (1897).

whom something of the bohemianism of an earlier generation re-
vives, offers a second escape from Naturalism; a third is the
neo-Romanticism of Edmond Rostand (1868–1918). The latter's
Les Romanesques (1894) borrows the theme of Romeo and Juliet
and transposes it into a cloying verse-comedy almost on the level of
the Pierrot show; *La Princesse Lointaine* (1895) exploits the theme
of ideal love in a medieval setting; with *Cyrano de Bergerac* (1897)
the tide of Romanticism seems at its height again: a central dramatic figure, pseudo-historical, hiding his secret love under a false air
of truculence and gaiety, a grotesque antithesis of a poet's soul
hidden in physical ugliness. Much the same may be said of
L'Aiglon (1900) except that here the hero has exchanged romantic
ebullience for the romantic melancholy of decline; in place of
truculent bravery he wears the aristocratic air of glacial detachment to hide his patriotic designs; in his relations with the vapid
Marie-Louise, his mother, with his entourage, puzzled by his Sybil-
line remarks,[122] the duc de Reichstadt is vaguely reminiscent of
Hamlet.

Only one important Romantic trait seems lacking: for the 1830
generation the hero they created was the image of something they
genuinely believed in: man the sport of fate, of society, or of some
other force beyond his control. Maybe they were too egotistical to
give that image much human or universal significance, but the
belief was genuine. Rostand does not persuade us of his sincerity.
In particular we may question it when we remember that the part
of L'Aiglon was originally played by a woman.[123] This may be
acceptable for the principal boy in pantomime or in an opera by
Mozart,[124] but in a drama with a supposedly historical basis?
The part was presumably written for the actress whose skill and
grace could be expected to give additional pathos to the role. This
serves to underline the essentially theatrical nature of Rostand's
art.

Cyrano de Bergerac remains Rostand's masterpiece, because here
there is a grain of genuine human pathos, particularly in the last
scene when the dying Cyrano inadvertently reveals to Roxane the
heroic imposture he has been living for years. Rostand was a talen-
ted playwright: skill in dramatic construction Hugo could not have
competed with, poetry which for rhetorical power, skilful versifica-
tion and ingenious rhyming vies with Hugo's, ability to exploit
human emotion[125] for theatrical effect; only the spark of sincerity
is generally lacking to lift his work from its rather trivial plane to

[122] Act I, Sc. 8.
[123] Sarah Bernhardt; she had also played 'Mélissinde' in *La Princesse
Lointaine*.
[124] e.g. Cherubino.
[125] Even political, e.g. Bonapartist patriotism in *L'Aiglon*.

a level where its dramatic impact would have more human significance.

Nor must we forget that the expansive days of the Third Republic
at its apogee provided an even better climate than the days of
Labiche for comedy to flourish independently; comedy of situation
in high life: Edouard Pailleron (1834–99),[126] Henri Lavedan (1859–
1940);[127] emotional comedy: Maurice Donnay (1859–1945),[128]
bourgeois comedy: Tristan Bernard (1866–1947),[129] farce: Georges
Feydeau (1862–1921);[130] satirical comedy: Robert de Flers (1872–
1927) and Arman de Caillavet (1869–1915) in double harness. Their
non-corrosive humour plays lightly on the gravity of the Academy,[131] on the 'Establishment' from crowned heads to aspiring
politicians,[132] on the Ministry of Fine Arts.[133]

Alfred Jarry (1873–1907) is in a class by himself; like Lautréamont, like Rimbaud, a shooting star, an enigma, one of the non-
conformists whose fate so often is to live miserably on the fringe
of the literary 'Establishments', to die unsung, and sometimes to
be picked up later, then hailed as prophetic geniuses. Jarry's *Ubu
Roi* was performed (1896) and failed; thereafter Jarry disappeared
from view until in recent years all his works were published.[134]

The grotesque 'Ubu' was born when Jarry was a schoolboy at
Rennes (1885–8); was he a schoolboys' collective joke? In any
case, Jarry's was the creative imagination that aimed at gathering
up 'tout le grotesque qui est au monde' in the character of Ubu,
inspired by one of Jarry's masters. The idea developed into a
veritable saga: *Ubu Cocu, Ubu enchaîné, L'Almanach du père
Ubu illustré* (with drawings by Bonnard and by Jarry himself, full
of the same grotesque vigour), *Ubu sur la butte*, and – best known
of all now – *Ubu Roi*. Here the scene is a fanciful Poland; a revolution overthrows the reigning monarch; Ubu, flanked by his down-
to-earth spouse, la Mère Ubu, becomes king. At no point did *Ubu
Roi* seem to make contact with a period emerging from Naturalism
and wedded to the neo-Romanticism of Rostand, the Symbolism of
Maeterlinck, the social theatre of Mirbeau, Hervieu, Brieux and
company, the various levels of comedy from the 'Vaudeville' of
Feydeau to the wit of Flers and Caillavet. If anything Jarry's
grotesque hammer-blows are more akin to the harsh irony of

---

[126] e.g. *Le monde où l'on s'ennuie* (1881).
[127] e.g. *Le Prince d'Aurec* (1894).
[128] e.g. *Amants* (1896), *La Douloureuse* (1897).
[129] e.g. *Un mari pacifique* (1901), *Triplepatte* (1905).
[130] e.g. *La Dame de chez Maxim* (1899), *Occupe-toi d'Amélie* (1907).
[131] *L'Habit vert* (1912).   [132] *Le Roi* (1908).   [133] *Le Bois sacré* (1911).
[134] *Oeuvres complètes*, edited by R. Massat; 'Editions du Livre' (Monte
Carlo, 1949). Also *Le Tout Ubu – livre de poche* (1962), and the *Cahiers
du Collège de pataphysique*.

Georges Courteline, but without Courteline's deliberate hold on reality.

In the fullness of time Ubu in his various manifestations has come to be recognized as a farce of epic grandeur. Departing entirely from the stage realism of its own day, it looks back to the Shakespearian stage and forward to Brecht.[135] This point alone makes it interesting; on a different plane, the vision it reveals has made a powerful impact. The truculent pantaloon Ubu, cruel, merciless, treacherous, grasping, inept, governing the state as in a Kafka nightmare, is seen to be a prophetic satire on our own day; the age of Hitler and Stalin, of lesser dictators black, white or yellow, has learned to recognize in Jarry's sinister buffoon a tragically relevant image.

Jarry's other works are a mixture of brilliant poetic imagery, fantastical invention and what in less percipient times would have been regarded no doubt as nonsense, now perhaps as post-Nervalian hermetic references, or deep pre-Surrealist and Freudian explorations; obscurities in any event.

Critics were not wanting to take up the torch from Sainte-Beuve and Taine.

Pedagogue *in excelsis*, Ferdinand Brunetière (1849–1906) believes in chastisement, order, authority; chastisement first, that order may be restored. Zola and the Naturalists are in the ascendant; Brunetière brings his ferule down on them – *Le Roman Naturaliste* (1883).[136]

Amongst his most characteristic works are three series of lectures subsequently published: *L'Evolution des genres* (1890), a history of criticism in France which its author intended should be the first part of a history of all the different literary 'genres'. He was unable to realize that plan in full, but the other two series of lectures fit in: *L'Evolution de la poésie lyrique* (1894), and *Epoques du Théâtre* (1896). The titles call up the shades of Darwin: 'Evolution', 'Genres', 'Epoques'.

The full statement of Brunetière's doctrine is given in his article on 'La Critique' (c. 1889):[137] 'L'objet de la critique est de juger, de classer et d'expliquer'. Explanation is the first person in this critical Trinity and here Darwin's influence shows itself; explanation means relating a work to its genre, showing its position in the

---

[135] 'Notez que je suis certain de la supériorité "suggestion" de la pancarte écrite sur le décor. Un décor, ni une figuration ne rendrait "l'armée polonaise en marche dans l'Ukraine" ' – extract of letter from A. Jarry to Lugné-Poe, Director of 'Théâtre de l'Oeuvre', 8 January 1896.

[136] Originally published as articles in *La Revue des deux mondes* from 1875. Brunetière became its editor in 1892.

[137] *Grande Encyclopédie.*

latter's development, what conditions, social and personal, may have affected its character. There are reminiscences of Taine and Sainte-Beuve, but the emphasis is more on the idea of art-forms which, like Darwinian species, have a life of their own, are exposed to the constant pressure of social forces, transform themselves in time, obey the law of evolution, without losing their characteristics as 'genres'.

The idea of evolution enables the critic to situate a work in relation to its kind; it also enables him to proceed to classification of 'genres' in relation to each other, and works in relation to others in the same genre. The notion of hierarchy is as pertinent to the arts and within the arts to literature and within literature to 'genres', as to species in botany or zoology; the hierarchy of the arts depends in the last resort on the degree of humanity that each can express, having regard to their respective media; *mutatis mutandis*, the same principle applies to art-forms and lastly to individual works.

On this basis judgment is as objective an exercise as the other two; in contrast to the critics (e.g. Taine) who refused to admit the critic's right to judge, thus reducing criticism to a branch of psychology or sociology, Brunetière insists that the aim of criticism is not fulfilled without judgment, that criticism parts company here with, one might almost say, other sciences of observation, which remain within the limits of explanation and classification. We may admit the claim, but scarcely that Brunetière's judgment is objective. Judgment, he says, means deciding to what extent a given work has exploited the potential of its own art-form and thus in the last resort contributed to the whole aim of literature, but Brunetière's personal attitude creeps in; literature's aim is to express in the most beautiful form the permanent universal aspects of humanity; his attitude is rigidly classical; the seventeenth century is his ideal.

Once the aim has been established, the function of the critic himself follows naturally: to guard the shrine, keep authors and public opinion within the bounds of truth, chastise (when necessary). Nor let anyone deny that right to the critic; not only is he armed with the tables of the law; literature itself clearly shows the superior position of criticism, since every great work is in itself a critical act; Racine's plays are a criticism of Corneille, Hugo's a criticism of the neo-classical tragedy, etc.

Brunetière exemplifies Thibaudet's dictum that critics from the ranks of academe tend towards politics. Literature has a moral function; the state is there to defend the moral values enshrined in a nation's history; the critics belong to the 'Establishment': 'N'est-ce pas le critique, en maintenant la tradition qui rend, non plus aux auteurs, ou à l'opinion, ni même aux lettres, mais à la race, mais à la nation ce dernier service d'entretenir et de perpétuer d'âge en âge l'identité de la conscience nationale.'

The political affinities of Brunetière are not difficult to guess; they appear in *Discours de Combat* and were to be sharpened by the Dreyfus Affair.

Academe was to provide other recruits to criticism, notably Emile Faguet (1847–1916) and Gustave Lanson (1854–1934). Faguet excels in analysis; he applies himself first to literary subjects, *inter alia, Etudes sur le 17e siècle* (1893), and lest anyone should be surprised to see this most unpoetic of men writing a history of French poetry, the reason is that Faguet was appointed to a chair of poetry at the Sorbonne (1897). Later, without abandoning literature, he turns to moralists and political thinkers: *Politiques et moralistes du 19e siècle* (three volumes, 1891, 1898, 1900).

Literary journalism also occupied him, as dramatic critic (1888–1907) in the *Journal des Débats* he wrote numerous reviews: *Notes sur le Théâtre* (1889–91), *Propos de Théâtre* (1903–10).

Twice at least Faguet expressed a view about the critics' role: in *Propos Littéraires 1e Série* (1902–10),[138] and *L'Art de Lire* (posth. 1920).[139] Doubtless literary studies incorporating large stretches of literary history, with writers treated more as moments in the literary continuum (Brunetière's method), have their value; at the same time Faguet remains suspicious of these broad perspectives. Like views from a hill-top, they may confer an intelligible structure on the literary landscape but we must not neglect the divergent currents, contradictory tendencies that appear, on closer inspection. Thus, Faguet tends to concern himself more with individuals than with movements. The method is apt to be uniform: the man, the work, the influence. The analysis proceeds with oiled precision, at its best in the studies of ideas or individual works. At the turn of the century Faguet, like Brunetière, was drawn into the political controversies of the day (*Questions politiques*, 1899; *Problèmes politiques*, 1900). The long habit of analysis applied to past political thinkers may have awakened his desire to influence political opinion in the present, and doubtless the Dreyfus Affair sharpened it.

The intellectualist Faguet was a liberal[140] and particularly an anti-democrat.[141] This fact explains why Faguet found himself in the same camp as the nationalist and Catholic Brunetière.

[138] Chap. I.
[139] Chap. IX.
[140] *Le Libéralisme* (1902).
[141] *Le Culte de l'incompétence* (1911), *l'Horreur des responsabilités* (1911).

Lanson does not conform to Thibaudet's dictum, previously mentioned, about academic criticism and publicism. His great strength is critical and historical erudition.[142] Doubtless all critics are learned. Unlike Brunetière who made his erudition serve his evolutionist theories, unlike Faguet who wears his learning lightly, Lanson makes erudition the solid basis for literary history; amongst his numerous writings – inter alia, Histoire de la littérature française (1894) – the most characteristic is his Manuel bibliographique de la littérature française moderne (1909–14). Lanson is the epitome of what Péguy disliked in the Sorbonne,[143] and of what was later to be the target of 'Agathon'[144] in the pamphlet L'Esprit de la Nouvelle Sorbonne (1911); unjust attacks; Lanson's achievements stand.

Criticism by creative artists also has its representatives in this period; the names of Zola, Mallarmé, Verlaine spring to mind. Zola scarcely ranks above the level of a propagandist; Mallarmé and Verlaine, particularly the former, have original things to say about poetry, but they can scarcely compare as critics with Baudelaire.

Other creative writers practised criticism in the strict sense to a greater or less extent. Amongst these mention may be made of Bourget and France, Jules Lemaitre (1853–1914), E-M. de Voguë (1848–1910), Gide (1869–1951). Finally there are the professional critics and journalists, notably Francisque Sarcey (1827–99), Hennequin (1858–99), Rémy de Gourmont (1858–1915).

Bourget's Essais de Psychologie Contemporaine (1e série, 1883, 2e série, 1885) are an important date in French criticism of the period. Much in the line of Taine, Bourget regards books as a means of analysing the psychology of their authors; aesthetic questions are secondary. Each of the writers Bourget studies reveals a spiritual flaw and therefore a danger: Renan – the intellectual dilettante, Flaubert – the moral nihilist, Baudelaire – theorist of decadence and glorying in it, Stendhal – black pessimism, Dumas fils – the analytical spirit that destroys the possibility of happiness, the Goncourt brothers – aesthetic dilettantism, etc. In one form or another Bourget denounces pessimism as a paralysing malady and a danger to the nation. The critic must be a moralist; Bourget's critical studies reflect fully the post-1870 spirit of anxious critical soundings: why defeat? How avoid another such experience?

Beneath the objective analytical approach the moralist with religious and traditionalist values, essential to withstand the dangers

[142] cf. his article in Revue du mois, October 1910. See H. Peyre, Essais de méthode ... de G. Lanson, 1966, chap. i.
[143] 'Qui n'a pas connu la douceur de M. Lanson ignore ce que c'est que du vinaigre sucré, et du fiel en confiture'. See also above, p. 107.
[144] Pseudonym of Henri Massis and Alfred de Tarde.

he has been diagnosing, appears. Bourget at this level rejoins
Brunetière.

Anatole France (*La Vie Littéraire*, 1888-92, *Le Jardin d'Epicure*, 1895, *Le Génie Latin*, 1918) and Jules Lemaitre (*Les Contemporains*, 1885-99, *Impressions de Théâtre*, 1888-98) have in
common their rejection of systematic criticism; both are impres-
sionists, both attack the dogmatists and traditionalists. The rate at
which systems succeed each other and throw over the claims of
what went before, scarcely encourages belief in their value as a
basis for criticism. Feeling and intuition, not reason, are the final
arbiters in artistic judgment;[145] moreover, as Lemaitre points
out,[146] we ourselves are changeable. What then is criticism to be?
Lemaitre replies: an extra source of enjoyment to be drawn from
literature, an enrichment of the reader's experience – 'la critique
est l'art de jouir des livres, et d'enrichir et d'affiner par eux ses
sensations.'[147] And France, in the same vein: 'le bon critique...
raconte les aventures de son âme au milieu des chefs-d'oeuvre.'[148]

Impressionism does not exclude preferences; Lemaitre is hostile
to Rousseau, harsh towards Chateaubriand, uncomprehending to
the Symbolists; France is equally uncomprehending towards the
latter; the seventeenth century is his ideal.

Voguë, diplomat and parliamentarian, critic and occasional
novelist (e.g. *Les Morts qui parlent*, 1899), is remembered for one
major critical work, *Le Roman Russe* (1886), which did much to
quicken French interest in the Russian novelists, particularly Tolstoy and Dostoïevsky.

Gide, the accomplished egotist, is an occasional critic when he
sees in some writer a reflection of his own attitudes (e.g. *Dostoïewsky*, 1923); at the same time he speaks with admiration of classicism (*Prétextes*, 1903, *Nouveaux Prétextes*, 1911) and sees modesty
as its essential trait; of classicism he himself has nothing except the
chaste beauty of form.

Sarcey is a journalist pure and simple who belongs in spirit to an
earlier generation. A passionate man of the theatre (*40 ans de
Théâtre*, *1860–99*), his ideal is the 'well-made play' as exemplified
in the school of Dumas *fils* and Augier; his considerable influence
was therefore thrown against the efforts by the Naturalists to give
renewed life to the theatre – witness his hostility to Becque.

Hennequin was a theorist; he had no time to apply his theory
set out in *La Critique Scientifique* (1888). Like Taine he is in

[145] See A.F., *Vie Litt.*, Vols. II and III, prefaces; Lemaitre, *Contemporains*, 6e serie, preface.
[146] *Contemporains*, 2e serie (A. France).
[147] Lemaitre, *Contemporains*, 3e serie (Bourget), see also A.F., *Le Jardin
Epicure*.
[148] *Vie Litt.*, Vol. I, preface.

search of objective scientific criteria but in fact he rejects as clumsy Taine's method of explaining a work by social background and historical momentum; neither criterion is uniform; social classes, different cultural levels and temperaments make background and historical pressures uneven; successful artists appeal to the affinities of certain types of people (e.g. Bunyan in seventeenth-century England, Béranger in nineteenth-century France) and so create their own background of readers who have become conscious of what they like or dislike through the artist. Taine's method should be applied in reverse; the critic should go from the known (the work) to the unknown that lies behind: the artist's own psychology and the social group he has in a sense created.

The parallel for Hennequin is less Taine than Bourget. Gourmont's pleasure as a critic is to take his readers for agreeable walks in the gardens of literature and thought (*Promenades littéraires*, 1904–27, *Promenades Philosophiques*, 1905–9).[149] Like Lemaitre and France, Gourmont has no system and follows the garden path wherever it lead, and, with such a voracious and penetrating reader, it leads to discoveries – forgotten writers, new views of familiar sites: 'le cerveau de M. Gourmont est comme l'oeil d'une mouche. Il voit tout et chaque fois différemment.'[150] Himself an occasional Symbolist poet, he became their champion and interpreter.[151]

A contributor to Péguy's *Cahiers de la Quinzaine* was André Suarès[152] (1866–1948). They had met at the turn of the century through Romain Rolland. The generous crusading spirit which animated Péguy and his friends had largely been engendered by the Dreyfus Affair ('Dire la vérité, toute la vérité, ... etc.'), but there were other contributory sources, both literary and political. Gobineau's theory on the superiority of the Aryan race, Nietzsche's ideas on the Superman were in the air. For young men living at a time when Europe was beginning to fall into the pattern of the 1914 alliances, here were stimulants that helped to produce a cult of the heroic and of greatness. It was to take many forms: aggressive monarchism, with Charles Maurras; nationalism with Barrès; carrying the civilizing mission of France to Africa with explorers and officers of the stamp of Savorgnan de Brazza and Psichari; the patriotism of the generous humanist Péguy.

Suarès reflects its literary and humanist aspect. He was united with Romain Rolland in the cult of great men, great music, great

---

149 New selected edn., 3 vols. (1963).
150 Quoted by E. Clancier: *De Rimbaud au Surréalisme*, Seghers (1961).
151 *Le Livre des Masques* and *Deuxième Livre des Masques*.
152 Real name Yves Scantrel.

literature and art. 'Si je pars le premier', he writes to Péguy in October 1911, 'faites mon oraison funèbre en fonction de l'art que j'ai fidèlement servi, et de la divine musique, qui est l'architecture du coeur'; in counterpoint, an aristocratic and equally Romantic disdain of the vulgar herd, 'la foule ignoble et féconde qui fait les enfants, les révolutions, le fromage, les gros souliers, le commerce et fortune avec.'[153] How well the scorn of the sentiment is emphasized not only by the disparate assemblage – children and revolutions, cheese and hob-nail boots – but also by the accumulation of 'fs' – mere coincidence from such a master of style? Suarès's response to his cult of great men is to be found in the series of biographical studies from his pen: *Tolstoï* (1899), *Wagner* (1899), *Tolstoï vivant* (1911), *Trois Hommes – Pascal, Ibsen, Dostoïevski* (1915), *A. de Musset* (1923), *Debussy* (1927).

In his own day Suarès remained an isolated figure, known only to a limited public. Of recent years he has awakened more interest; not, however, as biographer or as poet and dramatist (*La Tragédie d'Electre et Oreste*, 1905, *Cressida*, 1914), but as the vigorous letter-writer of a restless and unquiet soul,[154] in which role he is often both moralist and literary critic, acute though not necessarily always just, and as the author of *Le Voyage du Condottière* (1911), the passionate and eloquent traveller in quest of art – 'Comme tout ce qui compte dans la vie, un beau voyage est une oeuvre d'art: une création.'[155]

[153] To Romain Rolland, 25 August 1887. See *Cahiers Romain Rolland*, No. 5 (1954). The choice of letters in this volume gives not only portraits of both writer and recipient but is informed with the spirit of the time, when the influence of Schopenhauer was still active, and the impact of Nietzsche was strong.
[154] Op. cit.; also *André Suarès et Paul Claudel, Correspondance*.
[155] *Voyage du C.*, préface.

Part II

§ II RESTLESSNESS
AND RECONSTRUCTION

Chapter 8

THE FIRST WORLD WAR
AND THE INTELLECTUAL BACKGROUND
BETWEEN THE WARS

T HE war of 1914 destroyed the brilliant social life of the previous decade and swept away the ephemeral literature of the day. In that sense it clearly marks the end of an era.

But also, at the outset at least, it gave a great impetus to Nietzschean influence: life to be lived at a level of intense experience, the search for the deepest sources of energy and power in human nature as a basis, *inter alia,* of new moral values, heroism. The generation that went to war in 1914 was deeply imbued with these ideas and had found their most brilliant expression in the writings of Barrès. In that sense the war was not a break but a continuance, if only for a little, a flowering of the seeds that had been germinating before, an upsurge of patriotic emotion healing all differences and galvanizing the nation into a united thrust to repel the invader, not counting the cost in individual sacrifice.

This romantic response to war comprises inevitably the flood of ephemeral patriotic literature, journalistic and other, produced for home consumption. But a residuum of writings have a higher quality because conveying some aspect of authentic human experience under the stress of war: e.g. Cocteau's *Thomas l'imposteur,* Montherlant's *Le Songe,* Drieu La Rochelle's *La Comédie de Charleroi,* Larrouy's *L'Odyssée d'un transport torpillé* (1917).

Here, if the confusion, brutality and suffering of war are evoked, the purpose seems essentially to give an objective record of the adventure. Something of the same objectivity appears in the conversations between Marcel and his friend Saint-Loup, on leave from the front shortly before being killed.[1] Imaginative intelligence here successfully replaces direct experience to produce a sense of authenticity.

From an officers' mess come *Les Silences du Colonel Bramble* and *Les Discours du Docteur O'Grady* which made André Maurois's reputation, but these are national character studies, as seen in

---

[1] *Temps Retrouvé,* 1.

war conditions, rather than war novels. Soon, however, the war
settled into the stagnation of trench warfare, convulsed from time
to time by violent battles where the tremendous fire-power ensured
a holocaust.

The mood of war literature changes. The lyric poets, perhaps,
bring us closest to the sense of tragedy and suffering. Guillaume
Apollinaire expresses often the weird beauty of the desolate lunar
scene and with sober realism his pity for the sufferings of his
fellow soldiers;[2] equally moving is the sense of anguish and desolation that comes across to us from 'Prière des tranchées' by Jean
Marc Bernard[3] (1883–1915).

> Ah! rendez-nous l'enthousiasme . . .

or from his 'De Profundis'

> Du plus profond de la tranchée
> Nous élevons les mains vers vous,
> Seigneur! Ayez pitié de nous
> Et de notre âme desséchée.

Amongst prose works, a classic and sincere expression of the
tragedy and sacrifice of war, is Roland Dorgelès' *Les Croix de Bois*
(1919).

Equally characteristic of the changed mood is the note of pity,
e.g. Duhamel's *Vie des Martyrs* (1916), and especially the note of
protest, e.g. Drieu La Rochelle's *Interrogations* (1917), Vildrac's
Les Chants du désespéré (1920), and, on a more philosophic level,
Mars, ou la guerre jugée (1921), where its author 'Alain' speaks
as a moralist who has seen the war close at hand.[4] The outstanding
work in this category however is surely *Le Feu* (1916), by Henri
Barbusse (1873–1935).

Here, what romanticism of war might have been left after
nearly two years of trench warfare, has sunk in the mud. *Le Feu*
evokes the daily lives of the ordinary infantryman in the trenches
amidst the mire, the filth, the damp, the lice and the dead: '"Oui
c'est ça, la guerre, répète-t-il d'une voix lointaine . . ." Il veut dire,
et je comprends avec lui: "Plus que les charges qui ressemblent à
des revues, plus que les batailles visibles déployées comme des
oriflammes, . . . cette guerre, c'est la fatigue épouvantable, sur-
naturelle, et l'eau jusqu'au ventre et la boue et l'ordure et l'infâme
saleté. C'est les faces moisies et les chairs en loques et les cadavres
qui ne ressemblent même plus à des cadavres . . . C'est cela, cette
monotonie infinie de misères, interrompue par des drames aigus,

---

[2] See below, pp. 206–9.
[3] Also wrote *Sub Tegmine Fagi* (1913) and the very Barrèsian prose
meditation *Haut Vivarais d'hiver* (*Oeuvres*, posth., 1923).
[4] 'Alain', though over-age, joined up and served as a signaller.

c'est cela, et non pas la baïonette qui étincelle comme de l'argent, ni le chant de coq du clairon au soleil!'"[5]

The picture of war in *Le Feu* recalls the Naturalists' 'slices of life' of *Les Soirées de Médan* and the attitude is not dissimilar – a generous humanitarian indignation: 'L'avenir! L'avenir! L'oeuvre de l'avenir sera d'effacer ce présent-ci ... comme quelque chose d'abominable et de honteux. Et pourtant ce présent, il le fallait ... Honte à la gloire militaire, ... aux armées, ... au métier de soldat qui change les hommes tour à tour en stupides victimes et en ignobles bourreaux ...'[6] Indignation, but also, in contrast to the authors of *Les Soirées de Médan*, an element of hope in a democratic future, symbolized at the end by the thin ray of sunshine that breaks through the lowering clouds, as the narrator and his friends gird themselves once more for battle, just as at the beginning the consumptives in the mountain sanatorium at the outbreak of war are also a symbol – helpless victims before the onset of disease, helpless peoples before the onset of war.

Of a quite different and less sympathetic order of protest is Romain Rolland's article, *Au-dessus de la mêlée* (1914). Over military age, Rolland had gone to Switzerland so that his active pacifism should not be interfered with, but whatever justification there may be, Rolland's scolding attitude to the intellectuals on both sides for their betrayal of European culture was bound to draw angry attacks which duly came; many thought nothing better became a pacifist than silence at such a time; others stressed the moral courage needed to speak out as Rolland did; intellectual arrogance may masquerade as courage, blind a writer to faults of taste, and lead him to believe that whatever he chooses to say, whenever he decides to say it, is important to the listening earth.

When, after four years, the fighting ceased, the scene, which in retrospect appears more European than national, saw by turns the effort to enforce the Treaty of Versailles (1919), the calmer mood of Locarno, the growing menace of the Third Reich. The earlier years were bedevilled by the problem of Reparations and War Debts, the search for security to which, for a brief space, the Treaty of Locarno (1926) seemed a halting answer; the 'thirties were a restless, haunted decade, as the spectre of a new war arose and the Treaty of Versailles was progressively eroded by the brinkmanship of Hitler.

A salient feature of the inter-war years is the growth of rival ideologies that cut across frontiers and exerted a pull on men's loyalties, different from the older national allegiances; the quest for

---

[5] *Le Feu*, chap. 24.
[6] *Ibid.*, chap. 20. See also chap. 24. 'Ah! Vous avez raison, pauvres ouvriers innombrables des batailles ...'.

intellectual security organized by a fascist or communist system of ideas traversed the search for political security within treaty and national structures, and confirmed the all-pervading sense of insecurity, which the advances in the physical sciences had done nothing to allay.

From this aspect, too, the war of 1914 may be seen as an interruption rather than a break with the past.

Science itself had contributed to the sense of dissatisfaction that had been the feature of the pre-war years; far from fulfilling earlier optimistic promises of unlimited progress built on the notion of Nature's fundamental stability, science had been discovering a Universe of infinite complexity and uncertainty. No wonder the discontent produced a shift of allegiance from those exploring the world of matter to those who claimed priority for spiritual and moral values, to Bergson and Nietzsche.

Bergsonism remained rather as a diffused phenomenon, but Nietzsche's influence gathered strength both from the war and from conditions in the inter-war years. Beside Nietzsche stands another figure whose influence was to have equal power – Sigmund Freud (1856–1939). Every age has its 'fashions' in science as in anything else; the shift in emphasis no doubt arises from the belief the more or less informed public acquires about whence may come the greatest contribution to its welfare. In the 'twenties the answer was psychology and psycho-analysis. This development, too, seems in line with the prevailing insecurity engendered by the political situation and the human situation as it appeared from the latest views of the physicists – man, alone, in infinite chaos. Accordingly, he is driven inwards once more, but to a deeper level than had hitherto been dreamed of; like an iceberg of which only a small proportion emerges above the sea's surface, the psyche is shown to plunge deep in the subconscious 'id', whence come our profoundest urges, sexual and other; irrational compulsions dominate our lives. A new field of investigation is opened where there are no accurate standards of measurement in the strict sense and all is mysterious; there perhaps true human happiness lies hidden, and on it men may build a better social order. The psychologist must call in the statistician, the opinion pollster, the computer, to collect data and reduce them to a systematic pattern of behaviourism. Nay more, he may claim the wide expanse of literature, past and present, as his own. Men betray their mental mechanisms in their linguistic habits, writers 'discover' the true nature of their own psyche by the subtle and unwitting emphasis they give to this theme or that, by their choice of this aspect or that of the reality they portray. To whom if not to the literary critic falls the task of penetrating to the core of their secret through the smoke of their professed sentiments or those they lend to their characters. The creative artist, on his side, abandoning all the 'isms' of previous literary schools, will hold up his mirror to catch the true reflection of man's psyche and its chaos. Both creative artist and critic must be the servants of the psychologist in promoting the skills of true mental communication, on which all forms of effective publicity depend.

The literary scene between the two wars reflects something of the intellectual trends and the political conditions. Time has scarcely had an opportunity yet of separating the wheat from the chaff; hence the multitude of poets, novelists, dramatists, essayists and critics that crowd the stage and tend to reduce a literary history to a catalogue. None the less some pattern is discernible; according to their natures, writers reflect the conditions of their day and seek either escape or an appropriate moral attitude.

Peace naturally brought with it an immediate release of tensions and hence a feeling of euphoria; the dawn of a brave new world had broken at last. The new generation was determined to indulge to the full its long pent-up desires. Youth found in the pre-war teachings of Gide a revolt against traditional moral values and a praise of spiritual fervours that exactly fitted its mood; escape was the watchword, escape to adventure or escape from familiar scenes to the wide world which, as never before, lay at men's feet.

Revolt, too, was in the air; signs of it had appeared before the war elsewhere than in Gide, but then it had been little more than a quest, like others before it, for literary and artistic renewal; now was added a sense of violent grievance against the older generation, guilty of the criminal folly of war; their art and literature were equally condemned. Thus did the war give added impetus to the search for a new idiom freed from traditional artistic canons; Dadaïsts and Surrealists were to take the torch from the hands of the earlier Futurists, Freud pointing the way to the inner deeps.

But visions of a brave new world were soon to fade; a mood of despair reappears; in face of the harsh tragedies that seemed in prospect the Gidean interpretation of Nietzsche was too soft; stiffer moral attitudes were necessary and a philosophy more in keeping with man's isolation in a universe that reason had no hold over and was, in a word, absurd. The answers were to be various: the antidote of heroic action for ever straining human endurance to the limit, a deepened Christian faith that accepted life as a tragic adventure and the dear purchase of saintliness, a new Romanticism on a truly Nietzschean, non-Gidian level, that believed man could make sense of life only by vigorous commitment, by stamping the impress of his own will on its absurdity, by creating his own destiny.

Chapter 9

OUTSTANDING WRITERS OF THE AGE

I. VALÉRY LARBAUD

COSMOPOLITAN has been thought an ugly word ever since nineteenth-century nationalism created with it the image of a deracinated 'métèque', incapable of national loyalties. Eighteenth-century attitudes, more broad-minded, had seen their last flowering on the banks of Lake Geneva, in the favourable climate of matured Swiss Protestantism, and strengthened by opposition to Napoleon. A century and more later in what would seem at first the less favourable climate of the French 'H.S.P.',[1] rich, closed, conventional, Valéry Larbaud (1881–1957) provides another example of cosmopolitanism in the best sense of the term. But the Protestant tradition of non-conformity may provide a natural breeding-ground for protest, and in Larbaud's cosmopolitanism, as in Madame de Staël's, though for different reasons, there was an element of protest; protest against the narrow Protestant circle he was brought up in by a domineering mother, with whom his relations appear to have been compounded of resigned submission and the desire to escape.

No wonder Larbaud was a friend and admirer of the 'renegade' Gide, whose suffocated cry of revolt against family envelopment – 'familles, je vous hais!' – echoed his own feelings. The young Barrès, too, must have brought him spiritual comfort: 'Mais d'abord il m'a fallu détruire tout ce que l'expérience des autres avait construit en moi: la morale et les idées de nos éducateurs.'[2] Such sentiments could have come straight from the author of *Sous l'oeil des Barbares* and *Un Homme Libre*.

Escape from the family background, yes, but also from the burden of wealth, which was an isolating force, could become a tragic disadvantage and inspired in Larbaud a restless and guilty sense of uselessness: 'me regarder vivre, et passer toutes ces heures à écrire, avec un tel sentiment d'inutilité et d'isolement.'[3]

---

[1] 'Haute Société Protestante'.
[2] A. O. Barnabooth (pronounced Barna-bousse), *Journal Intime*: V.L., *Oeuvres Complètes*, Vol. IV, p. 377.
[3] Op. cit., Vol. IV, p. 161.

But protest, the desire to escape, the sense of guilt, could not have produced the cultured cosmopolitan Larbaud became, had they not been accompanied by a strong sense of quest, which on the intellectual level showed itself as a thirst for the realities, past and present, cultural and customary, of other countries.

The cosmopolitan Larbaud has the fervour Gide prescribes for Nathanaël (*Nourritures Terrestres*) when he encourages his disciple to go out into the world and enter into man's inheritance of beauty and potential experience: 'Que l'importance soit dans ton regard, non dans la chose regardée.' Fervour and an idealism transcending national frontiers. Reaching back to Voltaire, an early 'European', and forward to our own day, when the idea of Europe is making headway, Larbaud, with his strong belief in the international kinship and community of minds, had been one of the few French writers of the day to see in the 1914 war a monstrous civil war![4]

On a deeper and more intimate level of his being, Larbaud's quest was in search of his own true nature, in search of stable foundations to build a purpose in life on.

All these elements, negative and positive, of Larbaud's cosmopolitanism are reflected in his works which, poetry and prose, are intimately connected with his personal aims and experience. They fall broadly into three parts: first, the *Poèmes d'un riche amateur* (1908, renamed *Poèmes d'A.O. Barnabooth*, 1923) and the *Journal Intime d'A.O. Barnabooth* (1913), to both of which the moral tale in a Voltairian manner, *Le Pauvre Chemisier* (1902), is a kind of introduction; secondly the short novel *Fermina Marquez* (1911), the series of studies of childhood, *Les Enfantines* (1918), and *Amants, heureux Amants* (1923); thirdly the numerous translations of foreign works and critical studies, rich harvest of Larbaud's scholarship and passion for reading—*Ce vice impuni, la lecture* (1925), three parts welded together by Larbaud's cosmopolitanism, three facets of his personality.

Written in the free rhythms Larbaud had derived from Walt Whitman, of whom he was an admirer, and laced with flashes of dry humour (e.g. 'Prologue') very characteristic of Larbaud, the poems shuttle us by train hither and thither across Europe, on shipboard to other parts of the world, wherever the nostalgic whims and curiosity of the sensitive, observant Barnabooth direct:

> Prête-moi ton grand bruit, ta grande allure si douce
> Ton glissement nocturne à travers l'Europe illuminée
> O train de luxe! . . .
> Je parcours en chantonnant tes couloirs
> Et je suis ta course vers Vienne et Budapesth
> Mêlant ma voix à tes cent mille voix,
> O Harmonika-Zug! . . .   (Ode)

[4] See *Preuves*, No. 75 (May 1957); Y. Lévy, 'Valéry Larbaud'.

Various minor events in his own experience[5] had early suggested to Larbaud the personage of Barnabooth, native of South America, citizen of New York, and burdened with an income of ten million 450,000 francs (gold). If the poems give us some glimpses of his character (e.g. 'L'Eterna Voluttà'), his full portrait emerges in the *Journal*, which this millionaire of twenty-three, determined to wipe away the stain of his wealth by using it to enrich his intellectual and emotional experience, writes as he travels from Italy to England, to Russia, to Germany, to Scandinavia, to Spain.

The interior monologue, interspersed with reported conversations, is a treasure-house of observations on the passing scene, descriptions of men and things, reflections, ironic, cynical, moving, by turns. Like his creator, Barnabooth, a second but very Gidian Frédéric Moreau in search of his 'sentimental education', feels the lack of purpose in his life: 'Je n'ai rien fait. Je ne suis rien de bien; je ne suis qu'un ensemble de possibilités que j'ai mille raisons de mettre en doute',[6] and, since millionaire he is, is determined to be something more than a wealthy idler, a millionaire with ideas and knowledge, and indeed no more cultivated and stimulating cosmopolitan than young Barnabooth could be found; in his wake other authors will follow: Paul Morand, Blaise Cendrars, Giraudoux.

Fermina Marquez, largely drawn from personal memories of his school days at Sainte-Barbe-des-Champs (Saint-Augustin in the novel), and *Les Enfantines* are mainly concerned with children's hopes and ambitions (e.g. Joanny Léniot in *Fermina*) and the gulf of misunderstanding and even hostility that separates them from grown-ups (e.g. 'Le Couperet'). The link with his own adolescent experience is evident.

As linguist and critic, Larbaud, with innumerable critical studies and some translations to his credit, put his scholarship at the service of his cosmopolitanism and became a skilful intercessor in France for things foreign, an admirable intellectual liaison agent between France and England, Spain, Ireland, the United States, South America, Mexico, Italy, Portugal, a dedicated European.

II. GIDE

Calvinist bred, educated in the Parisian Protestant school – the Ecole Alsacienne, André Gide (1869–1951) is permeated by Calvinism and, to speak in its terms, Gide seemed predestined to literature, a vocation the family wealth made it easy for him to respond to. His first work, published anonymously, appeared in 1891 – *Les Cahiers d'André Walter*, in two parts: 'cahier blanc', 'cahier noir'. They contain the young poet André Walter's reflec-

[5] *Oeuvres Complètes*, IV, Introduction.   [6] Op. cit., Vol. IV, p. 390.

tions on his love for his cousin Emmanuèle; private confessions to a diary dated 1887–8 and not dissimilar in form from verses of a psalm, about a love that was never divulged; Emmanuèle marries another, dies; André's frustrated love redoubles but tries to find consolation in spiritual and emotional fervours: 'la vie intense voilà le superbe...'[7]

André Walter's solitary reflections and his poems (1892) passed unnoticed; only later when Gide had made a name was it apparent that much of his future doctrines lay in germ in the *Cahiers*: the many-sided nature of truth – 'Nous ne pouvons qu'opiner. L'Affirmation est coupable... Etroits esprits de croire que leur vérité est la seule. La vérité est multiple, infinie, nombreuse autant que les esprits pour y croire'; liberation from constraining disciplines – Gide seems already to be creating his peculiar brand of ethics by generalizing his own revolt against his puritan upbringing:

> Plan de conduite.
> Liberté: la raison la nie – Quand même elle ne serait pas, encore faudrait-il y croire. Les influences certes nous modèlent: il les faut donc discerner. Que la volonté partout domine: se faire tel que l'on se veut. Choisissons les influences?

In his autobiography, *Si le Grain ne meurt* (1926), Gide recalls his first steps in the literary world of Paris, where, in addition to his former school friend Pierre Louÿs, he met Maeterlinck, Huysmans, Henri de Régnier, Mallarmé, Paul Valéry, Francis Jammes. Symbolism, in the ascendant, kindled Gide's enthusiasm, reflected in *Le Traité du Narcisse* (1892): 'le Paradis est toujours à refaire; il n'est point en quelque lointaine Thulé. Il demeure sous l'apparence. Chaque chose détient virtuelle, l'intime harmonie de son être ... tout s'efforce vers sa forme perdue...' The poet's duty is to express the truths hidden within the heart of things.

The Symbolist influence extends to *Le Voyage d'Urien* (1893), in which a shipload of adventurers of the spirit embark upon a Symbolist voyage of 'escape'. Gide himself thereupon embarked on a journey of escape to North Africa from what to him at least seemed the oppressive atmosphere of the literary circles of the capital. He records in *L'Immoraliste* (1902), *Amyntas* (1906), later in *Si le Grain ne meurt* the impact the country made on him; thereafter North Africa did not cease to attract him, and he returned thither in 1895, the year of his marriage to his cousin Madeleine Rondeaux (Emmanuèle in *Si le Grain ne meurt*) and of *Paludes*, an ironical tale that opens the way to Gide's first considerable work, *Les Nourritures Terrestres* (1897).

Gide had now broken with his own Calvinist upbringing and with Symbolism; he had become an apostle of fervour; of spiritual

[7] *Oeuvres*, I, p. 36.

excitement at the potentials of this world; let the young man to
whom this manual of egotism is addressed go forth: 'le désir de
sortir – sortir de n'importe où, de ta ville, de ta famille, de ta
chambre, de ta pensée ...'; 'sortir ... de ta pensée ...', in short let
Nathanaël close his mind to no new aspects or new ideas that the
world may offer, let him above all accept no position as final and,
for that means in effect accepting bondage of some sort, no security.
'Je haïssais les foyers, les familles, tous lieux où l'homme pense
trouver un repos', declares Ménalque, Gide's mouthpiece, 'je disais
que chaque nouveauté doit nous trouver toujours tout entiers
disponibles.'

The message is like an echo of Nietszche and indeed in one of
his *Lettres à Angèle*,[8] Gide writes with enthusiasm of the German
moralist. Nietzsche, a demolisher? Perhaps, but only that others
may build; Nietzsche, like the author of *Les Nourritures*, hates anything savouring of self-complacency and rejection of restless effort;
Gide quotes with approval: 'Rien ne nous fait moins envie que la
Morale de ruminant et l'épais bonheur d'une bonne conscience.'

In line with Nietzsche, but in opposition to the message his contemporary Barrès was proclaiming; the apostle of traditionalism
and nationalism as safe harbours where, so Barrès thought, young
Frenchmen should cast anchor; and indeed, young Frenchmen of
the day who were not wedded to the gospel of Jaurès preferred
Barrès to Gide, as a spiritual attitude against the Germany they
believed – and were they so wrong? – to be preparing for war.

In 1897 Gide was still an isolated figure, unnoticed by the critics,
unknown to the public. Not till after the 1914–18 war was the book
to be seized on eagerly by the new generation, tired of sacrifice,
condemning the folly of their elders that had brought about the
war; here was a manifesto of revolt, of enlightened, enriching
individualism: 'Nathanaël, jette mon livre ... Ne t'attache en toi
qu'à ce que tu sens qui n'est nulle part ailleurs qu'en toi-même et
crée de toi ... le plus irremplaçable des êtres.' In form *Les Nourritures* are reminiscent of an epistle from the Scriptures – the Calvinist nourished on the Bible is apparent in many ways.

For *Prométhée mal enchaîné* (1899) Gide borrowed the medieval
word *sotie*; farce is a convenient term, which conditions the reader
to passing without protest from the realistic to the fanciful at the
author's pleasure; moralists from Voltaire to Anatole France
found the method convenient, Gide in whom the moralist was
quickly taking shape is no exception. In *Prométhée mal enchaîné*
the taste for spiritual restlessness for its own sake is again in evidence; the lesson of *Les Nourritures* in the form this time of
Prometheus's eagle. 'Il faut avoir un aigle', declares this Prome-

[8] No. XII, 10 December 1898.

theus in modern dress, 'Je n'aime pas les hommes; j'aime ce qui les dévore.'

Another theme too makes its appearance: the 'free act'. Prometheus, sitting at a café, is addressed on the matter by the waiter: 'Une action gratuite!... Moi, ça me paraît extraordinaire, j'ai longtemps pensé que c'était là ce qui distinguait l'homme des animaux... j'appelais l'homme: l'animal capable d'une action gratuite. Et puis après j'ai pensé le contraire: que c'était le seul être incapable d'agir gratuitement... sans motif...' Though echoing the ideas of *Les Nourritures* the latter's ecstatic tones are lacking; instead, irony, even flippancy. Is this merely a change of mood or does it not reveal a slight shift of attitude, a delicate operation of disengagement from earlier fervours?

From the turn of the century the rhythm of Gide's production quickens; critical reviews, essays and lectures collected in *Prétextes* (1903), *Nouveaux Prétextes* (1911), *Dostoïewsky* (1923), *Incidences* (1924); plays: *Philoctète* (1899), *Le Roi Candaule* (1901), *Saül* (1902), *Le Retour de l'Enfant prodigue* (1903), *Oedipe* (1931), *Thésée* (1946); stories: *L'Immoraliste* (1902), *La Porte Etroite* (1909), *Isabelle* (1911), *La Symphonie Pastorale* (1919), *L'Ecole des Femmes* (1929) and its sequel *Robert* (1930); another *sotie*: *Les Caves du Vatican* (1913); a novel (the only one of his works he thought could be so described), *Les Faux-Monnayeurs* (1926), in conjunction with which should be mentioned the diary he kept about the composition of the novel, *Le Journal des Faux-Monnayeurs* (1919-25).

The above list is not exhaustive; there are numerous miscellanea: e.g. *Souvenirs de Cours d'Assises* (1912), *L'Avenir de l'Europe* (1923), *Voyage au Congo and Retour de Tchad* (1928), *Retour de l'U.R.S.S.* (1936), *Journal* (1889-1939).

Some of these are referred to below; all bear witness to Gide's ceaselessly alert curiosity in human experience of many kinds, the breadth of his interests and, being a writer to the marrow, his desire to record and communicate them. But the essential Gide is to be found in the plays, in the best of his stories, in *Les Caves* and *Les Faux-Monnayeurs*.

The plays are little more than moral themes in dramatic form, and Gide is fond of using ancient legends or history, with a Gidian twist. Philoctète, abandoned by his companions on an island, learns the value of solitude, Candaule, the king, suffers for failing to keep private joys to himself; where Prometheus had made of his eagle a kind of domestic fowl, Saul assailed by devils learns to cherish the inner enemy. The parable of the Prodigal Son, particularly, shows how Gide shifts the emphasis; in Gide's play, if the attitudes of the father and the elder brother reflect the Bible story, the real interest attaches to the relations between the Prodigal and his younger brother, devoured as the Prodigal had been, by the desire to escape from the walled garden – itself a symbol. The Prodigal first admonishes him, but in the end, unlike his prototype, his repentance is not for his going but for his coming back, and when the time comes he encourages his younger brother to escape in his turn. The parable of repentance, of fatherly love not measured in terms of service rendered, is twisted into the typical Gidian message to youth: away! away!

All the stories have in common a form marked by rigorous economy of means, simplicity in style, an austere beauty such as might be found in a Calvinist *temple*, 'modesty' – to use Gide's own phrase in reference to the French classics.[9]

In substance Gide's best *récits* show the effects in specific cases of different ethical attitudes, those of Nietzsche, of puritan rigorism, of Christian charity.[10] *L'Immoraliste* is a story of the previous three years of Michel the narrator's life, told to two friends, a story that reflects Michel's new egotistic zest for life after recovering from illness and, in his efforts to satisfy it, the disregard of conventional moral values and his wife's health; she dies as a result. Michel, however, is ill at ease with his un-moral egotism; he is anything but the superman for whom alone it seems Nietzschean ethics are designed; characteristically, Gide has created a poor champion of harsh egotism, thus leaving the reader in doubt what the author's attitude really is.

La Porte Etroite leaves the reader with the same problem. Jérôme is as spineless as Michel, drifts, indecisively, between the two sisters, the austere Calvinistic Alissa, his betrothed, and Juliette who also loves him. Alissa decides to sacrifice her love for the sake of Juliette's, but Jérôme cannot bring himself to take advantage of Alissa's withdrawal and marry Juliette, who marries another; Alissa dies as though consumed by the inner fires of her faith. A study in self-torture and to what purpose? Are we to suppose that Alissa, in exchange for her rejection of the easy way to happiness ('O Seigneur! Gardez-moi d'un bonheur que je pourrais trop vite atteindre!' – a typical Gidian attitude), is rewarded by spiritual felicity, a dear purchase? Does Gide want us to admire Alissa's self-sacrifice or condemn it as useless masochism? The oracle replies in riddles and we are left with a taste of dust and ashes .

La Symphonie Pastorale, by its formal beauty and its more compelling or in any case more humanly understandable motivation, is Gide's masterpiece in pure narrative. The narrator, a Swiss pastor, whose capacity for self-deception masquerading as Chris-

[9] *Nouveaux Prétextes* (1911).
[10] See Ehrard, *Le Roman français depuis Marcel Proust* (1933).

tian charity is endless, destroys the happiness of his wife and son, unwittingly brings about the death of the blind Gertrude whom the pastor has welcomed into his home, and to whom an operation has restored sight and with it the knowledge that the world is not the innocent place the pastor had led her to believe in when she was blind. Thus, in the quest for happiness, none of the three tales provides a solution: Nietzschean egotism, puritan austerity, Christian charity alike end in bankruptcy.

The theme of the family is taken up again in *L'Ecole des Femmes* and *Robert*; the same situation as though reflected in parallel mirrors is seen through the mind first of the wife, then of the husband, both torn by excessive scruple – bankruptcy again.

Gide did well to call *Les Caves* a *sotie* and at the same time recall *Paludes*; *Les Caves* is a piece of serious nonsense, a subtle mixture of farce, fantasy and philosophy in the Gidian mode, suggested to the author in part by his literary relationships, notably with Claudel, and in part perhaps by French politics of the day. Claudel's relationships with Gide provide an interesting study of two able minds of different temper, the one powerful, fervent, not conspicuous for humour or tact, the other enquiring, hesitant, using scruple and doubt as a skilful defensive operation against the religious blandishments of the other, for Claudel the Catholic neophyte would fain have persuaded Gide into the fold.[11] The religious issue had indeed separated the two men since the days of the review *L'Ermitage* at the turn of the century, to which both contributed,[12] and especially since 1908 when Gide and his friend Jean Schlumberger had founded their own review *La Nouvelle Revue Française*, whose liberal orientation drove away the Catholics Claudel, Jammes, Ghéon. *Les Caves du Vatican*, as a kind of ironic echo of Claudel's *L'Otage* where an earlier Pope is also a prisoner, would be well within Gide's vein.

But the idea may also have been suggested to him by the policies of Leo XIII, the real one, who succeeding Pius IX, the great reactionary, applied a much more pliant policy, and did all he could to heal the breach between the Catholic Church and the French State. The French Catholics of the day were themselves divided about this policy, the liberal Catholics (e.g. Comte Albert de Mun) in favour, the high Catholics (e.g. Louis Veuillot) against. This division in Catholic ranks may have given Gide the idea of showing the false Leo XIII as an agent, no less, of freemasonry, adopting a policy which, in the eyes of a high Catholic like the comtesse de St Prix and simple souls like Fleurissoire, was hostile to the true interests of the Church.

---

[11] cf. Claudel – Gide letters.
[12] Other contributors: Copeau, Ghéon, Jammes, Valéry.

Skilfully interwoven with this buffoonery is the theme of 'L'acte gratuit'. Gide's interest in the subject had, as we have seen, already appeared in *Prométhée mal enchaîné*. Here it skilfully links together the Fleurissoire fantasy, Lafcadio's adventure and the subsidiary theme of Comte Julius de Baraglioul, the novelist who represents the moral and literary attitudes Gide most dislikes.

Gide's admiration for Dostoievsky is important here. In Dostoievsky's characters he saw a contrast with the French conceptions of psychology; the former full of contradictions, inconsequential, spontaneous, the latter trying to arrange human conduct into a unified logical pattern. 'Nous agissons sans cesse comme nous estimons que l'être que nous sommes, que nous croyons être, doit agir. La plupart de nos actions nous sont dictées non point par le plaisir que nous prenons à les faire, mais par un besoin d'imitation de nous-mêmes, et de projeter dans l'avenir notre passé. Nous sacrifions la vérité (c'est à dire la sincérité) à la continuité, à la pureté de la ligne.' Dostoievsky's characters, in contrast, 'cèdent ... à toutes les contradictions, toutes les négations dont leur nature propre est capable ...'[13] Here is the root of Lafcadio's erratic behaviour, his spontaneity following the whim of the moment, culminating in his final gesture to affirm, like Raskolnikov, his random freedom, the defenestration of poor Fleurissoire from the train; in contrast, the calculating Baraglioul who, hearing of the discovery of Fleurissoire's body, apparently a crime without a motive, suddenly has misgivings about the psychology he had given his characters to date? Here was the theme for his new book! As he explains to Lafcadio, whom he is far from suspecting of the crime, his ideas may be bold, but 'Puisque ce n'est que sur le papier, j'ose leur donner cours ...' That in itself condemns him, in Gide's eyes.

Baraglioul, who has been rejected by the Academy, is determined to give the Academicians a good reason for their injustice towards him, namely a book built on a crime without a motive, an absurdity in short. Nor can he accept his brother-in-law, Fleurissoire's murder – a crime apparently without motive – as proof that the idea for his new book, far from being absurd, reflects true human psychology; if robbery was not the motive (as the evidence shows) there must be another – in a flash the horrid truth, as Baraglioul thinks, comes to him; Fleurissoire – victim of the freemasons, a martyr! Thus may those who insist upon finding a rational motivation behind every action deceive themselves. Baraglioul will never be a great writer because he cannot believe in the virtue of his own discovery, in the virtue of spontaneity in life.

[13] 'Conférences sur Dostoïevsky', III (1911), *Oeuvres Complètes*, Vol. XI.

Gide's interest in the 'acte gratuit' may well have been quickened by his having been called as a member of an assize court jury.
Souvenirs de Cours d'Assises (1912) is the record of this experience,
and much more than a mere catalogue of horrors; in contrast to
the officers of the court who appear to take no interest in the
criminal, only in the crime, Gide believes that, rather than content
itself with punishing, society would find advantage in studying
criminal mentality and trying to assess what sort of compulsions
determine crime. As a Dostoievskian he is absorbed in the mystery
of actions not rooted in some form of self-interest and for which
'acte gratuit' is a convenient provisional label covering obscure
impulses.

But as he shows in his lectures on the Russian novelist, the apparently unmotivated actions of the latter's characters are often
due to a sense of humiliation suffered by them, perhaps obscurely.
Lafcadio suffers no such thing and in consequence is not a serious
contribution to the exploration of human psychology; he is merely
an entertaining exercise, more positive than the *récits*, in Gidian
ethics – liberation! spontaneity!

Les Faux-Monnayeurs, Gide's only novel, if we are to accept his
decision, is in any case his most important work of fiction. His
early stories, however skilful, were thin, linear creations with few
characters, and not many of these are three-dimensional. *Les Caves
du Vatican* has much more fictional weight. The different strands
of the story are skilfully brought together, thus creating a web of
events round the characters much more intricate than in any previous story. The illusion of life, into which the reader can plunge
as into a bath, is therefore greater at least where the author does
not deliberately break it either by direct intervention or by flight
into the fantastic. For the first time, too, appears the idea still in
embryo of a character (here, Baraglioul) aiming to write the book
the reader has just read.

These characteristics reappear with more emphasis in *Les Faux-
Monnayeurs*. The *Journal des Faux-Monnayeurs* is the record of
Gide's moral intentions, his ideas on the material and the technique
of his novel, the problems confronting him as he worked at this,
the most deliberate, intricate and intriguing of all his fictional
constructions.

On the surface level of reality there are a number of different
plots: the revolt of Bernard, the story of Vincent, the relations between Edouard, Olivier and Bernard and the novelist Passavant
(Baraglioul *redivivus*), the youthful coiners under the influence of
the sinister Strouvilhou (cf. Protos in *Les Caves*, but more developed), old La Pérouse, the Vedel-Azaïs boarding-house, the
Boris-Brondja idyll. All these are interwoven skilfully in the

manner of a fugue. Gide, accomplished musician and great admirer of Bach, takes the fugue as his model[14] and keeps all the plots moving together, like a juggler with several balls in the air. Gide wants to escape from the traditional linear plot developing in time, and substitute the impression of mobility, of life unfolding in a continuous present. Reducing to a minimum the purely descriptive elements, Gide invites the reader to help in creating this illusion for himself by supplying from his own imagination details the Realist novelist would have supplied in abundance.[15]

To help him in weaving the complex pattern of his fictional fugue, Gide took up again the idea embryonic in *Les Caves* of the novelist working at the novel the reader has in front of him and commenting on the characters. Edouard and his *Journal* put the reader at once on a different level, although Edouard himself has one foot on each.

But Gide does not resign his own right, as author, of direct intervention and at once we are on a third level, that of the novelist commenting on the characters in the novel, on Edouard's projects. Nor must we forget that in inviting the reader to rush constantly up and down stairs in this delicate three-storied house, Gide the moralist is always at his elbow.

The novel, at times exciting, is the most easily readable of all Gide's works; in admitting that, we recognize we have to a greater or lesser degree accepted the reality of the characters and given them existence in our imagination. Gide, however, wants them not only to exist but to mean something. 'Le titre même est déjà tout un programme' – to quote his own words. The novel really began to take shape in his mind when he saw how he could use the young coiners and the schoolboy suicides,[16] both as characters on the level of reality and symbols on the moral level;[17] he quickly applied the idea to other characters and thus the characters fall into two opposing groups – the coiners either in reality or metaphorically or both: the band of schoolboys, the older generation of the Profitendieu and Molinier families fixed in their conventional social values, the older Vedel's, whose narrow and exalted Calvinism blinds them to the unhappiness of the son and daughter, Passavant with his false artistic values; in the other camp, Edouard the sincere artist, Bernard and their friends, the younger generation in search of their destinies ('Dans un instant . . . j'irai vers mon destin. Quel beau mot l'aventure'[18]), in revolt against their elders.

And young Caloub? The author leaves us in ignorance, thus

[14] *Faux-Monnayeurs*, Part II, chap. 3.
[15] e.g. *F.M.*, Part I, chap. 11.
[16] Gide had kept amongst his papers newspaper cuttings from 1906, 1907 and 1909 reporting both types of case.
[17] *Journal des F.M.*, July 1919.   [18] *F.M.*, I, 6,

promoting the idea of the novel as no more than part of life's continuum, and safeguarding his own right to intervene: 'Je suis bien curieux de connaître Caloub.'

Les Faux-Monnayeurs evidently takes its place in the line of works charged with the Gidian message of sincerity, spontaneity, revolt, liberation.

But like the famous 'Chambre Introuvable' of which Louis XVIII complained, Gide is never quite where we expect to find him. He is not exclusively the apostle of individualism; he felt within himself the conflict between what a man owes to his true self (*la personne*) and what he owes to society (*l'individu*).[19] Just as the young post-war generation were eagerly climbing the slopes of *Les Faux-Monnayeurs*, Gide was moving down the other side towards society: 'C'est en se renonçant qu'on se trouve', he writes;[20] in 1927, at the request of the French Colonial Ministry, he undertook a journey to French Equatorial Africa, the record of which he gives in *Voyage au Congo* and *Retour de Tchad*, denouncing the exploitation of the natives by the big concessionary companies and the lack of supervision by the Ministry's servants, too few in number, and hampered by centralized control from Paris – thus too much power and too little responsibility, the worst of both worlds. Another aspect of Gide's social preoccupations is shown by his interest in Communism in the 1930's. Wishing to put his ideas to the test he went to Russia in 1936 and with characteristic honesty records his disappointment in *Retour de l'U.R.S.S.*

On the eve of the war Gide published his diary which, together with *Si le Grain ne meurt*, is an indispensable guide to Gide. The war years as expected yielded little – a few extra pages to the diary published in a second edition after the war, a philosophical tale, *Thésée*, an adaptation of Kafka's *Das Prozess*, a translation of *Hamlet*.

The 'thirties had seen a decline in Gide's influence for a variety of reasons. He himself had been uncomfortable at the image he had created of himself in the minds of the young and had sought to correct it – *Les Nouvelles Nourritures* (1935) and the preface (1927) to *Les Nourritures Terrestres*; new influences were making themselves felt (e.g. Malraux, Bernanos, Drieu La Rochelle); Europe was slowly dividing into fascist and anti-fascist camps, there seemed little room for the liberal attitudes Gide's image was identified with. Further, Gide's defence of homosexuality[21] and the confessions in *Si le Grain ne Meurt*[22] exposed him to attack.

---

[19] *Oeuvres*, Vol. VIII, preface, p. 20, by Martin-Chauffier.
[20] *Avenir de l'Europe.*
[21] *Corydon*, four Socratic dialogues, originally published privately, 1911.
[22] Part II.

His non-collaborationist position during the war, however, and his break with the *N.R.F.* because the review (with Drieu La Rochelle as editor) had taken the opposite position, refurbished his reputation and the Nobel Prize for literature (1947) crowned a literary career extending over nearly sixty years; he had become the 'Grand Old Man' of European letters.

Doubtless the image is a fair one in many respects; an open, alert, immensely cultivated mind, a fervent love – to speak in Gidian terms – of the beauties of life and the world; a work rich in variety: fiction, plays, essays – critical, political, criminological and *travelogical*, diaries, letters; the whole expressed in a style of great formal beauty and suppleness; at times austere, diamantine in precision, at others poetic and colourful, never opulent.

But if the overall formal impression is one of classical discipline, the substance is subjective; the work is largely a confession, first as a quest for liberation from what he regarded as the dead weight of his upbringing and heredity and then as a lesson to others; in short, Gide is a moralist above all who delights in surprising his disciples by the shifts and turns of his course from the quasi-religious mysticism of the *Cahiers d'André Walter* to the explosion of joy in nature of *Les Nourritures Terrestres*, back to the self-discipline of *Saül* and forward to the amoral egotism of *L'Immoraliste*, to the gospel of spontaneity and 'sincerity', in the Gidian sense, of *Les Caves du Vatican* and *Les Faux-Monnayeurs*. Nor is this the final position; *Les Nouvelles Nourritures*, and Gide's pro-communist leanings put him on the other tack, then the wind shifts again with *Retour de l'U.R.S.S.* and *Thésée*. Truly Gide speaks with conflicting voices, but, as chairman of his own discordant debate, he himself finds the expression that skilfully resolves it in a union of opposites: 'Il est bon de suivre sa pente pourvu que ce soit en montant.'[23]

III. CLAUDEL

The literary tradition of the Quai d'Orsay is distinguished; in the nineteenth century Chateaubriand, Lamartine, Gobineau, in the twentieth Claudel, Morand, Giraudoux, Saint-John Perse.

Lyric poet and dramatist, essayist and critic, Paul Claudel (1868–1955) was all of these, whilst at the same time an active and successful career took him to many parts of the world, as he steadily climbed the rungs of the consular and diplomatic ladder leading to ambassadorial rank.

If the *Poèmes de Guerre* and the fugitive pieces be set aside, Claudel's lyrical poetry is largely nourished by his triumphant

[23] *Faux-Monnayeurs*, chap. 14.

rediscovery of the Christian faith, which was his by upbringing but which he had lost in youth. In *Premiers vers* one poem at least – 'Pour la Messe des Hommes' (August 1886) – shows the poet pre-occupied with the problem but as yet unconverted. Christ tells the world he is not the son of God:

> Hommes! Mes frères! O mes enfants! je vous aime,
> C'est assez! 'Je ne suis pas Dieu le fils' dit-il
> Je suis celui, mort en rachetant votre exil
> Par son amour pour vous qui était suprême . . .

On Christmas Day 1886, at Notre-Dame in Paris, the poet was moved by divine grace. This first emotional impact was followed by a period of gestation and strivings, culminating in total sub-mission, heart and mind, four years later. 'Chant à Cinq Heures' (1891) seems to reflect the poet's joy:

> Je marchais en riant par le jardin en fête,
> Laissant derrière moi les arbres et les fleurs.
> Je marchais en riant sous le pays horrible
> Des astres que traverse une route de lait

A later poem in the same collection suggests that the poet was not immediately free from periods of doubting:

> Mes yeux sont pleins de nuit et mon coeur est plein d'eau![24]

But the mood of distress may have had a lesser cause, the impossi-bility for the traveller Claudel had by then become of putting down roots:

> Toujours le bruit, les voix diverses . . .
> Et le piétinement infini dans la poudre
> Et si je marche, ou que j'arrive! Il n'y a rien,
> Et le pied conduit l'autre pied d'où il vient.

Enriching though his experience of different civilizations was to be, Claudel was not insensitive to the traveller's inevitable isola-tion from home and family: 'Le voyageur rentre chez lui comme un hôte; il est étranger à tout, et tout lui est étrange . . . A la table de famille le voici qui se rassied, convive suspect et précaire . . .'[25]

The heartache of exile is not new: the Jews in Babylon, Du Bellay in Rome, the author of 'Home, Sweet Home';[26] Claudel's *Vers d'Exil*[27] seems at first to echo the same theme:

> Pour la dernière fois, acceptant leur étreinte,
> j'ai des parents pleurants baisé la face sainte . . .

[24] Attributed to the period 1896–1900. Notes, *Oeuvres*, I.
[25] 'Pensée en Mer' in *Connaissance de l'Est.*
[26] John Howard Payne. See the opera *Clair, the Maid of Milan* (Covent Garden, 1823).
[27] *Oeuvres*, Vol. I (1950).

The comparison is, however, deceptive. In the first poem, fleeting impressions of travel and foreign lands are indeed there:

> Tant d'attente et d'ennui, tant d'heures harassées,
> l'entrée au matin au port d'or les hommes nus,
> L'odeur des fleurs, le goût des fruits inconnus,
> Tant d'étoiles et tant de terres dépassées . . .

Despite the apparent clumsiness of the second line the stanza is rich in psychological and sensuous suggestion. But the poet's distress, of which the poems are full, seems to arise from a cause other than the exile's sense of isolation. In 1900, Claudel was in the toils of an adulterous love affair. None of the poems, significantly perhaps, is dated; all but one were first published in 1905,[28] and the torment they express points to the conflict in the poet five years earlier between his love and his faith which in 1900 or only a short time before had led him to the brink of the religious life.[29] Thus the exile is a spiritual one. The poet is isolated from God by a sense of physical guilt; the religious theme, but from another angle, is again present, as it was in *Premiers Vers*.

Though Claudel's moral robustness enabled him to recover quickly his sense of balance, the 'Brief Encounter' was to separate the mature man from his youth:

> Adieu, enfant! Adieu, jeune homme que je fus! . . .

and to mark the poet's work profoundly; there are clear allusions to it in 'Les Muses',[30] and in 'L'Esprit et L'Eau':[31]

> Et voici que, comme quelqu'un qui se détourne, tu m'as trahi
> Tu n'es nulle part, O rose!
> Rose, je ne verrai plus votre visage en cette vie!

cries the poet, in the latter ode, using the emblem of the bitter-sweet pain of love.[32]

In 'La Cantate à trois voix' the three women are uplifted by a love into whose plenitude they are prevented from entering;[33] *Le Partage de Midi* has clear elements of a discreet confession;[34] in

---

[28] *Oeuvres*, I, notes.

[29] At some time between 1898 and 1900 Claudel had visited Ligugé, with the idea of entering the novitiate; in September 1900 he asked to be accepted as a novice, but the Benedictines wisely refused his application because they believed that his attitude, which was to sacrifice his artist's inclinations and submit his will, in the hope that God would then implant in him the conviction of having a greater reward in the monastic life as a way to salvation, was not a true monastic vocation.

[30] First of the *Cinq Grandes Odes*; the closing stanzas where Erato is evoked.

[31] Second ode.

[32] But why the change from 'tu' in the first and second lines to 'vous' in the third? Doubtless because the image of the flower in the first has faded into the image of the woman.

[33] P.-A. Lesort: *Paul Claudel par lui-même*.

[34] The 1906 edition was very limited and circulated privately.

this and his other plays, as we shall see, runs the theme of human love unsatisfied or sacrificed, exchanged, one might almost say, for a higher.

After the passage of the emotional storm, Claudel, like Huysmans, became a Benedictine oblate.[35] His peace with God made, his lyrical poetry is uplifted in joy; the searing experience, though recalled, must be accepted as a part of the divine scheme of things.

With the *Cinq Grandes Odes* (1910) the poet enters fully into his own inheritance. The traditional rhymed alexandrines he had used hitherto give place to bold unrhymed and irregular metres that Claudel makes peculiarly his own, to be used thereafter in his poems and his plays:

> O mon âme impatiente, pareille à l'aigle sans art! Comment
> ferions-nous pour ajuster aucun vers? ...
> Que mon vers ne soit rien d'esclave! mais tel que l'aigle marin
> qui s'est jeté sur un grand poisson,
> Et l'on ne voit rien qu'un éclatant tourbillon d'ailes
> et l'éclaboussement de l'écume!
> Mais vous ne m'abandonnerez point, O Muses modératrices.[36]

The poet claims untrammelled freedom for his genius, relying solely on the guidance of the muses, in other words on his native sense of rhythm and on the delicacy of his ear, to create a perfect fusion between the form and substance of the poem, the impulse of the thought determining the measures of the line, as though it were a vision with a musical accompaniment; away with counting syllables! Terpsichore, to whom, significantly, the poet turns first, will give him natural rhythm:

> Terpsichore, trouveuse de la danse! où serait le choeur sans
> la danse? Quelle autre captiverait
> Les huit soeurs farouches ensemble, pour vendanger l'hymne
> jaillissante, inventant la figure inextricable.

But the poet claims all the muses as his handmaids:

> Les neuf muses! Aucune n'est de trop pour moi!

All the arts must contribute; rejecting the example of great poets of the past – Homer, Virgil, Dante, eschewing all traditional forms – 'nous n'établirons aucun chantier!', his poetry must be universal in its scope:

> Je regarde toutes choses, et voyez tous que je n'en suis pas
> l'esclave, mais le dominateur.[37]

But at the same time the second Ode shows the poet's soul drawn to God:

> O mon Dieu, mon être soupire vers le vôtre ...

[35] Shortly before the Benedictines were expelled from France, and left Ligugé for Belgium, September 1901.
[36] First ode.   [37] Second ode, 'L'Esprit et L'Eau' (1906).

Not only the rhythms but the spirit of the psalmist informs the poetry. The third Ode[38] is in similar vein. The poet glories in his own strength, yet is overcome by a greater:

> O mon Dieu . . .
> . . . je fus devant vous comme un lutteur qui plie,
> Non qu'il se croie faible, mais parce que l'autre est plus fort.

The image of the wrestler brought down by another seems characteristic of Claudel, robust in person and attitudes; how far removed too is this anthropomorphism from the romantic idea of man possessed by some mysterious force. Strong in his faith, and with a rotund humour which sometimes rolls around in his plays, he thanks the Almighty for saving him from false gods, so many of them adored by nineteenth-century intellectuals and writers:

> Soyez béni, mon Dieu, qui m'avez délivré des idoles,
> Et qui faites que je n'adore que Vous seul, et non point Isis
> et Osiris,
> Ou la Justice, ou le Progrès, ou la Vérité, ou la Divinité,
> ou l'Humanité, ou les Lois de la Nature, ou l'Art ou la Beauté . . .

Romantics, Naturalists, Parnassians are all contemptuously dismissed! In contrast to their static or fatalistic attitudes, the poet of the Odes, established by God in this harsh world, like a tenacious weed in the barrenest soil – 'Comme le sec et tenace chiendent invincible . . .', refuses to contract out of it and, illumined as he is by God's light, sees his role as that of interpreting the world, of fitting it into God's purpose:

> . . . il ne cesse de faire son oeuvre et chimie en grande patience et temps
> Car ce n'est pas de ce corps seul qu'il me faut venir à bout,
> mais de ce monde brut tout entier, fournir
> De quoi comprendre et le dissoudre et l'assimiler
> En vous et ne plus voir rien
> Réfractaire à votre lumière en moi!

Fully of this world but at the same time a temple of divine light, both ideas are taken up again in the last two Odes. The fourth – 'La Muse qui est la Grâce' (1907) – shows the poet filled anew with an intoxicating force of inspiration ready to glorify the divine order manifested in the world, and rejecting the plea of the Muse, revealing herself as God's grace, that he should dedicate himself to the religious life:

> Va-t-en! Je me retourne désespérément vers la terre!

In the fifth – 'La Maison Fermée' (1908) – the poet declares that in order to become that temple of light, that witness of God's purpose in the world, his soul must be as a shuttered house. Only

[38] 'Magnificat' (1907).

by looking inward into his soul can the poet achieve his ambition of uniting the world to God, in the faith.

The five Odes may be regarded as Claudel's greatest achievement in lyric poetry. 'La Cantate à trois voix' (1913), with all its suavity, the liturgical poems, e.g. 'Corona Benignitatis anni Dei' (1914) and 'La Messe Là-bas' (1919), are narrower in scope; the five Odes express Claudel's conception of poetry and of the poet's task; they are a beacon-light of his faith. Their form is equal in quality to their substance; every line weighted with meaning; no windy eloquence; each Ode a unit with every part essential to the whole. The result is compression, pithiness, strength, the beauty of wrought iron, weight but no heaviness because with all its solidity there is a dramatic quality about the verse, a vitality of talk that wastes no words, both spontaneous and highly-charged; that quality derives at once from the author's percipient intelligence and the verse form he has forged for himself; freed from the servitude, and perhaps the temptations, of traditional verse form – syllable counting, rhyme – the poet is attentive to the natural rhythms of speech, the ebb and flow of the speaker's thought, the cadences – themselves the result of the emphasis the speaker gives to the expression of his thought, the sound values and last but not least the breathing pauses:

> ... les Muses respiratrices ...[39]

To develop its full potential Claudel's poetry needs to be declaimed; it is an incantation; its appeal to the intellect is less through the inner eye of the reader, though this is far from being left unsatisfied, than through the ear.

With Claudel's belief in the tremendous drama of the Christian conception of the world, a drama in three acts – Creation, Incarnation, Redemption,[40] the drama as a vehicle of communication appealed to him early and often.

Claudel's plays fall by date into at least three groups: the early works – *Tête d'Or* (1890), *La Jeune Fille Violaine* (1892), *La Ville* (1893), *L'Echange* (1896); the plays of his early maturity – *Partage de Midi* (1906), *L'Annonce faite à Marie* (1912), and a trilogy, *L'Otage* (1911), *Le Pain Dur* (1918), *Le Père Humilié* (1920); *Le Soulier de Satin* (1928), an epic drama which stands by itself. To these a fourth, heterogeneous group could be added, consisting of a lyrical drama, *Le Livre de Christophe Colomb* (1933), an oratorio with music by Honegger, *Jeanne d'Arc au Bûcher* (1939), a morality, *L'Histoire de Tobie et de Sara* (1942). Nor should we omit, because of the evident influence of Greek drama upon his

[39] Les Muses.
[40] P. H. Simon, *Témoins de l'Homme* (1952).

own, his translations from Aeschylus, *Agamemnon* (1896), *Les Choéphores* (1920), *Les Euménides* (1920).

Written in the free verse that Claudel had so triumphantly made his own, his plays provide a tremendous variety. The early group are essentially symbolical plays. *Tête d'Or* has the flimsiest attachments to time and space: fields at the end of winter, a palace hall, the distant confines of Europe; the characters, or rather the character – for in fact only one counts – is drawn in bold outline; the whole human adventure of Simon Agnel is an allegory. Driven from an earthly paradise, by the death of the woman he loves, he sets out to fill the emptiness of his life by adventure; Agnelet becomes the victorious general, Tête d'Or; but military glory leaves his thirst unquenched, the soldier turns politician, Tête d'Or topples the Emperor (a pathetically comic figure, vaguely Shakespearian), becomes king, to find in the end that his attempt to conquer this world, like all human adventure, if it be an end in itself, ends in nothing. Tête d'Or had vigorously rejected belief in God:

> Je ne crois plus aux fables des mères...
> Et qu'il existe dans cette salle du monde
> D'autre dieu que l'homme ignorant...

As he lies dying he recognizes the emptiness of it all:

> ... je n'ai été rien!
> Car, pas plus que l'image ne retient l'image du feu,
> L'homme ne garde aucun bien.
> Oh! Je voudrais vivre encore et employer tout ce
> qui me resterait de vie
> A' prophétiser à chacun sa sottise!

Thus at this early stage the great Claudelian theme – life has sense only within the context of faith, is established, to reappear in *La Ville*, where the ruins encompassed by the godless Avare – Tête d'Or in a new guise – are rebuilt in faith by Ivors, son of Coeuvre the poet-builder, and the woman Lala. The city and its inhabitants are a symbol of destruction in the darkness of disbelief, of reconstruction in the light of faith.

La Jeune Fille Violaine provides another change; unlike *Tête d'Or* and *La Ville* it is firmly anchored in space. On the eve of leaving France to take up his first consular appointment, Claudel seems to be taking a fond farewell of his native Tardenois, and working into the bucolic background of the dramatic poem a theme of contrast between the creative value of adventure, of suffering, and the narrowing pressures of the diurnal humdrum: Violaine gives up her fiancé, Jacques Hury, because her sister is in love with him and because she believes in the value of suffering.[41]

---

[41] *La Jeune Fille Violaine, Seconde version* (1898).

L'Echange offers a similar idea in a starker form: Louis Laine betrays his wife Martha – well-named, worthy and reliable but dull that she is – with the heartless Lechy Elbernon. The situation foreshadows that of *Partage de Midi*: as previously pointed out, this play, rooted in Claudel's own experience, is a veiled confession.

In contrast to the early plays, the middle group are less evidently symbolical. *Partage de Midi* is in the first place a domestic drama with human characters shown in a very human situation, and caught up, though not directly involved, in political events; the latter are only a distant echo serving as background and end to the private lives of well-drawn characters. The same is true of the characters in *L'Annonce faite à Marie* and of those in the trilogy, whilst the domestic realism of *Le Partage de Midi* is matched in the latter cases by an admirable sense of period; this is not historical realism according to the old Romantic notion of 'local colour' but the evocation, by deft touches, of attitudes, mentalities and events of the times the plays' actions are placed in: *L'Annonce faite à Marie* conveys the burning faith of the Middle Ages, crusading in Anne Vercors, constructive – in the literal sense – in Pierre de Craon, saintly and ascetic in Violaine, superstitious and satanic in Mara. *L'Otage*, in spite of one thread in the plot that stretches credulity,[42] gives a picture, which has all the elements of psychological truth, of the conflict between the old order and the new. Sygne de Coufontaine, scheming to save what she can of the family inheritance from the wreck of revolution, and sacrificing first her happiness and then her life in defence of her overriding loyalties; Turelure, coarse-grained and ruthless, prototype of men who are revealed and discover their own potential in times of social flux. With the second and third parts of the trilogy the spirit of the times is again faithfully reflected; in *Le Pain Dur* the July Monarchy ('la Monarchie constitutionnelle; traditionnelle par son principe, moderne par ses institutions!', to quote a lapidary phrase of Turelure's, itself characteristic of an age when weighty apophthegms were current coin). Turelure, his son, a Coufontaine by his mother Sygne, and their entourage, are vivid reminders of different aspects of the period in France and elsewhere: the old man has become a pillar of the régime and a railway magnate, his mistress and her father Ali Habenichts represent the early wave of the Jewish penetration, social and economic, from beyond the Rhine,[43] his son, a land-developer, evokes the period when French colonizers and speculators were establishing themselves in Algeria in the wake of military conquest, the Countess Lumir represents the spirit of Polish patriotism aflame in 1848; a last and eloquent

[42] The 'kidnapping' of the Pope.   [43] Echoes of Balzac.

touch to the portrait of an age, when in bourgeois hearts like Turelure's the light of faith burned very low, is afforded by Turelure's
selling the old crucifix for its weight in metal to the haggling
Habenichts.

In *Le Père Humilié* history has moved on another twenty years
and again we are afforded vivid glimpses of the day. By placing his
action in the diplomatic world of Rome, Claudel can evoke some
of the great controversies and events that filled the European
scene: the Pope as bulwark of traditional Catholicism opposing the
new scientific spirit, Italian nationalism ready to reap the advantages the Franco-Prussian war affords.

The emphasis on history is less strong in *Le Soulier de Satin*, but
into the witches' cauldron of this play it is as though Claudel had
thrown the whole Spanish Renaissance; and out of it arise dancing
shadows: the legacy of Christopher Columbus and Cortez, Lepanto,
the Armada, sword thrusts and blunderbusses, brigands, Spanish,
African, Mexican scenes; a veritable kaleidoscope.

In scope and variety nothing in Claudel's dramatic works equals
Le Soulier de Satin. Divided into 'days' in the Spanish manner,
the spectacle is as rich in fantasy and surprises, comedy and
tragedy, as any sword and dagger novel of Dumas the elder or –
to put the play in its true context – as a picaresque novel of the
seventeenth century, or the most turbulent play of Lope de Vega;
Don Quixote would have been an approving spectator;[44] the play
is a grand epic drama in the spirit of the baroque age, bolder and
more imaginative than anything from the pen of Rotrou or Corneille. Claudel alludes in his preface to 'le désordre . . . délice de
l'imagination'; confusion perhaps, but contrived; around the central theme, Prouhèze-Rodrigue, are woven supporting sub-plots:
the romance of Doña Musique and the viceroy of Naples, the
destinies of Doña Isabel, Don Camille, Doña Sept-Epées.

Whatever dramatic form Claudel adopts, the direct Symbolism
of the early plays, the realism of *Le Partage*, the emphasis on
history in the *Otage* trilogy, the reflection of the ethos of an age
in *L'Annonce*, the same but on a colossal epic scale in *Le Soulier*,
underlying them all and binding them together is the author's
faith. One way or another the plays must show the working of
Providence; whether in the narrow compass of individual lives or
on the broader scene of an age, history must be made to have a
meaning – a difficult task in view of the apparent chaos in the
world, the sin, suffering, violence, the unbridled passions of men.
For a dramatist to ignore them would be unrealistic, for a Christian
dramatist, it would be both unrealistic and lacking in robust faith;
Claudel will be neither. His plays are built on the idea of suffering;

[44] R. Kemp, 'Chronique théâtrale', *passim*; *Le Monde*, 22 April 1949.

its most usual form – man and woman drawn towards each other by all the force of nature that is in them but separated by compelling circumstance: Ysé and Mésa, Sygne and Georges, Louis and Lumir,[45] Pensée and Orian,[46] Violaine and Jacques Hury, Prouhèze and Rodrigue.

The sacrifice all these characters make of their love reflects Claudel's own espousal of Catholic doctrine in the exalted form defended by Bloy and the high Catholics: life means the sacrifice of human desires, the submission of human wills to the divine order. Marriage is seen as one form of that order.[47] Thus Claudel's characters sacrifice their love and submit to marriage: Sygne will marry Turelure (L'Otage), Pensée will marry Orso (Le Père Humilié), Prouhèze will marry Don Pélage and then Don Camille (Le Soulier de Satin).

In a letter to Le Temps[48] about L'Otage, Claudel speaks of 'la force tragique qui résulte de l'intervention dans notre vie individuelle et quotidienne d'un appel extérieur et supérieur à nous. Les circonstances plus ou moins misérables au milieu desquelles nous vivons tous nous laissent cependant le sentiment qu'il y a en nous quelque chose d'inemployé, quelque chose qui n'est pas sorti . . .'; in short 'the slings and arrows of outrageous fortune' produce suffering, but that suffering releases our hidden potentials and provides us with the means of grace; a synthesis of proximate pessimism and transcendental optimism. In all the cases cited this is how Claudel resolves the antinomy: the sacrifice of human love, deceptive and fragile in the contingencies of this world, excites the desire of imperishable love in the next; if Prouhèze had been unfaithful to Don Pélage, then, she tells Rodrigue, 'Je n'aurais été qu'une femme bientôt mourante sur ton cœur, et non pas cette étoile éternelle dont tu as soif.'[49]

Claudel's philosophy is his own affair, but inevitably it affects his characters and the whole economy of his plays. Claudel is not interested in his characters as human beings but as representing a point of view; fanaticism lies at the end of that road and although Claudel is too intelligent and percipient to fall into that trap, there is sometimes more than a suggestion of inhumanity in the apparent lack of sympathy he shows towards his characters as human beings.

In the symbolical plays, the reader is prepared for that and

[45] Le Pain Dur.   [46] Le Père Humilié.
[47] 'Un homme non marié ou non consacré n'a pas reçu d'ordre. Il reste ouvert et imparfait. Le sacrement remplace la sainte clôture.' Letter from Claudel to Louis Massignon, the great Arabic scholar, 19 November 1908. Quoted by R. Griffiths, op. cit., p. 324. See also the words of the Pope on marriage, to Orian and Orso (Père Humilié, II, 2).
[48] June 1914. Positions et Propositions, I; Oeuvres, Vol. 15.
[49] P. H. Simon, Le Monde, 27 March 1963.

accepts it because the characters are so evidently un-human symbols, but the very skill with which Claudel paints human situations, in the second group for example, is apt to cause a disturbing tension, dramatically speaking, between the human and theological levels, astride which the action may be uneasily poised, or between groups of characters, some earthy, others touched by grace, or in the characters themselves.

L'Annonce is a good example. It is a particularly sombre drama of human jealousies, suspicion and murder, and on the human plane perhaps the most convincingly motivated of all Claudel's plays; but do Violaine's progress to saintliness and the rising of divine love through suffering and sacrifice hinge easily on to the human action, or is she not living and speaking on a different level? Is she not, good Claudelian theologian that she is, too busy adjusting her attitudes to what she knows her creator (Claudel) wants, to be convincing as a human character? Is the miracle of the child's resuscitation, however much it may be within the logic of the faith that moves mountains, convincing dramatically or could it give the impression of a conjuring trick? We may at least question whether Claudel's particular form of 'involvement' (ghastly word) is shown here to be the natural or at least possible extension of human life or whether as in a bad landscape painting the horizon dividing earth and sky is a harsh line such as is not found in nature.

Nor is L'Annonce an exception in this way. Mésa (Le Partage), Sygne (L'Otage), Pensée, Orian and Orso (Le Père Humilié) are all good theologians in the Claudelian sense, all convinced in one way or another that they are predestined, that they must show in their lives the latent and unused element of their natures responding to the divine call ('sentiment qu'il y a en nous quelque chose d'inemployé, quelque chose qui n'est pas sorti . . .'). 'Il est nécessaire', exclaims Orian to Pensée, 'que je ne sois pas un heureux . . . pas un satisfait! Il est nécessaire que l'on ne me bouche pas la bouche et les yeux avec cette espèce de bonheur qui nous ôte le désir.'[50] But not everyone will be convinced of the necessity of their sufferings, and consequently of the latter's dramatic force.

Yet when all is said and done, Claudel's drama is an experience one cannot be indifferent to; the impact is perhaps greatest in a purely symbolical play like Tête d'Or or in the grand epic vigour of Le Soulier de Satin, where Claudel is not bound by the need to bring a realistic human situation into his theological context, and where his poetic and imaginative gifts have free rein.

Amongst Claudel's prose-works particular mention should be made of those devoted to the Far East. Claudel first set foot on

[50] Act III, Sc. 2.

Chinese soil in 1895. His service in China lasted with intervals till 1909. Japan he had visited in 1898 and he returned thither in 1922 as Ambassador for four years.

Connaissance de l'Est (1902, 1907) is a collection of essays, mostly about China, but with some inspired by his visit to Japan in 1898; *L'Oiseau noir dans le Soleil Levant* (1927) relates to Japan.

China's impact on Claudel may have been all the greater in that he went there from the United States, a country where western civilization and liberal values had but comparatively recently taken root – and were developing in luxuriant profusion; in contrast, here was a civilization rooted in the depths of time:

> La vieille Chine des taotaïs et des chaises à porteur, pleine
>   d'ordures, de lanternes et de diableries,
> Ce radeau une seule chose avec l'immense passé dont j'ai hanté
> le bord un moment et dont j'ai fait partie...
> Ah, laissez-moi rejoindre une dernière fois derrière moi ce
> pays plein de délice et d'amertume.[51]

Thus in a poem that serves as preface to the two collections of essays does Claudel look back nostalgically over the years to the China he had known. Nothing could be more alert, observant and penetrating than these essays. This is not the banal travelogue of some itinerant journalist but a series of prose poems, stimulating alike by the sensuous impressions that pack them tight and by the responses of a subtle mind to what the poet sees. Claudel's prose has all the merits a reader could wish for in this sort of composition: a wealth of language and hence a suppleness of descriptive power that is always vivid, never abstract. No better example of solid fusion between image and thought can be found than in 'Le Pin'. The reader cannot fail to evoke the titanic struggle between the trees and the elements along the Tokkaido road: 'En vain le vent de l'Océan les couche: agriffé de toutes ses racines au sol pierreux, l'arbre invincible[52] se tord, se retourne sur lui-même, et comme un homme arc-bouté sur le système contraire de sa quadruple articulation, il fait tête... il semble s'accrocher à l'antagoniste, se rétablir, se redresser sous l'assaut polymorphe du monstre qui l'accable...'

In comparison with this prose so full of sap and rustic vigour, how anaemic appears the work of another great traveller who, spoilt child of fortune that he was, enjoyed a great reputation in his day – since mercifully deflated. Pierre Loti's forty volumes are bathed in tears, full of confidences in elegiac mood, have a style

---

[51] Hong-Kong, 1927.
[52] The change from the plural to the singular here is significant. The reader cannot 'see' all the trees at once; his attention is fastened on one, his impression all the more vivid.

as vaporous as fog that blurs all outline and sharp definition. Nor is Claudel content to register his sense impressions of the Far East. He interprets Chinese and Japanese attitudes to life. What more percipient than his essay on the Japanese traditional theatre?[53] Here Claudel reveals himself as good a critic as he was poet, and, if further proof of that be required, it is afforded in ample measure by the two volumes of critical essays: *Positions et Propositions* (I, 1928; II, 1934) and *L'Oeil Ecoute* (1935 and 1946).

'Bois, O mon coeur, à ces délices inépuisables...' – a Baudelairian line, indeed, and yet the joys referred to are not Baudelairian. The prose poem, whence the line comes,[54] brings out another aspect of Claudel's 'conquest' of the East, his joy in God's creation:

> Tant de beauté me force à rire! Quel luxe! Quel éclat!
> quelle vigueur de la couleur inextinguible ...

and the poet adds at the end of the paragraph: 'ce qui me trouble comme un amant, ce qui me fait frémir dans ma chair, c'est *l'intention* de gloire de ceci, c'est mon *admission*, c'est l'avancement à ma rencontre de cette joie.'[55]

The glory of God's creation; the poet may enter in, he has but to look, and the brilliant splendour of it all is spread before his eyes. The very word *connaissance* has great importance for him; it appears in several sub-titles of *Art Poétique* (1907), in one of them, significantly, he makes a play on the word, 'Traité de la conaissance au monde et de soi-même' – knowledge of oneself is inextricably bound up with faith, whereby we are, as it were, reborn to the world, reborn in a new understanding of God's creation. This attitude provides the key to all Claudel's work. In the preface to his complete works Claudel speaks of 'La Cité qu'elles font ensemble'; a kind of 'civitas Dei', and perhaps the image was inspired by St Augustine.

Whether this philosophy is the cause or the result of that spiritual and intellectual robustness that is everywhere in Claudel, who is to say, a robustness be it said in passing that is not devoid of a certain egotism; Claudel's work may be full of God's creation, but that creation is also very full of Claudel; in his many-sided work one form is absent, the novel. Could it be that the novel, to be great, requires an objective study of other men?

None the less, Claudel's worship of this world as God's creation uplifts in song his lyric poetry, his dramatic work, his essays, and gives them cosmic significance.

---

[53] 'Noh' in *L'Oiseau noir*.
[54] 'La Descente' (*Connaissance de l'Est*).
[55] The italics are Claudel's.

IV. PROUST

The young man about town, squandering his time and substance on frivolous pursuits, the hermit of the Boulevard Haussmann struggling against time and illness to complete the great work of his later years, these images of Marcel Proust (1871–1922) are like two unconnected panels of a diptych. Recalling Pascal suddenly renouncing the world after his mystical experience, they date from the time when little was known of Proust's writing apart from *Les Plaisirs et les Jours* (1896), his first work (if earlier ephemeral reviews,[56] in which he collaborated with his friends, be excepted), and *A la Recherche Du Temps Perdu*, the first part of which – *Du Côté de chez Swann* (1913) – was published at the author's own expense, after four publishers had refused the manuscript.

During the 1914–18 war a small literary circle learned to appreciate the originality and importance of *Du Coté de chez Swann* but not till the Prix Goncourt had crowned *A l'Ombre des Jeunes Filles en Fleurs*, the second part of *A la Recherche*, in 1919 did Proust make an impact on a larger public. Thereafter his reputation grew apace; he had won his wager against time, had the joy of knowing that his labours had not been in vain, that the impression, if it still existed, of an aimless life had been fully expunged.

Four more parts of the gigantic work appeared before Proust's death (November 1922): *Le Côté De Guermantes I* (1920); *Le Côté de Guermantes II* and *Sodome et Gomorrhe I* (1921); *Sodome et Gomorrhe II* (1922); the remainder posthumously: *La Prisonnière* (1923); *Albertine disparue* (1925), *Le Temps Retrouvé* (1927). Six volumes of letters appeared from 1930 to 1936; since then, two important earlier works, never previously published: *Jean Santeuil* (1952) and *Contre Sainte-Beuve* (1954).

The publication of these 'documents' shows that the years between *Les Plaisirs et les Jours* and *Du Côté de chez Swann* were not a desert with here and there an unnoticed oasis – the translations from Ruskin in 1904 and 1906 – but years of labour, of progressive enrichment, years spent in an unremitting search for the appropriate form of what he wanted to express. The diptych with two separate panels does not at all correspond with the facts; the literary vocation had appeared early; thereafter, he had been engaged all his life on a quest, the object of which seemed constantly to elude him but which in the end, after turning down successive side-roads, he found and embodied in the vast complex of *A la Recherche*.

Les Plaisirs et les Jours, in spite of its elaborate presentation – preface by Anatole France, illustrations by the fashionable artist

[56] e.g. *La Revue Verte* (1887); *La Revue Lilas* (1888).

Madeleine Lemaire, four pianoforte pieces by Proust's friend, Reynaldo Hahn — made scarcely a ripple. The reader likes a story with a beginning, a middle and an end; the critics like a work that has form and fits into a recognized category. *Les Plaisirs et les Jours* did none of these things; it seemed the work of a dilettante, unworthy of notice. Yet *Les Plaisirs et les Jours* can be seen to have a place, if only a minor one, in the pattern of Proust's development. There is an understanding of the structure of Parisian, and more generally of French, society in 'Mondanité et Mélomanie de Bouvard et Pécuchet' that foreshadows, if only dimly, what is to come; there is, too, a strong vein of irony and social caricature, some skilful pastiche in the presentation of an aspect of Flaubert's two worthies, that their creator, lacking musical sensibility, had not drawn. Proust, as he was later to show,[57] possessed the art of pastiche, the art of penetrating so intimately the mental attitudes of another writer that one can adopt them at will and write, as it were, with his pen.

Nor was this capacity of Proust's limited to writers; he was to give abundant proof of it by his subtle analyses of the painting of Elstir, of the Sonata and the Septet of Vinteuil, and he was to exercise it too on the society he lived in. 'Un dîner en ville' provides an early sketch of what was to be a background to the gallery of characters of *A la Recherche*, characters that are not key-portraits of Proust's friends and acquaintances; he was careful to point out that they are composite constructions drawn with the help of his powerful memory from his perceptive and ironical understanding of the men and women he moved amongst.

But if a Proustian outline is discernible in *Les Plaisirs et les Jours*,[58] how much truer this is of *Jean Santeuil*. *Jean Santeuil* represents a euphoric moment in Proust's life. His health was adequate, he had a position in Parisian society and the wealth to enjoy it; above all a confident mood that launched him squarely on the creative tide. Unlike *A la Recherche*, *Jean Santeuil* is not told by a narrator in the first person, yet it is more autobiographical than *A la Recherche*. It is the latter in embryonic form: the characteristic Proustian style, its long serpentine sentences, as yet lacking the masterly handling of a later day, themes and scenes that will reappear in *A la Recherche* (the goodnight kiss, calf-love, jealousy with its twin effects of self-torture and cruelty, 'high life' and snobbery in the 'noble Faubourg', the pregnant significance to be

[57] In *Pastiches et Mélanges* (1919).
[58] Especially with its suggestion of Proustian themes: the power of habit ('Violante ou la Mondanité'), snobbery ('un dîner en ville'), jealousy that lives and dies with the changing psyche ('La fin de la jalousie'), the stimulating power of sound on memory ('La Mort de Baldassar Silvande', last pages), the impossibility of getting at the truth ('La fin de la Jalousie').

found in a musical phrase, the effluxion of time, involuntary memory,[59] garrison life at Provins – Orléans in Proust's own experience, the Doncières of *A la Recherche* – with Prince Borodino and Bernard de Réveillon, alias Saint-Loup).

Two important characters are missing: Swann and Madame Verdurin; some of what will be projected into Swann's experience here forms part of Jean's, and there is a trinity of hostesses who will merge their identity in the ineffable Madame Verdurin, tyrannical, bullying and so sensitive (says she) to music that an evening with Wagner means bed, with a migraine.

Such is the profusion of *Jean Santeuil* that much of its wealth will have to be sacrificed in *A la Recherche*: attitudes that may well be drawn directly from the young author's own experience: e.g. Jean's harshness to his parents, the latter's dislike of Jean's idleness, scenes such as a Parisian lycée, military service,[60] the Chamber of Deputies during a financial scandal (?echoes of Panama), the courts during the Dreyfus Affair.

Proust worked at *Jean Santeuil* from 1896 until 1900. What made him stop? Did its very profusion weigh him down and create difficulties that appeared insurmountable? It would seem so. 'Je travaille depuis très longtemps', he writes to Marie Nördlinger in 1899, 'à un ouvrage de très longue haleine, mais sans rien achever. Et il y a des moments où je me demande... si je n'amasse pas des ruines'[61] – a melancholy thought for anyone after three years' work. Then, as though with relief, he continues: 'Depuis une quinzaine de jours, je m'occupe à un petit travail absolument différent de ce que je fais généralement, à propos de Ruskin et de certaines cathédrales?'

Proust's interest in Ruskin in fact dates from some years before; already in 1896 he had read everything by Ruskin, translated into French,[62] and could quote long passages from memory, but now as his creative urge flags, temporarily at least, he turns aside to translation and critical commentary. For the next six years Proust was to be preoccupied with Ruskin. Despite his shaky knowledge of English he was, with the help of Mme Nördlinger, to translate two of his hero's works; in 1904 appeared *La Bible d'Amiens* with abundant notes and, as preface, an article Proust had published (1900) in the *Mercure de France*, entitled 'Ruskin à Notre-Dame d'Amiens'; in 1906 appeared *Sésame et Les Lys*. This too carries

---

[59] The vital significance for Proust of this phenomenon is particularly emphasized, e.g. in Vol. II, chap. vi, sec. ix, 'Impressions retrouvées'.

[60] Proust joined up as an under-age volunteer and did a year's service at Orléans in 1889, the last year in which the volunteer service still existed.

[61] Proust, *Lettres à une amie* (Letter No. II, 5 December 1899).

[62] Mme Marie Nördlinger, 'Note on Proust and Ruskin', catalogue of exhibition, *Proust and His Time* (London, 1955).

a preface as long as the lecture it accompanies, again an article of
Proust's, this time published in *La Renaissance Latine* (1905) and
entitled 'Sur la lecture'. In these prefaces, Proust's ideas on art
are to be found in embryo.[63]

What in Ruskin enthralled Proust? His enthusiasm for Turner
or the pre-Raphaelites? His hatred of the Industrial Revolution
and the enslavement, as he saw it, of man in the factories? His
passion for art and architecture, and his dream of bringing art into
the life of the people, as a kind of religion of beauty with stimulating social value?

A pointer to the answer is provided by the works Proust translated and by his prolonged sojourn in Venice (spring 1900), the
only considerable journey abroad Proust's health ever allowed him
to undertake;[64] a pilgrimage to see 'The Stones of Venice' through
the eyes of Ruskin, to see 'en des palais défaillants, mais encore
debout et roses.'[65] Ruskin's ideas on architecture take solid form;
a dream come true, and yet, as we shall see, not wholly true.

We may safely say that Ruskin's belief in the therapeutic value
of the handloom or the hand printing-press set up in some cottage,
cradled in the bosom of nature, the social mission of art – a gospel,
understandable against the background of grime and poverty in
Victorian England, was not destined to interest in 1900 a Parisian,
lapped in luxury, in whom nature, its flowers and their scent provoked, as likely as not, an attack of asthma; but Ruskin's enthusiasms for architecture, notably Gothic, for painting, notably the
Italian primitives whose bright fresh colours were the pretext for
the gorgeous palette of the pre-Raphaelites, Ruskin's loving study
of detail, in depth, as a vital basis for an informed opinion of any
work of art or style – in general his genuine adoration of art, here
were attitudes and beliefs that could and did awaken an eager response in Proust.

The love of the plastic arts was not innate in Proust; several of
his artist friends, notably Jacques-Emile Blanche, bear witness to
that.[66] Ruskin, by transposing works of art, painting or architecture, into literary terms, showed Proust the way. The use Proust so
often makes in *A la Recherche* of works of art as a basis of descriptive comparison derives from the insight he obtained from Ruskin's
'close-looking' at a picture, or a sculptural motif (e.g. a small
figure over the Portail des Libraires at Rouen cathedral), and the
elaborate literary analyses of his characters' feelings at the sight of
some picture or on hearing a piece of music are masterly in their

[63] See A. Maurois, 'Proust and Ruskin', in *Essays and Studies by members of the English Association*, Vol. XVII (Oxford).
[64] He did spend a few days in Belgium and at Geneva.
[65] Quoted by Maurois, op. cit.
[66] Maurois, op. cit.

finesse; his initiation into this process of investigation is due to Ruskin; the slow elaborate convolutions of style that result from such microscopic slow-motion viewing is similar in both authors, but pushed to its extreme in Proust.

From a note to his translation of *Sesame and Lilies* Proust appears, too, to have drawn from Ruskin what was later to form the essential structural idea of *A la Recherche*, the need of guiding themes; 'Mais c'est le charme... de l'oeuvre de Ruskin', he writes, 'qu'il y ait entre les idées d'un même livre, et entre les divers livres, des liens qu'il ne montre pas, qu'il laisse à peine apparaître un instant et qu'il a d'ailleurs peut-être tissés après coup, mais jamais artificiels cependant puisqu'ils sont toujours tirés de la substance toujours identique à elle-même de sa pensée. Les préoccupations multiples mais constantes de cette pensée, voilà ce qui assure à ces livres une unité plus réelle que l'unité de composition, généralement absente, il faut bien le dire.'[67] This foreshadows the pattern of *A la Recherche*. *Sesame and Lilies* (1865) deals with the place of literature in Ruskin's scheme of things – literature is a treasure-house open to all; great books multiply our friendships, are a sum of human experience. Here, however, comes a parting of the ways between Proust and Ruskin, his initiator. Proust's preface 'Sur la lecture' does not accept Ruskin's thesis. Great books indeed may play a vital part, but it is limited because whereas for an author, his book is a conclusion of wisdom and experience, for the reader it should be an incentive, a starting point: 'notre sagesse commence où celle de l'auteur finit...' This idea runs like a golden thread through the preface: 'la lecture est au seuil de la vie spirituelle; elle peut nous y introduire; elle ne la constitue pas...'. There is, indeed, Proust tells us, a certain danger in reading: 'Quand la vérité ne vous apparaît plus comme un idéal que nous ne pouvons réaliser que par le progrès intime de notre pensée et par l'effort de notre coeur, mais comme une chose matérielle, déposée entre les feuillets des livres comme un miel tout préparé par les autres.' This is what Proust calls 'idolatry'; the idolatry of art is a danger he has come to see in Ruskinian attitudes. Thus, without rejecting Ruskin who was both a revelation and a stimulus to Proust, we find the latter gradually forming his own aesthetic ideas in contrast to him.

That process is continued in *Contre Sainte-Beuve* (1908–10). The great nineteenth-century critic suffers in the encounter. To the standard reproaches made against him (his injustices, e.g. to Balzac and Beyle; his lack of understanding for Nerval and Baudelaire) Proust adds his own: Sainte-Beuve's taste for anecdotes about the man he is studying, his efforts to see him as a reflection of his

[67] Quoted by Maurois, op. cit.

family, his friends, his time and even of his vices, means that Sainte-Beuve goes from society to the author and from the author to his work, as though the latter were the product of his talk, of the surface layer in the author's psyche, the social man, that part of him in fact that is the same (only more so) as in anyone else. Proust's idea is the opposite: the work reveals the man; only thus can we achieve an insight into the deeper strata of a writer's psyche whence the work springs, that account for his uniqueness and consequently for that of his writing: 'Un livre est le produit d'un autre moi que celui que nous manifestons dans nos habitudes, dans la société, dans nos vices,'[68] – and yet, be it said in passing, who better than Proust has portrayed the society he knew, the men and women his contemporaries, creatures of habit, as he so often tells us we are, and the vices that flourish in 'the cities of the plain'?

The 'contemporaneity' of a work of art is indeed in Proust's view a necessity of great art – Baudelaire thought no differently[69] – but his stricture on Sainte-Beuve is the latter's unawareness that a book draws its essence from deeper levels. Proust's certainly will, but, in the Proust-Sainte-Beuve debate, we may not feel inclined like Proust to dismiss Sainte-Beuve's method as irrelevant, even though it may be superficial and tend, subtle nuances, moral finesse, roving curiosity, genuine scholarship and all, to the commonplace.

What contact, Proust seems to ask, could Sainte-Beuve make with a Nerval or a Baudelaire, two of the most original writers in the nineteenth century? Proust's interest in the former is particularly important; the penumbra between consciousness and sleep, the dream world, leading in Nerval's case to a kaleidoscopic confusion between dream and reality (his form of madness), these were to have an important part in *A la Recherche*; Proust's reflections on Nerval are like a small rough sketch for part of the finished picture. Indeed this applies to the whole book – not so much an attack on Sainte-Beuve as a series of studies presently to find a place, rewritten and rearranged, in the great work; in the meantime woven disconcertingly around Sainte-Beuve.

Proust set his *Contre Sainte-Beuve* aside in 1910. Ten years had elapsed since in what seemed a mood of discouragement he had given up *Jean Santeuil*, ten years which on the surface look barren: two translations, accompanied by prefaces and textual notes, a few newspaper articles; obituaries, literary reviews and the like, and, attached to Sainte-Beuve, a disjointed group of studies, like *Jean Santeuil*, unpublished.

[68] Chap. 8, 'La Méthode de Sainte-Beuve'.
[69] His essay on Constantin Guys.

But Ruskin and more indirectly Sainte-Beuve had helped Proust to find his own originality and the form that suited it – the narrator speaking in the first person, the future Marcel, appears in *Contre Sainte-Beuve* for the first time; Ruskin, Sainte-Beuve and physical suffering; asthma, which had begun when Proust was ten, grew more frequent from 1906 and drove him more and more into seclusion and invalidism. Illness brought constant interruptions to his work; on the other hand, in his cork-lined room, insulated from noise, isolated from society, but keeping in touch with the world by his voluminous correspondence, free almost of all physical movement, he was driven in on himself and able to achieve the pin-pointed concentration needed to record the results of his deep inner exploration.

An added spur may have come from a sense of remorse towards his parents[70] whose desire to see Marcel with a career – law, diplomacy, the magistrature – failing which, at least to see him achieving something in literature, had scarcely been realized. Be that as it may, he was ready, conscious as he now was of the urgency his own precarious grip on life created, to embark upon the final, exhausting but triumphant enterprise.

Du Côté de chez Swann, itself divided into three sections – 'Combray', 'Un Amour de Swann', 'Noms de Pays: le Nom', is, together with the last part, *Le Temps Retrouvé*, the most important and in many people's view the best part of *A la Recherche Du Temps Perdu*. Its importance or, to be more accurate, the importance of 'Combray', is that it gives the clue to the structure of the whole work.[71] This is no novel developing in the traditional form with a series of events arranged in a casual chain developed over a given time-space; there is no plot, only a series of moments in Marcel's stream of consciousness, a series of expanding circles as the small boy grows up and takes an adult hold on the world.

The basis for this original treatment of the novelist's material – human experience – is prepared in Combray. When the reader first meets Marcel he is a middle-aged man exploring as he lies in bed in the dark the borderlands that lie between sleep and consciousness:[72] as semi-consciousness merges into sleep, he has enchanting glimpses of his past; he sees himself at the centre of past experiences he can reach out to at any point of the circumference. A series of rooms he has occupied from childhood[73] emerge. He becomes fully awake and, rather than try to find sleep again, he

---

[70] His father Adrien Proust, a distinguished physician, d. 1903, his mother, née Weil, d. 1904.

[71] See *Combray*, edited by G. Brée and C. Lynes, Introduction, pp. 19 *et seq.*

[72] cf. *Contre Sainte-Beuve*, chap. 1, 'Sommeils'.

[73] cf. op. cit., chap. 2, 'Chambres'.

determines to go out in search of the memories he feels are mysteriously stored up in the rooms that have been conjured up at Combray, at Balbec, at his parents' flat in Paris, at Doncières, Venice, Tansonville.

In a manner that suggests the fading-out technique of the cinema, the picture we have in our minds of the middle-aged Marcel merges into that of the small boy he had been at Combray.[74] The voice of the middle-aged narrator persists but from now on his image returns only occasionally to the screen; with one exception, referred to below, the sequence of scenes that passes before us in the succeeding parts of *A la Recherche* are cut from the unending film of his memory: 'Combray', where we see the small boy in the family circle, eagerly reading George Sand in the summer afternoons, dreaming of the country and its feudal lords that lay in some ideal place where the rainbow ends, along the way to Guermantes; of the less mysterious Méséglise, inaccessible only because beyond the horizon; the way to Guermantes, the way to Méséglise, the two ways that seemed to lead to places different in essence, but which were to unite in Marcel's later experience, and again at night waiting in anguish to know whether his mother will come and give him her good-night kiss.

The second section, as its title implies, is the exception just mentioned; here the narrator speaks from hearsay about his parents' neighbour, Swann, the *châtelain* of Tansonville; accordingly the narrator abandons the first person for the third, as Swann comes to the centre of the stage. We have taken a step back in time and follow the ascending and falling graph of his infatuation for the *demi-mondaine* he was later to marry, Odette de Crécy.

This step back in chronological time is seen later to be essential to the whole scheme of the work, partly because many of the characters Swann falls in with in the course of his love affair subsequently come into Marcel's own life: Swann himself, M. and Madame Verdurin and their sycophantic circle – 'le petit clan', Odette; partly because the exhaustively studied course of Swann's love for Odette provides a pattern that Marcel's own for Albertine closely conforms to – that perhaps we all inevitably conform to? Does not human behaviour conform to set patterns, thinks the later disillusioned Marcel?

In the third section, 'Noms de Pays: le Nom', the narrator returns once more to his own memories. With each successive part new areas of Marcel's experience are added; *A l'Ombre des Jeunes Filles*: again Balbec and a new circle of acquaintance – Madame de Villeparisis; new friendships – Albertine and her circle, Robert de Saint-Loup, the strange and disquieting M. de Charlus, the tire-

[74] Illiers, in Proust's own experience.

some Bloch; *Le Côté Guermantes*: Marcel's first and gradually more assured steps in the 'high life' of the Faubourg Saint-Germain; *Sodome et Gomorrhe*, his discovery of unnatural vice; *La Prisonnière* and *Albertine disparue*, his love for Albertine and her death. *Le Temps Retrouvé*: glimpses of Paris at night in war-time, in 1916, when Marcel, after years of illness spent in a nursing home, returns thither. In the last section of this final part an invitation from the princesse de Guermantes to a musical matinée just after the end of the war tempts Marcel to take up the threads of his interrupted life, with vital results for himself.

At this point the wheel of time, having gone full circle, catches up with the narrator's present, and we leave him ready at last with a strong sense of urgency to embark on the work we have just read. The whole structure, where no details – and they are countless – are fortuitous, with its crowd of characters, its complex of family, social and passionate relationships, its elaborate themes interwoven as in a Wagnerian music-drama, with varying moods, comic and poignant, is complete.

What is the purpose of it all? If the various parts *A la Recherche* is divided into are convenient as indicating the various areas of experience Marcel uncovers in the course of his long exploration, a better division perhaps in the context of Proust's purpose is to think of it in three parts: 'Combray' which gives the clue to what the quest is about and lays the foundations the structure is built on;[75] the quest that takes Marcel from his childhood at Combray to the musical matinée at the princesse de Guermantes' (*Le Temps Retrouvé*, chapter 3); and, finally, the solution of the whole matter, which fills the remainder of that long chapter.

The clue in 'Combray' is two-fold; as Marcel recalls his child-hood he notes that whenever he thinks of the old family house, always one little section of it at one moment in time flashes on the screen of memory: 'à la base assez large, le petit salon, la salle à manger, l'amorce de l'allée obscure par où arriverait M. Swann ... le vestibule où je m'acheminais vers la première marche de l'escalier ... et au faîte ma chambre à coucher avec le petit couloir à porte vitrée pour l'entrée de maman.' The reason for this peculiar trick of memory is that these parts of the house are the ones intimately connected with what was always a moment of tense emotion for the child, his going to bed, of tense emotion because the question-mark always stood at the end: would his mother come to kiss him good-night, so that he could go to sleep happy, or would that tiresome 'M. Swann' by his evening call prevent her coming?

Of course, Marcel recognizes that with a minimal intellectual

[75] G. Brée and C. Lynes, *Combray*, Introduction.

effort he can recall the house in all its detail, but this intellectual voluntary act of memory merely means an assemblage of facts, and Marcel notes no desire in himself to make that small voluntary effort: 'comme les renseignements qu'elle [i.e. la mémoire de l'intelligence] donne sur le passé ne conservent rien de lui, je n'aurais jamais eu envie de songer à ce reste de Combray. Tout cela était en réalité mort pour moi.' But some time later Marcel gets his second clue, the incident of 'la petite madeleine' dipped in tea: 'à l'instant même où la gorgée mêlée des miettes de gâteau toucha mon palais, ... Un plaisir délicieux m'avait envahi, isolé, sans la notion de sa cause ...' The experience is so arresting that Marcel is obliged to examine it attentively; satisfied that the cause does not lie in any particular virtue of the madeleine, he sees that it must be in himself, that a relationship exists between the taste and aroma of the madeleine dipped in tea and a mysterious something in his mind. Suddenly the answer comes: the madeleine recalls the identical savour of the madeleine dipped in tea or lime that his Great Aunt Léonie used to give him when he went to see her in her room on Sunday mornings at Combray. The madeleine that Marcel is eating is the key that has opened a door in his involuntary memory; memories of Combray come crowding through, not merely an assembly of facts but a totality of experience, a veritable resurrection.

The pages wherein Marcel describes this key experience[76] end on a passage that seems to vibrate still with his emotion; it is a moment of poignancy that cannot leave the reader unaffected: 'Mais, quand d'un passé ancien rien ne subsiste, après la mort des êtres, après la destruction des choses, ...'.

But why the joy? Marcel feels there is more in it than the mere pleasure of reliving a past experience and sets out to seek the answer in 'l'édifice immense du souvenir', finding it at last during the musical matinée at the Princesse de Guermantes'.

Marcel will have to undertake an arduous pilgrimage before the answer to that question – Why the joy? – is vouchsafed to him. In the course of it – and on the surface, the intellectual level of Marcel's experience – the reader gets a fascinating picture of French society at a distinct period of its history, the Third Republic in its heyday. Numerous topical details from 'le Jockey', to Charvet ties, references to historical persons and events from Mac-Mahon to the Prince of Wales, from the bank crash of the Union Générale to the Dreyfus Affair, from Delcassé to the Great War, in which, incidentally, Robert de Saint-Loup, hetero- and homosexual, faithful friend, faithless husband, intelligent, courteous, heroic, a typical member of his class, is killed; all these and count-

[76] See *Combray*, chap. 1, last pages.

less others provide the work with a framework of reference in historical time.

The society portrayed is one where money plays no part because it presents no problem, having been acquired generations earlier ('des fortunes bien digérées'), a society where everyone seems to have an appointed station in the hierarchy from the duc and duchesse de Guermantes, Charlus and the princesse de Parme at the peak down the nicely graded steps to the small fry and 'country cousins': Madame de Saint-Euverte, and the Cambremer family ('dont le nom finit juste à temps', as Oriane de Guermantes, the cruellest tongue in the Faubourg, remarks), and to well-connected persons whose earlier escapades have lost them caste, e.g. Madame de Villeparisis (pronounced vi-parisis by those in the know); and in another world outside the noble Faubourg, equally moneyed, making up for lack of aristocratic by intellectual pretentions, the bourgeois society – Monsieur and Madame Verdurin and their hangers-on; last, but not least in skill of characterization, the satellites revolving round the greater luminaries, the hôteliers and purveyors, coachmen and domestics: Aimé and 'le lift', Jupien and his niece, above all Françoise – as faithful and tyrannical as any Toinette of Molière.

From the secure if unpretentious bourgeois background whence he sprang, Marcel, like his creator a reader of Saint-Simon, had in his childhood looked at high society with admiring awe; in his imagination he had peopled it from the pages of the *Mémoires*; the great names that had adorned the court of Louis XIV had the same magical effect upon him as those of Venice, Florence and Balbec. Like Proust, Marcel determined to break into this mysterious world, and like Proust whose intellectual gifts and brilliant conversation made him so welcome, he succeeds easily; ever since the seventeenth century at least, talent, for want of high birth, has been a passport to the great salons.

Yes, on the surface level, a fascinating picture of a vanished time seen by an observer with a radiographic eye, a companion-piece to the court of Louis XIV in Saint-Simon, and to the society of the Restoration and July Monarchy in Balzac, with the duchesse de Langeais as counterpart to the duchesse de Guermantes. Balzac had been the first to conceive the idea of novels grouped together as one structure with characters seen on two levels, the social level as members of the background crowd, and the moral level when his magnifying eye reveals the burning passions within. Proust's work is more tightly knit, not a group of novels, but one novel; the social scene may be less broad (what mention for example of the Church? Religion plays no part in Marcel's world), but it is seen in greater depth; on closer scrutiny the noble Faubourg turns out to be not the impregnable fortress Marcel had imagined; he sees it now as a living organism subject like any other to the law of change. The process is of course continuous but in Marcel's span of memories there are two moments of acceleration: the Dreyfus Affair, of which there are constant echoes, and the 1914 war. The violent cleavages of opinion wrought by both have created strange and unstable groupings in society, providing opportunities of social advancement to some, causing the eclipse of others.

Monsieur Verdurin, harmless ass, having discreetly died, Madame Verdurin brings the much-needed support (and consolation?) of her fortune first to the duc de Duras and then to the widowed prince de Guermantes; as the second princesse de Guermantes she 'queens' it in the ranks of those who in the old days she had dismissed (in jealousy) as 'les ennuyeux'. Madame Swann, also widowed, has become Madame de Forcheville – no great advance perhaps in itself, but, like the second duchesse de Duras, Odette knows that to change one's name twice instead of only once is much more than twice as effective; Madame Swann, the ex-cocotte Odette de Crécy (ye gods!), was not 'received'; Madame de Forcheville, the former Madame Swann, has long since nosed her way into the Faubourg and her daughter Gilberte is the widowed marquise de Saint-Loup. Jupien has become the baron de Charlus's indispensable factotum; his niece, adopted by the baron as Mademoiselle d'Oloron, has married well. Legrandin, snob of snobs, has achieved 'la particule' ('Monsieur de ...'); Morel, Bloch – mere nobodies, have consolidated their uncertain positions; others have been touched by age or social decline; with the years and change of fashion the salon of the duchesse de Guermantes is not quite the pinnacle it was; as for poor Charlus – a physical and mental ruin.

Marcel's awareness of the change is rendered particularly acute when, having been taken, as it were, out of the time process by his long illness, he is injected into it again at the princesse de Guermantes' matinée. As he enters the salon he carries in his memory the images of his friends and acquaintances as he had known them; confronting him now are rows of shrunken forms and wrinkled or bloated faces, pitilessly mirrored in his eyes. Only with difficulty do images and reality merge in the process of recognition; nor does he forget that as he looks at them through the images in his mind they are looking at him in the same way. He too must be old; he too has death at his elbow.

Thus the Faubourg's reality destroys the ideal; it is full of ordinary people who cannot measure up to the ideal society Marcel as a child had created for himself with the romantic names in Saint-Simon; it is a society hedged about with convention and formality, a frivolous society with nothing to do but dine in or dine out, receive or be received, be seen everywhere – especially by the social columnists for the Press next morning; a society regularly going through the accepted but meaningless movements of a minuet.

The reality, closely experienced, has destroyed the ideal. As we follow Marcel in his exhaustive (and sometimes exhausting) exploration of his experience we see him constantly disappointed in this way: the luminous mental picture he has created for himself of Venice is destroyed by the mosquitoes, at Balbec he is disappointed not to find the confirmation of the image he had formed from what Legrandin and Swann had told him about the wild coastline and the church, like Swann he discovers in his attachment for Gilberte and in his passion for Albertine that love is a subjective emotion that cannot hope to coincide with that of the partner in the experience, that it inevitably follows a set pattern, souring into jealousy, drying up in indifference. Moreover, like Swann in his jealous cross-questionings of Odette, Marcel finds it quite impossible, as he taxes Albertine with his suspicions, to get at the truth. Just as he comes to what he believes a firm conclusion, someone else says something that puts a totally different complexion on the matter; Swann's experience had been just the same. Perhaps we are inevitably imprisoned in our subjective impressions; even these vary, Marcel notes, with our moods or physical condition.

Relativity, flux, patterns, seem to control our lives, and individuals must be insignificant mechanisms all controlled in their behaviour by the mysterious laws that govern the species; a glaring example of behaviour pattern is provided by the remarkable scene, that Marcel from his look-out post is witness of, when Charlus meets Jupien.[77] Without a word they recognize each other for what they are and, partners in their sexual aberration, begin a kind of 'courtship pattern': 'on eût dit deux oiseaux...'.

Yet against the pessimism Marcel's explorations lead to, he can set the experience of the little madeleine dipped in tea and a number of other experiences, including the musical experience of Vinteuil's sonata and the septet, which accumulate in the course of the work and which share the common characteristic of filling Marcel with intense joy. He had understood, as we have seen, that they released the mechanism of involuntary memory and resurrected a moment of past experience, but, engaged as he has been for years in society life, he had not until the musical matinée fastened his attention on the phenomenon. On that morning these moments of intense joy crowd in upon him with such force as a result of small incidents – walking on unlevel paving stones, the clinking of teaspoons on cups in the next room, etc. – that he is forced to re-examine them, and so the revelation comes: deep down in the

[77] See *Sodome et Gomorrhe*, I.

subconscious beneath the surface being, living in the relative, enslaved to time and change, there must exist a spiritual being outside time who, unknown to Marcel, stores up the total experience obtained by Marcel in time and of which intuitive flashes only have so far been granted to him. This wonderful conviction must be conveyed to men and at once Marcel's life as an artist is transformed, makes sense, has a purpose, that of recapturing the totality of the inner spiritual vision in its unending stream, giving it form and meaning, in fact creating it. The role of intelligence is subordinated; it must accept the material intuition provides; but it retains the important function of giving that material a significant form.

Intuition and intelligence, both have been at work in the creation of *A la Recherche*. The connection with Bergson needs no stressing; the time stream, the changing nature of the psyche in the time continuum, the hidden wealth of the sub-conscious which intuition alone can reveal, the roles of intelligence, and art, all these ideas derive from Bergson.[78] The impression of the stream of consciousness is strengthened by the very form Proust's intelligence devised for his matter: sinuous labyrinthine sentences extending sometimes to a paragraph, even a page; page after page with scarcely a paragraph to relieve the eye let alone the attention; the author admits no compromise; once embarked, we move inexorably on the leisurely tide.

V. VALÉRY

The work of Paul Valéry (1871–1945) as poet and essayist falls into two main groups. The first group comprises the early poems, originally published in divers ephemeral reviews (e.g. *La Conque, L'Ermitage, La Revue Indépendante*, later collected under the title of *Album de vers anciens* (1920), and a number of prose writings, notably: *Introduction à la méthode de Léonard de Vinci* (1895), *La Soirée avec M. Teste* (1896). The second group, besides containing a number of new editions of earlier writings, comprises two major poems, *La Jeune Parque* (1917), *Le Cimetière Marin* (1920), the shorter poems of *Charmes* (1922) and a great number of collected essays, prefaces and reflections: *inter alia* two Socratic dialogues, *Eupalinos ou l'Architecte* (1921), *L'Ame et la Danse* (1921); *Variétés I–V, 1924–39* (critical essays on literature, music, painting and the sciences); *Regards sur le monde actuel* (1931); *Analecta* (1926), *Tel quel I, II* (1941, 1943), *Rhumbs* (1927), *Autres Rhumbs* (1934), *Mauvaises Pensées* (1942), *Mon Faust, ébauches* (1941) – some forty volumes in all; in addition, a photostat edition in twenty-nine volumes (1956) of the *Cahiers*.

[78] See Léon Pierre-Quint, *Marcel Proust*, chap. 2.

Born of a French father with Corsican forbears, and an Italian mother, Valéry lived his early years in the South of France, first at his native Sète and from 1884 to 1892 at Montpellier; he also spent frequent holidays at Genoa.

The early poems bear the Mediterranean stamp of his heredity and environment. Theorists of the 'Latin genius' could find much support for their thesis[79] in poems such as 'Hélène', 'Orphée', 'Naissance de Vénus', 'Narcisse Parle'. Classical traditions, without obtruding, are in close attendance, the impact of the Mediterranean landscape is evident; nor were these characteristics to disappear from his later poetry where they are if anything more emphatic.

Of equal importance in the earlier poems are literary influences of the day. Baudelaire had attracted him, the Parnassians moderately, he had discovered Edgar Allan Poe whom he admired, but the Symbolists Valéry at once recognized as his masters. *A Rebours*, which he read in July 1889, revealed to him Verlaine, Mallarmé, the Decadents, all still unrecognized by the pedagogues of the day as worthy of their attention. Thanks to Pierre Louÿs, a chance acquaintance and later friend, Valéry met André Gide[80] who introduced him to the works of Rimbaud and gave him his first appreciation of music. Louÿs also put Valéry in touch with Mallarmé, at whose Tuesday gatherings he was to be a regular visitor when he moved to Paris (1892).

In contrast to the poems mentioned above, 'La Fileuse' (1891) is a Symbolist poem in treatment and feeling: daylight fading into night, consciousness merging into dream, the soft music of the poem enhanced by the feminine rhymes throughout; there are reminiscences of Verlaine in the very vocabulary: 'la caline Chevelure...', of Mallarmé in indirect description:

> ... une source vive
> Qui ... arrose
> De ses pertes de fleurs ...

In his articles on Mallarmé, Valéry recalls the impact the older poet made on him, the joy of progressive discovery Mallarmé's hermeticism produces – poems such as 'Baignée' and 'Au Bois Dormant' are clearly in the idiom of the master; they are static, exclusively descriptive of material objects, suggested by deft and indirect touches that reveal them progressively to the co-operative reader. As so often in Mallarmé, the difficulty lies on the surface of these sonnets; like intricate mechanisms they open smoothly when the key is found, and discover nothing of significance within; but

[79] See Valéry Larbaud, *Oeuvres*, VII, Essay on P.V.
[80] For Gide's contacts with Montpellier, see *Si le Grain ne meurt*.

in the process the reader has been forced to re-create the image for himself; therein lies his pleasure. The early poems were all written between 1890 and 1892. In the latter year Valéry changed his course. An unhappy love affair was not foreign to his doubts and dissatisfaction. The crisis point occurred in August, at Genoa, during a night of thunderstorms, that seem a fitting background to the dramatic decision to abandon poetry in favour of more rigorous intellectual exercise. In what would look like a symbolic gesture of renouncement, if Paris had not been the goal of his ambitions since his discovery of the Symbolists and Mallarmé, he left the south for the capital.

The *Introduction à la méthode de Léonard de Vinci* and *La Soirée avec M. Teste* are important guides to Valéry's new orientation. In the *Introduction*, which is no biography of Leonardo, nor even a study in the first instance of his work as artist, architect and engineer, the author constructs an ideal intellect like some delicate piece of mental machinery ('Je me propose d'imaginer un homme...'), which he then fits into the body of Leonardo, like an engine in a car ('Un nom manque à cette créature de pensée... Aucun ne me paraît plus convenir que celui de Léonard...').

The *Introduction* is a dive into the inner labyrinth in search of pure consciousness, as yet untouched by intellectual activities, be they scientific or other ('à la profondeur d'un trésor, la permanence fondamentale d'une conscience que rien ne supporte...'); the purpose? – to establish the nature of this deep inner prism capable of instantaneously splitting up the intellectual rays that fall on it, for, if that mystery were penetrated, we should indeed stand at the very heart of all activity, our radius of intellectual power would be multiplied, our mental processes greatly accelerated ('Si ce mode d'être conscient devient habituel, on en viendra, par exemple, à examiner d'emblée tous les résultats possibles d'un acte envisagé, tous les rapports d'un objet conçu...'). The whole passage suggests nothing so much as the prophetic vision of a modern electronic computer, with its immediate and multiplied responses to an initial impulse. Valéry seeks 'l'unité de méthode', the phrase seems Cartesian, but Descartes is satisfied to establish the presence of the thinking principle to authenticate his existence, and thereafter to conquer the real world as the indispensable step to wisdom and beatitude; Valéry is absorbed in pursuit of the inner citadel of consciousness alone.

For Leonardo let us now substitute M. Teste. No more than Valéry's Leonardo, M. Teste scarcely comes alive as a fictional character; we see him through the eyes of the narrator, later through those of his widow; the narrator's interest in him stems from his conviction that Teste has the secret the narrator is searching for: 'A force d'y penser, j'ai fini par croire que M. Teste était arrivé à découvrir des lois de l'esprit que nous ignorons.' He is consciousness, crystallized out, keeping inward vigil on itself; the narrator quotes him as saying: 'Je suis étant et me voyant; me voyant me voir, et ainsi de suite ... Pensons de tout près ...'.

To what end? To an ordinary mortal the question comes naturally; he is tempted to imagine M. Teste in an heroic Promethean role, seeking to steal the forbidden fire for the good of humanity, or on a lower level as a villain of science fiction in pursuit of power, undreamed of, over humanity by his mastery of mind mechanism. He is neither; he is a peaceful bourgeois, content with the satisfaction this inner 'cleanliness', this hygiene of consciousness, whence all intellectual impurities have been distilled, gives him. Madame Teste pertinently describes her late husband as 'un mystique sans Dieu.'

The narrator's 'confession' in the opening pages is evidently Valéry's own; it recalls the intellectual position he had reached in October 1893, and had set out from to write the *Introduction* and *M. Teste*. We can understand the arduous debate he had held with himself during 'la nuit de Gênes', so-called, when he had noted 'tout mon sort se jouait dans ma tête. – Je suis entre moi et moi.' Intellect had conquered; like M. Teste, Valéry was to become 'un mystique sans Dieu'!

Valéry remained for some years in the literary circles of Paris, but as an onlooker respected for his early achievements. After Mallarmé's death (1898) he gradually withdrew. A post in the Ministry of War, later with Havas, marriage (1900), children – Valéry seemed to have buried his former self under office paper and family responsibilities. But the passionate pilgrim of the inner labyrinth was in fact actively pursuing his 'avancement en soi-même', studying physics, mathematics, the psychology of mind concentration, inner awareness, attention and memory; there perhaps lay the path leading to the understanding of consciousness?[81]

Yet, in spite of his silence, the reputation of this poet, buried alive, was treasured by a 'happy few'. In the winter of 1912–13 Gide invited Valéry to collect his early poems in view of an edition under the imprimatur of *La Nouvelle Revue Française*. Valéry's rejection of the idea did not discourage his friends who, having collected the poems themselves, submitted a typed copy to Valéry with the suggestion that he should write an introduction. Then only did Valéry consent to look at them again: 'Contact avec mes monstres', he comments,[82] 'Dégoût ... je me mets à les tripoter.

[81] The 270 *Cahiers*, edited in 1956 in twenty-nine volumes, mostly belong to these years.
[82] Valéry Larbaud, op. cit.

Retouches...' His interest was aroused enough for him to consider writing a short poem of twenty-five lines as a farewell to poetry. Here is the germ of what after over four years of work and a hundred versions finally became a poem of 500 lines and Valéry's acknowledged masterpiece, *La Jeune Parque.*

Of the three fates of mythology, Clotho, the youngest, presided at men's birth, and held the distaff from which Lachesis spun their lives' thread, cut in due course by Atropos with her scissors. Valéry seems to have had Clotho in mind,[83] because she stands at the outset of the human adventure, a point of vantage therefore before any commitment or direction has been taken. Thus the Clotho of the poem symbolises Valéry's own constant quest for that inner point of vantage, pure consciousness, whence he could see at once all the options lying at the circumference of his being.

In the opening section of the poem, Clotho is discovered standing on some Mediterranean shore within sound of the waves ('la houle me murmure...[84]), during the last watches of the night, beneath the stars, 'diamants extrêmes'.[85] She ponders not men's fate but her own. She has been aroused by the horror of a dream in which she had suffered a serpent's bite. With that capacity the psyche has in the dream state of being both subject and object, she had watched her conscious self following the serpent, symbol of self-knowledge, into the inner jungle:

> Je me voyais me voir,[86] sinueuse, et dorais
> ...mes profondes forêts
> J'y suivais un serpent qui venait de me mordre.   (ll. 35–37)

She dismisses the serpent, figment of her dream:

> Va! Je n'ai plus besoin...   (l. 50)

and embarks upon a soliloquy; she floats down her stream of consciousness, identifying herself now with her 'Harmonieuse Moi' or lucid conscious self, now with her 'Mystérieuse Moi' or the self of her senses, the physiological mechanism; Clotho hovers between the options provided by the two shadow beings in her psyche; the intense inner debate is resolved as dawn breaks after a night of anguish that had led her conscious self to contemplate escape from her other self by the latter's suicide:

> O n'aurait-il fallu, folle, que j'accomplisse...   (ll. 381–405)

Under the kiss of the rising sun, Clotho herself rises to calm acceptance of the inescapable union of her conscious and sensuous selves; without the body, consciousness cannot be:

> Alors, malgré moi-même, il le faut O Soleil...   (l. 508)

[83] cf. *J.P.*, II, 416, 417.   [84] I, 9.
[85] I, 2.   [86] Almost the very words of M. Teste.

La Jeune Parque may well be described as Valéry's quintessential 'sum', with a formal beauty that yields nothing to the substance.[87] Yet it may be thought that *Le Cimetière Marin* welds form and substance into an even tighter and more beautiful unity. 'Ce toit tranquille...' (l. 1) – the sea seen through the pines and glittering with diamonds in the noonday sun, the parched earth that covers the desiccated dead, the grating insects, the sails like distant doves pecking at corn: 'Ce toit tranquille où picoraient des focs' (l. 144), the heat, the silence accentuated by the murmuring sea – this clear-cut, vivid, Mediterranean vision, which stimulates a strong, sensuous response in the reader, is the poet's joy and reward after his meditation.

In the stillness which seems – familiar thought to Valéry – absorbed in self-contemplation:

> Midi là-haut,...
> En soi se pense...   (ll. 63–4)

the poet sees himself as the only changing, impure element:

> Je suis en toi le secret changement...   (ll. 65–8)

soon to join the multitude that peoples the cemetery:

> Tout va sous terre et rentre dans le jeu   (l. 80)
> Et vous, grande âme...   (l. 81)
> Chanterez-vous quand serez vaporeuse?   (l. 84)

The archaism, recalling the sixteenth century when classical influences were strong and Ronsard sang of the myrtle groves and his own shade taking his ease there:

> Je seray sous la terre et, fantosme sans os,
> Par les ombres myrteux je prendray mon repos...

the archaism reinforces the pagan materialist spirit of the poem, echoing that of *La Jeune Parque*; it accepts unperturbed the ultimate absorption of the individual being in the universal living impulse, 'passé dans les fleurs' (l. 73). The poet's curse is the worm of consciousness that feeds on his living spirit, but he rejects the momentary despair: 'Le vent se lève!... il faut tenter de vivre!' (l. 116).

Almost unknown, at any rate forgotten, Paul Valéry was revealed to the general public as a poet with *La Jeune Parque*; as poet his reputation was enhanced by the *Album* and the twenty-one poems, including *Le Cimetière Marin*, of *Charmes*, where familiar Valéryan themes reappear: consciousness and its modes,

---

[87] Some lyrical passages are particularly noteworthy: e.g. 'La renaissante année...' (ll. 222–42); 'Je n'implorerai plus...' (ll. 280–309); 'Salut! Divinités...' (ll. 348–69); 'Si je viens, en vêtements ravis...' (ll. 496–512).

its relationship with knowledge, the senses, poetic creation. The classical, Mediterranean spirit that informs Valéry's poetry, both earlier and later, has already been emphasized. It is also a very cerebral poetry. This applies both to the Mallarméan poems of the first group where the impact on the reader is so skilfully calculated and in a greater but different measure to those of the second where the difficulties lie deeper and move from the heart of the poems outward to the surface, the esoteric thought expressing itself in a rigorous metrical form. In both groups, as befits cerebral poetry, direct personal emotion is absent; the reader's responses are aesthetic and intellectual, not affective. Valéry once described *La Jeune Parque* as: 'copulation monstrueuse de mon système, de mes méthodes, de mes exigences musicales et de mes conventions classiques.'[88] In brief, a deliberate controlled 'exercise'.[89] No poet has given more thought to the nature of poetry, of his own poetry, of the poet, of himself watching himself, 'me voyant me voir', to quote Teste, in the creative act of writing poetry.[90]

As early as 1889 Valéry had expressed his idea of the modern poet, and he did not substantially vary from what he had written then: 'une conception toute nouvelle et moderne du poète. Ce n'est plus le délirant échevelé, celui qui écrit tout un poème dans une nuit de fièvre, c'est un froid savant, presque un algébriste, au service d'un rêveur affiné...'[91] Away with the old romantic conception of the poet as a medium writing under the dictation of the muse. Inspiration – 'le rêve' – provides the initial impulse; thereafter the 'froid savant' takes control, weighs, triturates, distils and produces the quintessence of 'pure poetry', whence all impure elements – emotion, didacticism, story-telling, description, etc. – have been removed.

From the Symbolists he was to borrow the idea of poetry as music and to this too he remained constant; later he was to emphasize the idea of design and structure in a poem as in architecture, and insist that poetic rhythms were as important as the rigorous measures of the dance, but in 1889 he had already created the image of the poet-scientist which was to arise again in the poet of *La Jeune Parque* and *Charmes*.

In the meantime the dramatic reorientation of 1892 becomes clear; his poems to date did not conform to his ideal of scientific precision;[92] the *Introduction, M. Teste*; the years of self-investiga-

---

[88] See V. Larbaud, op. cit.
[89] See dedication of *La Jeune Parque* to Gide.
[90] e.g. 'Poésie et pensée abstraite' in 'Variété; théorie poétique et esthétique'. *Oeuvres*, I (Pléiade).
[91] 'Sur la technique littéraire'; *Oeuvres*, I, notes, p. 1,786 (Pléiade).
[92] As a good example of this ideal, cf. *La Jeune Parque*, ll. 280–97, the welling up of tears. cf. 'Contact avec mes monstres...' see above, p. 201.

tion; the delight in mathematics and the exact sciences; the joy in architecture[93] – surely the harmonious materialisation of precisely calculated risks; in the dance[94] – precise balance and controlled movement; the dislike of history – chaos that contains everything, teaches nothing therefore and justifies anything;[95] all this forms a coherent intellectual structure; the triumphant return to poetry provides the pinnacle: 'un diamant fermant le diadème...' (*J.P.*, 1, 182) and the paradox of the poet with one small volume of poetry and forty volumes of prose is resolved.

But slowly from the poet and the official personage success had made him,[96] emerged the image in the last years of an intellectual sage and moralist, astringent, ascetic, which his innumerable essays abundantly justify. The image is noble, pure, characteristic of an age that places human endeavour between the poles of truth and error and attaches supreme importance to the investigation of the psyche, but it lacks warmth. In pursuit of pure intelligence and sensuous, sometimes very sensual, beauty, Valéry has forgotten the values of the heart. 'Je m'étais fait une île intérieure', he writes in the preface to *Monsieur Teste*; perhaps if as writer and poet he had remembered Donne's 'No man is an island', the final note of unfulfilment and despair[97] would not have sounded.

[93] Already in the *Introduction*, see chap. 3; later *Eupalinos*.
[94] *L'Ame et la Danse*.
[95] *Remarques Extérieures* (1927).
[96] French Academy (1925), later professor of poetics at the Collège de France, delegate at conferences, national and international. 'Le reste est vacarme', he writes amusingly in the autobiographical notes he gave V. Larbaud, and which stop at *La Jeune Parque*.
[97] *Ebauches de mon Faust*.

Chapter 10

POETS AND DRAMATISTS

THE cafés of Montparnasse and their habitués, the poets, writers and artists of the Parisian left bank in the decade before 1914, such is the background evoked by the name of Guillaume Apollinaire[1] (1880–1918). Journalist, short story writer, poet and minor playwright, he found a favourable intellectual climate amongst the members of the artistic 'avant-garde'; Matisse, van Dongen, Picasso, Bracque, Derain, Dufy, Vlaminck, Fauvists, Cubists, Futurists and 'Art-nègrists', all found a ready champion in the art reporter and critic Apollinaire had become by 1908. Even that naïve neo-primitive with the 'innocent eye', Henri Rousseau the 'customs man', enjoyed his friendship and support, without which the 'douanier' might not have attracted the attention he eventually received.

Such apparent prescience was not due so much to the discernment of the art critic with artistic training – he lacked it – as to a natural orientation towards the experimental and the imaginative, a characteristic discernible both in his prose and poetry. As a prose writer Apollinaire is unlikely to survive. The short stories of *L'Enchanteur pourrissant* with their medieval flavour have little merit except for the wood-cuts by Derain in the luxury edition (1908); the macabre and cruel stories of *L'Hérésiarque et Cie* (1910) are his best collection; *Le Poète Assassiné* (1916), a disjointed fantasy that can scarcely rank as a novel, owes something to Rabelais, much more to the sardonic humour of Apollinaire's friend Alfred Jarry, whose influence is also discernible in the two-act play, *Les Mamelles de Tirésias* (1917); *La Femme Assise* (posth. 1920), another ill-assorted collection of stories, adds nothing to Apollinaire's reputation. To this list may be added the short poems of *Le Bestiaire ou Cortège d'Orphée*, a collection of modernized medieval legends that were a good pretext for the wood-cuts of Raoul Dufy in a luxury edition (1911), and *Le Flâneur des deux Rives* (1918), where the charming day-to-day chronicler of Parisian life that Apollinaire could be reveals him at his best.

Only as the poet of *Alcools* (collected poems, 1898–1913) and

[1] Real name, G. de Kostrowitsky.

Calligrammes (collected poems, 1913–16) does Apollinaire achieve some stature. Many of the poems are inspired by his love of the moment,[2] as fleeting as time, flowing away like the Seine:

> Sous le pont Mirabeau coule la Seine
> Et nos amours ...   ('Le Pont Mirabeau', *Alcools*)

or again:

> Je passais au bord de la Seine
> Un livre ancien sous le bras
> Le fleuve est pareil à ma peine
> Il s'écoule et ne tarit pas ...   ('Marie', *Alcools*)

At moments of lyrical tenderness, Apollinaire often achieves a song-like quality reminiscent of Villon:

> Mon beau navire O ma mémoire
> Avons-nous assez navigué ...
>   ('La Chanson du Mal-Aimé')

He is at his best when he notes down a quick impression, usually visual, from a direct personal experience. The 'Rhénanes' and 'A la Santé'[3] sequences (*Alcools*) are noteworthy in this context, and his war experience as a gunner, later as an infantry officer,[4] inspired some of the best poems of *Calligrammes*, surely unique as war poems in that so often they convey not the horror or the suffering of war but its visual beauty, provided, for example, by star shells and Very lights:

> Feu d'artifice en acier
> Qu'il est charmant cet éclairage ...   ('Fête')

or again:

> Que c'est beau ces fusées qui illuminent la nuit
> Elles montent sur leur propre cime et se penchent pour regarder ...
>   ('Merveilles de la Guerre')

Or realistic details, unemotionally noted. The idea of danger and sudden death is recorded unsentimentally:

> Allons Adieu messieurs tâchez de revenir
> Mais nul ne sait ce qui peut advenir.
>   ('Le Vigneron Champenois')

[2] Anne Playden, whom he met in Germany (1901–2) and wished to marry; Marie Laurencin ('Lou'), the painter, Madeleine Pagès, whom he was to marry but he broke off the engagement (1916); Jacqueline Kolb 'La Jolie Rousse', whom he married a few months before he died, a victim of 'Spanish flu'.

[3] He spent a week in prison there (1911), having been arrested on the suspicion, in due course officially recognized as groundless, of being implicated in thefts from the Louvre Museum.

[4] He enlisted in December 1914 for the duration; was dangerously wounded in the right temple in March 1916.

and on the rare occasions when a note of pity sounds, the poet's eye is never turned inwardly in self-pity, but on others – an African gunner ('Les Soupirs du Servant de Dakar') or four young soldiers who in spite of their youth speak of past memories rather than future hopes:

> Tous quatre de la classe seize
> Parlaient d'antan non d'avenir
> Ainsi se prolongeait l'ascèse
> Qui les exerçait à mourir   ('Exercice')

This unsentimental astringency is perhaps Apollinaire's most moving quality as a war poet, yet it is neither as love nor war poet that he achieves particular importance; extrovert that he was, he does not communicate to us any deep spiritual experience. His significance is rather as an experimental poet, uneven perhaps on that account. His refusal to use punctuation and the poems arranged to represent the objects they are about – *Calligrammes*, as he called them – add nothing to his originality; what is important are his attempts, bold and not always successful, to apply new techniques to his poetry; 'Zone' (*Alcools*) for example, with its successive pictures drawn from his childhood onward, suggests a cinema technique; the poet seems to be watching the screen of his own memory. Other poems, with their lack of organization round a given theme, their sense of being a random collection of visual data, suggest the Cubist dislocation of objects and their reconstruction according to an intellectual conception of 'simultaneousness', aiming to give the viewer a richer experience of reality than representational art, or again the *collage* technique of an arbitrary assemblage of objects into significant patterns.

More important than such poems is Apollinaire's evident conviction that he and his contemporaries stood at a turning point:

> Nous partimes alors pèlerins de la perdition
> A travers les rues, à travers les contrées, à travers la raison...
>   ('Poème lu au mariage d'André Salmon', *Alcools*)

or again:

> Voici le temps de la magie
> ... attendez-vous
> A des milliards de prodiges...
>   ('Les Collines', *Alcools*)

His vision is prophetic and foreshadows Surrealism:

> Profondeurs de la conscience
> On vous explorera demain
> Et qui sait, quels êtres vivants
> Seront tirés de ces abîmes...   (*Ibid.*)

The last two poems of *Calligrammes*, 'La Victoire' and 'La Jolie Rousse', are something of an artistic Testament:

La Victoire avant tout sera
De bien voir au loin . . .
Nous voulons nous donner de vastes et d'étranges domaines
Où le mystère en fleurs s'offre à qui veut le cueillir
Il y a là des feux nouveaux des couleurs jamais vues . . .

The emphasis is on colour. The Symbolists had looked towards music. Apollinaire and the Surrealists after him looked towards painting.

Surrealism may justifiably rank as an important sign-post of the post-war years. Literature and painting both reflect its influence, both figure in the long ancestry that the Surrealists, like other literary schools before them, claimed as theirs – the haunted world of Hieronymus Bosch (c. 1450–1516), the bizarreries of Arcimboldi (1527–93), the Romantic 'horror' of Fuseli (1741–1825), the Satanism of Goya (1746–1828), the dream paintings of Odilon Redon (1840–1916); Nerval's twilight land between sanity and madness, Lautréamont's nightmare phantoms of cruelty, Rimbaud's bold experiments in poetic communication.

Artists and writers whose inspiration often came from mystery and horror, magic and dreams, beyond the boundaries of normal experience, may indeed have affinities with Surrealism, but to the Surrealists goes the credit of a conscious shift of emphasis in what literature and painting should be investigating and expressing. Futurism, Cubism and Dadaïsm had already shaken traditional structures to their foundations. Futurism (1909–c. 1915), launched by an Italian writer, Marinetti, was not in the first instance an art but an intellectual, indeed a moral, movement which must be seen in the context of the languid atmosphere of the pre-war years – Naturalism and Symbolism in decay, the society novels of Bourget and Marcel Prévost, the ironic scepticism and mild sensuality of Anatole France, all very popular in a wealthy society eager in its idleness for moral or psychological problems intermingled with 'bon ton' salaciousness, all suitable for discussion over the tea cups or the dinner table but not disturbing to comfortable habits of mind and life.

Marinetti's article in *Le Figaro* (20 February 1909) recalls Stendhal's 'coup de pistolet dans un concert'. He announced 'a new beauty . . .'; 'a roaring motor-car, which runs like a machine-gun', said he, 'is more beautiful than the "winged Victory of Samothrace" . . . we wish to glorify war . . .'[5] – in short the dynamism of the bull in a china shop, and it was the dynamism, the idea of movement, that appealed to the painters. The *Manifesto of Futurist Painting* (1910) proclaims: 'that universal dynamism must be

[5] See *Dictionary of Art and Artists*, by P. and L. Murray (Penguin, 1959).

rendered as dynamic sensation; that movement and light destroy the substance of objects . . .'.[6]

We need not concern ourselves here with the artistic worth of the paintings included in the Futurist Exhibition of 1912, but only with the disruptive impact of Futurism on representational art and with its contribution to the problem of communication between artist and viewer.

Traditional conceptions of representational art received an almost simultaneous blow from Cubism (1906–14), which derives from Cézanne and condemns the idea of representation as traditionally conceived, unsatisfactory first in its very limited recording of the object chosen – one moment in time, one angle of vision – and secondly in its effort to give a third dimension. Painting should reject the lure of perspective, and instead exploit the potentialities of the two-dimensional surface it works on; create patterns satisfying to the eye in colour and form, satisfying to the intellect as a synthesis or total account of the 'structure of any given object and its position in space'.[7]

Cubism is evidently an intellectual form of art; to a greater extent than Futurism, it revolutionizes the idea of representation and develops a picture's potential of communication to the viewer.

Dadaïsm (c. 1915–22) was little more at first than an anarchic attitude, born of the war, in its senselessness and horror, a measure of the wickedness of the liberal bourgeois society that had launched it. Good Dadaïsts must show their contempt for that order of society by rejecting its authority in their domain – art; all the accepted canons of beauty must be swept away, its products humiliated.[8] The only positive, perhaps accidental, result to emerge from this nihilistic aim to outrage and scandalize was the potential of stimulating suggestion to be derived from the association of random objects.

The three-pronged attack delivered by the movements just considered on traditional ideas in art and literature created a climate of intellectual ferment and dissatisfaction for Surrealism to flourish in. The word had been coined by Apollinaire in 1917 to describe the inconsequential Ubuesque humour of his play *Les Mamelles de Tirésias*. André Breton (1896–1966) took up the word again as a mark of friendship for the poet who as art critic had been a champion of Futurism and Cubism, and gathered the remnants of the Dadaïsts round the new standard.[9]

[6] *Ibid.*   [7] *Ibid.*
[8] *Ibid.*; e.g. a reproduction of the Mona Lisa decorated with a moustache and the caption LHOOQ (=Elle a chaud au cul).
[9] 'En homage à Guillaume Apollinaire, qui venait de mourir . . . nous désignâmes sous le nom de Surréalisme le nouveau mode d'expression pure' (*Manifeste du Surréalisme*).

Dominating the scene now was the towering figure of Freud who placed the origin of our attitudes and actions deep in the sub-conscious – 'Car nous sommes, comme le dit Freud, des masses d'inconscient légèrement élucidées à la surface par la lumière du soleil . . .'.[10] The new group, with the example of Proust before them, and the Freudian compass in hand, would plunge into the subliminal world of the psyche; induced hallucinatory states, auto-matic writing were the key for unlocking the hidden mechanisms; Freudian psychology was seen not only as the means whereby man could acquire complete knowledge of his ego and thereby full con-trol of himself – 'L'homme propose et dispose. Il ne tient qu'à lui de s'appartenir tout entier'[11] – but as a new source of inspiration and beauty in literature and painting: 'Il s'agissait de remonter aux sources de l'imagination poétique et ... de s'y tenir.',[12] to the sources, that is, in the sub-conscious, where, as across a screen, im-pressions from the exterior world, blind compulsions and obscure desires rooted in sexual instincts, all acting and reacting upon each other, flash past in an endless, rationally unrelated, chain. Here at last was the inner truth about the psyche; by observing it atten-tively, by recording it faithfully without reference to artificially arranged patterns, painting and literature could hope to give an account of the inner chaos, as dynamic as Futurism could want, as total as Cubism aimed to provide of any object, as unpredictable and rationally unrelated as any Dadaïst could hope for, a higher reality, a synthesis between the conscious logical-pattern-making mind and the mind-object, similar to that of a dream in which the dreamer is at once actor in an irrational chain of events and spec-tator of them.

Such in essence are the claims André Breton, the theorist and acknowledged leader of the group, made in his *Manifeste du Surréalisme* (1924), and since did not cease to defend, by precept and example, in prose and poetry.

Stimulating though the Surrealist ideas are, the difficulty of building on them a work which shall both be a true reflection of man's chaotic inner dream-states and have enough coherence to make communication with the reader possible, as art must, is shown by the rarity of creative Surrealist prose works.

Breton's *Poisson Soluble* (1924) consists of a series of chapters unrelated to each other, each full of disconnected thoughts and images – the whole could be the result of automatic writing and perhaps the title is intended to suggest the idea of the poet afloat, as it were, in his own mind, like a fish in water, but at the same time absorbed in the visions he finds there. Very Surrealist, no

---

[10] Pierre-Jean Jouve, *Sueur de Sang*, Avant-propos (1933).
[11] A. Breton, *Manifeste du Surréalisme*.   [12] *Ibid*.

doubt, but significant art? More doubtful. Louis Aragon's *Le Paysan de Paris* (1926) has only a tenuous link with Surrealism and belongs more to the prevailing literary impressionism made popular by the novels of Morand,[13] with a generous admixture of fantasy, in the manner of Cocteau.

By 1928 the first wave of Surrealist enthusiasms had almost spent itself, but in that year Breton published what remains the only readable Surrealist work of fiction, *Nadja*, the study of a young woman who floats through the story as in a dream, as in a dream fits her day-to-day experience into a pattern of subjective references, inaccessible to others, and, in consequence, appears to them incoherent; 'Elle est, je le veux bien, un désenchaînement perpétuel', comments the narrator.

Inaccessibility leads to a breakdown in communication with others, to isolation in a word, which, interpreted as an insecure hold on life, leads Nadja to a mental home – unjustifiably, claims the narrator, invoking the undefined frontiers of sanity and the view that mental homes create what they aim to cure: 'Il ne faut jamais avoir pénétré dans un asile pour ne pas savoir qu'on y fait les fous, tout comme dans les maisons de correction on fait les bandits ... Tous les internements sont arbitraires.'

Nadja could be regarded as no more than a clinical study in fictional form of mental twilight. In the absence of any other surviving Surrealist work of fiction, one is tempted to wonder what other subjects in prose fiction the principles of the *Manifeste* could lead to. But *Nadja's* survival as something more than a literary curio is partly due to the pathos that attaches to the fragile phantom and the love-story that might have been, partly to the value Breton finds for Surrealism in her mental processes; Surrealist magic springs from the capacity to see unsuspected significance in ordinary things, relationships that stimulate meditation – 'Il se peut que la vie demande à être déchiffrée comme un cryptogramme' – and lead it to a higher reality.

This esotericism gave a powerful stimulus to poetry.[14] A galaxy of poets clusters round André Breton, himself poet as well as doctrinaire: P. Reverdy (b. 1889); Philippe Soupault (b. 1897), Breton's collaborator in automatic writing experiments, and co-author with him of *Les Champs magnétiques* (1920); the vitriolic A. Artaud (1896–1948) who like Nadja ended in a mental home; P. Eluard (1895–1952), who expressed vividly the nightmare of the Occupation in *Couvre-Feu* (1943); L. Aragon (b. 1897)–

---

[13] See below, chap. 11.
[14] Also to painting and sculpture, e.g. Arp, Chirico, Ernst, Dali, Miro, Picabia, Giacometti.

Surrealist poet in the 'twenties, novelist in the 'thirties and Communist Party member, Resistance poet during the war, abundant and powerful novelist thereafter; T. Tzara (b. 1896), the active Dadaïst; Henri Michaux (b. 1899), the macabre humorist of the straight face, the brilliant juggler with words, painter withal, having affinities with Paul Klee; B. Péret (b. 1899); R. Char (b. 1907); R. Desnos (1900–45), victim of the Gestapo; R. Vitrac (1901–52).

As a school of non-conformity and revolt – and on that account sympathetic in the 'thirties to Communism – Surrealism made a collective impact that remains active.

The non-rational, the obscure forces in man's psyche, which surface from time to time as though by chance in French literature, quickly to be submerged by the Cartesian authority of reason and order, achieve a right of citizenship, are indeed proclaimed as the essence of poetry and the graphic arts. Poetry was no longer to be a vehicle of lyrical emotion, or confession, above all never to be descriptive, never mere versified rhetoric; it was to be an instrument of investigation into the sub-conscious source and controller of our conscious lives. To it could be applied the lines Eluard addressed to Picasso:

> Dur Contempteur avance en renonçant
> Le plaisir naît au sein de ton refus
> L'art pourrait être une grimace
> Tu le réduis à n'être qu'une porte
> Ouverte par laquelle entre la vie.
>
> ('Le Travail du Peintre')

Max Jacob (1876–1944), a Jew from Quimper, who had made Paris his home, became a Christian as a result of a mystical experience and a vision of Christ (1909). The Catholic Church prudently made him wait five years before accepting him. Thereafter he lived in the shadow of the old Benedictine Abbey Church of St Benoît-sur-Loire until the Gestapo arrested him and sent him to die in the concentration camp of Drancy.

In the bohemian circles of Montmartre and Montparnasse he had become the friend of Apollinaire and Salmon, of Picasso and the Cubists; with his mixture of burlesque, deliberate naïveté and lyrical emotion, he gives the impression of an amiable, sometimes skilful, pantaloon faintly reminiscent of *Ubu*. He extended, if in a minor way, the range of contemporary poetry and may be counted as one of the links in the chain leading from Jarry to the Surrealists, though in a letter to his friend Cocteau he denies all knowledge of modern poetry: 'la poésie moderne que j'ignore, bien loin (comme on prétend) d'en être l'inventeur.'[15]

[15] *Lettres à Cocteau.*

Jacob's conversion to Christianity gave an additional dimension to his poetry without altering the formal mixture he affected:

> C'est pas boulonné comme un pont en fer, les églises.
> C'est un objet en améthyste
> Dont l'entrepreneur en bâtisse
> Est le fils de Dieu.   ('Renaissance de l'Esprit religieux')

The nimble humorist is at his best in *Le Cornet à dés* (1917), a collection of prose poems, and a further good example of his vein is provided by his Saint Matorel,[16] that saintly figure of fun, who might seem to owe something to Anatole France's M. Jérôme Coignard.

Nor did Jacob's conversion immediately alter his way of life: 'Flegmatique et sensuel, je l'étais, je le reste'. To the doubts this attitude aroused on the sincerity of his faith he replied in his *Défence de Tartufe – Extases, visions, prières, poèmes et méditations d'un juif converti* (1919), where he claims that if contrast there be between his way of life and his faith, it is no different from that of other Christians, and does not affect his sincerity. His nature is akin to Verlaine's but more robustly persistent in the chosen path, and is there not something reminiscent of the poet of *Sagesse* in lines such as these:

> J'ai peur que tu ne t'offenses
> Lorsque je mets en balance
> Dans mon coeur et dans mon oeuvre
> Ton amour dont je me prive
> Et l'autre amour dont je meurs.[17]

Of his stories – *Cinématoma* (1920), *Le Roi de Béotie* (1921), *Filibuth ou la Montre en or* (1922), *Le Terrain Bouchaballe* (1923) – the last named is particularly characteristic of Jacob's verve as a story-teller, exploiting the full potential of burlesque in the internecine rivalries produced at the town of Guichen (his native Quimper) over the use to be made of a garden bequeathed by a worthy and wealthy citizen to the municipality. The tale is worthy of the best seventeenth-century heroi-comical tradition in the vein of Sorel, Scarron and Furetière.

Jean Cocteau (1889–1963) has the brilliance of a firework display, its multi-coloured arabesques bursting into activity now here, now there.

As early as 1908 he had a precocious reputation in Paris high society as a youthful poet; Cubism, Diaghilev's Russian ballet, the music of Stravinsky – all that was new and adventurous attracted

---

[16] *Saint Matorel* (1911), *Les Oeuvres burlesques et mystiques de Frère Matorel* (1912), *Le Siège de Jérusalem, grande tentation céleste de Saint Matorel* (1914), *Matorel en Province* (1920).
[17] See Pierre Andreu, *Max Jacob*, Wesmael-Charlier (1962).

him. *Le Potomak* (1913) is an early example of inconsequential fantasy, much assisted by drawings reminiscent of Edward Lear.

The war was a different kind of adventure. Though rejected as unfit for military service, Cocteau managed to get to the front in a Red Cross unit. His experiences were to inspire the poems of *Discours du Grand Sommeil* (1916, published 1925) in memory of his friends the Fusiliers-Marins, defenders of Dixmude and Nieuport, who had adopted him as one of themselves, and *Thomas L'imposteur* (1922) which, despite its deliberate air of unreal adventure tale, conveys against the lunar desolation of trenches and no-man's land much of the grim realities the author had been involved in; it deserves to rank as an authentic piece of war literature.

Less significant is *Le Grand Ecart* (1922), another tale, this time on the theme of adolescent 'sentimental education', where fact is heavily diluted with fancy; but together the two tales, almost at the outset of Cocteau's career, have something symbolic; Thomas, the gallant mock-soldier, killed at the front, and Jacques Forestier, the maturing adolescent, suggest their author leaving his youth behind him and ready to ride, as indeed he did, the euphoric wave of creative talent, feverish activity and revolutionary experiment that mark the immediate post-war years.

Poetry, ballet, novel, drama, films, criticism, journalism, interior decoration – to all these Cocteau brought his original fantasy, as light and unpredictable as Ariel, but with some darker colours in the weave, derived from a brief excursion into drugs, and from Ancient Greek themes, which attracted a number of authors between the wars.

Nor should we omit to mention his return to the Catholic fold under the influence of Jacques Maritain (*Lettre à Jacques Maritain*, 1926), though this did not affect his creative work.

The poems of *Le Cap de Bonne-Espérance* (1919), partly derived from his experience of flying with his friend Roland Garros, a pioneer of aerobatics, of *Vocabulaire* (1921) – a gesture towards 'Dada', of *Plain-Chant* (1923), of *Opéra* (1927), are not particularly arresting; genuine experience (some of it from opium[18]) is intermingled with verbal acrobatics that evidently fascinated him.[19] On his return from the front, Cocteau – with the Russian ballet in mind – had designed a ballet, *Parade* (1917), with music by that brilliant musical humorist, Erik Satie, and décor by Picasso; considered at the time as an offence to all accepted canons, it has none the less maintained itself in the repertoire. Cocteau's liking for this type of art is further shown by his mime, *Le Boeuf sur le Toit* (1920),[20] with music by Darius Milhaud and décor by Raoul

---

[18] e.g. 'Prairie Légère' (*Opéra*).   [19] e.g. 'L'Hotel' (*Opéra*).
[20] It was to give its name to a Parisian restaurant.

Dufy, and another ballet performed by the Swedish troupe, *Les Mariés de la Tour Eiffel*.

But he was now to turn from these brilliant clownings, in search of other conquests. The orientation towards antiquity already appears in *Musée Secret*, last section of *Opéra*; the ancients were to offer him a rich field of experiment which produced some of his most solid achievements: *Antigone* (1926), a one-act synthesis of Sophocles's tragedy, an adaptation of *Oedipus Rex* (1926, performed 1936), *Orphée* (1926), a play inspired by the ancient legend but in a characteristically Cocteau idiom that exploits anachronisms between the present and the past as a source of dramatic effect; it had been done before, for its comic value[21] and was to be used again.[22] Most successful of Cocteau's dramatic excursions into antiquity was *La Machine Infernale* (1932), of which his *Oedipe* had been a first sketch.

In the meantime he had written a one-act realistic play, *La Voix humaine* (1929), for only two characters, a woman and her telephone, which draws its pathos from a classic situation – the mistress, cast aside. Ancient Greek themes are successfully blended with modern actions in *Les Enfants Terribles* (1929), a novel, and *Les Parents Terribles* (1938), a play. With their brilliant economy of means, their complex thematic patterns, incestuous and Freudian, the suggestion of drug addiction, the excellent psychological motivation, these works may well rank as Cocteau's masterpieces, at once Greek, Racinian and modern. The characters in each seem to be executing a ritual dance of death, at once fascinating by its precision and compelling by its mounting tension, and yet, despite the dramatic power of both works, the characters seem too far out on the fringe of life to have much human substance. Cocteau seems to delight in putting distance between his work and life; poetic fantasy sometimes, preciousness, verbal and intellectual gymnastics at others, call it what you will, it deprives him of the compelling relevance his originality and inventiveness might otherwise have entitled him to.

Jules Supervielle (b. 1884) is a native of Montevideo, like Laforgue and Lautréamont. Like the latter he is a visionary, but the vision, if it dwells on the mysteries of love and human behaviour, is of light, not of darkness. Both in his prose stories, e.g., *L'Enfant de la Haute Mer* (1931), *L'Arche de Noé* (1938), or in his poetry, e.g. *Poèmes de l'humour triste* (1919), *Débarcadères* (1922), *L'Homme de la Pampa* (1923), *Gravitations* (1925), *Le Forçat Innocent* (1930), *Les Amis Inconnus* (1934), a fairy-like fantasy

---

[21] e.g. *Orphée aux Enfers* (1858), *La Belle Hélène* (1864).
[22] Gide, Giraudoux, Sartre, Anouilh.

dwells in him and draws him to quiet confidence and hope, though in company with other poets the misfortunes of France inspire his *Poèmes de la France malheureuse* (1941).

A fastidious poet both in quantity and by the quality of his taste and humour, Léon-Paul Fargue (1878–1947) reaches back to Mallarmé, in whose circle he had moved as a young man, and the Symbolists, forward to the Surrealists. His poetic contribution and that of his two greatest contemporaries is admirably characterized by Saint-John Perse in a preface to a recent two-volume edition of Fargue's main works:[23] 'Entre la masse basaltique d'un Claudel et les pures cristallisations d'un Valéry il y eut un soir, et à la ville, en lieu fiévreux et féerique, ce déroulement soudain, comme d'une crosse de fougère ivre, ce dépliement soudain, comme d'une aile de névroptère séchant au feu des lampes son fin lacis de gaze verte.'

Fargue had come to maturity in the post-Symbolist years when the claims of the non-rational, the sub-conscious, were beginning to be heard. *Suite Familière*, that brilliant series of random thoughts about writers and literature, flavoured with the 'do's and don'ts' of style and of the poet's craft, shows Fargue almost in the vanguard of modernism: the power of words to go deep and tap hidden springs ('les mots sont artésiens... Quand tu lis un livre pèse les mots, regarde les objets qu'ils veulent représenter, joue au furet derrière l'auteur...'), the contrast between the meagreness of a clear style so-called, and the wealth underlying a style that is difficult ('Pauvre phrase claire! Ça coule, ça se démaille, ça file comme du cousu machine. Vous ne paîrez jamais assez le cousu main'), the suspicion of pure intelligence in poetry ('Je n'aime pas l'intelligence pure, pepsine qui se digère elle-même').

Suite Familière is indeed a treatise on poetics in miniature, reflecting modern attitudes but astringent, tempered by discernment.

Fargue deserves to be remembered as more than a door-keeper at the temple of modern poetry. He has his own originality, as the poet of Paris in 'la Belle Époque' (*Le Piéton de Paris*), mingled often with a note of discreet personal melancholy:

> Un long bras timbré d'or glisse du haut des arbres
> Et commence à descendre et tinte dans les branches.
> D'autres verront cela quand je ne serai plus;
> La lumière oubliera ceux qui l'ont tant aimée....[24]

Pierre-Jean Jouve (b. 1887) had begun in the Parnassian tradition of rigorous form and rich rhyme. Later, as he recalls in *En*

[23] *Poésies* (containing: 'Tancrède', 1894; 'Ludion', 1886–1933; 'Pour la Musique', the prose poems and *Suite Familière*) and *Le Piéton de Paris*. Gallimard, 1963.
[24] *Sous la Lampe*, Postface (1930).

miroir, journal sans date (1954), a record of his development as a
poet, Baudelaire, Rimbaud *(Illuminations)*, Mallarmé *(Vers et
Prose)*, Gourmont *(Livres des Masques)* showed him new poetic
possibilities: 'un voile se déchira'.[25] The Unanimist fervours attracted him momentarily but he subsequently rejected the influence
of the Abbaye group: 'l'influence fut néfaste...me détourna de
ma recherche, à la fois de mon réel et de mon possible.'[26] Not
until after the First World War, which inspired his *Danse des
Morts* (1917) and *Tragiques* (1923), did he feel, in the artistic
turmoil of the post-war years in Paris,[27] that he was beginning to
see where his poetic independence and purpose lay: 'je fus orienté
vers deux objectifs fixés:...obtenir une langue de poésie qui se
justifiât entièrement comme chant – pas un des vers que j'avais
écrits ne répondait à cette exigence – et trouver dans l'acte poétique
une perspective religieuse – seule réponse au néant du temps.'[28]
Prière (1924), *La Symphonie à Dieu* (1930), *Les Noces* (1931) mark
the stages of Jouve's spiritual crisis and conversion. These years
were also those of Freudian impact which, in company with the
Surrealists, he felt strongly.[29]

Of Valéryan complexity, and emphasizing the poetic value of
symbols – 'Bien des pièces ne sont que des chaînes de symboles',[30]
Jouve's poetry (e.g. *Sueur de Sang*, 1935; *Kyrie*, 1938; *Diadème*,
1949; *Ode*, 1950; *Langue*, 1952; *Ténèbre*, 1965) expresses the pitiless struggle in all human experience between man's spiritual self,
his search for God, and his sexual compulsions, emerging from his
sub-conscious. The inescapable contradiction provides a permanent
source of despair; yet despair has its value as a means of achieving
a lucid view of the human situation; poetry as a revelation of
beauty is a way to spirituality.

Gloire (1942) and *La Vierge de Paris* (1946) are strongly marked
by the tragedy of France in defeat.

Like Jouve, Saint-John Perse[31] (b. 1887) is a poet whose experience stretches across two world wars; unlike Jouve, he was unaffected by Freud or the Surrealists; he does not accept the formlessness Surrealists tended to justify as the sign of genuine investigation into the inner chaos: 'céder à l'inflexion musicale, sans
répudier jamais le grammairien secret que porte en lui tout vrai
poète articulé.[32]

No more than Valéry does he admit of compromise with the
facile in any form, but whereas Valéry remained faithful to the
traditional alexandrine, Saint-John Perse, like others of his genera-

[25] *En miroir*, p. 21.   [26] Op. cit., p. 26.   [27] Op. cit., p. 29.
[28] Op. cit., p. 29.   [29] *Sueur de Sang*, preface.   [30] *En Miroir*, p. 132.
[31] Alexis Léger.   [32] Article on L-P. Fargue, *N.R.F.*, Nos. 128, 129.

tion, notably Valéry Larbaud in the footsteps of Walt Whitman, breaks away from traditional prosody, and expresses himself in the rhythmical strophes, compressed, complex, gorgeously apparelled in a wealth of words.

Un-Freudian that he is, his inspiration is not drawn from the inner depths but from 'the Isles',[33] where, like some young prince from afar, he spent his childhood (cf. 'Pour Fêter une Enfance', 1910, in *Eloges*, 1911), from the sunlight and the wind, the savour of the earth and its infinite spaces (cf. *Anabase*, 1924; *Vents*, 1946), from dreams of power and empire that make of Anabase himself, the unseen narrator, Saint-John Perse's *alter ego*, and an epic character, a modern Alexander or Genghis Khan, fired by some grand and undefined design,[34] from political relations and the interplay of forces on the chess-board of international affairs (cf. *Vents*), statecraft in a word, the core of Alexis Léger's experience as a man of government.

Saint-John Perse looks neither inward nor upward, but outward; man's inner chaos, his relationship with God do not interest him; God is absent, but the gods are there – and what are they, if not the personified forces of nature, the glories of this world in which as man and poet Saint-John Perse feels involved?

Nor must we omit Patrice de la Tour du Pin (b. 1911). Already before the war, his published work was considerable – *Les Enfants de Septembre* (1932), *La Quête de Joie* (1933), *D'un Aventurier* (1934), *L'Enfer* (1935), *Le Lucernaire* (1936), *Le Don de la Passion* (1937), *Psaumes* (1938), all of which have since the war been built into his *Une Somme de Poésie* (1946), a poetic construction on a great scale, where the poet aims to realize the ideals he had expressed in his essay, *La Vie recluse en Poésie* (1938). Poetry is no mere literary exercise, nor, especially, a flight from this world ('le mot d'évasion ne nous plaisait guère...'), it must be born of man's total experience ('notre base n'est pas la poésie, notre base est l'homme; nous ne cherchons pas à connaître la poésie, mais l'homme...'; an idea echoed in *Psaumes*, xxi, 8: 'La poésie n'est pas notre rêve – ou d'une incantation magique – elle est de notre vie active et du travail de nos mains'). Thus *Une Somme* is an effort to bear witness to the poet's experience of both the exterior world with its joys and of the inner world of the spirit, its mystical leanings and religious aspirations.

The actor-manager is a prominent figure in the theatre world between the wars. His importance goes back to the days of Antoine

---

[33] b. in Guadeloupe.
[34] See E. Clancier, *De Rimbaud au Surréalisme* (1953), p. 351.

and the 'Théâtre libre'. Antoine's simple enthusiasm for the theatre had been the faith that moves mountains; just as some sixty years earlier that 'happy band of brothers', described by Théophile Gautier,[35] had launched the assault on the citadel of classicism at the Comédie Française, so Antoine, pushing his go-cart, had given the signal for the overthrow of the Dumas *fils*-Augier empire and its critic-in-ordinary, Francisque Sarcey.

But important as Antoine was as a liberating force, his own vision of the theatre was at one with that of the Naturalist dramatists; the 'slice of life' formula reduced to a minimum the artistic contribution to a play by the producer. Antoine's impact was limited to bringing the theatre and the acting style more into relation with everyday life. He could also, once established as theatre-manager, look for inspiration beyond the frontiers, but Antoine's sympathies were limited to writers who reflected his own ideas – Ibsen, Hauptmann – and, hampered as he was by finance, could go little faster than the public, conservative as always, would let him.

Symbolism had given wider scope; plays were no longer a slavish representation of physical reality in the raw, the aim was to communicate a sense of foreboding, fear, joy, in short to suggest atmosphere and a reality underlying the surface of things; the producer could come into his own with his knowledge of theatrical techniques, his imaginative use of lighting and décor.

Lugné-Poë (1869–1940) at the 'Théâtre de l'Oeuvre' is a case in point. Production becomes an art in its own right. But Symbolism, which had never made a great impact on the stage, had tended to produce there a climate of mystification, with the producer as chief magician. In contrast Jacques Copeau (1879–1949), one of the leading spirits of the *Nouvelle Revue Française* at its foundation, strove for a root and branch reform in acting, production and the character of the plays performed.

He had given the signal for a new departure by his production in 1911 of a dramatic version of *The Brothers Karamazov*; the strong impetus came when he established himself as manager-producer-actor at the 'Vieux Colombier' (1913–24), with a troupe of actors, as humbly dedicated as he to the art of drama. As leader of his troupe, Copeau demanded, with naturalness in acting, equality in anonymity. Away with the 'star', so pronounced a feature of the day – 'the immortal' Sarah, Mesdames Bartet and Réjane, Mounet-Sully, the Coquelin brothers; whatever part the individual actor may take, the production is a collective effort; the credit, if any, is the company's. Elaborate stage settings as a realistic background to a Naturalist play, or as a *demi-mondaine*'s

[35] *Histoire du Romantisme.*

boudoir in some social comedy, or the mysterious halls of a Symbolist dream castle, all were alike swept away; instead, severe simplicity – curtains, lighting effects, the barest indication for the audience to conjure up the scene with. Copeau, in short, was returning both by taste and financial necessity to a simple classical conception, with playwright, actors, producer – and spectators – contributing to the dramatic synthesis.

Like all innovators, Copeau had mainly to contend with the reigning dramatists and their allied critics entrenched behind conservative public opinion. In retrospect the French theatre at the turn of the century appears remote. Its centre of gravity was not with the experimenters but on the boulevards. In the comfortable heyday of the Third Republic, the boulevard theatre managers could afford to neglect all influences from outside, and cater for the tastes of a wealthy clientèle content like Narcissus to contemplate the image, its own, of a society for whom love intrigue, grave or gay, was the great pastime, thrilling with Bernstein, salacious, erotic and sentimental with Lavedan, Donnay and their compères, uproarious and naughty with Feydau; for good measure an occasional moral conundrum from Hervieu or Bataille and the mention of an unmentionable disease from Brieux; the drama was a polite convention: the 'pursuit of love' in a 'closed shop'.

In face of this in-bred, if well-bred, convention Copeau began a revolution in public taste which the war completed. After the war, although the 'Vieux Colombier' soon closed its doors, Copeau's influence remained vigorous thanks to the younger generation of producers, the Cartel des quatre, Georges Pitoëff (1884–1939), Gaston Baty (1892–1952), Charles Dullin (1885–1949), and Louis Jouvet (1887–1951), the last two trained by Copeau. Since then others have taken their place – J. L. Barrault (b. 1910) notably. Nor has Copeau's influence remained confined to the studio type of theatre. The new spirit touched the state theatres and gave great impetus to the popular theatre movement which goes back to Romain Rolland and Gémier (1865–1933), was revived after the First World War by Henri Ghéon (1875–1944) with his Compagnons de Notre-Dame and productions of medieval miracle plays; it achieved its high point of success after the Second World War with Jean Vilar (b. 1912), sometime director of the Théâtre National Populaire. In Copeau's footsteps, the new generation of actor-managers expanded the time and space horizons of the French theatre public in a manner impossible a few years earlier. The Russians, the Scandinavians, the Spaniards, the Irish, the Ancient Greeks, the Elizabethans, Shaw, Pirandello, invaded the Parisian stage as never before.

In the French dramatic repertory only the classics firmly held

their ground – Corneille, Molière, Racine, Marivaux. The nineteenth century's contribution was largely swept away. Of the Romantics, only some of Musset remained; Hugo was to get a new
lease of life after the Second World War thanks to Jean Vilar at
the T.N.P. Augier had been and remains a total loss; only an occasional revival of *La Dame aux Camélias* saves Dumas *fils* from
bankruptcy; of the Naturalists, only Becque's *La Parisienne*, the
comedies of Courteline and the realistic cameos of Renard (e.g.
Poil de Carotte, Plaisir de rompre, La Bigote) can hope to survive;
of the post-Naturalist period, nearest in time but perhaps remotest
in spirit, Georges Feydeau has enjoyed a revival for 'period'
charm; the same reason might favour the wit of Flers and Caillavet; although in that period, Jarry, grotesque and brutal, has
acquired relevance and is seen to appeal to deeper, human levels,
limited though they may be, than his contemporaries did. Bernstein
(1877–1953) and Sacha Guitry (1885–1957), alone of the surviving
pre-war playwrights, were still writing for the stage, the former
skilfully trimming his sails to the fresh winds (e.g. *Félix le Mes-
sager*, 1927), the latter on the same rose path that had led to his
pre-war successes (e.g. *Le Veilleur de Nuit*, 1911; *La Prise de
Berg-op-Zom*, 1913), and that led to an enchanted theatrical world,
shut away from contemporary relevance (e.g. *Faisons un rêve*,
1916; *La Pèlerine Ecossaise*, 1922), or to a series of musical plays
based on the lives of famous men, e.g. *La Fontaine* (1916), *Pasteur*
(1919), *Mozart* (1925).

Author, manager, producer, actor, in Sacha Guitry all the
strands were united; the temptation was irresistible to build plays
around himself or as pretexts for the lovely singing voice of Yvonne
Printemps. Later the films provided a valuable new medium for
this supreme entertainer, in a class apart, and his inexhaustible inventiveness (e.g. *Le Roman d'un tricheur*, 1935; *Les Perles de la
Couronne*, 1938).

The new generation of French dramatists falls broadly into
three categories: those who are content to build new plays, comic
or serious, within old forms and humanist attitudes; those who seek
a renewal of dramatic forms; and those who look for new interpretations of human character or of the human situation.

Light comedy, comedy of manners, comedy of character flourish
as ever, the first in the plays of, for example, Jacques Duval (b.
1894); his most successful play, *Tovaritch* (1934), is like a variation
on *Lord Richard in the Pantry*[36] of the London stage, or indeed
on any plays exploiting the old theme of social levels temporarily
upset by some external cause; in this, Russian *émigrés* are in the
leading roles. The plays of Edouard Bourdet (1887–1944) and

[36] By Sidney Blow and Douglas Hoare, Criterion Theatre, 1919.

Marcel Pagnol (b. 1895), as comedies of manners, have more weight. Bourdet's *Vient de paraître* (1927) is a satire on the intrigues in the world of publishers and writers around the award of literary prizes, *Le Sexe faible* (1929) a satirical portrayal of the lounge-lizards to be found in the Paris luxury hotels of the post-war years. In all his plays Bourdet is a master of dramatic construction. It may be added that as director of the Comédie Française (1936–40) he showed himself very open to the influences from the experimental theatres. Pagnol's *Topaze* (1928) is an entertaining satire on the corrupting power of money – honest schoolmaster into financial rogue; in more lyrical mood, Pagnol evokes the life of Marseilles; we can almost smell the garlic and the bouillabaisse in *Marius* (1928) followed with equal verve by *Fanny* (1929) and *César* (1931).

Jules Romains's contribution to post-war comedy is a brilliant mixture of farce and comedy of character.[37] Jean Sarment (b. 1897) and Marcel Achard (b. 1899), both from the Copeau 'stable', write a romantic type of comedy, the former in e.g. *La Couronne de Carton* (1920) and *Le Pêcheur d'Ombres* (1921), the latter in a series of plays of which the most successful was *Jean de la lune* (1929). A number of dramatists portray human relationships without probing deeply into the human psyche. Charles Vildrac (b. 1882), the one-time Unanimist poet, chooses characters that reveal themselves for what they really are under the stress of circumstances (e.g. Ségard and Bastien in *Le Paquebot Tenacity*, 1920). Paul Géraldy (b. 1885) evokes the emotional conflicts of two or three characters, e.g. in *Aimer* (1921), *Robert et Marianne* (1925), *Do, mi, sol, do* (1934). Jean-Jacques Bernard (b. 1888) portrays secretive, inward-looking characters (e.g. *Le Feu qui reprend mal*, 1921; *Martine*, 1922). Stève Passeur (b. 1899) presents erotically obsessed characters in dramatic situations (e.g. *Suzanne*, 1929; *L'Acheteuse*, 1930); the plots vary but the formula is reminiscent of Bernstein.

Of the dramatists who sought a renewal of dramatic forms Paul Claudel is the outstanding example.[38] He had entered the field of poetic drama when Rostand's romantic verse plays were in fashion; his masterpiece – *L'Annonce faite à Marie* – had been written before, but not till after the First World War was the full measure of his originality appreciated – his Christian assessment of man in creation, expressed in rich poetic prose, now in symbolic, now in realistic, now in historical terms.

In the same field stand Gide,[39] Cocteau,[40] André Obey (b. 1892) and Giraudoux, all of whom re-express themes from the Bible or

---

[37] See below, chap. 11.
[38] See above, chap. 9, iii.
[39] See above, chap. 9, ii.
[40] See above, pp. 214–16.

the drama of the Ancients. Obey's *Le Viol de Lucrèce* (1931) and *Noé* (1931) are restatements of the old stories, the former with the classical chorus, the latter in the form of a rustic philosophic farce. Jean Giraudoux (1882–1944) is more likely to survive by his plays than his novels.

Debout Simon! On peut écouter debout les derniers conseils de son père . . .
Je me levai.
Inutile, Simon, de t'encourager au travail.
Ou tu travailleras, ou tu te passeras de pain . . .
Regarde-moi, Simon! Laisse ces noix.
Je regardai.
Tu entres dans la lutte avec une chance incroyable . . .
Félicite-toi de tous ces privilèges et pose cette pomme.
Je posai la pomme . . .

The valedictory scene, so charmingly evoked, that opens the bio-graphical *Simon le Pathétique* (1918), between father, cloaking his solicitude in severity, and son, who, in the manner of small boys no doubt, has, besides the nuts and apple referred to, a pocketful of useless treasures, gives promise of a novelist with an eye for the details that create a character or evoke a scene, in clear outline. But the expectation is not fulfilled; Giraudoux does not evoke reality as we know it so much as a world of fantasy, nourished in varying degrees by personal memories (e.g. *Provinciales*, 1909; *L'Ecole des Indifférents*, 1911; *Simon le Pathétique*, 1918; the early pages of *Suzanne et le Pacifique*, 1921; *Juliette au Pays des Hommes*, 1924), the experience of the war-time soldier (*Lectures pour une Ombre*, 1917; *Amica, America*, 1918; *Adorable Clio*, 1920), the experience of the diplomat, involved in the conflict of personalities and rival politics (e.g. *Bella*, 1926) or close witness of events on the international level (e.g. *Aventures de Jérôme Bardini*, 1930). It is a rich world in which the prism of Giraudoux's brilliant imagination adorns reality with bright colours, a fairy-land reality where the unexpected, the whimsical, the gay, the sad, the pene-trating, the precious and the far-fetched greet, stimulate and sometimes, yes, fatigue the reader.

To call these works or others (e.g. *Suzanne et le Pacifique*, where the heroine, a castaway on her Pacific island, plays the role of a new Robinson Crusoe, or *Siegfried et le Limousin*, 1922, set partly in post-war Germany and partly in Giraudoux's native Limousin) novels seem a misnomer, by any traditional standards; they fall rather into the category of long philosophical tales and indeed an author like Giraudoux, who weaves the multi-coloured skein of impressions experience gives him into his own pattern, evidently feels within him the urge to don the mantle of the moralist. Thus Simon's Odyssey teaches him the value of fitting into the existing order; Suzanne, despite the beauties she discovers in her island cluster, yearns in the end for the homely peace and changelessness of her native Bellac; Siegfried, the 'coming man' in German politics, returns by choice to the humble life in Limousin as the Jacques Forestier he had been before a war wound and loss of memory had turned him into a German citizen in a German hospital.

Giraudoux the moralist turned naturally to drama and wisely, for Giraudoux the playwright is superior to Giraudoux the spinner of philosophic tales. Fresh and original as tales such as *Simon le Pathétique, Suzanne et le Pacifique, Siegfried et le Limousin* were when they first came out, their author's brilliant fantasy runs away with him like a high-mettled horse apparently out of control; the reader's attention flags and in the end the tales are remembered not so much for themselves as for occasional passages which for one reason or another retain their relevance, or pen portraits that remain historically interesting.[41] Much the same impression of gratuitous brilliance, preciousness in the last resort, is conveyed by Giraudoux's critical studies (e.g. *Racine*, 1930; *Les Cinq tentations de La Fontaine*, 1938; *Littérature*, 1941). But the theatre gives little room for 'free-wheeling' fantasy; to be effective this needs to be geared to the action. In contrast to his other writings, his plays gain immeasurably by the compression imposed by the dramatic form. What better evidence can we have than *Siegfried* (1928), Giraudoux's first and one of his most successful plays. In contrast with the dilution of *Siegfried et le Limousin* whence it is distilled, the characters are well drawn, the action vigorous. The initial data, mainspring of the action – Siegfried's amnesia, the consequent depression into the subconscious of his French personality and the superimposition of a new German personality, stretch credibility, Freudian in inspiration though they may be; none the less, the argument for understanding between former enemies, inspired no doubt by the ideas of Briand and Berthelot as against the prudential policies of Poincaré, is clear enough.

Not the least attraction of the theatre for Giraudoux was the actor-manager Jouvet whose personality, by its mixture of wit and seriousness, was so closely in sympathy with Giraudoux; and who became the principal dramatic interpreter of Giraudoux's plays from *Siegfried* to the posthumous *La Folle de Chaillot* (1945), including *Amphytrion 38* (1929), *Judith* (1931), *Intermezzo* (1933), *Tessa* (1934), *La Guerre de Troie n'aura pas lieu* (1935), *Electre* (1937), *Ondine* (1939), *Sodome et Gomorrhe* (1943). Of these, *La Guerre de Troie n'aura pas lieu* is outstanding for

---

[41] e.g. Bolny (*Simon le Pathétique*), or Bunau-Varilla of *Le Matin* to whom Giraudoux had been secretary (1907); 'Rebendart' or Poincaré and 'mon père' or Philippe Berthelot in *Bella*; Briand in *Combat avec L'Ange* (1934).

the brilliance of its dialogue, its mixture of penetrating wit, serious purpose and underlying pessimism. To the ancient story of the Trojan war, Giraudoux has added an earlier chapter, a new overture, as it were, to a familiar opera. Shall Helen be sent back whence she came and Troy be spared the war? The question divides Trojan opinion. Hector, professional soldier that he is, knowing from direct experience what war is like, is not pacifist, but pacific: 'Tous ceux des Troyens qui ont fait et peuvent faire la guerre ne veulent pas la guerre' (I, 3), to which Andromaque, with tragic foreboding, replies: 'Il reste tous les autres'. Her prescience is confirmed; the civilians are bellicose, as only men ignorant of war can be, Paris and Helen live isolated in their lovers' indifferent egotism. The clash of opinions, the motives of the contending parties, are movingly and clearly expressed, as the debate moves to its climax, and Hector's efforts, even at the price of accepting insults, to keep the peace, are vain, too great the forces against him: the power of beauty over men (cf. I, 6; Priam to Hector: 'regarde seulement cette foule, et tu comprendras ce qu'est Hélène . . .'), blind chauvinism, and, in the end, a lie that precipitates the conflict (Demokos, in the last scene).

Nor should we omit to recall here Montherlant's efforts to re-create high tragedy in the stark terms of conflict between political or religious necessity and love, as the motivation of human action.[42]

In the third category come the Freudians and the Existentialists; the latter are discussed in the next chapter; for the former, characters who, however closely studied, are seen as human beings with 'des âmes de verre', i.e. acting on transparently rational motives, are out of favour; instead the Freudians aim at a deeper exploration of the human personality, interpreted as a complex of subconscious urges, a potential of violence. The early plays of Henri Lenormand (1882–1951), e.g. Poussière (1914), obey the Naturalist canon – a slice of life (low). Les Ratés (1919), which portrays a company of down-at-heel actors, is in the same tradition, but Le Temps est un Songe (1919), with its plot based on the heroine's precognition leading to the suicide of her fiancé, recalls both Pirandello's theme of illusion becoming reality and the blind compulsions of Freud. Le Simoun (1920) and especially Le Mangeur de rêves (1922) also derive their dramatic intensity from compulsive forces and thwarted longings in the psyche of the characters, the drama being played out against exotic backgrounds chosen to heighten the effect. Similar impulses emerging from the depths are at work in the plays of Julien Green.[43]

Of all the inter-war dramatists one of the richest in substance and varied in the expression of his themes, in the tone of his plays, is surely Armand Salacrou (b. 1900). Here we are no longer on Freudian territory; running through all his plays from the early Surrealist *Le Casseur d'assiettes* (1925) onwards, runs the author's anguished quest for an answer to the problem of man's destiny, expressing itself now in a bitter comedy such as *Atlas-Hôtel* (1931), now in the tragedy of Savonarola (*La Terre est ronde*, 1937), now in the sardonic humour of *L'Archipel Lenoir* (1947), so markedly Existentialist – 'il n'y a qu'un scandale, un seul . . . la vie. L'Existence. La Naissance qui n'est qu'une promesse de mort.'[44]

Of the few dramatists of this generation that have made a reputation beyond the frontiers of France, one of the most prominent is Jean Anouilh[45] (b. 1910). The sometime publicity agent quickly turned playwright divides his plays into four categories: *Pièces Noires* (1942),[46] *Pièces Roses* (1942), *Pièces Brillantes* (1951), and *Pièces Grinçantes* (1957). Two other plays were published separately: *Ardèle* (1949) and *La Valse des Toréadors* (1952). Anouilh's youthful heroes and heroines seem at first to owe something to Musset, the gossamer-like texture of the plays might suggest a comparison with Marivaux, but the complexity of the characters' attitudes to one another and the sophisticated preciosity of the sentiments reveals influences much closer at hand – Pirandello and Giraudoux.

Anouilh however does not share Giraudoux's fundamental optimism, his confidence in man. Like other prominent writers of the 1930's, Anouilh has lost the sense of euphory evident and possible in the writers of the post-war decade; forthcoming events seem to cast their cold shadow across the path. Whilst some writers brace themselves with the tonic of heroic action and high tension endeavour on the individual level (Saint-Exupéry, Montherlant, Malraux), others find a metaphysical background to this position in Existentialism. Anouilh's plays reflect the general pessimism; his characters, the young with their sorrows and pride, their elders with their cynicism, if they share with the Existentialists the sense of man's fundamental isolation – 'Ah! On est seul, tu ne trouves pas qu'on est trop seul',[47] show no inclination to stamp their own seal on life, and prefer renunciation in death or in life with disillusion.

Love is the essential theme but love is not companionship or a shared joy; it is another form of egotism, a means of escape from our solitude, a fragile thing forever menaced or traversed ('Une

<hr>

[44] *Archipel Lenoir*, Part II. Salacrou, *Théâtre*, VI, p. 68, Gallimard. See also the pages to the memory of Charles Dullin, *Théâtre*, VI, pp. 97–122.

[45] See J. H. Watkins, 'Twenty-one years of Anouilh', *Modn Langs.*, vol. xxxiv, No. 3, Sep. 1953.

[46] A second group, *Nouvelles Pièces Noires*, was published in 1946.

[47] *Eurydice*, III.

lutte de chaque jour' – *Roméo et Jeanette*, 1945), now by difficulties of our own imagining, now by outside circumstances – wealth on one side, poverty on the other, reputation, convention.[48] 'S'aimer, c'est lutter constamment contre des milliers de forces cachés qui viennent de vous ou du monde – contre d'autres hommes, contre d'autres femmes.'[49] *Antigone*, though the theme of love is present (Antigone and Hémon), raises another question – the restatement of the conflict starkly portrayed by Sophocles between duty to the divine law (Antigone) and duty to the State (Créon), but a restatement on Anouilh's level between a harassed politician, convincing but not uplifting in his humanity and a petulant girl – 'Moi, je veux tout, tout de suite . . . ou alors je refuse'[50] – unconvincing in her determination to die, when she doesn't have her way. In subsequent plays, e.g. *Roméo et Jeanette, Ardèle* (1948), *La Répétition ou l'Amour puni* (1950), *Colombe* (1951) and *La Valse des Toréadors* (1952), love is once more the dominating theme, and, as always in Anouilh, the quest, revealed as impossible to attain, or, if attained, impossible to preserve, of purity. Faced with this impasse the result is cynical disillusionment or renunciation of high hopes for spiritual peace on a low level of contentment (e.g. *L'Invitation au Château*, 1947; *La Répétition ou l'Amour puni*, 1950; *La Valse des Toréadors*, 1952; and particularly the one-act tragedy, *Médée* – written 1946, performed 1953 – in which Jason concludes, as he watches the flames consuming Medée's body: 'Il faut vivre maintenant, assurer l'ordre, donner des lois à Corinthe et rebâtir sans illusions un monde à notre mesure pour y attendre de mourir' – a mixture of Goethean *Entsagung*, civic duty and hopelessness in an Existentialist world with no certainty but death). Anouilh's skill in dialogue is real but the range is limited.

[48] cf. *L'Hermine*, 1931; *La Sauvage*, 1934; *Eurydice*, 1942; *Antigone*, 1942.
[49] *L'Hermine*, II.
[50] Antigone to Créon, *Antigone*, p. 97, Table Ronde edn.

Chapter 11

NOVELISTS AND CRITICS

NO better proof of the public appetite for escapism at the end of the war could be provided than by the success of Pierre Benoit (1886–1962). Between 1918 and 1961 – date of his last novel (*Les Amours Mortes*) – he wrote some forty novels, of which the early ones (e.g. *Koenigsmark*, 1918, *L'Atlantide*, 1919, *La Châtelaine du Liban*, 1924, *Axelle*, 1927) show the value, when the conjunction of external circumstances are favourable, as they were, of the well-worn romantic formula of passionate love and exoticism – the lonely Prussian shore of the North Sea (*Koenigsmark*), the mysterious Hoggar (*L'Atlantide*), Martinique (*Fort-de-France*, 1933). Benoit was elected to the French Academy in 1931; he was at the peak of his success. Thereafter his almost annual novels are like so many steps downhill to oblivion. The art of the story-teller with a dash of mystery here and there, in the manner of Mérimée, remains constant, but the tide of public favour had receded.

Like many novelists of his generation Benoit was or became a world-wide traveller, but his novels rely rather on imagination whereas other writers who may be mentioned in the same bracket draw more on direct experience: Maurice Constantin-Weyer (b. 1881), with his Canadian background – *Un Homme se penche sur son passé* (1928), Maurice Bedel (1884–1954), who satirizes the Scandinavian way of life in *Jerome 60° latitude Nord* (1927), Roland Dorgelès (b. 1886) who whether in his war experience – *Les Croix de Bois* (1919) – or in his knowledge of Montmartre – *Le Château des Brouillards* (1931) – or in his travels – *La Caravane sans chameaux* – has a more accurately descriptive art, which is also that of Marc Chadourne (b. 1895), author of *Vasco* (the intellectual who combs the South Seas in the footsteps of Gauguin only to find disillusionment). The note of authenticity is unmistakable too in the work of Pierre MacOrlan[1] who from his early harsh experience of poverty in Montmartre and at Rouen, where the quayside and ships quickened his imagination, built up a series of adventure stories played out by sailors, bootleggers, prostitutes and

[1] Real name Pierre Dumarchey.

down-and-outs, against a background of sordid hotels and cafés in
dingy streets; poetry and realism. 'J'ai besoin d'authenticité pour
moi, le roman doit être mêlé directement à la vie. C'est une
chronique où il faut introduire un élément romanesque.'[2] There
are reminiscences of Stevenson and Conrad in works such as *Le
Chant de l'Equipage* (1918), *Abord de l'Etoile-Matutine* (1920),
Quai des Brumes (1927).

Blaise Cendrars (1887–1961), poet, novelist and journalist, had
a keener appetite for travel than MacOrlan. Swiss by birth, he belonged to the generation of artists and writers – Picasso, Léger,
Salmon, Apollinaire, Jacob – who had 'invented' Montmartre and
Montparnasse.[3] He is in the true line of Valéry Larbaud, but, unlike the latter, not at the luxury end of the train. *Bourlinguer* is
the title of one of his autobiographical novels; the fever of vagabondage had seized him young:

> En ce temps-là, j'étais en mon adolescence
> J'avais à peine seize ans...
> J'étais à mille lieues du lieu de ma naissance
> J'étais à Moscou...
> (*Prose du Transsibérien et de la petite Jeanne
> de France*, 1913)

As a poet (*Prose du Transsibérien, Poèmes Elastiques*, 1919), Cendrars has evocative skill, by rapid notation – the essence of the impressionistic style fashionable in the post-war years; but his short
stories – *Histoires Vraies* (1937), *La Vie dangereuse* (1938) – and
his novels – e.g. *L'Or* (1925), *Moravagine* (1926), *Rhum* (1930)
and, more recently, *L'Homme foudroyé* (1945), *Dan Yack* (1946),
La Main Coupée (1946), *Bourlinguer* (1948), *Le Lotissement du
Ciel* (1949) – are more like 'reportage' on the grand scale, where
impressions of people and places jostle each other in a turbulent
disjointed torrent, with here and there a calmer pool of reverie.
Cendrars' fictional characters with the exception of Suter (*L'Or*)
are little more than inconsistent shadows.

In contrast to the 'rolling stone' variety of travel, which is Cendrars', Paul Morand (b. 1888) offers travel on the diplomatic level,
with kaleidoscopic impressions: '50,000 kilomètres, 28 pays nègres.'[4]
Paul Morand is the true cosmopolitan, at home wherever he goes,
but for whom the world is getting too small, too round, humanity
too similar (*Rien que la Terre*, 1926). The impressionistic verses of
Lampes à Arc (1919) and *Feuilles de Température* (1920) were
followed by the short stories of *Tendres Stocks* (1921), reminiscent

---

[2] Interview published in *Le Monde*, 4 November 1961.
[3] Article by J. Duvignaud, *Preuves*, No. 124, June 1961. Cendrars enlisted in the Foreign Legion in the 1914 war and lost his right hand and
forearm.
[4] *Magie Noire*, Avant-propos.

by its heroines of Giraudoux, and by those of *Ouvert la Nuit* (1922), *Fermé la Nuit* (1923) and *L'Europe galante* (1925), where the night-life in bars and dance halls, with prostitutes and drug traffic, seems much the same and equally synthetic whether in Paris or London, Berlin, Moscow or Constantinople. His three novels, *Lewis et Irène* (1924), *Bouddha vivant* (1927), and *Champions du Monde* (1930), show Morand in the role of moralist, either pointing out to men the dangers of feminine competition in business, or, by the failure of Prince Jâli to find disciples of his Oriental wisdom in occidental capitals, the gulf fixed between East and West. But Morand is less effective in the novel than in the short story. Like the brilliant draughtsman, who, less at home with the detailed picture, can in a few strokes of his pencil suggest features, depth and movement, Morand excels at the kaleidoscopic effect of sketches and scenes with the minimum of plot and character analysis.

A distinctive feature of the early post-war years was the fashion for African art. Its bold designs and constructive rather than figurative interest had attracted the Cubists and sculptors, its garish colours refreshed the modern painter's palette, the disjointed rhythms of its tunes inspired the strident discords of modern music; and beneath the outward forms lurked the primitive psyche drawn to magic and such-like practices by the obscure compulsions of the subconscious which the Surrealists were busy exploring. While the Negress dancer, Joséphine Baker, became queen of the Paris night clubs, Paul Morand collected impressions, pen portraits of the Negro world in *Magie Noire* (1928) and *Hiver caraïbe* (1929). Not less skilful is the manner in which he evokes the characteristic atmosphere of New York (*New York*, 1930), of Paris in its heyday (*1900*, 1931), of London (*Londres*, 1933).

An older Morand, full of stylistic skill, knowledge of the world and moral savour, has recently appeared in a collection of short stories, mingled with earlier ones in an anthology, *Nouvelles d'une Vie (I et II)* (1966) and a novel, *Tais-Toi* (1966).

Another form of escape is provided by Francis Carco[5] (b. 1886), with whom we travel to the fringes of the criminal world – 'le milieu' so called. His early poems – *Instincts* (1911), *La Bohème et mon coeur* (1912), *Chansons aigres – douces* (1912) – already suggest a theme that appears in his post-war novels (e.g. *L'Homme traqué*, 1922; *Rien qu'une femme*, 1924; *Rue Pigalle*, 1928; *Dans la Rue*, 1930), the compulsive power of instinct in settings that owe something to the Naturalists. Carco's characters are usually the victims of an obsessive passion that destroys them – e.g. Lampieur (*L'Homme traqué*), the baker's man, who has committed

[5] François Carcopino-Tusoli.

murder, Claude (*Rien qu'une femme*), Valentine, murdered by her lover (*Rue Pigalle*), Louise, the prostitute (*La Rue*). He explores their mentalities with less sympathy than interest in the phenomenon and with an all-pervading ironic pessimism on the uselessness of life.

The jungle beyond the law is inhabited not only by the criminal and his moll but by the human sleuth, their brother-enemy. In the gallery of fiction's detectives, Inspector Maigret has achieved a place not far below that of Sherlock Holmes. Admittedly he comes into his own only after the Second World War, but the career of his creator began in the early 'twenties. The achievement of the Belgian-born Georges Simenon (b. 1903) as purveyor of detection stories is impressive by its sheer mass.[6] Between 1922 and 1930 some one hundred and fifty stories, signed by diverse fictitious authors, *inter alia* Georges Slim, Christian Brulls, Aramis, Georges Martin-Georges, Jean du Perry, thereafter some one hundred and eighty under the author's own name and of these a third approximately form Maigret's 'geste'.

Simenon has been described as a 'Balzac sans les longueurs', a description that is unfair to Balzac and sits ill on Simenon whose interest is not, like Balzac's, in society as a living organism, but, appropriately enough for a detective story writer, in the individual's crime. Here, however, Simenon's art has developed, characteristically for a post-Freudian, from the early type of crime conundrum, to exploration of the human mystery underlying it, and, in adding this dimension to the detective story, Simenon has moved to a sense of sympathy, of human responsibility for the criminal, isolated from society by his crime (e.g. *Les Feux Rouges*, *L'Horloger d'Everton*).

Ever since Rousseau a persistent form of escapism has been the flight to nature, the simple peasant life. Prominent among the literary 'rustics' are C. F. Ramuz (1878–1947), who in his native Swiss canton of Vaud feels drawn to a communion with nature and expresses it in a rugged style that becomes fatiguing (e.g. *La Guérison des Maladies*, 1917; *L'Amour du Monde*, 1925; *La Grande Peur dans la Montagne*, 1926); Henri Pourrat (b. 1887), author of a peasant chronicle in verse, *Les Montagnards* (1919), and painter of life in Auvergne in *Gaspard des Montagnes* (1922) and *La Ligne Verte* (1929); and Jean Giono (b. 1895). Giono's trilogy – *Colline* (1929), *Un de Baumugnes* (1929) and *Regain* (1930) – portrays the peasants of Upper Provence close to nature, which is endowed by the author with animistic life; a lyrical pantheism emerges in *Le Chant du Monde* (1934) and *Les Vraies Richesses* (1937). Paradoxically enough, whilst writing these peasant

[6] P. H. Simon, article in *Le Monde*, 5 June 1963.

novels, Giono was preparing a series of historical tales which have
since become a second manner (e.g. *Le Hussard sur le toit*, 1951;
Le Moulin de Pologne, 1959). The pacifist sage of Manosque,
communing with the god Pan, evokes the horrors of a cholera outbreak at Marseilles (*Le Hussard*), and delights in battles (*Le
désastre de Pavie*, 1963).

Closely allied to the 'rustics' are the regionalists of whom there
are enough to plant out in every corner of France. Some, like A.
de Châteaubriant (1877–1951) in *La Brière* (1923), and J. de Pes-
quidoux (1869–1946) in *Chez Nous* (1921) and *Sur la Glèbe*
(1922), essentially descriptive of their home country, almost forsake the novel form; others, like Jean de la Varende (b. 1887) in
Nez de Cuir (1937) or Henri Bosco (b. 1888) in *Le Mas Théotime*
(1946) and *Malicroix* (1948), use a regional background, the former
the Ouche Country (Normandy), the latter Provence, as the scene
for their historical or contemporary story-telling; another prominent story-teller is Henri Béraud (1885–1958), who uses his native
Lyons either for his own reminiscences (*La Gerbe d'Or*, 1928) or
for a tale, evoking the narrow lives of the silk magnates (*Ciel de
Suie*, 1934). Within the regionalist context, too, comes André
Chamson (b. 1900), who recalls his Protestant background and
boyhood (*Les Quatre Eléments*, 1935, and *Le Chiffre de nos Jours*,
1954) at Le Vigan, Gard, paints a pen-portrait full of local savour
in *Histoires de Tabusse* (1930) and, in what he later called *Suite
Cévenole*, has written three stories – *Roux le bandit* (1925), *Les
Hommes de la Route* (1927) and *Le Crime des Justes* (1928) – that
have a human significance beyond their regionalist framework –
in the first, the protest of the individual conscience and the form
of heroism it may produce, in the second, the value of dogged collective effort, 'crime and punishment' in the third; powerful tales
all three, that deserve to survive and that outstrip in quality all
Chamson's subsequent novels (e.g. *La Galère*, 1939; *La Neige et
La Fleur*, 1951) in which he abandons the two themes he was born
and bred to – Cévennes and Protestant mentality.

Novelists are not lacking during the period under review who
follow the best established tradition in French literature, that of
psychological analysis. An early post-war example is provided by
Raymond Radiguet (1903–23), truly a shooting-star, quickly gone,
leaving behind a short but brilliant trail – two short novels: *Le
Diable au corps* (1923) and *Le Bal du Comte d'Orgel*[7] (1924). As a
coup d'essai, the former is remarkable enough, but the latter, built
like its predecessor on a triangular situation, but a virtuous one,
faintly recalls *La Princesse de Clèves* and, richer in characters,
fulfils the early promise. The scope, though greater than in *Le*

[7] Also a book of poems: *Les Joues en feu* (posth. 1925).

Diable au corps, remains small, the field of analysis narrow, but the psychological insight is penetrating, the investigation of motive in the characters precise and satisfying; the effect is that of a brilliantly constructed mechanism, in miniature.

Jacques Chardonne[8] (b. 1884) has made his own the study of the married couple, the psychological relationships created by two lives lived in common and bonded together less by their initial love than by the minutiae of everyday life that contribute to imponderable shifts of attitude, form a solid texture of common experience, acceptance, tolerance, and provide some knowledge of the life partner – 'vivre ensemble, quelle expérience! que de larmes, de luttes, de méprises, avant de s'ouvrir un peu l'un a l'autre.'[9] This is the dominant theme of *L'Epithalame* (1921), Chardonne's masterpiece, and, with variations, of *Les Varais* (1929), *Eva ou le Journal interrompu* (1930), *Claire* (1931).

André Maurois's[10] novels (*Bernard Quesnay*, 1926; *Climats*, 1929; *Le Cercle de Famille*, 1932) are not compelling; the author's tolerant scepticism, deriving from a pessimistic belief in the inevitable inconstancy of human attitudes, is reflected in characters, who, as a result, lack purpose.

Where the lack of personal philosophy allied to interpretative skill, from being a weakness becomes a strength, is in biography; *Bramble* and *O'Grady* have something of fictional biography and these works remain his best.[11] The type of biography that became fashionable in the 'twenties, in which a man's fame is used alternatively as a pretext to build up a very human story or to reflect the author's own attitudes, owes much to Maurois. In *Ariel* (1923) and *Byron* (1930), Shelley and Byron are seen more as victims of the English social code than as great poets, in *Disraëli* (1927), the great Victorian statesman's tolerant scepticism, shown in such advantageous contrast with Gladstone's rigidity, is Maurois's own. The series has continued.[12]

Some authors, whilst interested in the psychological mechanisms of their characters, enlarge their canvas to the family, in one or more generations, a social class, a society at a given period. Jacques de Lacretelle (b. 1888) shows the passage from the study of individual mentalities in *Silbermann* (1922) and *Le Retour de Silbermann* (1930), in *La Bonifas* (1925), to that of a family in *Les Hauts-Ponts* (1932–6). In the former he portrays two characters, shunned by the group they would like to identify themselves with: Silbermann, the young Jew, and the unfeminine Marie Bonifas,

[8] Jacques Boutelleau.   [9] *L'Epithalame*, vol. ii, p. 258.
[10] Emile Herzog.   [11] See below, p. 266.
[12] e.g. George Sand, Hugo, the Dumas family (father, son and grandson), La Fayette, Proust, Balzac.

suspected of lesbianism. In *Les Hauts-Ponts*, the author tells the story of the Darembert family over three generations who struggle to regain and maintain the family estate in Vendée, only to lose it in the end. The destinies of a landed family are also portrayed by Jean Schlumberger (b. 1877) in *Saint Saturnin* (1931).

Both Roger Martin du Gard and Georges Duhamel have written family sagas. Born of Catholic bourgeois stock, Roger Martin du Gard (1881–1958), after some scientific studies under the notable biologist Le Dantec, was trained as an archivist paleographer at the 'Ecole des Chartes' (1903–5) and for his diploma wrote an archaeological thesis (1909) on the ruins of the Abbey of Jumièges. Though both branches of study may be said to have influenced him indirectly (e.g. the determinist attitude of certain of his characters, his taste for historical accuracy), literature was to claim him early. A first novel, *Devenir*, appeared in 1908. In 1910 came the unsuccessful short story *Une de Nous*, pulped during the war, and in 1913 the first important work, *Jean Barois*, and a peasant farce, *Le Testament du Père Leleu* (performed 1914, published 1920).

After war service Martin du Gard published *Les Thibault* (1922–40), the central pillar of his work, *La Confidence Africaine* (1931), a short story, *Vieille France* (1933), scenes of peasant life, two further plays – *La Gonfle* (1928), which is another peasant farce, and *Un Taciturne* (1931), a sombre drama. The author's correspondence, his *Journal*, covering thirty years from 1919, and an unfinished novel, entitled *Le Journal du Colonel Maumort*, remain unpublished.

First novels are often more interesting as signposts than for their performance. The interest of *Devenir*, later condemned by its author,[13] is of that order; the story of André Mazerelle, prodigal of ambitions that remain unfulfilled, and his more successful friend Grosdidier, is like a meagre preliminary sketch for the much bigger canvas of *Les Thibault*, with its pivotal characters, the brothers Jacques and Antoine.

Jean Barois, on the other hand, is an important work. That it should have made an immediate impact is natural; it recalls for a generation that had experienced them both, the intellectual struggles and the dramatic events of the closing years of the nineteenth century and the early years of the twentieth, the struggle between Christians and Rationalists, and the Dreyfus Affair. The author has most skilfully intertwined the spiritual conflict of his hero caught between the religious habits of his upbringing and the imperatives of contemporaneous scientific philosophies, with the events and polemics of the time. Whether *Jean Barois* may be regarded as a wholly successful work of art is more debatable. With

[13] 'Un mauvais roman de jeunesse'.

its series of dramatic dialogues and its quick changes of scene it is if anything a film scenario rather than a novel; the technique is well chosen, indeed inevitable in view of the scope of the subject to be brought within the limits of one volume, but as a result the author has scarcely done justice either to the portrayal of the characters and their relationships to each other or to the historical events they are involved in; the work hovers between a study of psychological and domestic conflict, and 'flashes from the news room', as elements of period evocation. For anyone who had lived through the period, the work would surely have evoked as vigorous a response as a dentist's drill touching a sensitive nerve, but for later generations to whom the events suggested in Jean Barois's own spiritual pilgrimage or evoked by the 'news flashes' are history not personal experience, the case is different; the artistic skill of an author alone can communicate to them the emotions aroused at the time by a drama like the Dreyfus Affair or produce in them that sense of identification with a character which is the test of great fiction. To do either of these things, *Jean Barois* attempts too much or too little, too much in the scope of the historical picture, too little in the exploration of individual religious experience.

The fusion of these two elements, evocation of period and character study, is more richly successful in *Les Thibault*. The ten volumes of this novel fall broadly into three groups: the first (Parts I to VI inclusive[14]) gives the inter-connected stories of two families, the Thibaults and the Fontanins, the attention being mainly concentrated on Oscar Thibault, an elderly widower, and his two sons, Antoine and Jacques; the second group (the three volumes of *L'Eté 1914*) broadens the canvas from the family level to the European scene. The author skilfully weaves the story of his main character and a host of secondary characters into a documented chronicle, Tolstoyan in proportions, of the events that occurred week by week, almost day by day between 28 June and 10 August 1914. The third section consists of *Epilogue* (1940) alone, which takes up the story of the surviving members of the two families at the end of the war and focusses interest on Antoine Thibault, who, knowing his days to be numbered as a result of the effects of mustard gas, keeps a diary, in which, as a doctor, he notes the progressive deterioration of his condition and tries to come to terms with the mysteries the exercise of his profession has, hitherto, given him no time for, the mysteries of life and death; his final position similar to Jean Barois's, in spite of his conversion

---

[14] Part I, *Le Cahier Gris* (1922); Part II, *Le Pénitencier* (1922); Part III, *La Belle Saison* (1923); Part IV, *La Consultation* (1924); Part V, *La Sorellina* (1928); Part VI, *La Mort du Père* (1929).

in extremis, and doubtless reflecting the author's, is that life has no individual significance.

Les Thibault is a family saga, the first in French literature if one excludes Zola's *Rougon-Macquart* series, where the family is scarcely more than a convenient means of studying different levels of society and applying, when the author remembers, a theory of heredity, and *Jean-Christophe*, which pivots on the life of one character only. Martin du Gard's novel follows out the intricate pattern of the Catholic Thibaults and the Protestant Fontanins. Each family has its 'conformers' and its rebels, those (e.g. Oscar Thibault, Madame de Fontanin) who struggle to uphold the family tradition as, to quote Oscar Thibault, 'la cellule première du tissu social et le pivot de l'état bourgeois', and those who either by lack of principle (e.g. Jérôme de Fontanin) or by reaction against parental discipline (?tyranny) struggle to destroy it. By nature Antoine Thibault is a traditionalist – less his father's religious bigotry; reinforcing his instinctive sense of conservation is the discipline of his profession. Daniel de Fontanin, too, after a period of hesitation under the influence of his friend Jacques, finds salvation (much as his creator perhaps?) in an external discipline, that of art.[15]

La Confidence Africaine is the story of an incestuous relationship between a brother and sister; in *Un Taciturne* the author studies the psychopathic Thierry who chooses suicide as an escape from life; *Vieille France,* Naturalistic in its pessimistic portrayal of a low-grade humanity, is a collection of scenes from village life at the fictional Maupeyrou.

There is indeed much of the technique and spirit of Naturalism in the art of Martin du Gard: the skilful weaving together of rapid and diverse scenes into a complex whole by an individual (*Devenir, Jean Barois*) or family (*Les Thibault*) thread; the predilection for medicine and biology, with the determinism that can accompany them, not without struggle against faith (Jean Barois, Antoine Thibault).

The human sympathies that had no doubt helped Georges Duhamel (b. 1884) to choose medicine as a career and had drawn his interest to the Abbaye de Créteil experiment in 'Unanimism' (1906)[16] inform his writings – whereas Roger Martin du Gard aims to give the reader an objective account of his characters, their careers in the family, social and historical background. Duhamel, whilst doing much the same, shows more solicitude; du Gard has the detachment of the historian, Duhamel (in novels, essays and memoirs) is a moralist imbued with charity and pity. Christian in spirit, humanist in belief, he remains interested primarily in the

---

[15] See *Les Thibault,* Part III, *La Belle Saison.*   [16] See above, p. 106.

individual. These attitudes are evident in *Les Aventures de Salavin* (1920–9) and in his *Chronique des Pasquier* (1933–44).

As dutiful son and humble employee (*Confession de Minuit*), as friend (*Deux Hommes*), as seeker after saintliness without religion (*Le Journal de Salavin*), as social and political worker (*Le Club de Lyonnais*), Salavin is one of this world's *ratés*, studied with quiet humour and what in the end – 'Tel qu'en lui-même?' – amounts to fraternal affection for the earnest plodder who in his foibles, his dreams and temptations, his sufferings, has so much in him of the host of little men that people the earth, and who, according to their humble lights, struggle for salvation; Salavin's significance extends beyond his own poor little life's adventure.

The Pasquier Chronicles have a social background anchored in time to the first twenty years approximately of the twentieth century and touch upon events (e.g. memories of Unanimism and the Abbaye de Créteil in *Le Désert de Bièvres*) and aspects of society (e.g. Institut Pasteur in *Combat contre les Ombres*) which were within Duhamel's own experience.[17] But though the canvas is broader than in Salavin, the members of the family as individuals claim our attention, the choleric but likeable Raymond Pasquier and his children, of whom Laurent as child and adult is a transposition of Duhamel.

Unable like his sister Cécile, the musician, to find solace in Christian belief,[18] Laurent achieves something like it in the ideal of service to his neighbour. There speaks the resigned and melancholy humanist that Duhamel remains, intent in his latter day, as the tireless traveller he has become, to extend unceasingly his experience and understanding of humanity, that he may the better warn us against the danger, in the development of our material civilization, of undervaluing liberty. *Scènes de la vie future* (1930), that not very understanding essay on America, had already been a cry of alarm; it persists in his *Problèmes de civilisation* (1962), but in an age where torture and kidnappings across frontiers have become current forms of political behaviour, the annoyance of the telephone and the noise of the petrol engine which Duhamel continues to inveigh against with benign melancholy, have become a little out of focus.[19]

Much more ambitious in social scope is the work of Jules Romains[20] (b. 1885), a Southerner by birth,[21] a Parisian by upbringing, a schoolmaster by training, as his father had been. But teaching he soon abandoned. Unanimist ideas were to be a fertile

---

[17] See his memoirs, *Inventaire de l'abîme* (1944); *Biographie de mes fantômes* (1945).

[18] *Cécile parmi nous*, Chronique, Vol. VII.

[19] See article in *Le Monde*, February 1964, P. H. Simon.

[20] Louis Farigoule.   [21] From the Velay region, in N. Languedoc.

source of inspiration for him, both in poetry and prose. All the poems in his first volume of poetry, *La Vie unanime* (1908), derive from them; the theme, not evident in the more subjective *Odes* (1913), re-emerges in *Europe* (1916); *L'Homme Blanc* (1937), which is an epic of the white races, is mainly inspired by the ideas of progress, reason, liberty, a Universal Republic, and recalls the beliefs of Victor Hugo in *La Légende des Siècles*.

But Jules Romains will be remembered as dramatist and novelist rather than as poet: in these fields his Unanimistic inspiration flows strongly, in the lyrical verse drama *Cromedeyre le Vieil* (1920), in comedies such as *M. Le Trouhadec saisi par la débauche* (1921) and *Knock ou le Triomphe de la médecine* (1924) or *Donogoo*[22] (1930). Romains's comic verve is at its best in *Knock*, surely his stage masterpiece, and in *Donogoo*. The adventurer Knock deserves to join Molière's gallery of great comic characters. With no more knowledge of medicine than is provided by 'les annonces médicales et pharmaceutiques ainsi que les prospectus intitulés mode d'emploi'[23] and a little experience as a fraudulent ship's doctor, he transforms the decaying practice of Doctor Parpalaid into a veritable community of patients, enjoying (in the fullest sense) ill-health, by instilling into them a shared reverence in medicine – unanimism at work!

Donogoo, described by its author as a 'conte cinématographique', is the story of how a band of colonizers, deceived by the fraudulent publicity of one Lamendin, set out for an Eldorado in South America which does not exist and once there, beyond the point of no return, have no alternative but to create it, greatly to the spiritual comfort of the worthy Le Trouhadec whose reputation as a geographer is at stake for having described what was, at the time of writing, the inexistent Donogoo, in volume three of his *Géographie de l'Amérique du Sud*. Another unanimist miracle! – although in fact, both plays might be seen equally well as triumphs of individual ascendancy or energy.

Unanimism is at the source of Romains's amusing early novel, *Les Copains* (1913), may indirectly be attached to the trilogy, *Psyché* (1922–9), intended as a study of 'the married couple', in the context of unanimistic thought but too overweighted with eroticism and verbosity to be anything but pedestrian, and more particularly to *Les Hommes de Bonne Volonté* (1932–47) which with its twenty-seven volumes must rank as Romains's most colossal achievement. Volume I is entitled *Le 6 Octobre*, volume XXVII *Le 7 Octobre*, a twenty-four hour period which in fact extends over twenty-five years, from 1908 to 1933, and in which

---

[22] Originally published as a story, *Donogoo-Tonka* (1920).
[23] Act I, scene 1.

Romains aims to give a 'total' view of French life. Echoes of the Agadir and the Balkan war, religious and social quarrels, the impact on the worker of the extension of the machine age, scenes of the 1914–18 war (Volume XVI, *Verdun*, rises in parts to epic grandeur), the difficult post-war years with their diplomatic, economic crises and financial scandals are amongst the historical themes that, together with the personal stories of his crowd of characters, go to make up this modern historico-fictional epic.

Romains has not resisted the temptation of attacking the literary fashions of the 'twenties – e.g. Dadaïsm and Surrealism. 'Pris en eux-mêmes', notes Jallez, one of the reader's constant companions throughout the work, 'ces signes manquent d'importance. Mais comme indice d'un état de santé, ils ne sont pas négligeables, comme des boutons sur la peau.'[24] Vorge the young aesthete,[25] in Gidian ecstasies, admires Quinette's crime[26] and extols murder as one of the fine arts.

Romains draws his characters from all levels of society: the nobility – the Saint-Papoul and Champcenais families; the Church – l'Abbé Mionnet future Archbishop; politics – Gurau, deputy, and Jerphanion who enters politics (Vol. XXI) and becomes Minister of Foreign Affairs (Vol. XXV); the world of commerce and finance – Haverkamp, Champcenais; of the small trader and workman – Quinette, Wazemmes; of the intellectuals – Jallez, Jerphanion, Clanricard.

In the multitude two are in the forefront, Jallez and Jerphanion, products like Romains of the Ecole Normale Supérieure, who, in their conversations, often most protracted, their interchange of letters, or their interior monologues noted *in extenso* for the reader's benefit, are the constant witnesses of their day. In the vast pageant there is much suffering, vice, sordid ugliness, and yet the ultimate impression, as the title implies, is not one of pessimism, though this is more the result of the author's own philosophy than a logical conclusion from the chronicle itself. Like Balzac's, Romains's attitude towards human activities, good or mischievous, seems essentially one of interest, and this suggests in the last analysis a love of the human scene. Though there can evidently be no conclusion to such a work on the historical level, on the level of the individual his two *Normaliens*, and Haverkamp, the financial 'go-getter', all marry and – we may presume – live happily ever afterwards.

A chronicle planned on such a wide scale demands direct per-

[24] Vol. XVII, *Vorge contre Quinette*.
[25] The critic A. Thérive sees in him a composite portrait of Jean Cocteau and André Breton (article in *Le Temps*, 18 April 1940).
[26] Committed in Vol. II.

sonal experience, if it is to appear authentic. Romains's personal experience is no doubt broad, but parts of his large canvas (e.g. the world of politics, ecclesiastical circles, the nobility) give the impression of being sketched in from imagination rather than observation, the characters are wooden (e.g. the Saint-Papoul family). Often, too, the characters suffer from Romains's verbosity and – supreme misfortune for the creator of M. Le Trouhadec and the great Knock – they seem neither endowed nor observed with humour; a little self-criticism, essential to humour, would come as a relief from Jallez. Romains is at his best in his descriptions of supra-individual anonymous life on the scale of the community, be it small town, city quarter, city or nation or even continent, in a word 'unanimist' life (e.g. 6 October 1908, the opening scene in Vol. I; France in July 1914, Vol. XIV, chap. 26; the crowd movement in the Champs Elysées in 1922, Vol. XIX, chap. 1; Paris goes to work, Vol. XXVII, chap. 1; Europe in 1933, Vol. XXVII, chap. 24) – such scenes give an impression of great evocative power. Jallez, so often the author's mouthpiece, surely discloses Romains's aims and philosophy when he writes: 'La vie collective, la société respirante est toute autre chose que l'histoire et se passe fort bien d'elle. La vie collective s'abreuve très volontiers à ce mélange de quotidien et d'éternel qui a toujours signifié pour moi la poésie, la grâce, la contemplation, le repos divin.'[27] This is what gives the whole work its peculiar *cachet*, so different from other 'romans-fleuves' of the period – Proust's *A la Recherche Du Temps Perdu*, with its profound exploration of the inner world; Duhamel's *Les Pasquier* and Martin du Gard's *Les Thibault*, family chronicles essentially; or Lacretelle's *Les Hauts-Ponts*, with its theme of struggle between conflicting loyalties.

In contrast to the novelists who portrayed the bourgeois either as individual or in the social context, without criticism of the social structure or the material and moral values the bourgeois represents, a number of writers are critical of the bourgeois order. Marcel Arland (b. 1899) attacks false values (money, security, position) in *L'Ordre* (1929). Philippe Hériat (b. 1898), whilst conforming to the family saga genre in the first volume of his *La Famille Boussardelle* (1944), which traces the building up of the family's fortunes in the nineteenth century, shows (less convincingly) its progressive decline and disintegration in the twentieth (*Les Enfants gâtés*, 1954; *Grilles d'or*, 1957) under the pressure of events and the revolt of

[27] Vol. XXV (chap. 17). For those who are in search of eroticism spread thickly, this volume will provide it. Jallez, in obedience to 'la douce alimentation sexuelle', pursues his amorous adventures in Europe. Essential or even valuable to the 'unanimist' historical character of the work? Doubtful. Cynically one is tempted to wonder whether there was a need at this point to boost sales!

some of its members against the ideas that had been the dynasty's strength – the respect for money and family strategy controlled by it.

The bitterest attack came from Louis-Ferdinand Céline (1894–1961). His flow of words, and flood of vituperation reminiscent of Léon Bloy, but deliberately on a lower linguistic register, that of the people, were overwhelming. But this doctor of the poor, who in *Voyage au bout de la nuit* (1932) and *Mort à credit* (1936) seemed to espouse the anti-bourgeois cause, subsequently became a nihilist who in his furious despair rends all comers: *Bagatelles pour un massacre* attacked the Jews (1937) and *L'Ecole des cadavres* predicts France's defeat (1938); *Les Beaux draps* (1941) rejoices in it – paroxysms of hate that seem pathological and in the end fatiguing, but that cannot be forgotten or dismissed.

Very different from the writers just mentioned who, whether portraying man as an individual or in the framework of family relationships or against a background of society, remain on the human plane, are the moralists, prominent amongst whom are Mauriac and Bernanos.

We may be pardoned for thinking that the greatness of Mauriac (b. 1885) as a writer is not beyond dispute. What cannot be questioned is his success; his must be one of the most personally satisfying literary careers of this century, acclaimed by a chorus of approval with few discordant notes, and crowned by academic honours (elected to the French Academy, 1933, Nobel Prize for literature, 1952). Like many other writers Mauriac first published two volumes of poetry: *Les Mains jointes* (1909), which excited the enthusiasm of Barrès,[28] and *L'Adieu à l'adolescence* (1911). Two other volumes of poetry were to be added some years later: *Orages* (1925) and *Le Sang d'Atys* (1940), but Mauriac's real success derives from his substantial contribution to the novel. His first two novels, *L'Enfant chargé de chaînes* (1913) and *La Robe Prétexte* (1914), are, naturally enough, drawn largely from personal sources, but, immature though they are, they are signposts to the world of sin and temptations of the flesh the later novels introduce the reader to.

After the war, in which Mauriac served as a medical orderly in Salonika, begins the series of novels his reputation is built on, notably *Préséances* (1920), which paints an unloving picture of Bordeaux's merchant circles; *Le Baiser au Lépreux* (1922), the first novel to win success with critics and public, the first, too, which is truly in the Mauriacian manner – the study of a frustrated

[28] 'Je voudrais le dire au public. Je suis profondément heureux que nous ayons un poète.' *Echo de Paris*, 21 March 1910.

woman, Noémi Pélueyre, murderess of her crippled husband, in spirit if not in fact; *Génitrix* (1923), a drama of maternal jealousy, destroying the happiness of son and daughter-in-law; *Le Désert de l'Amour* (1925) where father and son compete for the love of the same woman; *Thérèse Desqueyroux* (1927), the heroine of which, the would-be poisoner of her husband, Bernard, is of all Mauriac's sombre characters the darkest; *Le Noeud de Vipères* (1932), a tale of conflict between an old miser and his family; *Le Mystère Frontenac* (1933), which is in part an autobiography in fictional form and where a ray of pale sunshine sheds some light on the encircling gloom of the other novels; *La Fin de la Nuit* (1935) where Thérèse Desqueyroux re-appears.[29] These novels do not exhaust the list but provide a clear indication of Mauriac's world, and its tonality, also reflected in *Asmodée* (1938), a successful *coup d'essai* for the stage, which encouraged Mauriac to write three further plays: *Le Mal Aimé* (1945), *Passage du Malin* (1948), *Le Feu sur la terre* (1951).

Amongst Mauriac's autobiographical writings, some (e.g. *Commencements d'une vie*, 1932, and *Mémoires Intérieurs*, 1959) help us to understand the influence his background and upbringing had upon his work, others (e.g. *Bloc-Notes*, 1958 and 1961, and *Journal*, Vols. I–IV, 1934, 1937, 1940, 1950) show us Mauriac's evolution towards active journalism, the strengthening in him of the moralist and political commentator he has, in his later day, successfully become.

There remain a number of biographical and critical works, e.g. *La Rencontre avec Pascal* (1926), *La Vie de Jean Racine* (1928), *Dieu et Mammon* (1929), and *Souffrances et Bonheur du Chrétien* (1930); in the spiritual experiences of the two great seventeenth-century writers he saw reflected something of his own, whilst the two essays are inspired by the same theme. In a newspaper article,[30] Mauriac refers to 'le monde étroit et janséniste de mon enfance pieuse, angoissée et repliée et la province où elle baignait.' Here are the two constants that run through his work. His father, a free thinker, had died in François' infancy, leaving him to be brought up by his mother and grandmother in an atmosphere of exalted Catholic piety. We are reminded of Gide, and like Gide who was soon in revolt against the Protestant puritanism that had moulded him, so Mauriac revolted against his equally puritanical but Catholic background. The parallel with Gide soon ceases, however, for Gide's revolt takes the form of an ever-shifting quest in search of his own nature's core and a perpetual invitation to youth to be 'sincere' to itself: a peculiarly Protestant individualist revolt

---

[29] Also in *Plongées* (1938), short stories.
[30] 'Vue sur mes romans', *Figaro Littéraire*, 15 November 1952.

driving him away from the religion that had nurtured him. Mauriac's revolt takes a different form.

In the earlier group of novels, from *Le Baiser au Lépreux* to and including *Thérèse Desqueyroux*, Mauriac's vision is darkened by an exclusive preoccupation with sin from which there is no escape, his characters are devoid of charity. Mauriac is in conflict with himself: the old Adam, drawn towards the temptations of the flesh and the rewards of this world, at grips with the moralist unable to escape from his Jansenist upbringing, yet revolting against it and deriving some psychological compensation by depicting the society he had known as composed of pharisaical *bien-pensants*, sunk in material interests.

In the late 'twenties, a more balanced Christian view began to prevail in his work and with it the strengthening of Christian hope; his *Vie de Racine*, the essays *Dieu et Mammon* and *Souffrances et Bonheur du Chrétien* reflect the change; thereafter he was prepared to soften his attitude towards human beings (e.g. *Le Mystère Frontenac*) and though sin in one form or another remains the central theme (e.g. *Le Noeud de Vipères*, *La Fin de la Nuit*), a faint hope is left with the reader that Louis, the old miser of the former novel, finds faith and human affection before he dies, and Thérèse Desqueyroux of the latter may find forgiveness and spiritual peace. But Christian though Mauriac may be as an artist, his main preoccupation is to write novels that make a powerful impact. With his intimate knowledge of Bordeaux and its surroundings, a country of vineyards, pines and sand, he has wisely chosen to place his characters against that background, and the background is excellent, but Mauriac cannot be classed as a regionalist writer for he aims to portray characters as fatally charged with passions as those of a Racinian tragedy. Whether he succeeds in communicating to the reader the same sense of crisis and urgency is debatable; the characters are too limited in their psychology, they seem to be rather the product of a preconceived plan than of careful observation. This criticism is particularly applicable to a novel like *Le Mystère Frontenac* where for once Mauriac comes down from the stark heights of sin and aims to portray normal human relationships in a family circle, but the characters move along their pre-ordained course, they are poorly observed, stereotyped and not alive.

Power, dedication, on the other hand, these and similar words come to mind when we read Georges Bernanos (1888–1948). His work falls broadly into two groups: the novels, the political writings. The former are *Sous le Soleil de Satan* (1926), *L'Imposture* (1927), *La Joie* (1929), *Un Crime* (1935) – a detective tale, of which *Un Mauvais Rêve* (1935, published posth.) is another version, without the detective element, *Journal d'un curé de campagne* (1936), *Nouvelle Histoire de Mouchette* (1937), *Monsieur Ouine* (1943); to this list must be added a group of short stories: *Dialogues d'Ombres* (1928), and the dramatic dialogue, finished just before his death – *Dialogues des Carmélites* (1948).

The second group includes the polemical newspaper articles written when he was a journalist before 1914 and the book-size pamphlets of later years: e.g. *La Grande Peur des Bien-pensants* (1931), *Les Grands Cimetières sous la lune* (1938), *Les Enfants humiliés* (1940, published posth.), *Lettres aux Anglais* (1942), *La France contre les robots* (1944).

When he was writing these, he had established his reputation as a novelist; he had in consequence numerous audiences ready to listen to his views on politics. But with the passing into history of the urgent or tragic events that provoked them, these pamphlets have lost their emotional impact. The historian interested in Edouard Drumont, that violent anti-semitic journalist, admired by Bernanos and unenviably prominent in the early days of the Dreyfus Affair, is unlikely to find much of value in *La Grande Peur*, nor the historian of the Spanish Civil War in *Les Grands Cimetières sous la lune*; the hindsight provided for us by time may not compel our agreement with the prophet Bernanos becomes in *Les Enfants humiliés* or *La France contre les robots*, nor will the reader in search of a coherent political system on which to pin his faith find much reward. Bernanos was at the outset a passionate monarchist, with a nostalgic vision, arising from a flimsy historical notion about Saint Louis and his reign, of paternalist, 'popular',[31] Christian monarchy where the extremes of Right and Left might meet to the exclusion of a bourgeois-ridden democracy. And a passionate monarchist he may at heart have remained, but, in the interval, his own contradictions – the extravagant praise and later violent denunciation of Maurras, his admiration of Drumont and his denunciation of Franco, whom Drumont would probably have approved of, his hatred of the modern world, where in some respects at least conditions for the humble and disinherited are better than under the *ancien régime* – all this leaves the reader with the conviction that the pamphlets remain more revealing as documents on their author than anything else, revealing his passionate admiration for men and causes that reflected his ideals: Edouard Drumont, Charles Maurras and *L'Action Française* – until he broke with both, the British at war, the French Resistance; revealing too his equally passionate denunciation of what he regarded as some manifestation of sin – the smug prudential 'do-good-ism' of the

[31] In the continental political sense.

'bien-pensants', for example, a lie in the soul if ever there was one. 'Le mensonge' is a key-word to the Bernanosian world.

Passion, dedication, a massive weight of words, poured forth in a lyrical torrent; something of the power of Léon Bloy without the vituperation, such is the impression of the pamphlets, and such is the impression of the novels, where, in the world conjured up by his powerful imagination, Bernanos shows us human happiness poised between the poles of righteousness and sin; Bernanos's vision is coloured by Christian beliefs which were his as a boy and which his experience as a soldier in the war of 1914 gave added power and definition to.

Some of the early short stories (notably 'La Muette', 'Madame Dargent', 'Une Nuit'[32]) are a good introduction into the stark, uncompromising world that was presently to unfold in the novels. The economy imposed by the short story reinforces the impact of the violence always present in Bernanos, but which in the novels is no more than an incidental extension into the hard material world of the searing spiritual experiences his characters live through.

The immediate success of his first novel (*Sous le Soleil de Satan*) persuaded Bernanos to exchange insurance agency for writing; a gamble on the material plane the decision was, and perhaps a greater slavery ensued, pen, paper and ink being the most indispensable items in his baggage, as this nomad moved from France to Majorca, from Majorca to Paraguay, thence to Brazil, where he spent the years of the Second World War, back to France and on to Tunis. But behind the decision lay the spiritual compulsion of a vocation; an early idea of the priesthood had been quickly abandoned; here at last was the revelation of his true vocation, his way, that is, of testifying to the truth, as he saw it, about human life in its relationship with God. Thus, for Bernanos literature may have meant material slavery but it was also a spiritual revelation, fulfilment, an ultimate joy such as some of his characters achieve through suffering. Here surely lies the secret of the spiritual intensity that informs Bernanos's novels; the issue is the soul's salvation, than which for Bernanos no more urgent problem faces us.

That Bernanos should in these circumstances have been led most often to choose priests as his main characters, portraits inspired perhaps by priests he had known as a boy in his native Artois, seems natural; apart from the saints they, more than most men, must be peculiarly sensitive to the spiritual gamble life sets us, they whose initial choice in life is a kind of gamble on the presence of God – 'l'effrayante présence du divin à chaque instant de notre pauvre vie',[33] on the power of his grace to preserve their souls

[32] *Dialogues d'Ombres.*   [33] *Journal d'un curé de campagne.*

against the powers of darkness, and implies an unceasing battle against those powers for the souls of others. Two other reasons may have contributed to the choice; first the immense value Bernanos attaches to spiritual innocence like that of children, for whom Bernanos incidentally had great reverence, an innocence that must possess the priest at the outset, that in the armour of his faith and in virtue of his training, both intellectual and moral, he of all men is likely to preserve. The second reason is connected with Bernanos's choice as a novelist; man's spiritual salvation being his theme, the priest, as a front line soldier in this battle, is both a natural and a valuable choice.

The quality of spiritual innocence distinguishes the central characters of the novels, young priests for the most part: the Abbé Donissan (*Sous le Soleil de Satan*), the Vicar of Ambricourt (*Journal d'un curé de campagne*), the Vicar of Fenouille (*M. Ouine*), but not always: the Abbé Chevance (*L'Imposture*), Chantal de Clergerie (*La Joie*), Soeur Blanche de L'Agonie du Christ (*Dialogues des Carmélites*).

'Notre ami appartenait à cette espèce d'innocents dont nous viennent abondamment tous les maux' – thus Monsieur Ouine to the Vicar of Fenouille, about his predecessor. M. Ouine, like all the worldly-wise, moves on a different plane, and judging from his level, he is right; amongst those who live on lower moral planes, the spiritually innocent may cause discomfort, confusion, havoc, from which they themselves are the first to suffer; their simplicity exposes them in worldly terms to suffering and humiliation, they are the butt of ridicule, victims of petty persecution, misinterpretation of motive, unjust censure from superiors, isolation, death (e.g. Chantal, murdered by M. Fiodor); they are not 'Establishment' men. Yet, only those who, like the Abbé Donissan, the Vicar of Ambricourt and the Abbé Chevance, have these spiritual gifts are really capable of stirring men to the depths; they alone can penetrate to the secret recesses of the soul (e.g. the Abbé Donissan's impact on Germaine Malorty; that of the Vicar of Ambricourt on both Mademoiselle Chantal and the Countess; Chevance's discovery of the abbé Cénabre's secret apostasy in *L'Imposture*); they alone can become sanctuaries of light, in a word – saints (e.g. Donissan – 'le Saint de Lumbres').

As a foil to these, the salt of the earth, Bernanos has a number of priests, older men, who have learned something of the ways of this world; e.g. the Vicar of Torcy, that splendid fighter, the Canon of La Motte-Beuvron (*Journal d'un curé de campagne*), and the Abbé Menou-Segrais (*Sous le Soleil de Satan*). They endeavour vainly to counsel their younger colleagues, but they recognize the latter's rare spiritual qualities: 'Que voulez-vous, mon enfant, ces gens ne haïssent pas votre simplicité, ils s'en défendent, elle est comme une espèce de feu qui les brûle' – thus the Canon of La Motte-Beuvron to the Vicar of Ambricourt.

Finally Bernanos has a gallery of characters, who are spiritually null and void (the apostate Cénabre,[34] M. Ouine[35]). Many of them are doctors and men of letters: Delbende (*Journal*), La Pérouse (*La Joie*), Lipotte (*Un Mauvais Rêve*), M. de Clergerie (*La Joie*), Ganse (*Un Mauvais Rêve*), Antoine Saint Martin[36] (*Sous le Soleil*). They are not bad men, indeed Delbende is in his way a lay saint, but at best their lives lie between the poles of mere goodness and badness, they are mere humanists with no hope, no light, no charity in the strict sense. Even out-and-out sinners like Mouchette (*Sous le Soleil, Nouvelle Histoire de Mouchette*) are more worthwhile because in the last resort they recognize saintliness when they see it and by inference at least their own position in the divine scheme; they are therefore not beyond hope of forgiveness. Evidently Bernanos will have none of the idea that, by repentance and good works alone, happiness in this world or the next may be purchased, as Balzac would have us believe.[37]

The Vicar of Ambricourt, in his pastoral action, calls forth deeper spiritual responses from the local chatelaine than the abbé Bonnet from Madame Graslin;[38] we cannot feel sure that for all her good works and public penance Madame Graslin dies comforted, whereas at the end of a scene of Dostoievskian power, whence the humble Vicar of Ambricourt emerges exhausted, he knows (and we do), from the Countess's own admission, that he has conquered her secret sorrow and her arid sense of divine injustice, by giving her a new understanding of life: 'il n'y a pas un royaume des vivants et un royaume des morts, il n'y a que le royaume de Dieu, vivants ou morts, et nous sommes dedans'; where was hatred, she finds charity, where revolt, resignation, where despair, hope; Grace comes, and with it peace. She has discovered man's true relationship with God, his complete spiritual dependence on God's grace for preservation of the soul's innocence, for ultimate forgiveness and salvation. The final humiliation and suffering reserved for the Vicar of Ambricourt is to die, absolved only by an unfrocked priest because a brother priest cannot get to him in time, but he does not lose hope: 'Qu'est-ce que cela fait', he murmurs to his friend, 'tout est grâce.'

Bernanos's preoccupations being what they are, the chances of his characters' salvation are what concern him; the material frame-

[34] ? L'Abbé Bremond, see below, p. 269. But if so, with what justification?
[35] Originally modelled on André Gide.
[36] A portrait full of irony; surely of Anatole France.
[37] cf. *Curé de Village.*
[38] Op. cit.

work of their lives, as often as not a village in the Flanders he had
known as a boy, is subsidiary, nor is he concerned with the linear
development of a story – some of the novels seem roughly thrown
together, e.g. *Monsieur Ouine*. The vital matter is to communicate
attitudes of mind, the intellectual or moral atmosphere that sur-
round the characters at crucial moments in their lives; then the
power in Bernanos develops its full potential.

In calmer waters but of compelling analytical quality is the
spiritual journey described by Joseph Malègue (1876–1940) in
Augustin ou le maître est là (1934), a story, banal enough, of a
young Catholic intellectual who loses and regains his faith, as he
dies of tuberculosis. The Auvergne background of *Augustin* recurs
in the uncompleted mass of Malègue's second novel *Pierres noires
ou les classes moyennes du salut* (posth. 1958) which even in its unfinished state has great social interest (especially Book I, 'Les
Hommes couleur du temps') and provides in the character of
Félicien the study of an unquenchable thirst for a revelation of
God which was to lead him to become a missionary and a martyr
(Book III fragments).

Marcel Jouhandeau (b. 1888), whose style recalls the technique
of a dry-point engraving, pursues his relentless way,[39] now evoking
the small town tragi-comedy of Chaminadour, 'la bienheureuse' –
his native Guéret (*Chaminadour*, 1934, *L'Oncle Henri*, 1943), dis-
secting the mean little souls of its inhabitants, now analyzing the
conjugal infelicity of one of its citizens, Monsieur Godeau (*Monsieur Godeau intime*, 1926, *Monsieur Godeau marié*, 1927, *Chroniques Maritales*, 1938, *La Faute plutôt que le Scandale*, 1949,
L'Imposteur, 1950), now noting his own reflections (*Journaliers*,
Vols. I–VI, 1960–4). The moralist of these latter volumes
is a lucid egotist who, in the host of events that make up the daily
round, in the talk and attitudes of those around him, finds an inexhaustible subject of commentary, of deeper self-knowledge, his aim
above all – 'en dehors de Dieu et de soi, tout n'est qu'illusion ou
mensonge'.[40]

In contrast to the bitter, inward-looking attitudes of the moralist
Jouhandeau, may be cited that of Maxence van der Meersch
(1907–51), consumed[41] with zeal for the relief of human misery.
His novels, for the most part placed in the industrial north of
France,[42] suggest in tonality the paintings of Vlaminck, in treatment the work of Zola. Like Zola, he develops from vigorous melodrama in *La Maison dans la dune* (1932) to social themes: a textile
strike (*Quand les sirènes se taisent*, 1933), a child dragged up in

---

[39] Some 100 volumes to date – see P. H. Simon, article in *Le Monde*,
27 January 1965.　　　　　　　　　　[40] *Journaliers 1960*, p. 145.
[41] The word has its full sense, he died of consumption.
[42] He was born at Roubaix.

poverty and degradation (*Le Péché du Monde*, 1934), a documentary on life under German occupation (*Invasion '14*, 1935), an indictment of the inhumanity in medical care as a result of mass methods in public health institutions (*Corps et Ames*, 1943).

But though these novels appear to owe much to Naturalism in treatment, the spirit is not the same; in place of determinism, charity to individuals, pity for their suffering, the intention to arouse these emotions in the reader as the best hope of remedying the evils portrayed in works which in some cases are more documentary than fictional (e.g. as in the three novels cited above) – in short a Christian social spirit, without formal adherence to a Church. That van der Meersch was not only a social reformer but also a novelist in the true sense is shown by *L'Empreinte du Dieu* (1936) which won the prix Goncourt.[43]

Social reformer, too, something of a Péguyste, but without the latter's 'leftism', stands Daniel-Rops (1901–65). As essayist and journalist (e.g. *Notre Inquiétude*, 1928, *Le Monde sans Ame*, 1931) Daniel-Rops writes as a moralist, analyzing the evils of his generation, both on the individual and the political planes, condemning its egotism and materialistic attitudes that choke all feelings of humanity towards the disinherited, both as souls and bodies.

His search for some steadfast beacon (e.g. *L'Ame obscure*, 1929) led him to the Christian faith and Catholicism, revealed for the first time in his novel *Mort, où est ta Victoire?* (1934). Thereafter, without abandoning fiction (e.g. *L'Epée de Feu*, 1939), Daniel-Rops was mainly engaged in building his monumental *Histoire de l'Eglise du Christ* (six volumes, 1945–65). A collection of early short stories, *Contes Pour le Cristal* (posth. 1966) reveal Daniel-Rops's interest in the area of disquieting human experience that lies on the frontier between the normal and the mysterious, and where the events related hover between rational explanation and the supernatural.

Julien Green (b. 1900) is a novelist of skill and power. With him we move from the Christian plane of righteousness and sin to the plane of good and evil; his characters are the prey of the evil within them, violence and crime its consequence.

Of Scots and Irish descent, born in France, of American parents in whom the Secessionist spirit of the South still burned, Julien Green enjoys the rare distinction of having published important works in both English and French, critical essays in the former,[44] in the latter, seven volumes to date of his *Journal*, covering the years 1928–58, autobiographical works – *Partir avant le jour* (1963) and *Terre Lointaine* (1966), an important series of novels and a

---

[43] See F. A. Hedgcock, *Modn Langs.*, xxxiv, No. 3.
[44] e.g. on the Brontës, Blake.

number of plays. Like Gide, Green's *Journal* is a valuable and absorbing commentary on his work, on the evolution of his ideas, on everything that comes within the scope of his experience, on the surface and intellectual planes of his being; we meet there the mature writer, giving only that part of himself that society has a right to know of. He compares his diary to a room: 'réservé aux bonnes pensées';[45] the deeper springs of his being he tells us are to be found in his novels: 'Il n'y a que ce que je passe sous silence qui s'exprime dans mes romans', and indeed the gap seems wide between the cultivated, brilliant commentator of the *Journal* and the creator of those tortured beings in the novels whom the artist seems to have endowed with his secret compulsions. In *Partir avant le jour*,[46] Green has set out to bridge the gap.

There, we have a picture of his childhood and adolescence, under the wing of an adoring mother and five elder sisters. Another Lamartine? Perhaps, but a very twentieth-century Lamartine, over whose cradle brooded not only maternal devotion but the spirit of Freud, of Proust, and who came to maturity in the days of Surrealism. As though puzzled at the dark spirit of evil that demanded expression from the artist, Green, in the manner of Proust, sets out in quest of the child Julian. This is not a sheaf of memories so much as a dive into the psyche with the determination that whatever the murky depths yield up shall be exposed to the light. 'Je me propose de regarder là où je n'ai jamais tourné les yeux que par hasard, je veux tâcher de voir dans cette partie de la conscience qui demeure si souvent obscure à mesure que nous nous éloignons de notre enfance ...'.[47] Pitilessly and with scrupulous sincerity Green examines the child he had been, his sexual obsessions, his imaginative taste for violent crime and the horrific in the manner of Poe, his religious fervours.

Terre Lointaine recalls Green's student years in the homeland of his parents' families, the 'Deep South', where time seemed to have stood still, the nineteenth century to have lived on into the 'twenties of the twentieth. Beneath the nostalgic and beautiful evocation of this peaceful corner of an aristocratic and puritan world, runs the theme of the author's own development, his growing recognition of the inner tensions set up by his homosexual leanings, alongside the ardours of his recent conversion to Roman Catholicism.

Evidently the novels derive from these substrata of his being – *Mont Cinère* (1926), *Adrienne Mesurat* (1927), *Léviathan* (1929), more especially *Moïra* (1950), and the play *Sud*. The tragedies of

---

[45] Cited by P. H. Simon, *Le Monde*, 17 April 1963.
[46] The title is presumably taken from Florian's short poem 'Le Voyage'? See Vol. IV, p. 21 n. 6.
[47] *Partir avant le jour*, pp. 97-8, Grasset: Cahiers verts 64, 1963.

Joseph Day (*Moïra*) and of Lieutenant Ian Wiczewski (*Sud*) seem rooted in the experience of the young student portrayed in *Terre Lointaine*. For those that enjoy traumatic experiences, these, Green's first three novels, are recommended. As we watch Emily Fletcher (*Mont Cinère*) caught in the crossfire of mutual hatred that divides her mother and grandmother, consumed by her own hatred of the man she marries to spite her own mother, Frank Stevens,[48] or Adrienne Mesurat in her slow but sure descent, after murdering her father, from isolation to suspiciousness, from suspiciousness to terror, from terror to madness; or the complex and fatal relationships that ensnare the unhappy Guéret (*Léviathan*) and drive him to his crime, we are drawn irresistibly into a claustrophobic atmosphere, by the author's skill in combining cogent analysis of his characters' states of mind with descriptions of scene that are both exact in detail and richly evocative. Characters and scenes are vigorously impressed on our imagination and we accept without question whatever the author's story demands.

Adrienne Mesurat, Guéret, Madame Grosgeorge[49] are characters whose secret desires burn with all the more intensity because repressed: 'Si froide et si grave qu'elle (Madame Grosgeorge) parût aux yeux inattentifs du monde, elle n'était qu'inquiétude et cachait un coeur rebelle sous les apparences d'une vie bien réglée.'[50] Their repressions build up unbearable pressures that must find a channel of escape; hallucinatory states ensue in which the characters seem to live on two levels, lucid consciousness, and a lower level whence erupts a sudden compulsive act of violence: 'Quelque chose en lui (Guéret) était demeuré éveillé, alors que tout le reste de son être était plongé dans une sorte de rêverie effroyable où des actes s'accomplissaient qu'il n'avait pas crus possibles, des actes de meurtre et désir.'[51] Green's stories have been criticized as sometimes unconvincing;[52] unusual certainly by their dramatic intensity, abnormal often; at moments of high tension, too, the surroundings seem to recede, leaving the characters imprisoned in the hideous loneliness of their own minds, acting mechanically as in a dream; the word somnambulism often recurs as a term of comparison under Green's pen.

As the novels succeed each other, Green's interest seems to focus more insistently on these hallucinatory states, where the subconscious mechanisms take control (e.g. *Le Visionnaire*, 1934, *Moïra*). Perhaps in the subconscious, which the Surrealists had been exploring, is the truth not only about our natures, but also the

---

[48] Reminiscent of the sinister Heathcliff (*Wuthering Heights*). One understands Green's interest in the Brontës.

[49] *Léviathan*. [50] *Ibid.*, Part II, 2. [51] *Ibid.*, Part I, 13.

[52] e.g. Clouard, *Hist. de la Litt. frse.*, Vol. II, p. 358.

unexplored potential of awareness that would enable us to seize the mystery that lies beyond, the mystery of death?[53]

Varouna (1940), perhaps the least successful of Green's novels, endeavours to clothe in fictional form, the idea, derived from Indian mythology (hence the title of the work), of a brooding fate that watches over men, and ensures that the results of their actions are carried on and fully worked out in successive generations, individuals being but links in the unending chain of human destinies. Here, as before, emerges the idea of mysterious forces controlling men, but, from the sub-conscious, they are raised to a cosmic level.

The writers mentioned in the foregoing pages, the story-tellers and escapists, the psychologists and social novelists, the moralists who see man's nature and his actions within some broader context, the denunciators, none are positive moralists providing some code of behaviour. To find one we must go to a veritable school of energy and heroism – Montherlant, Drieu La Rochelle, Saint-Exupéry, Jean Prévost.

From the outset Montherlant (b. 1896) revealed himself as one of the leading writers of the inter-war period, whether in works that are on the borderline between fiction and autobiography: *La Relève du matin* (1920), *Le Songe* (1922), *Les Bestiaires* (1926); or in articles honouring the fallen: *Chant funèbre pour les Morts de Verdun* (1924); or in his novels: *Les Célibataires* (1934), *Les Jeunes Filles*[54] (1936-9), *Le Chaos et la Nuit* (1963); or in his plays: *La Reine Morte* (1942), *Le Maître de Santiago* (1947), *Malatesta* (1948), *La Ville dont le prince est un enfant* (1951), *Port-Royal* (1954), *Le Cardinal d'Espagne* (1960), *La Guerre Civile* (1965); or in his essays and reflections: *Le Paradis à l'Ombre des Epées* (1924), *Les Onze devant la porte dorée*[55] (1924), *Aux Fontaines du désir* (1927), *La Petite Infante de Castille* (1929), *Service Inutile* (1935), *L'Equinoxe de Septembre* (1938), *Le Solstice de Juin* (1941), *Un Voyageur solitaire est un Diable* (1961).[56] Whatever form Montherlant uses to express his forceful personality, the image he creates is that of an austere moralist, bearing, much as a saint his stigmata, the marks of aristocratic tradition, Catholicism, and war.

The determination to be master of every situation whether on the battlefield (e.g. *Le Songe*) or in the bull-ring (e.g. *Les*

---

[53] e.g. *Le Visionnaire*, Part II, *Le Récit de Manuel*.

[54] Four volumes: I, *Les Jeunes Filles*; II, *Pitié pour les Femmes*; III, *Le Démon du bien*; IV, *Les Lépreuses*.

[55] Published with *Le Paradis à l'ombre des Epées* as *Les Olympiques* I and II, 1938.

[56] Collection of essays written between 1925-9 and intended to form, with *Aux Fontaines du désir* and *La Petite Infante*, a trilogy entitled *Voyageurs Traqués*.

Bestiaires), the testing nature of all adventure whatsoever, aloofness from the vulgar, the demand for quality in all things, the refusal to be blinded by illusions, fastidiousness, all these forms of exalted individualism combine to form Montherlant's aristocratic attitudes, which also have their defects – striving after effect, harsh egotism, inhumanity, lack of charity. There is much in all this to remind us of the young Barrès or Nietzsche. 'Je suis peu accessible à la pitié et voudrais ne l'être point du tout' – if La Rochefoucauld had not written those words,[57] Montherlant could have done.

Of the Catholicism he had imbibed by family tradition and at the College of Sainte-Croix, he retained especially what fitted his 'inner aristocratic necessities', as Barrès might have said, the idea of discipline attached to the name of Rome, rejecting the inner core of faith, subordinating all that comes from the heart as weak and unvirile – shades of Nietzsche! The essay entitled 'Tibre et Oronte'[58] is crucial to an understanding of Montherlant's attitude, as he emerged from the war holding fast to the experience of war as a school of heroism, of moral fibre, of energy, and to sport, as its pale image, with its competitive disciplines of control, of self-expenditure to the limits of exhaustion and beyond; to the tradition of Rome of which he sees Catholicism only as a part, and to the image he has of Spain, epitome of all his values, realized peculiarly in the cult of bull-fighting: 'Rien n'est plus simple ... que ces grandes divisions, à la fois, superficielles et ... profondes, qui ont partagé ma vie: 1° la symphonie catholique formée par un collège religieux, les auteurs de Rome ancienne, l'Espagne et essentiellement, l'esprit taurin; 2° la guerre; 3° le sport – Chacun de ces ordres m'a versé, pièces mêlées, son trésor de félicité et de malheur.' In a manner recalling Barrès's elaborate allegory of the high and the lowlands,[59] Montherlant sees in the Tiber and the Orontes the symbols of the two types of philosophy that have flowed down the ages: 'Deux philosophies se disputent le monde, où elles ont tour à tour installé leur empire...'

'Tibre et Oronte' seems to sum up Montherlant's early moral attitudes which are fully reflected in *La Relève du matin*, *Le Songe*, and *Les Bestiaires*. Montherlant had gone from school to the trenches. In *La Relève*, as the title suggests, he is thinking particularly of the generations younger than he who, as a result of their elders' sacrifice, will not have their energies harnessed by war in the single national thrust to repel the invader; all the more reason, thinks the young soldier,[60] that they should be schooled to

---

[57] In *Portrait par lui-même*.
[58] *Le Paradis à l'Ombre des Epées*, chap. 1.
[59] *Jardin de Bérénice*.
[60] Particularly chapter entitled 'Dialogue avec Gérard'.

develop their full spiritual potential by the spirit of war and sport
– heroism, disciplined team spirit.

In *Le Songe*, Alban de Bricoule is Montherlant's *alter ego*, much
as Philippe, André Malterre, Del Rio are by turns the mouthpiece
of Barrès in his early years, but by temperament, education, and
experience of war, Alban de Bricoule is more virile than the
neuropaths of Barrès's young invention, trying to invigorate their
little egos with emotional or aesthetic nourishment (*Du Sang, de la
Volupté et de la Mort*). Self-reliance, born of discipline in war and
sport, is his supreme value and to this is allied the cult of bodily
beauty, symbolised in the athletic Dominique Soubrier; strictly
subordinated, as a natural necessity, the instincts of the flesh,
divorced from any emotional tie.

Though written later, *Les Bestiaires* is an earlier chapter in
Alban's life, taking the reader back to Montherlant's youth before
the 1914 war, when he discovered Spain and communed in spirit
with the *aficionados* in the *mystique* of bull-fighting, to which the
book bears passionate and exciting testimony, derived from the
direct experience of one who had himself faced bulls in the ring
as a matador and knew the cloak and sword play – that kind of
ritual *pas de deux* from which man usually and beast sometimes
emerges the victor. 'Ce n'était plus un combat, c'était une incantation religieuse qu'élevaient ces gestes purs ... Et celui qui les
dessinait, soulevé de terre comme les mystiques par un extraordinaire bonheur corporel et spirituel se sentait vivre une de ces
hautes minutes délivrées où nous apparaît quelque chose d'accompli
que nous tirons de nous mêmes et que nous baptisons Dieu.'[61]

Supreme delectation to which Montherlant's values all contribute: aloofness, nay isolation, in the face of danger, physical skill
and courage, endurance stretched to the full, spiritual domination
over brute force, beauty of colour, gesture, speed and control in
movement, and withal an element of tense horror that Baudelaire
might have recognized as his own.

But a change comes over the lyrical moralist of aristocratic
values. After exaltation comes flat disillusion; *Les Bestiaires* closes
a period. The earlier values are seen as so many empty husks,
Barrès as fraudulent. The cult of bodily beauty alone remains; the
vanity of human things, the nothingness that is their end dictate a
cult of pleasure; energy, stretched in pursuit of desires – echoes of
Stendhal's 'Chasse au bonheur'!

Aux Fontaines du désir, La Petite Infante de Castille, and *Un
Voyageur solitaire*, which is like the third panel restored after being
lost for thirty years to complete the triptych, evoking the anguished
traveller; Spain, Italy, North Africa witness the restless spirit

[61] Chap. 8.

hounded on by the search for a happiness that eludes him because not in his own heart.

This nihilistic pessimism is clearly discernible in Montherlant the novelist, creator of *Les Célibataires* and *Les Jeunes Filles*. The ironic misanthropy of the former easily takes the form of 'Rochefoucauldian' aphorisms: 'tout commerce entre deux humains est un dangereux équilibre';[62] 'c'est une grande erreur que faire une confiance illimitée à la méchanceté des hommes: il est rare qu'ils nous fassent tout le mal qu'ils pourraient.'[63] The futile Monsieur de Coantré and the old bear, his uncle, M. de Coëtquidan, are truly Balzacian characters, admirably drawn; equally well drawn are the characters in *Les Jeunes Filles*: the brutal egotist Costals and his various feminine correspondents; skilful letter-writers all of them, and creating clear-cut images of themselves in the reader's mind by their letters. M. Dandillot, though a minor character, suggests an artist's small self-portrait painted into a corner of his crowded canvas as a memorial to himself. M. Dandillot, dedicated in his youth, we learn, to the cult of sport, now in his latter day and dying of cancer, believes his life's work to be vanity and is left with nothing to hold on to but the hope (not even the conviction!) that his strivings in themselves raised him above his own norms: 'Si ce que j'ai fait est vain, qu'il me reste au moins de m'être dépassé en le faisant.'[64]

By creating living characters, Montherlant shows himself to be a true novelist, yet, if the earlier Montherlant has habituated us to look for some positive moral in these novels, we shall be disappointed. The two old bachelors' stubborn refusal to move with the times has not a grain of dignity, the deliberate cynicism of Costal's relations with women seems gratuitous; none of these, the principal characters, draws our sympathy and in consequence we tend to relegate them all to the outer fringe of our experience and give them correspondingly little significance in our lives.

The ruins of his early philosophy left Montherlant in the uncomfortable position of a moralist without a moral. Montherlant the essayist of *Service Inutile*, a prey once more of his earlier lust for action, endeavours to build anew; if action there is to be, either it needs some conscious aim or its pointlessness itself requires a rationale. Even earlier[65] indications emerge, of how he will, if not surmount, at least attenuate his nihilism – an instinctive wish to keep some hold on what he claims to have thrown overboard, and why, if not because former beliefs and attitudes may be fitted into a pattern, as truths of no absolute but only of relative value, at

---

[62] *Les Célibataires*, p. 296.   [63] *Ibid.*, p. 307.
[64] *Jeunes Filles*, Vol. II, *Pitié pour les femmes*, p. 195.
[65] e.g. *Les Olympiques* (1924).

successive times. Thus does he achieve a new philosophy,[66] which gives him a fragile foundation for action and service. Useless in themselves these may be, but they are the result of some momentary natural impulse to be obeyed, and joy taken in the quality of the doing itself – M. Dandillot's words quoted above exactly reflect this attitude, which opens the way to the 'morale de la qualité' of *L'Equinoxe de Septembre*, a studied aristocratic refusal to accept anything as important, apart from the manner of its accomplishment; a loyalty, in short, to nothing outside one's own pride: 'Peu importe la cause, il s'agit de savoir si, sous sa bannière indifférente, on s'accomplira.' Aristocratic hedonism in short. Is this lofty attitude so very different from the earlier one, stripped of the youthful enthusiasm for the heroisms of war and sport? The emphasis on quality may have a negative value as an antidote against vulgarity, but equally it explains Montherlant's sour delectation in defeat – hope of a new era of greatness established on individual quality.[67]

In contrast to these masochistic contortions of Montherlant the moralist, the plays reveal a genuine vein of tragedy. The circumstances of the time, Montherlant's own *espagnolisme*, as Stendhal would have called it, and his *morale de la qualité* are all reflected in *La Reine Morte*; King Ferrante and the Infanta of Navarre are characters of Cornelian stamp, there is for Montherlant an unusual but sincere vein of tenderness in Doña Inès; all the characters are caught up in a convincing interplay of inward motive and outward events.

Exalted souls debating authentic problems in a vigorous style, their conflicts presented with a severe economy of means, such is the formula in *La Reine Morte* and succeeding plays, notably *Le Maître de Santiago*, *Port-Royal*, *Le Cardinal d'Espagne*. In his most recent play, *La Guerre Civile*, Motherlant's moral nihilism re-appears strongly; subject, scene, characters are skilfully chosen to that end: Civil War; the rivals' camps south of Dyrrachium; Pompey and his so-called friends, driven by jealousy (Pompey), self-interest (Acilius, Laetorius), by aristocratic disdain (Caton). In Cato, consoled by his superior perspicacity, drawn to Pompey's cause by his conviction, deliciously excited at the sight of the disintegration on every hand, of the futility of human things, we see the most faithful (and rather sententious) practitioner of *service inutile* ethics.

Montherlant's black pessimism and aristocratic attitudes so evident in *La Guerre Civile* had been strongly re-emphasized two years earlier in a novel *Le Chaos et la Nuit*. This study of a Spanish bourgeois intellectual, the anarchist Celestino Hernandez, who lives a proud solitary life in Paris as a refugee from the Civil

[66] cf. *Service Inutile*, 'Avant-propos', *passim*.　[67] cf. *Solstice de Juin*.

War and returns to Spain after twenty years, only to die mysteriously (?murder ?suicide), is like a triumphant 'sum', as well as a triumphant return to the novel form, of Montherlant's ideas: total despair, proudly, heroically accepted.

Pierre Drieu La Rochelle (1893–1945) and Montherlant are kindred souls. Rather inferior to Montherlant as a stylist, Drieu has one superiority: rather than contract out of life into disdainful individualism, the love of action he shared with Montherlant leads him to a restless search for some principle of moral regeneration through political ideas. Like many other writers Drieu's first works were two collections of poems: *Interrogation* (1917) and *Fond de Cantine* (1920). Thereafter his writing took the form now of autobiography proper: *Etat-Civil* (1921), *Le Jeune Européen* (1927), to which may be added the posthumous *Récit secret* (1961); now of political essays: *Mesure de la France* (1922), *Derniers Jours* (1927), *Genève ou Moscou* (1928) and articles in the wartime *Nouvelle Revue Française*, so alien in spirit to the original; now of personal confession, thinly disguised as fiction: *Plainte contre inconnu* (1924; short stories, notably *La Valise vide*), *L'Homme couvert de femmes* (1925), *Blèche* (1928), *Une Femme à sa fenêtre* (1930), *Feu Follet* (1931), *La Comédie de Charleroi* (1934), *Rêveuse Bourgeoisie* (1937), *Gilles* (1939), *L'Homme à Cheval* (1943). Five short stories: *Journal d'un délicat, la Duchesse de Friedland, L'Agent double, Le Souper de réveillon* and *Intermède romain*, were published posthumously under the title *Histoires Déplaisantes* (1963);[68] also posthumously (1966), an unfinished novel, *Mémoires de Dirk Raspe*.

For Drieu even more than for Montherlant, to get away from himself and create independent fictional characters is difficult, his feelings are too intense. 'Saurai-je un jour raconter autre chose que mon histoire' (*Etat-Civil*, N.R.F., p. 7). Thus, whatever the forms of his self-expression, and whether he is speaking in his own name or through a character – Gonzague (*Valise vide*), or Gilles (*L'Homme couvert de femmes, Gilles*) or Blaquans (*Blèche*) – his writings are in reality chapters in the development of his personality and thought.

'Né mélancolique et sauvage',[69] he writes of himself in *Récit Secret*, and *Etat-Civil* shows him from his adolescence a solitary in his generation, full of doubts about the future of France. The outbreak of war in 1914 was like a tonic to him, a tonic of violence, man, as he then thought, being born for war. The poems of *Inter-*

---

[68] All these stories except the last (unfinished) had appeared in diverse reviews. See F. Groin, *Drieu La Rochelle*, Bibliothèque idéale, *N.R.F.*, 1962.
[69] N.R.F., p. 14.

rogation, in the manner of Walt Whitman, whom he admired, outline a philosophy of action and, fore-shadowing Drieu's later attitudes, express admiration for German strength:

> A vous Allemands . . . je parle.
> Je vous ai combattus à mort . . .
> Mais vous êtes forts. Et je n'ai pu haïr en
> vous la Force, mère des choses . . .

But looking back on the war, Drieu recognized that science, financial and industrial power are the sinews of modern war – 'tuerie
anonyme, bureaucratique et sédentaire.'[70] Like Montherlant, he
turns to the cult of sport, where man can measure his strength
against man, and he adds to it an element of frank eroticism –
Fond de Cantine, La Valise vide, L'Homme couvert de femmes.
  At the same time, unlike Montherlant, he sets out on the quest
for a political principle that could be an inspiration for France
(*Mesure de la France*). The euphory of victory in no way blinds
him to the realities; France, bled white by her losses in men,
needs more children if in the future she is to keep her commanding
position, the reward of a victory her own unaided strength could
not have achieved: 'Son corps exsangue ne l'aurait pas soutenue si
la force de vingt nations n'avait accru ses membres énervés.' Could
the Russian Revolution be the example to follow? Drieu had
thought so but was quickly disillusioned. The revolution in art –
Surrealism – and the idea of faith left him equally dissatisfied: a
surfeit of eroticism reveals to Gonzague (*Valise vide*) and Gilles
(*L'Homme couvert de femmes*) its ultimate emptiness. Drieu's
spiritual odyssey in search of some principles of regeneration – cry-
ing need of the decadent West – is described in *Le Jeune Européen*; after turning his back finally on the idea of revolution
(*Genève ou Moscou*) he is led to seek salvation in a party of intellectuals of the Right, supermen with bodies like Grecian athletes
and minds moulded by Nietzsche. As the title *Le Jeune Européen*
indicates, Drieu is thinking not only in terms of France, but of
Europe, which between the giants Russia and the U.S.A. must
unite.
  Drieu's own lust for action wells up; he sees himself (*La Comédie de Charleroi*) as an agent at once of destruction – destruction of
the decadent liberal bourgeois values – and of reconstruction, regardless of national frontiers, by the virtues of physical strength
as a principle of unity in joy (*Gilles*). Fascism was the haven, and
when the war came, his welcome to the Germans, his campaign in
the wartime *Nouvelle Revue Française* in favour of Fascism as the
way to regeneration and the only hope for France, in a Europe
united under Hitler, were to be expected. The final apologia for

[70] *Etat-Civil*, N.R.F., p. 154.

his action is to be found in *Récit secret*: 'Je suis fier d'avoir été de ces intellectuels là.[71] Plus tard on se penchera curieusement sur faible s'amplifiera ... Oui, je suis un traître. Oui, j'ai été apporter nous pour entendre un autre son que le son commun. Et ce son l'intelligence française à l'ennemi – ce n'est pas ma faute si cet ennemi n'a pas été intelligent ... Nous avons joué, j'ai perdu – je réclame la mort.'

As the first essay in *Récit secret* shows, suicide had long been a familiar idea, indeed a temptation to him. To a whole complex of reasons, physical – dislike of old age – and metaphysical – death seen in Oriental fashion as a re-absorption into the eternal source of life, was now added the desire to escape the humiliation of being condemned by judges, blinded by passions and intellectually incapable of understanding the disinterested motives of his actions. After an unsuccessful attempt in April 1944, this courageous and ultimately pathetic figure, at once political prophet, eroticist and mystic, took his own life in March 1945.

In the few months preceding his suicide, however, when he had gone into hiding to elude arrest and certain execution, Drieu gave the fullest measure of his controlled courage and literary gifts; rising above his desperate circumstances, he wrote what bids fair to be his masterpiece, even though, with only four parts written out of the seven planned, it remains fragmentary. Inspired by the life of van Gogh, Drieu has drawn a hero, in whom, at the outset at least, we recognize the author. But gone are Drieu's old political preoccupations; between the service of men and the service to art, Dirk Raspe finally chooses the latter, and in his struggle to express his vision of the world by painting, finds nourishment for his unquiet soul.

In contrast to Montherlant's 'aesthetics of heroism', as they might be called, and the heroism of Drieu, that chooses action in politics and does not shrink from death when the dice fall wrong, the message of Antoine de Saint-Exupéry (1900–44) seems more human, more compassionate, without losing one jot of the heroism he was so shining an example of, from the days when, with his co-pilots,[72] he blazed the air trails over the North and West African deserts, the Southern Atlantic, the jungles and mountains of South America, to his war experience and the mission he did not come back from.

Saint-Exupéry's best writing (*Courrier-Sud*, 1928, *Vol de nuit*, 1931, *Terre des hommes*, 1939, *Pilote de guerre*, 1942) is not fiction

---

[71] i.e. the 'new Europeans' under Hitler. N.R.F., pp. 98 *et seq.*
[72] Notably Mermoz (1901–36; lost over the Southern Atlantic), and Guillaumet.

but life's experience, his own and that of his friends, simply, realistically, sometimes lyrically told, in a series of episodes, moving as
tales of human courage, human endurance driven to its extreme
limits ('ce que j'ai fait, je le jure, jamais aucune bête ne l'aurait
fait'[73]), human skills offering the opportunity of extending human
action with calculated risks, human responsibility and solidarity,
as meditated on from the height of the Southern skies.[74]

Where message is closely hinged to action, the result is good. But
Citadelle (posth. 1948) where Saint-Exupéry, who worked on it
from 1936–43), has chosen to clothe his message in the form of a
long apologue, an ancient oriental monarch handing out wisdom
to the young prince, his heir, is less effective. In *Le Petit Prince*
(posth. 1946) the moralist has turned, momentarily, from his more
serious purpose, and revealed a delicate side of his nature in a
tender fairy tale.

Whereas Saint-Exupéry's humanism is founded on the heart,
that of Jean Prévost (1901–44[75]) is rooted in the joy of physical
strength (*Plaisirs des Sports*, 1926, *Dix-huitième année*, 1930) and
intellectualism. He is more convincing as essayist and critic (e.g.
Les Epicuriens français, 1931, *La création chez Stendhal*, 1942),
than as novelist (e.g. *Les Frères Bouqinquant*, 1930).

Lunes en papier (1921), *Ecrit pour une idole à Trompe* (1921),
Royaume farfelu (1928), the very titles inspired by fantasy and
make-believe seem out of tune with the harsh tragic reality that is
the world of André Malraux (b. 1901). These works belong to the
time when, as a student in Sanskrit, Chinese and archaeology,
Malraux was also open to diverse literary influences – the literary
Cubism of Apollinaire and André Salmon, enjoying a passing
vogue, the spirit of adventure of MacOrlan, the whimsicality of
Max Jacob, German expressionism, older writers (Anatole France,
Barrès, Gide, even Laforgue, of whom he published an edition of
selected works). By 1928, Malraux was launched on a career,
packed tight with intense experience: archaeology and travel, revolution and war, literature and art, history, journalism and politics.

To this career, with its sense of Promethean revolt expressed in
heroic action, the three early works are like an overture where
themes that will appear later are delicately indicated: the tragic
absurdity of life, the weight of history bearing on man's destiny,
art as expression and custodian of the dignity of the human spirit.

Thereafter Malraux's novels are like chapters out of his adventurous life, closely integrated with his philosophy and action: *Les*

---

[73] *Terre des hommes*, chap. 2, Guillaumet's struggle and endurance in
the Andes.
[74] cf. *ibid.*, chap. 8, *passim*.   [75] Killed in the Resistance.

Conquérants (1928) and *La Voie Royale* (1928) – action in Indo-China; *La Condition Humaine* (1933) – action in China; *L'Espoir* (1937) – action in Spain; *Les Noyers de l'Altenburg* (1943–8) – fragments of action in France. Into these chapters of action the essays fit as projections, on to the plane of ethics, politics or art, of the philosophy that is the mainspring of his doing: *La Tentation de l'Occident* (1926), *Le Temps du mépris* (1935), *L'Adresse aux Intellectuels* (1948), and diverse writings on art, notably *Les Voix du Silence* (1951), *La Métamorphose des Dieux* (1957).

La Tentation de l'Occident expresses the pessimistic nihilism of which Garine is the mouthpiece in *Les Conquérants*. In the chaotic Indo-Chinese scene with its ruthless exploiters, commercial adventurers and an arbitrary colonial administration, Garine is driven by a 'will to power' – '... j'ai désiré la puissance ... Déterminer. Contraindre, la vie est là',[76] his purpose none but to stamp a pattern on the formless magma that life is, to give meaning to his own.

The young archaeologist of *La Voie Royale* with an eye to the commercial value of the ancient sculptures he believes lie hidden in the jungles of the interior, and Perken the older colonial adventurer who wants to leave his mark on the map – 'Je veux laisser une cicatrice sur cette carte'[77] – are cast much in the same mould as Garine; they are vigorous individualists despising their fellow men for their inert acceptance of the servitudes of life, for their non-existence, in a word.

As the novels succeed each other, the heart of the matter as Malraux sees it becomes abundantly clear; life has no meaning other than what man gives it; this he has always striven to do, first by setting up God in his own image and then by believing in man and the power of his reason to create an earthly Utopia. One after another these idols have crumbled; we are left face to face with the tragic truth: man's only escape from the absurdity of life is to forge his own destiny by affirming his will in some deliberately chosen option; imprisoned in his own solitude, man is the sum of his own actions; only by thus building his own existence and accepting all the calculated risks, including death, can his spirit prevail against the power of death, against the servitudes of his mortal human condition.

The message, already clear enough in *Les Conquérants* and *La Voie Royale*, runs like a deep furrow across the pages of *La Condition Humaine* and *L'Espoir*. Do the four novels then suffer

---

[76] *Les Conquérants*, Part iii, 'L'Homme'. Power! The theme is constant; other passages from the novel can be quoted.

[77] *Voie Royale*, Part I, chap. 4.

from a certain sameness? In a note on a critical study of his work,[78] Malraux writes: 'Le roman moderne est à mes yeux, un moyen d'expression privilégié du tragique de l'homme, non une élucidation de l'individu.' To deny the vast area of individual character and motive, as a field for the novelist's investigation, is evidently to make a big sacrifice and to run the risk of that sameness just mentioned.

But the starkly tragic situation of man as Malraux sees it, indeed reduces individual differences to trivial insignificance; only his attitude to that situation counts, whether and how he can 'take arms against a sea of troubles'. Thus the suspicion of sameness may be avoided only by the differences of the scene and situation against which the struggle between man and his destiny is fought out, and by the quality of perception the characters display in their assessment of their own heroic acts of 'liberation'. Of the four novels, *La Voie Royale* is probably the closest to the traditional novel structure; it has a clear linear development and can be read as an absorbing, at times gripping adventure story; the other three have a similarity of treatment: successive scenes, short, often thrilling dramas on their own, an impression of brilliant, vigorous reporting or of pages from the diary of a man of action, recording his experience, as it were, red hot; this is particularly true of *L'Espoir*, but whether we are witnessing scenes in the struggle for mastery in China between the Kuomintang and the Communists (*La Condition Humaine*) or scenes in the Spanish Civil War (*L'Espoir*), the purpose is not to record events, it is to show how men of courage use the tragic events they are involved in to give significance to their lives. All the characters are as a result not only heroic men of action, but also metaphysicians; in some, we may more easily recognize Malraux's own image – Claude Vannec (*Voie Royale*), Magnin (*L'Espoir*), the narrator of *Les Noyers*, but all the protagonists to a greater or lesser extent reflect his philosophy; those in *La Condition Humaine* are perhaps the most successfully individuated: Kyo and Katow the idealist revolutionaries who triumph over defeat by their heroic deaths; Tchen the nihilist seeking to assert his personality by dedication to the murder of the Revolution's enemies; Ferral the capitalist; the sage Gisors whose deliberate choice is opium, Clappique the pantaloon. A little underlying sameness perhaps, but there is no denying that by their tragic fervour, by the intensity and variety of experience, the novels make a powerful impact. Moreover, if the imperious call to heroism remains constant to men determined to exist in any worthwhile sense, a certain shift in moral values seems detectable between the individualistic heroism of a Claude Vannec in search of a fortune

---

[78] Gaëtan Picon, *Malraux par lui-même*, p. 67, note 25.

because, for example, 'Etre pauvre empêche de choisir ses enne-
mis',[79] and the dedication to a cause that inspires Kyo[80] or Katow,
Magnin, Manuel and Ximenes (L'Espoir), or the narrator of Les
Noyers. Doubtless the reason for the shift lies in Malraux's own
heroic revolt against destiny, which, from the early days of adventure in the jungles of Indo-China,[81] identified itself for many years
with mass movements of liberation[82] and, after the Communist
betrayal,[83] with patriotic loyalties against the traditional enemy[84]
and Gaullisme.

'J'ai vécu quarante ans dans l'art et pour l'art... Est-ce une
chose si difficile... que d'attendre la mort (qui ne viendra peut-
être pas!) en buvant tranquillement et en lisant des vers ad-
mirables...'.[85]

Here, in the character of the old art dealer Alvear, is another
projection of Malraux's rich personality, his passionate dedication
to art, itself rooted in man's endless search for truth. The sympo-
sium in Les Noyers de l'Altenburg and the paper contributed to it
by Möllberg the ethnologist[86] develop the same theme. Les Voix
du Silence, La Métamorphose des Dieux transpose it from fiction
to scholarship, but, with all the breadth of knowledge that these
works display, this is not art history so much as a passionate exploration of the visible forms men, known and unknown, have
striven to create as witness to the truth.

The domain of criticism between the wars is as full of distinguished names as it ever was.

The giants of academic criticism of an earlier generation –
Brunetière, Faguet, Lanson – have their younger contemporaries
and successors: medievalists such as Joseph Bédier (1864–1932) and
Gustave Cohen (1879–1958); a historian of ideas, Daniel Mornet
(1878–1954); scholars in foreign fields such as the Germanists
Andler (1866–1933) and Legouis (1861–1937); the Anglicist Caza-
mian (1877–1965); the historian of comparative literature Paul
Hazard (1878–1944); the historian of the French language Ferdin-

[79] Voie Royale, Part I, chap. 2.
[80] 'Il (Gisors) pensa à l'une des idées de Kyo: tout ce pour quoi les
hommes acceptent de se faire tuer, au-delà de l'interêt, tend plus ou moins
confusément à justifier cette condition en la fondant en dignité: christian-
isme pour l'esclavage, nation pour le citoyen, communisme pour l'ouvrier.'
(Condition Humaine, Part IV, 1949 edn., pp. 270–1.)
[81] Which brought him into conflict with the French authorities, for
carrying off some bas-reliefs from the temple of Banteaï-Sney (Le Monde,
11 April 1964).
[82] 'Young Annam League', Assistant Sec.-Gen. Kuomintang, Communist
Propaganda chief in Kwangsi and Kwantung; Commander Republican Air
Force in Spanish Civil War.
[83] Stalin-Hitler pact.   [84] Noyers de l'Altenburg.
[85] L'Espoir, Part II, Sec. 1, chap. 7.   [86] Les Noyers, Part II.

and Brunot (1878–1944). Outstanding amongst the historians of literature is Albert Thibaudet (1874–1936), author of a series of penetrating studies of individual authors,[87] crowned by a final synthesis of literary history.[88] Nor should we forget his analysis of criticism itself,[89] and, in a different field, of the ideas that are the constants, from generation to generation underlying French politics,[90] or of the French intellectual, dominant factor in the French political scene since the turn of the century till the 'twenties.[91] Thibaudet is one of the completest modern academic critics; for him the word generation is important; in political ideas and literary criticism the notion of a continuum with each generation of writers like successive waves on the surface of the sea.

Amongst the multitude of journalist critics and essayists mention may be made of men such as Paul Souday (1869–1929) – a power in the land of letters as critic of *Le Temps*, of André Billy (b. 1882), novelist, critic and chronicler of literary life (*L'Epoque 1900*), of Edmond Jaloux (1878–1949), novelist and critic, in *Les Nouvelles Littéraires*, a man of broad liberal temper, treading mainly in the footsteps of Sainte-Beuve, though more generous perhaps to young contemporaries, sharing Sainte-Beuve's tireless curiosity and liking for impressionistic criticism where the portrait of an author and the analysis of his work are united; 'tel arbre, tel fruit'.

Julien Benda (1867–1956), a doughty champion of rationalism and opponent of Bergsonism, never ceased to inveigh against writers and attitudes that offended his Cartesian passion for clarity or show any betrayal of the disinterested calling of the 'clerk', by some 'commitment' in what was later to be the Sartrian sense (e.g. *Belphégor*, 1918, *La Trahison des clercs*, 1927, *La France bizantine*, 1945). Paradoxically Benda was connected for a number of years with the *N.R.F.*, although the review was out of sympathy with his own attitudes: 'Et en effet, mon mode d'esprit mathématique, était à l'antipode de celui de la maison, tout épris de doute, de "disponibilité", d'inquiétude, fervent de pensée précieuse, de logique sibylline, d'ésotérisme verbal, méprisant de l'affirmé, du net, du rectiligne, et dont Gide et Alain, à des titres distincts, sont les incarnations.'[92]

But more prominent than any by the number and success of his

---

[87] e.g. *La Poésie de Mallarmé* (1913), *Flaubert* (1922), *Valéry* (1924), *Stendhal* (1931).
[88] *Histoire de la littérature française de 1789 à nos jours* (posth. 1936).
[89] *Physiologie de la critique* (1922).
[90] *Les Idées Politiques de la France* (1922).
[91] *La République des Professeurs* (1927).
[92] *Exercice d'un Enterré vif*, 1940–4, 1946.

writings is André Maurois[93] (b. 1885), no mean novelist but essentially an essayist. Ever since the days of *Colonel Bramble* (1918)
whose silences were as eloquent as the eloquence of his friend,
Docteur O'Grady (1922), André Maurois, on the pattern of these
two essays in national mentality, which have achieved by their
success – the first, at least – the level of fictional biography, has
made a speciality of biography, to be classed as 'vulgarization in
the best sense'. From *Ariel, ou la vie de Shelley* (1932) the list of
illustrious writers, statesmen, soldiers, whom he has recalled to
literary life is long: *Byron, Lélia, Olympio, Les Trois Dumas,
Proust, Disraëli, Lyautey, La Fayette, Edouard VII et son temps*,
and now a Promethean *Balzac* (1965), which is, he says, to be the
last.

All these are humanists, critics and essayists in that they study
their chosen subject without reference to any pre-established
framework of ideas, in contrast for example to the traditionalist,
Henri Massis (b. 1886).

Two of the best literary critics of the inter-war period are the
Catholics Charles Du Bos (1882–1939) and Jacques Rivière (1885–
1925).

Du Bos, English by his mother, was an amateur critic turned
professional by necessity, dedicated to the study of the arts and in
particular to literature, of which he had a wide knowledge, ranging
not only over French, but also over English, American, German
and Russian writers.

Pascal, Constant, Baudelaire, Claudel, Proust, Gide, Valéry were
amongst the French writers he particularly admired – all moderns,
be it noted, except Pascal – but his most fervent loyalties were
abroad: Goethe 'le plus beau de mes étrangers',[94] as he called him,
Novalis, Emerson, Shelley, Keats, Walter Pater, Browning, Ruskin,
Eliot, Chekov.

He strode across frontiers[95] in search of kindred souls, and soul
is the right word in speaking of Du Bos, who had little interest in
the background of an author or the period he lived in, only in
the man himself, a soul whose delicate labyrinths must be explored
through their works, a soul to be loved and understood as closely
as possible – *Approximations* (1923–37) is the significant title he
gives to the seven volumes of his literary studies, *inter alia*, on
Shakespeare, Shelley, Goethe, Stendhal, Amiel, Anna de Noailles,
Proust.

In addition to *Approximations* there are eight volumes of his
diary, covering the years 1908–33, and a few individual studies

---

[93] Emile Herzog.
[94] Cited by Max Rychner, article in *Preuves*, November 1955.
[95] See M. Rychner, op. cit.

such as *Grandeur et misère de Benjamin Constant* (posth. 1946), *Byron et le besoin de la fatalité* (1949). In spite of the weight of matter, Du Bos was not a facile writer: 'Cette hésitation intérieure, cette difficulté à écrire qui me paralyse', he notes in his diary. Du Bos seems to secrete his criticism, like an oyster with a pearl. His diary which he began keeping on Gide's encouragement gives the best clue to Du Bos's value and originality as a critic. It is essentially an exhaustive record of his own literary experience in the company of past authors by their books or contemporary authors by their books and their society.

'Toute pensée', he writes, 'qui est soit la sécrétion due à un acte vital, soit la réflexion contre un acte accompli...importe au maximum. Une morale expérimentale...tel est mon domaine propre.' Ideas as such interested him little; the given writer's individual approach to life, his way of experiencing and communicating it, was all-important, and the key to that was his impact upon the sensitive and sympathetic critical mechanism that Du Bos himself was.

Of less universal culture than Du Bos, Jacques Rivière is equally distinguished as a critic. In the service of the *N.R.F.* since 1910, he became its director in 1919, on his return from a prisoner-of-war camp. From before the war dates the exchange of letters between him and his brother-in-law Alain-Fournier;[96] besides giving an intimate picture of an agreeable family relationship, they throw light on *Le Grand Meaulnes* and more generally on the literary ideas prevalent in the two correspondents' circle. From before the First World War, too, date a collection of Rivière's critical studies –*Etudes* (1912).

But not till after the war did Rivière come into prominence. *L'Allemand, Souvenirs et Réflexions d'un Prisonnier de Guerre* (1918), an acute work, shows his particular critical strength, psychological analysis. Hence no doubt his early recognition of the significance of Freud in literature and the pertinence of his lectures on the affinities of Freud and Proust, the latter of whom he was amongst the first of French critics to assess at his true value. As a psychologist too he claims (*De Dostoïevski et de L'Insondable*, 1922) that many French novelists are not the psychologists they claim to be, but rationalists whose unconscious desire for unity and clarity blind them to the true depths of the mind.

Not the least of Rivière's titles to distinction is to have brought the *N.R.F.*[97] to its peak of prestige and influence, partly by his

[96] Four vols. 1905–14, N.R.F. (posth. 1927).
[97] 1908–43. During the remaining years of the Second World War the *N.R.F.*, under different control and management (Drieu La Rochelle), became collaborationist. Since the war, Arland and Jean Paulhan have 're-created' the original *N.R.F.* with its old character and distinction.

own critical contributions, partly by those of other critics, drawn from widely different points on the critical compass, whom he gathered round him, notably M. Arland (b. 1899), novelist and critic (*Une Epoque*, 1930); Benjamin Crémieux (1888–1944), a victim of Buchenwald, a great humanist, to be found at his best in *Inquiétude et Reconstruction* (1931), where he analyzes the contemporaneous literary scene; R. Fernandez (1894–1944), the philosophical critic of *Messages* (1927), who despite his love and knowledge of English literature became a war-time collaborationist.

The contribution of Catholics to the intellectual life of France between the wars is great and stems from the days of the religious revival, already noted, at the turn of the century.

In the medieval field, Etienne Gilson (b. 1884) is particularly prominent, as belonging to the group of Catholic intellectuals who, in the wake of that revival, renewed the study and influence of St Thomas Aquinas.

Most noteworthy amongst the neo-Thomists is the philosopher Jacques Maritain (b. 1882). Of liberal Protestant origin, Jacques Maritain, as a young man, knew Péguy who introduced him to the philosophy of Bergson (1902). He remained a fervent Bergsonian until 1906, when, after his scientific studies in Germany, he was converted to Roman Catholicism by Léon Bloy, together with his wife Raïssa Oumançoff, of Russian Jewish extraction.[98]

Maritain recognized later that Bergson had released in him the sense of the absolute, but after his conversion he came to reject the anti-intellectual aspects of Bergson's philosophy (*Philosophie bergsonienne*, 1913), his distinction between intuition and intelligence, and to restore reason to the position the Catholic Church had always ascribed to it, namely the indispensable auxiliary of faith. Thomist thought alone provided him with the philosophic principles that accorded with his faith, and just as St Thomas in his age worked to reconcile Aristotle with Christian theology, so Maritain in his philosophical works – *Introduction générale à la Philosophie*, 1922, *Reflexions sur l'intelligence et sur sa vie propre*, 1926, *Docteur angélique*, 1930, *Distinguer pour unir, ou les degrés du Savoir*, 1932, *De la philosophie Chrétienne*, 1933, *Science et sagesse*, 1935 – aimed to show that faith is compatible with the modern world, and to show the value of Thomist thought as a framework for life today, not only from a religious point of view but also politically.

Maritain's interest in politics was first aroused by Pope Pius XI's condemnation of *L'Action Française* (1926). 'Alors a commencé

[98] For her childhood at Marioupol, and French friends at the time of the conversion–Psichari, Péguy, Bergson, Léon Bloy, Georges Rouault and others, see *Les Grandes Amitiés* by Raïssa Maritain.

pour moi', he wrote, 'une période de réflexion dédiée à la philosophie morale et politique où j'ai tâché de dégager les traits d'une
politique chrétienne authentique.'

Primauté du Spirituel (1927) and *L'Humanisme intégral* (1936)
defend the idea of a Christian democracy. The Second World
War naturally increased his political interests (*A Travers le
désastre*, 1940), which were further stimulated by his being appointed French Ambassador to Rome immediately after the war.
Thence he returned to Princeton, where he had been during the
war.

Maritain's prolonged sojourn in the United States has cut him
off from the younger generations of Frenchmen, but between the
wars he was one of the guiding lights in French intellectual circles
who sought for springs more refreshing than those that flowed
from Marx or welled up from the 'libido' at the call of Freud.
Some of his works (e.g. *L'Humanisme intégral*) had an influence
extending beyond Catholic circles, and it was strengthened by
direct personal influence. The Maritains' house at Meudon was an
intellectual centre of international standing that attracted men of
widely different intellectual disciplines.

The Catholic polemist in Maritain was active, too, not only
against Bergson but against Descartes, Rousseau, Kant, Blondel
and others. His *Trois Réformateurs* (1925) is a good sample of his
verve in this field.

Nor should we omit to mention his critical interest in poetry,
under the influence no doubt of Raïssa Maritain who was a poetess
in her own right,[99] with an element of mysticism, reminiscent of
Simone Weil, and who was co-author with Maritain of *Situation
de la poésie* (1938).

The debate on the nature and art of poetry was active between
the wars; in the lists were Valéry, Claudel, Thibaudet and a
scholar of repute in the religious field, the Jesuit Abbé Henri
Bremond (1865–1933), editor of the review *Etudes*, and author of
the authoritative *Histoire du Sentiment religieux en France* (1916–
32). Interested as he was in the humanistic pietists and the mystics
of the seventeenth and eighteenth centuries, estranged from his own
order, perhaps because of his too indulgent attitude towards Pascal,
we find him in *La Poésie pure* (1925) and *Prière et Poésie* (1927)
defending the view against Valéry that the essence of poetry like
true religious experience is emotional.[100]

[99] Three short collections of poems: *La Vie donnée, Lettre de Nuit, Au
creux des Roches.*
[100] For the foregoing chapter, see P. H. Simon, *Hist. de la Litt. Française
contemp^e, passim.*

Chapter 12

EXISTENTIALISM AND ITS IMPACT ON DRAMA AND NOVEL

T HE terms essence and existence are inseparable, but all previous philosophies tended to explain the nature of living
beings in terms of an essence: 'The essence refers to the
nature of things, the humanness of man, the horseness of a horse'.[1]
The concept itself might change in the human context, with different philosophies; what was mind for Aristotle was soul for St
Thomas,[2] what was soul for the Christians became reason for the
eighteenth-century Rationalists and the later Humanists, and if in
the nineteenth century, under the impulse of their discoveries,
scientists claimed to have discarded abstract reasoning in favour
of objective data, the tendency at least remained, to see individual
phenomena within the framework of some general intellectual
concept, an absolute therefore, which if it did not claim to explain,
at least controlled them, gave them direction and unity: Progress,
Evolution, Heredity, Determinism.

The revolution wrought by Soeren Kierkegaard (1813–55), the
first Existentialist philosopher,[3] and creator of the word Existentialism, lies in his having shown that, underlying the variations of
terminology in previous philosophies, the terms essence – existence
remained and that to give the former priority as both enclosing
existence and at its core was in fact a rationalist process that ignored the fundamental nature of individual human experience.
Experience is an inseparable part of life, *is* existence in fact, and
thus the terms must be reversed, existence must take priority over
essence; only by moving from the subjective experience that existing gives, can men proceed to take hold of life, that glutinous
magma they are suspended in, shape their destiny, give meaning
to the absurdity.

'L'existence précède l'essence ... il faut partir de la subjectivité',
writes Sartre.[4] This implies freedom of choice, as an indispensable
element of the human condition, and freedom of choice creates in-

---

[1] P. Roubiczek, *Existentialism. For And Against* (1964), p. 11.
[2] R. Lacour-Gayet, *La France au XXe Siècle* (1954), p. 298.
[3] Though Pascal, if born in a different age, might have been.
[4] *L'Existentialisme est un humanisme.*

escapable individual responsibility, 'Le destin de l'homme est en lui-même'.[5] Thus far Existentialists are at one, but from this subjective starting-point Christian and atheist Existentialists, the two opposing groups, move in different directions. The former, being both Christian and Existentialist, are inevitably in the position of trying to escape from their initial subjective position in order to be united with God. This appears strongly in the example of Soeren Kierkegaard, from whom the Christian Existentialists derive. Kierkegaard had early concluded that faith and philosophy were irreconcilable, but in youth he hesitated between the two. The influence of Hamann (1730–88) and Jacobi (1743–1819), two German mystics, led him (1838), after two years of spiritual conflict, to 'take the mortal leap of faith' (Jacobi) and to see that 'Faith is a personal relationship between a given particular man and God' (Hamann).[6]

Ardent in his faith he looked with loathing on the comfortable 'Establishment-minded' attitudes of the Danish Lutheran Church of his day. For Kierkegaard, being a Christian meant strict obedience to the teaching of Christ, even to martyrdom, and if, in nineteenth-century Denmark, martyrdom could scarcely mean death on the cross, it could, and for him did, mean witness, struggle, persecution and despairing spiritual loneliness on a pinnacle of faith no one around him could attain to. His life was ravaged by controversy; its tensions destroyed him. If ever the belief in the miracle of divine grace and salvation had burnt up its chosen human vessel, that happened to Kierkegaard. Christianity, in its zeal for extension, had become spread too thin; Kierkegaard believed in the need of deeper individual intensity,[7] stimulated by a re-discovered awareness of a man's individual existence as the primary all-important fact, with faith at its core, like the positive charge within the proton. 'As thou believest so art thou; to believe is to be.'[8]

The atheist Existentialists derive from Nietzsche. Kierkegaard's attack, however general its application, was directed at the Danish Lutheran Church, Nietzsche's at Christianity. For Kierkegaard life achieves meaning only with God and direction only from the adventure of uncompromising obedience to Christ's words, for Nietzsche, man in his utter solitude must himself give it meaning and direction. Although Nietzsche knew nothing of Kierkegaard and his use of the word 'Existence', both start from that point, both see man's existence in the starkest terms, as having no meaning in itself, in a word absurd; for both the cardinal preoccupation is to renew man's attitudes in the light of his situation as they see it, force him to be always at the extreme point of spiritual alertness.

---

[5] Sartre, op. cit.
[6] See C. Bonifazi, *Christianity attacked* (London, 1953).
[7] See C. Bonifazi, op. cit., chap. 2.   [8] Quoted by C. Bonifazi.

Whether directly or not, Kierkegaard's sense of mission and adventure regardless of cost has been a force in Christian thought and action in France during this century. The Gallican Church had learned much from its years of tribulation at spasmodic intervals in the nineteenth century, years of increasing severity and culminating in the separation of Church and State (1905). Far from this measure being the death blow the Church's opponents believed, it delivered the Church from unhealthy worldliness and clericalism, leaving it to pursue vigorously its pastoral action and to be a witness of the faith by the example of its members.

Re-invigorated Christian attitudes are also evident in certain writers, e.g. Péguy, Psichari, Claudel, Malègue, above all in Bernanos in whom the idea of grace as a consuming fire, of Christian faith as an arduous and exacting adventure, is evident.

Behind these attitudes must lie an intense awareness of a personal relationship with God, as the core of life. This awareness informs the work of the Christian existentialist Gabriel Marcel (b. 1889), whose thinking is expressed in two forms: plays (*inter alia*, *Un Homme de Dieu*, 1925; *La Chapelle Ardente*, 1925; *Le Monde Cassé*, 1932; *Le Chemin de Crète*, 1936; *Le Dard*, 1936; *Rome n'est plus dans Rome*, 1951) and philosophical writings (*Journal Métaphysique*, 1928; *Etre et Avoir*, 1935; *Homo Viator*, 1945; *Le Mystère de l'Etre*, 1951).

That Marcel's first published work is a play underlines the fact that, philosopher though he is, he is not using the drama merely as a vehicle for his philosophy, as for example Renan in *L'Abbesse de Jouarre* or *La Fontaine de Jouvence*. As a dramatist Marcel is intent upon creating authentic characters who as a result of the conflicts they are involved in are forced to seek the truth about their mixed motives and thus disentangle for us the mystery of behaviour: 'Je n'espère rien, je ne compte sur rien; j'ai besoin de voir clair en moi', exclaims Osmonde (*Un Homme de Dieu*, III, 7) and the concluding words of the piece, 'Etre connu tel qu'on est', reveal Claude's sincere wish to face up squarely to his true motives, when, after having forgiven his wife's infidelity years before, he forces her to meet the father of her child. The same sympathetic exploration of conflicting motives appears in other plays; e.g. Ariadne's attitude to her husband's mistress (*Le Chemin de Crète*), Aline Fortier's to her husband Octave and to Mireille, the former fiancée of her dead son (*La Chapelle Ardente*).

Doubtless Marcel is not the first dramatist to have appreciated and shown the complexity of motives in human behaviour, but what gives his plays their distinctive character is the underlying conviction that only by the closest awareness of his innermost experience can man escape from the 'exile' Marcel sees as the normal human condition. His plays are like different aspects of 'the tragic solitude of man among the debris of a broken world . . . exiled from God; . . . but first from other people, and in consequence of this . . . exiled from a true understanding of himself.'[9] 'The drama of the soul in Exile' is the title of a preface by Marcel to an English translation of his plays.[10]

Marcel describes himself as *Homo Viator*[11] (1944); if as a dramatist he explores the mystery of behaviour, as a philosopher he journeys in quest of 'the mystery of being'. His first published philosophical work is in the form of a diary; the very word suggests an itinerant attitude, the pursuit of philosophical 'clues' as the day-to-day experience of living may present them. Thus Marcel's method in philosophy is parallel to his method as a dramatist; philosophy becomes an intense awareness of living; the true metaphysician embraces life to the full, and if Marcel, like all Existentialists, emphasizes the importance of liberty of choice, this for him is essentially a free acceptance in hope of a world order, to which he is inevitably committed. Hope is to the soul what breathing is to the living man, it engenders the act of faith and thereby gives meaning to an otherwise meaningless existence.

Kierkegaard by his 'leap' across the abyss, Marcel by his image of man in exile or journeying, manage to escape from their subjective prison. In one sense at least the atheist Existentialists' position is easier; the straight denial that God exists leaves them free to build up their position in a logical manner from the starting-point – existence, essence. Sartre defends it by comparing the human situation with that of an inanimate object,[12] e.g. a book or a paper-knife. A paper-knife is made by reference to certain pre-established concepts, e.g. lightness, ease of handling, etc., and for a purpose, i.e. to cut paper. These are of the essence of 'paper-knifedom', conceived in the mind of a man before even any given paper-knife is made. There cannot be any pre-existing qualities or essences of human nature conceived in the mind of a creator before man was made because there is no creator: *ergo*, man exists first and builds up his own essences afterwards: 'l'homme existe d'abord, . . . surgit dans le monde et . . . se définit après . . . l'homme n'est rien d'autre que ce qu'il se fait.' Without a creator or some force, e.g. Nature to whom we ascribe mind, life has no teleological significance, is absurd; man alone can give it significance. Nietzsche said much the same.

We may recall in passing the powerful impact of German

---

[9] R. Speaight, 'Philosophy in the French Theatre today', *The Listener*, 19 February 1953.
[10] *Three Plays* (Secker and Warburg).   [11] Title of a collection of essays.
[12] See *L'Existentialisme est un humanisme*.

philosophers upon French intellectuals and writers throughout the nineteenth century: Kant on the Romantics, Hegel on Taine and Renan, Schopenhauer on Decadents and Symbolists, Nietzsche on the pre- and post-1914 generations, on Gide notably, and indirectly on the Existentialists, Freud on the Surrealists. Jean-Paul Sartre (b. 1905), learned in German philosophy, walks in the footsteps of Heidegger. He expounds his philosophy in *L'Etre et le Néant* (1943) and, more accessibly, in the essay *L'Existentialisme est un humanisme* (1946). Its first expression is in fact a novel – *La Nausée* (1938) – which purports to be pages from the diary of one Antoine Roquentin. Why does Roquentin suffer periodic bouts of nausea as he looks with a jaundiced eye on the sights and scenes of Bouville: the Sunday parade of the citizenry, the restaurant where he takes his meals, the public gardens with its statue of Veleda, the worthy 'autodidact' building up his knowledge alphabetically by wading through the Encyclopaedia in the town library, where Roquentin himself is engaged in writing the biography of M. de Rollebon, native of Bouville, *émigré* during the Revolution, secret agent of the Tsar, imprisoned on an unproven charge of treason by Louis XVIII? Why, oh why these bouts of nausea? Only when Roquentin gets to the truth about the objects around him is the mystery of his attacks of nausea revealed to him: his is a philosophic nausea. As he contemplates the root of a tree in the public gardens, he understands that there is no way of explaining its existence: 'J'avais beau répéter: "c'est une racine" – ça ne prenait plus. Je voyais bien qu'on ne pouvait pas passer de sa fonction de racine, de pompe aspirante, à ça, à cette peau dure et compacte de phoque, à cet aspect huileux, calleux, entêté. La fonction n'expliquait rien: elle permettait de comprendre en gros ce que c'était – qu'une racine, mais pas du tout celle-ci.'[13] Its existence has no necessity, is therefore gratuitous, and in the last analysis absurd.

The absurdity of existence without cause or purpose is what produces his nausea and his revulsion against all who in one way or another (e.g. the citizenry of Bouville, and the 'autodidact' whose name is not revealed, presumably to make him the more symbolical of the anonymous human herds, men who cherish as he does idealist values) live in a false state of intellectual security and upon whom Roquentin-Sartre claps the unlovely epithet: 'Salauds'.

Once Roquentin has understood the truth about life he throws up his biography of Rollebon (three years wasted!) – 'Jamais un existant ne peut justifier l'existence d'un autre existant',[14] and

---

[13] *La Nausée*, N.R.F., 1938, p. 169.
[14] *Ibid.*, p. 228. To write history whatever the form, biographical or others, means looking back, i.e. looking at events in reverse. They therefore take on a pattern and seem to lead to conclusions, in short they seem to have a purpose they could not have had in reality.

goes to Paris with a vague idea of writing not history but a novel perhaps, some sort of 'action' to give meaning to his own existence.

Existentialist themes: the absurdity of existence, man's freedom of choice and his inescapable personal responsibility, appear in many different forms in Sartre's subsequent work: in the novels *Les Chemins de la Liberté* (three volumes, 1945–9); in the short stories of *Le Mur* (1939); in the plays – *Les Mouches* (1943); *Huis Clos* (1944), *Morts sans sépulture* (1946), *La Putain respectueuse* (1947), *Les Mains sales* (1948), *Le Diable et le Bon Dieu* (1951), *Nékrassov* (1957), *Les Séquestrés d'Altona* (1959); in the critical essays, collected in *Situations*[15] (three volumes, 1947–9).

Sartre offers us his largest canvas in the trilogy of *Les Chemins de la Liberté*.

Against a background of Parisian life before the Second World War (Vol. I, *L'Age de raison*), of the feverish week from 23 to 30 September 1938 (Vol. II, *Le Sursis*), of the fall of France in 1940 (Vol. III, *La Mort dans l'âme*), what Sartre is concerned to show us is the progress in Existentialist wisdom of his main characters, notably Mathieu Delarue. 'Je voudrais ne me tenir que de moi-même', he explains to his mistress Marcelle, 'Si je n'essayais pas de reprendre mon existence à mon compte, ça me semblerait telle-ment absurde d'exister.'[16] The action in *L'Age de raison*, which materially is concentrated in twenty-four hours and is concerned with Mathieu's search for a loan to enable Marcelle to hire the services of a skilled abortionist, shows him and his friends, futile, parasitic, perverted (Daniel) and shrinking from the responsibility of committing themselves to any positive activity.

Le Sursis shows us the attitudes of his characters during the fate-ful week when Europe was balanced on a knife-edge between peace and war. Incidentally, Sartre's technical brilliance is shown here at its best; the multiplicity of scenes, now on the high diplomatic or political, now on the private level, merge without warning into one another; there is no linear development of a story; the deliberate effect is of the vast stream of existence flowing on without inter-ruption in meaningless confusion, bearing the reader and Mathieu and his friends along and giving them an illusory sense of escape from the duty of personal decisions by the force of external events (mobilization).

Only in *La Mort dans l'âme* does Mathieu finally rise to his full potential. His decision, his commitment to join the small band of

---

[15] First published in Sartre's review, *Les Temps Modernes*. *La Nausée*, be it noted, is itself presented as Roquentin's diary; in other words it is the presentation, day by day, of someone giving meaning to his life as he lives it, not of a story in the past, therefore with a pattern which the Existen-tialist does not accept as possible.

[16] Vol. I, p. 18, N.R.F.

soldiers who under the leadership of their officer are determined to fight to the end against the advancing Germans, reveals to him, at the moment of death, what true freedom means: 'Il s'approcha du parapet et se mit à tirer debout. C'était une énorme revanche; chaque coup de feu le vengeait d'un ancien scrupule... Il tira: il était pur, il était tout-puissant, il était libre.'[17]

Nowhere does Sartre express his ideas more powerfully than in his plays; Oreste defies Jupiter: 'je ne reviendrai pas sous ta loi: je suis condamné à n'avoir d'autre loi que la mienne... je suis un homme Jupiter, et chaque homme doit inventer son chemin...'[18] Inès echoes much the same idea but goes further in taunting Garcin for his cowardice (in life): 'Seuls les actes décident de ce qu'on a voulu... Tu n'es rien d'autre que ta vie.'[19] Henri the resister, facing torture and death with his companions, is glad when he learns that their leader, Jean, subsequently captured, has not been recognized; their concealing Jean's identity will thus give sense to their death: 'Si tu n'étais pas venue, nous aurions souffert comme des bêtes, sans savoir pourquoi – mais tu es là, et tout ce qui va se passer à present aura un sens.'[20]

Goetz von Berlichingen and Heinrich the renegade priest,[21] the former in choosing good on the throw of a dice (cheating to ensure the right answer), the latter in choosing evil, as their principle of action, lose their essential humanity, the twin absolutes must be swept away, for man to be free and humane.

Sartre's plays are the work of a brilliant, passionate craftsman; the situations are tense, often brutal; the dialogue compelling. In contrast to Marcel's exploration of 'men in exile', his is a drama designed to exemplify a number of clear-cut ideas. Like all his work, they are part of Sartre's apologia for atheistic Existentialism.

Nor should we forget the two essays in biography, one on *Baudelaire* (1947), the other, *Les Mots* (1964), autobiographical. To those who see in Baudelaire the victim of weak character and family circumstances, drawing forth poetry from his suffering, Sartre opposes the image of a man who deliberately chose an attitude. Our belief in the sincerity of the poetry may suffer in consequence, but the Existentialist liberty of choice and individual responsibility are saved. A similar thought, if unexpressed, pervades *Les Mots*. This beautifully written essay is not autobiography in the strict sense, it is a brilliant and penetrative piece of autobiographical interpretation. Sartre the mature man goes in search of Jean-Paul, 'Poulou', the darling of his widowed mother and his Schweitzer grandparents.

---

[17] Op. cit., Vol. III, p. 193, N.R.F.
[18] *Les Mouches*, III, 2.   [19] *Huis Clos*, scene 5.
[20] *Morts sans sépulture*, Tableau I, scene 5.   [21] *Le Diable et le Bon Dieu*.

The Protestant[22] idealist background to his childhood, mainly created by the powerful personality of his grandfather, Charles Schweitzer,[23] rather unsympathetically portrayed, seems a wholly improbable milieu for the Existentialist Sartre to have developed in. The inference is that the boy 'Poulou' was not father to the man; the latter, in a sense, achieved significance by an act of his own will and free choice.

No doubt the desire to write developed early, but not until Sartre had seen the light of Existentialism could his writing take on the value of action, for literature in Sartre's view must be a commitment, like any other. Literature written for entertainment and escape, anything that savours of 'art for art's sake' – Mallarmé's remark that everything in this world has as its only purpose to end in a beautiful book, such ideas are abhorrent to Sartre; they are a class phenomenon, part of the bourgeois scheme of things, which Sartre, the revolutionary, wishes to see abolished.[24]

Beside Sartre stands Albert Camus (1913–61). In spite of his Nobel Prize for literature (1957), not everyone will agree that his work equals in density or power the work of his slightly older contemporary and sometimes comrade in Existentialist arms – in the Resistance too – until Camus's *L'Homme révolté* and Francis Jeanson's diatribe[25] against Camus which that book provoked led to the severance of relations. But we must remember that Camus's career was brutally cut short by a car smash.

Camus's work falls broadly into three periods:[26] before, during and after the war. The early writings consist of two groups of essays: *L'Envers et l'endroit* (1937) and *Noces* (1938), and a play *Caligula* (1938, produced 1945); the middle group comprise the novel, *L'Etranger* (1942), a play, *Le Malentendu* (1943, produced 1944) and an essay, *Le Mythe de Sisyphe* (1942). Another shift in Camus's intellectual position, foreshadowed in *Lettres à un ami allemand* (1945), is reflected in the works of the last group: the novels, *La Peste* (1947) and *La Chute* (1956), the collection of stories entitled *L'Exil et le Royaume* (1957), amongst which *La Chute* originally figured, two plays, *L'Etat de Siège* (1948) and *Les Justes* (1949), and the essay previously referred to, *L'Homme révolté* (1952).

The extent to which Camus is a moralist intent on making his attitudes clear – a concern he shares with other Existentialists – is shown by the volumes *Actuelles* I (1950) and II (1954), consisting of fugitive pieces, written or originally spoken between 1944–8

[22] Madame Charles Schweitzer, his grandmother, was in fact a Catholic.
[23] Cousin of Albert Schweitzer.
[24] See *Situations*, II – 'Qu'est-ce que la littérature?'
[25] Published by Sartre in *Les Temps Modernes*.
[26] See S. John, article on Camus, *Mod. Langs.*, December 1954.

(Vol. I) and 1948–53 (Vol. II).[27] These writings are in effect commentaries and reflections, constituting a diary of Camus's thought over nine years.

The early essays foreshadow much of what was to come. Camus records (*Noces*) the impact Nature made on him along the coast of Algeria;[28] there is a frank paganism in his sensuous enjoyment of the intense effects of sunlight, sea and sky, in the mysterious life he endows them with and echoes of which will occur in *L'Etranger* and *La Peste*. But we move quickly to the metaphysical level – what is man's place in Nature? The enigma of death has a horrifying fascination for Camus. In the pagan symphony a discordant note is heard, a note of revolt; destined to total destruction in death, life has no meaning, man is a victim.

The war, the occupation, the Resistance – the impact of these events could do nothing but deepen the tragic view of man's destiny foreshadowed in the early essays. Its most powerful expression is to be found at this time in *L'Etranger*. The story is related throughout in the first person by Meursault from the death of his mother to his trial and condemnation for the murder of an Arab.

But in spite of Meursault's thus being in the forefront of the scene we get little idea of him as a human being, only a strong impression of him as a strangely detached observer of what happens to him; he seems absent from himself as in a dream: 'la bizarre impression que j'avais d'être de trop, un peu un intrus ...'.[29] He makes no sense of events. What made him kill the Arab? No rational motive explains his action; we are left to make what we like or can of Meursault's account: the light playing on the Arab's knife, the sweat pouring down his brow and blinding him, the sun, the oppressive heat reverberating on the sea.[30]

Was it an impulse of self-defence, the effect of a heat-stroke, or, as *Noces* might encourage one to think, a mysterious compulsion from the sun? If anything, the text encourages the latter suspicion: 'Il m'a semblé que le ciel s'ouvrait sur toute son étendue pour laisser pleuvoir du feu ... J'ai secoué la sueur et le soleil. J'ai compris que j'avais détruit l'équilibre du jour ...'. But whichever way it is, Meursault is a victim of fear or of a temporary physiological disequilibrium or of an hallucination. In the light of that, the efforts (successful) of the prosecution to wrest a conviction from the jury by imposing a flimsy pattern of rationality on the affair appear tragically absurd. With Kafka in mind, no doubt that was Camus's intention. But has he succeeded in making Meursault

[27] Vol. II contains, *inter alia*, Camus's letter to Sartre, in reply to Jeanson's article, which started the series of acrimonious, often ironical (Sartre), open letters between them.
[28] He was born at Mondovi.
[29] Part II, chap. 3.   [30] Part I, chap. 6.

a symbol of man's condition? In Kafka we never know what the case against his hero is. Our attention is therefore concentrated on the mental suffering of the victim as he struggles against unknown forces; the facts of Meursault's case are known to us and, far from accepting the position as inevitable, we may simply regard it as a monstrous miscarriage of justice in a given case, or alternatively as an interesting commentary on the effect on State Prosecutors' mentality both of the Inquisitorial system of justice, which seeks to establish the truth, or, to be more precise, a rational chain of motives, even at the price of truth, and of the structure of French justice which stimulates the zeal of State Prosecutors, by the lure of advancement on the number of convictions achieved – payment by results.[31] If we adopt either point of view *L'Etranger* really fails in its main purpose of illustrating the absurdity of life; the theme is given more powerful expression in *Le Malentendu*. Meursault describes how in his cell he had found a scrap of newspaper relating the story of a murder inspired by greed, followed by a double suicide, none of which would have occurred if the identity of the victim had been discovered in time. On such flimsy chances do our lives depend. Where is the sense of it?

But, no more than Sartre does Camus contract out of 'commitment'. On the plane of reality he was in the Resistance, which implies the recognition of some ideal worth dying and, by extension, worth living for; on the intellectual plane he discusses in *Le Mythe de Sisyphe* what in face of life's absurdity is the proper attitude for man to adopt, and, after discussing and rejecting both suicide and hope (i.e. religious faith) as a way of escape from nihilistic despair, decides that it lies in 'revolt', the refusal to give way, the moral equivalent in fact of the Resistance, and the acceptance of life on those terms, just as Sisyphe accepts his unending labour because he knows, as Pascal does and the Universe does not, that he is the latter's victim. From knowledge comes superiority and liberation. Between the works of the middle and those of the last period there is no fundamental break; the 'absurdity' of life, the total absence of God from creation remain, but a more positive attitude develops. In his *Lettres à un ami allemand* he defends his ideal of justice; why, one wonders, if all is absurd? Camus seems prepared to admit two levels of argument; whatever the ultimate absurdity, on the relative level the attitude of revolt is henceforth to be nourished by a sense of fraternity in suffering and human pity.

The most vivid expression of this revised position is *La Peste*, as a novel, richer in texture than *L'Etranger*. The story of plague-ridden Oran cut off by its own decision from the world and its

[31] e.g. Brieux, *La Robe Rouge*.

citizens all 'dans le coup', as Sartre would say, is conjured up with enough imaginative power for us to believe in it as a story in its own right; this is the prior condition of our moving willingly on to the symbolic levels of the work: France, beleaguered by the Occupation? – possibly, but in any case suffering humanity, beleaguered and crushed in an indifferent universe.

In this situation what is to be our attitude? The individuals in Oran, whose behaviour is singled out for our attention – the Jesuit Father Paneloux, Rambert the journalist, Tarrou, Grand, and Rieux the doctor, all have different attitudes, at the outset, but all[32] in the end under Rieux's leadership dedicate themselves to the relief of suffering, regardless of proximate or ultimate hopes. Rieux, that saint without God, and the reasons which prompt him to write the story of the plague, clearly reflect Camus's ideal: 'pour ne pas être de ceux qui se taisent ... pour dire ... ce qu'on apprend au milieu des fléaux: qu'il y a dans les hommes plus de choses à admirer que de choses à mépriser.' The message is clear enough, but whether its bearer himself, Rieux, carries much conviction as a living fictional character is doubtful. He has the same inertness as Meursault; here, as in *L'Etranger*, the secondary characters are more alive than their principals, who suffer in their vitality from the symbolic weight they have to carry.

In *Le Mythe de Sisyphe* Camus says pertinent things on the artist whose work is the product of a vision of the world and the lesser writer who merely puts forward a thesis.[33] Even if we assume that Existentialism has provided Camus with a tragic vision of the world, as novelist or dramatist he scarcely measures up to the greatest artists he cites; his important characters are not explored enough to have more than a shadowy life. This impression is not materially altered by the long monologue of *La Chute*.

The six short stories of *L'Exil et le Royaume* can scarcely be expected to develop character studies, and there is no denying the disturbing impact of some of them – e.g. 'Le Rénégat' and 'l'Hôte'. In both *La Chute* and the short stories the search, often vain, by lonely human beings for companionship, solidarity amongst men, the preoccupation that had become uppermost in Camus the moralist, is clearly implied. This 'positive change' in his philosophy had been given its full power in *L'Homme révolté*. Camus denounces the parties of the Left for bad faith. He analyses the evolution of their ideologies, notably the Marxian; in their decadence they have betrayed the sacred charge of man's liberation they claim to be working for.

---

[32] Except Cottard, who having a crime to hide, feels liberated by the plague from his own particular worry – the police – and terrified when, with the plague's abatement, the city reopens its gates. [33] 'La création absurde'.

Man has the right to revolt even against Revolution if it merely substitutes one form of injustice for another. No wonder Camus was to call down upon himself the thunders of Sartre, against such a renegade; the tide of Camus's moral development had borne him away from Existentialist orthodoxy of the Left. Metaphysical despair, absurdity – absolute, unheeding, incomprehensible – man's duty to create his own order in the total chaos, these Existentialist constants underlie his work, but unlike Sartre, where the emphasis is all on man's moral responsibility and inevitable freedom, Camus comes to recognize the value of justice, of service to others, to the community – Christian charity seems close at hand, stoic human-ism, in any case; in fine, the values held by those that Sartre would doubtless call 'les Salauds'.

The emphasis placed by Existentialism on the individual's iso-lation in a world of absurdity is in effect a Romantic upsurge. That it should have made such an impact during the Occupation is natural; whether in the Resistance or not, but especially in the Resistance under the threat of deportation, torture, violent death, man's inevitable and lonely responsibility for his own decisions was starkly evident. With the post-war relaxation of tension, the moral imperative of atheistic Existentialism, less urgent, was superseded by others, less direct. We have seen the issue, between the intel-lectuals' conscience and party loyalty (scarcely a new one), already raised by Sartre himself (e.g. *Les Mains sales*) and Camus (*L'Homme révolté*).

Simone de Beauvoir (b. 1908), strictest, in the Sartrian obedience, of post-war Existentialists, raises the same question in *Les Man-darins* (1955), a stodgy work full of eroticism which seems adoles-cent and valueless, except perhaps from the sales angle. Without it, the essential themes would have come out more clearly: Europe between the post-war options of American capitalism and Russian socialism, yet again the choice for leftist French intellectuals be-tween individual liberty and party loyalties, and beneath these ideological problems the varied lives of numerous individuals, notably that of Anne, the emancipated wife of the rigidly ortho-dox party philosopher Robert Dubreuil; abandoned by Lewis, her lover (not the first), she contemplates suicide, but, good Existen-tialist though she has shown herself to be, she ends by rejecting the idea; perhaps her death would distress her family, perhaps some crumbs of happiness may still be in reserve for her: 'Qui sait! Peut-être un jour serai-je de nouveau heureuse . . .'

An Existentialist novel ending on a note of hope recalls Pan-dora's box and suggests some loss of steam in atheistic Existential-ism, at least on the moral plane, nor does the black pessimism of Beckett's vision of a bankrupt world (*En attendant Godot*, 1952;

Fin de Partie, 1957) do much to raise it. Ionesco draws good effects of comedy, in his plays from *La Cantatrice Chauve, anti-pièce* (1950) to *Rhinocéros* (1960), by reducing the metaphysical idea of the absurd to the level of the unexpected and the incongruous, but is it of compelling human significance? Of all art forms, the novel has shown itself the most sensitive to the implications on the artistic level of Existentialist ideas. Nathalie Sarraute, Claude Simon, Alain Robbe-Grillet, Michel Butor, J. P. Faye, Bertrand Poirot-Delpech, Michel Bernard, the members of the 'Tel Quel' group, are amongst the pioneers in following up the logical consequences of the new philosophy.

Since the world is a meaningless absurd chaos, the novel must show this. No doubt Sartre had done great things: 'il fallait attendre Sartre pour voir enfin la nature humaine chassée du roman, et l'individu non plus se définir mais se faire par rapport au monde',[34] but Sartre had not completed the revolution he had begun; to show characters as he does at grips with the chaos, 'crispés sur la volonté d'exister',[35] is not enough; his novels as such still retain a unity in their own structure, they have a coherence either in time (by the linear development of a story) or in space (by e.g. simultaneity of events), usually in both. Sartre as we have seen is mainly concerned to communicate a view of life, a natural attitude for a dominant personality, especially in the circumstances of the time.

But the writers of the new brigade do not feel such preoccupations pressing close upon them and are concerned to create a novel 'form' which shall reflect Existentialist truth in its own economy; it shall in fact have no pre-existent structure (in the mind of the artist), it shall not be a novel in the old sense, but an 'anti-novel' which in its extremest form would come to mean an object composed of paper with words printed on pages, to which the reader himself must give a pattern of significance. Such a book in fact exists: *Composition No. 1* by Marc Saporta[36] who invites the reader to create the novel: 'C'est à vous de jouer. Le lecteur est prié de battre ces pages, comme un jeu cartes.'

But without indulging in this form of self-immolation, the pioneers are bravely following out other lines. The idea of presenting characters must clearly be dismissed; a character by definition is a formed meaningful being whom we get to know as his creator explores his personality for us more and more deeply. This conception is against Existentialist beliefs; however vague a character may be, the fact that he is there gives him some significance in relation to the world he is placed in, whereas the reader

---

[34] L. Janvier, *Une parole exigeante,* Edns. de Minuit, 1964.
[35] *Ibid.*   [36] Editions du Seuil.

must create his own significance from the objects the novelist gives him. The novelist must accordingly place the reader in the centre of a meaningless collection of objects; he becomes a kind of impersonal all-seeing eye that moves forward into the book, into the future, as though he were advancing into a labyrinth as devoid of emotion as in a dream, creating his own patterns of significance as he goes. After destroying humanist values, and establishing their philosophy on the ruins, atheist Existentialists are proceeding to break up the old art forms. What will emerge is anybody's guess; perhaps, after this orgy of destruction, a literary renaissance, less cerebral, more humane, for without humanity, art perisheth.

Bibliography

BIBLIOGRAPHY

1. Histories of Literature

Boisdeffre, P. de, *Métamorphose de la Littérature – Une Histoire vivante de la Littérature d'Aujourd'hui 1939–64.*

Bouvier, E., *Les Lettres françaises au XXᵉ siècle*, 1962 (2 vols.), 5th edn., 1964.

Clouard, H., *Histoire de la Littérature Française du Symbolisme à nos Jours* (2 vols.), 1947–9.
Petite Histoire de la Littérature Française, 1966.

Girard, M., *Guide illustré de la Littérature Française Moderne de 1918 à 1949*, 1949.

Lagarde and Michaud, *Collection Textes et Littérature, XIXᵉ siècle*, 1964, and *XXᵉ siècle*, 1965.

Lalou, R., *Histoire de la Littérature Française Contemporaine (1870 à nos Jours)*, 2 vols., 1941.

Montfort, E., *Vingt-cinq Ans de Littérature Française (Tableau de la Vie Littéraire de 1895 à 1920)*, 1925.

Picon, G., *Panorama de la Nouvelle Littérature Française*, 1949.

Simon, P-H., *Histoire de la Littérature Française Contemporaine 1900–1950* (2 vols.), 1956.

Thibaudet, A., *Histoire de la Littérature Française de 1789 à nos Jours*, 1936.

2. Political and Social History

Brogan, D. W., *The Development of Modern France 1870–1939*, 1940.

Bury, J. P. T., *France 1814–1940*, 3rd edn. revised, 1954.

Chastenet, J., *La France de Monsieur Fallières*, 1949.

Dreyfus, R., *La République de Monsieur Thiers 1871–73*, 1930.

Elton, Lord, *The Revolutionary Idea in France 1789–1878*, 1923, 2nd edn. 1931.

Gaxotte, P., *Histoire des Français* (2 vols.), 1951, vol. ii.

Halévy, D., *La République des Ducs*, 1937.

Madaule, J., *Histoire de France* (2 vols.), 1945–7, vol. ii.

Rémond, R., *La Droite en France de 1815 à nos Jours*, 1954.
Siegfried, A., *Tableau des Partis en France*, 1930.
Thibaudet, A., *Les Idées Politiques de la France*, 1932.

3. *Religion and the Church*

Dansette, A., *Histoire religieuse de la France Contemporaine* (2 vols.), 1948–51, vol. ii.
Phillips, C. S., *The Church in France: A Study in Revival*, 1929.
Weil, G., *Histoire de l'Idée Laïque en France au dix-neuvième siècle*, 1925.

4. *Intellectual Background*

Albérès, R. M., *L'Aventure intellectuelle du vingtième siècle; Panorama des Littératures Européennes, 1900–59*, new edn., 1959.
Barrière, P., *La Vie intellectuelle en France du seizième siècle à l'époque contemporaine*, 1961.
Bosworth, W., *Catholicism and Crisis in Modern France: French Catholic Groups at the Threshold of the Fifth Republic*, 1962.
Earle, E. M., *Modern France. Problems of the Third and Fourth Republics*, edited by E. M. Earle, 1951.
Faguet, E., *Politiques et Moralistes du dix-neuvième siècle* (3 vols.), 1891–9.
Griffiths, R. M., *The Reactionary Revolution 1870–1914*, 1966.
Hanna, T., *The Bergsonian Heritage*, 1962.
Lacour-Gayet, R., *La France au vingtième siècle*, 1954.
Manuel, F. E., *The Prophets of Paris*, 1962.
Picon, G., *Panorama des Idées Contemporaines*, 1957.
Raitt, A. W., *Life and Letters in France. The Nineteenth Century*, 1966.
Simon, P. H., *Témoins de l'Homme. La Condition Humaine dans la Littérature Contemporaine*, 1951.
Le Domaine héroïque des Lettres Françaises du dixième au dix-neuvième siècles, 1963.
Wright, C. H. C., *The Background of Modern French Literature*, 1926.

5. *Literary Movements*

a. *Naturalism:*

Beuchat, C., *Histoire du Naturalisme Français* (2 vols.), 1949.
Dumesnil, R., *L'Epoque Réaliste et Naturaliste*, 1945.
Le Réalisme et le Naturalisme, 1955.

Henriot, E., *Réalistes et Naturalistes*, 1954.
Martino, P., *Le Naturalisme Français 1870–95*, 1951.

b. *Symbolism:*

Décaudin, M., *La Crise des Valeurs Symbolistes, vingt ans de Poésie Française 1895–1914*, 1962.
Gourmont, R. de, *Le Livre des Masques* (2 vols.), 1896–8.
Guichard, L., *La Musique et les Lettres au temps du Wagnérisme*, 1963.
Michaut, G., *Message poétique du Symbolisme* (3 vols.), 1947.
Martino, P., *Parnasse et Symbolisme, 1850–1900*, 9th edn., 1954.

c. *Unanimism:*

Guisan, G., *Poésie et Collectivité 1890–1914. Le Message Social des oeuvres poétiques de l'Unanimisme et de l'Abbaye*, 1938.

d. *Surrealism:*

Carrouges, M., *André Breton et les données fondamentales du Surréalisme*, 1950.

6. *The Novel*

Albérès, R. M., *Histoire du Roman Moderne*, 1962.
Brombert, V., *The Intellectual Hero: Studies in the French Novel 1880–1955*, 1962.
Ehrard, J., *Le Roman Français depuis Marcel Proust*, n.d.
Lalou, R., *Le Roman Français depuis 1900*, 1941.
Rousset, J., *Forme et Signification. Essais sur les Structures Littéraires de Corneille à Claudel*, 1962.
Zola, E., *Le Roman Expérimental*, 1880.
Les Romanciers Naturalistes, 1881.

7. *The Drama*

Doisy, M., *Le Théâtre Français Contemporain*.
Faguet, E., *Notes Sur Le Théâtre Contemporain* (3 vols.), 1888–90.
Propos De Théâtre (5 vols.), 1903–10.
Guicharnaud, J., and Beckelman, J., *Modern French Theatre from Giraudoux to Beckett*, 1961.
Knowles, D., *La Réaction Idéaliste au Théâtre depuis 1880*, 1934.
Lalou, R., *Le Théâtre en France depuis 1900*.
Lemaitre, J., *Impressions de Théâtre* (9 vols.), 1888–98.
Lénient, L., *La Comédie en France au dix-neuvième siècle* (2 vols.), 1898.

Lintilhac, E., *Histoire Générale du Théâtre en France*, Vol. V, n.d.

Peters, R., *Le Théâtre et la Vie sous la Troisième République* (3 vols.).

Pillement, G., *Anthologie du Théâtre Français Contemporain* (2 vols.), 1945–6.

Pronko, L. C., *The Experimental Theatre in France*, 1962.

Simon, P. H., *Théâtre et Destin. La Signification de la Renaissance Dramatique en France au vingtième siècle*, 1959.

Surer, P., *Le Théâtre Français Contemporain*, 1964.

Zola, E., *Le Naturalisme au Théâtre*, 1881.

Nos Auteurs Dramatiques, 1881.

8. *Poetry*

Bever, A. van, and Léautaud, P., *Poètes d'Aujourd'hui 1880–1900*, 1903.

Brandin, L., and Hartog, W., *A Book of French Prosody*, n.d.

Brunetière, F., *L'Evolution de la Poésie Lyrique en France au dix-neuvième siècle* (2 vols.), 1894.

Clancier, E., *De Rimbaud au Surréalisme*, 1953.

Hackett, C. A., *Anthology of Modern French Poetry from Baudelaire to the Present Day*, 2nd edn., 1964.

Hartley, A., *The Penguin Book of French Verse*, ed. A. Hartley, 1957.

Mansell Jones, P., *The Oxford Book of French Verse XIII–XXth Century*, 2nd edn. ed. P. Mansell Jones, 1957.

Mansell Jones, P., and Richardson, G., *A Book of French Verse. Lamartine to Eluard*, edited with Introduction and Notes by P. Mansell Jones and G. Richardson.

Parmée, D., *Twelve French Poets 1820–1900*, Introduction and Notes by Douglas Parmée, 1957.

9. *Criticism*

Baldensperger, F., and Craig, H. S., *La Critique et l'Histoire Littéraire en France au début du vingtième siècle*, 1945.

Belis, A., *La Critique Française à la fin du dix-neuvième siècle*, 1926.

Brunetière, F., *L'Evolution de la Critique*, 1890.

Carloni, J-C., and Filloux, J-C., *La Critique Littéraire*, 1955.

Giraud, V., *La Critique Littéraire; le Problème, les Théories, les Méthodes*, 1946.

Michaud, G., *L'Oeuvre et ses Techniques*, 1957.

Peyre, H., *Essais de Méthode de Critique et d'Histoire Littéraire de G. Lanson, présentés par*, H. Peyre, 1966.

Thibaudet, A., *Physiologie de la Critique*, 1930.

10. *Miscellaneous*

Bourget, P., *Essais de Psychologie Contemporaine*, 1883–5.
Carré, J-M., *Les Ecrivains Français et le Mirage Allemand, 1800–1940*, 1947.
France, A., *La Vie Littéraire* (4 vols.), 1895–7.
Giraud, V., *Les Maîtres de l'Heure*, 1911.
Gourmont, R. de, *Promenades Littéraires* (7 vols.), 1904–28.
Huret, J., *Enquête sur l'Evolution Littéraire*, 1913.
Lemaitre, J., *Les Contemporains. Etudes et Portraits Littéraires* (8 vols.), 1886–1918.
Tiegham, P. van, *Les Influences Etrangères sur la Littérature Française 1550–1880*, 1961.
Zola, E., *Mes Haines*, 1866.

Appendix to Chapter 2

Les Rougon-Macquart 1871–93 (Selection)

 La Fortune Des Rougon (1871).
 La Curée (1871).
 Le Ventre De Paris (1873).
 La Conquête De Plassans (1874).
 Son Excellence Eugène Rougon (1876)*.
 L'Assommoir (1877).
 Pot-Bouille (1882).
 Germinal (1885).
 La Terre (1887).
 La Bête Humaine (1890).
 L'Argent (1891).
 Le Docteur Pascal (1893).

Select Bibliography for Chapter 2

Antoine, A., *Mes Souvenirs sur le Théâtre-Libre*, 1921.
 Mes Souvenirs sur le Théâtre Antoine et sur l'Odéon, n.d.
Baldick, R., *Life of J. K. Huysmans*, 1955.
Benoit-Guyod, G., *Alphonse Daudet. Son Temps. Son Oeuvre*, 1947.
Billy, A., *Les Frères Goncourt. La Vie littéraire à Paris pendant la Seconde Moitié du dix-neuvième siècle*, 1954.
Bollery, J., *Villiers De L'Isle-Adam. Correspondance Générale... Présentée par* J. Bollery (2 vols.), 1962.
Burns, C-A., *Henry Céard. Lettres inédites à Emile Zola. Publiées et annotées par* C-A. Burns, 1958.
 Emile Zola. Pages D'Exil. Publiées et annotées par C. Burns, 1964.

Daireaux, M., *Villiers de L'Isle-Adam. L'Homme et l'Oeuvre, avec des documents inédits*, 1936.

Descotes, M., *Henry Becque et son Théâtre*, 1962.

Dubeux, A., *A travers l'Oeuvre de Rosny Aîné. Préface par* A. Dubeux, 1961.

Frazee, R., *Henry Céard: Idéaliste détrompé*, 1963.

Fricker, E., *Alphonse Daudet et la Société du Second Empire*, 1937.

Gille, G., *Jules Vallès (1832–1885) Ses Révoltes, sa Maîtrise, son Prestige*, 1941.

Guichard, L., *Renard*, 1961.

Guillemin, H., *Présentation des Rougon-Macquart*, 1964.

Laver, J., *The First Decadent. Being the Strange Life of J. K. Huysmans*, 1954.

Lebois, A., *Villiers De L'Isle-Adam. Révélateur du Verbe*, 1952.

Ricatte, R., *La Création romanesque chez les Goncourt, 1851–1870*, 1953.

Robert, G., *Emile Zola. Principes et Caractères Généraux de son Oeuvre*, 1952.

Sabatier, P., *Germinie Lacerteux des Goncourt*, 1948.

Sullivan, E. D., *Maupassant: The Short Stories. Studies in French Literature 7*, 1962.

Ternois, R., *Zola et son Temps. Lourdes-Rome-Paris*, 1961.

Thérive, A., *J. K. Huysmans. Son Oeuvre*, 1924.

Vial, A., *Maupassant et l'Art du Roman*, 1954.

Vivent, J., *Les Inspirations et l'Art de Courteline*, 1921.

Ternois, R., *Les Cahiers Naturalistes*, Nos. 1–22, 1955–62.

Select Bibliography for Chapter 4

Adam, A., *Verlaine. L'Homme et l'Oeuvre*, 1953.

Bernard, Mme S., *Rimbaud Oeuvres...Introduction...par* Suzanne Bernard, 1960.

Chassé, C., *Les Clés de Mallarmé*, 1954.

Chisholm, A. R., *Mallarmé's Grand Oeuvre*, 1962.

Compère, G., *Le Théâtre de Maeterlinck*, 1955.

Dédéyan, C., *Alain-Fournier et la Réalité secrète*, 1948.

Etiemble, *Le Mythe de Rimbaud* (3 vols.), 1954–61.

Fontaine, A., *Verhaeren et son Oeuvre*, 1929.

Frohock, W. M., *Rimbaud's Poetic Practice. Image and Theme in the Major Poems*, 1963.

Gourmont, R. de, *Livre des Masques* (2 vols.), 1896–8.

Guiomar, M., *Inconscient et Imaginaire dans 'Le Grand Meaulnes'*, 1964.

Houston, J. P., *The Design of Rimbaud's Poetry*, 1963.

Jones, P. M., *Verhaeren*, 1957.

Michaud, G., *Mallarmé. L'Homme et l'Oeuvre*, 1953.

Mondor, H., *Vie de Mallarmé*, 1943.

Nadal, O., *Paul Verlaine*, 1961.

Niklaus, R., *Jean Moréas, Poète lyrique*, 1936.

Noulet, E., *Dix Poèmes de Stéphane Mallarmé*, 1948.

Reboul, P., *Laforgue*, 1962.

Ruchon, F., *Jules Laforgue (1860–1887). Sa Vie. Son Oeuvre*, 1924.

Starkie, E., *Les Sources du Lyrisme dans la Poésie d'Emile Verhaeren*, 1927.

Arthur Rimbaud, 1961.

Thibaudet, A., *La Poésie de Stéphane Mallarmé. Etude littéraire*, 13th edn., 1938.

Select Bibliography for Chapter 6

Barko, J. P., *L'Esthétique littéraire de Charles Maurras*, 1961.

Halévy, D., *Charles Péguy et les Cahiers de la Quinzaine*, 1918.

Jussem-Wilson, N., *Charles Péguy*, 1965.

Larnac, J., *Comtesse de Noailles. Sa Vie. Son Oeuvre*, 1931.

Rousseaux, A., *Le Prophète Péguy*, 1946.

Mallet, R., *Francis Jammes. Sa Vie. Son Oeuvre*, 1961.

Le Jammisme, 1961.

Select Bibliography for Chapter 7

Barrère, J-B., *Romain Rolland, l'Ame et l'Art*, 1966.

Bollery, J., *Léon Bloy* (3 vols.), 1947.

Burne, G. S., *Rémy de Gourmont. His Ideas and Influence in England and America*, 1963.

Cattaui, G., *Léon Bloy*, 1964.

Chauveau, P., *Alfred Jarry ou la Naissance, la Vie et la Mort du Père Ubu*, 1932.

Cheval, R., *Romain Rolland, l'Allemagne et la Guerre*, 1963.

Dargan, E. P., *Anatole France, 1844–96*, 1937.

Ekström, P. G., *Evasions et Désespérances de Pierre Loti*, 1953.

Fahmy, S., *Paul Hervieu. Sa Vie et son Oeuvre*, 1942.

Fernandez, R., *Barrès*, 1943.

Fowlie, W., *Ernest Psichari*, n.d.

Gaffiot, M., *Les Théories Sociales d'Anatole France*, 1923.

Giraud, V., *Anatole France*, 1935.

Paul Bourget. Essai de Psychologie Contemporaine, n.d.

Hok, R. C., *Edouard Estaunié. The Perplexed Positivist*, 1949.

Jean-Desthieux, F., *Le Dernier des Encyclopédistes. Paul Adam*, 1928.

Lory, M-J., *Léon Bloy et son Epoque*, 1944.

Marks, E., *Colette*, 1961.

Masson, G-A., *A. France. Son Oeuvre*, 1923.

Miéville, H-L., *La Pensée de Maurice Barrès*, 1934.

Robichez, J., *Romain Rolland*, 1961.

Shattuck, R., and Taylor, S. W., *Alfred Jarry, Selected Works*, 1965.

Sutton, H., *The Life and Work of Jean Richepin*, 1961.

Thibaudet, A., *La Vie de Maurice Barrès*, 1921.

Trahard, P., *L'Art de Colette*, 1941.

Select Bibliography for Chapter 9

Bemol, M., *Paul Valéry*, 1949.

Benoist, P-F., *Les Essais de Paul Valéry. Etude et analyse par* P-F. Benoist, 1964.

Blankenhorn, G., *Der Kosmopolitismus bei Valéry Larbaud*, 1958.

Brée, G., *André Gide, L'Insaisissable Protée. Etude critique de l'Oeuvre d'André Gide*, 1953.

Cattaui, G., *Marcel Proust. Proust et son Temps. Proust et le Temps*, 1953.

Fowlie, W., *Paul Claudel*, 1957.

Guichard, L., *Introduction à la lecture de Proust*, 1956.

Hytier, J., *La Poétique de Valéry*, 1953.

Ince, W. N., *The Poetic Theory of Paul Valéry*, 1961.

Jean-Aubry, G., *Valéry Larbaud. Sa Vie et son Oeuvre. La Jeunesse. 1881–1920*, 1949.

Lafille, P., *André Gide Romancier*, 1954.

Lawler, J. R., *Lecture de Valéry. Une Etude de Charmes*, 1963.

Lesort, P. A., *Claudel par lui-même*, 1963.

Mackay, A. E., *The Universal Self. A Study of Paul Valéry*, 1961.

Madaule, J., *Le Drame de Paul Claudel*, 5th edn., 1964.

Marchand, M., *Le Complexe pédagogique et didactique d'André Gide*, 1954.

Painter, G. D., *Marcel Proust. A Biography* (2 vols.), 1959–65.

Picon, G., *Lecture de Proust*, 1963.

Pierre-Quint, L., *Le Comique et le Mystère chez Proust*, 1928.
Proust. Sa Vie et son Oeuvre, 1922–46.
André Gide. L'Homme, sa Vie, son Oeuvre, 1954.

Richthofen, E. von, *Commentaire sur 'Mon Faust' de Paul Valéry*, 1961.

Soulairol, J., *Paul Valéry*, 1952.

Vachon, A., *Le Temps et l'Espace dans l'Oeuvre de Paul Claudel*, 1965.

Select Bibliography for Chapter 10

Anders, F., *Jacques Copeau et le Cartel des Quatre*, 1959.
Balakian, A., *The Literary Origins of Surrealism*, 1947.
Surrealism: The Road to the Absolute, 1959.
Blair, D. S., *Jules Supervielle. A Modern Fabulist*, 1960.
Callander, M., *The Poetry of Pierre-Jean Jouve*, 1965.
Carrouges, M., *André Breton et les Données fondamentales du Surréalisme*, 1950.
Crosland, M., *Jean Cocteau*, 1955.
Davies, M., *Apollinaire*, 1964.
Debidour, V-H., *Jean Giraudoux*, 1955.
Décaudin, M., *Le Dossier d' 'Alcools'*, 1960.
Dubourg, P., *Dramaturgie de Jean Cocteau*, 1954.
Esch, J. van den, *Armand Salacrou*, 1947.
La Rochefoucauld, E. de, *Léon-Paul Fargue*, 1959.
Loranquin, A., *Saint-John Perse*, 1963.
Marsh, E. O., *Jean Anouilh, Poet of Pierrot and Pantaloon*, 1953.
Mercier-Campiche, M., *Le Théâtre de Giraudoux et la Condition Humaine*, 1954.
Parent, M., *Saint-John Perse et quelques Devanciers. Etudes sur le Poème en Prose*, 1960.
Rousselot, J., *Max Jacob au sérieux*, 1958.
Robichez, J., *Le Symbolisme au Théâtre. Lugné-Poë et les débuts de L'Oeuvre*, 1957.
Sénéchal, C., *Jules Supervielle, Poète de l'Univers Intérieur*, 1939.

Select Bibliography for Chapter 11

Anet, D., *Antoine de Saint-Exupéry, Poète-Romancier-Moraliste*, 1946.
Beaulieu, P., *Jacques Rivière*, 1955.
Berry, M., *Jules Romains. Sa Vie, son Oeuvre*, 1953.
Boak, D., *Roger Martin du Gard*, 1963.
Chaigne, L., *Georges Bernanos*, 1954.
Cruickshank, J., *Montherlant*, 1964.
Cuisenier, A., *Jules Romains et l'Unanimisme*, 1935.
Jules Romains et Les Hommes de Bonne Volonté, 1954.
Eustis, A., *Marcel Arland, Benjamin Crémieux, Ramon Fernandez. Trois Critiques de 'La Nouvelle Revue Française'*, 1961.
Glauser, A., *Albert Thibaudet et la Critique Créatrice*, 1952.
Gorkine, M., *Julien Green*, 1956.

Gouhier, M-A., *Charles Du Bos*, 1951.
Grover, F., *Drieu La Rochelle*, 1962.
Hartman, G. H., *André Malraux*, 1960.
Hebblethwaite, S. J. P., *Bernanos: An Introduction*, 1964.
Hogarth, H., *Henri Bremond. The Life and Work of a devout Humanist*, 1950.
Hourdin, G., *Mauriac, Romancier chrétien*, 1945.
Kolbert, J., *Edmond Jaloux et sa Critique littéraire*, 1962.
Laprade, J. de, *Le Théâtre de Montherlant*, 1950.
Majault, J., *Mauriac et l'Art du Roman*, 1946.
Picon, J., *André Malraux*, 1945.
  Malraux par lui-même, 1953.
Robidoux, R., *Roger Martin du Gard et la Religion*, 1964.
Roux, D. de, *Louis-Ferdinand Céline. Textes réunis et présentés par* Dominique de Roux, 1963.
Scheidegger, J., *Georges Bernanos Romancier*, 1956.
Simon, P-H., *Georges Duhamel ou le Bourgeois sauvé*, 1947.
Sipriot, P., *Montherlant par lui-même*, 1953.
Suffel, J., *André Maurois*, 1963.
Turnell, M., *Jacques Rivière*, 1953.

Select Bibliography for Chapter 12

Chenu, J., *Le Théâtre de Gabriel Marcel et sa Signification métaphysique*, 1948.
Cranston, M., *Sartre*, 1962.
Cruickshank, J., *Albert Camus and the Literature of Revolt*, 1959.
Haggis, D. R., *Camus: La Peste*, 1962.
Kingston, F. T., *French Existentialism. A Christian Critique*, 1961.
Murdoch, I., *Sartre, Romantic Rationalist*, 1953.
Roubiczeck, P., *Existentialism For and Against*, 1964.
Thoday, P., *Jean-Paul Sartre. A Literary and Political Study*, 1960.
  Albert Camus 1913–1960. A Biographical Study, 1961.

Index

INDEX

Printed in Great Britain
by Western Printing Services Limited
Bristol